Millicent

Millicent

By Millicent Collinsworth and
Jan Winebrenner

WRS
PUBLISHING

A Division of WRS Group, Inc.
Waco, Texas

First published in the United States of America in 1993 by WRS Publishing, A Division of WRS Group, Inc., 701 N. New Road, Waco, Texas 76710
Book design by Kenneth Turbeville
Jacket design by Talmage Minter and Joe James

10 9 8 7 6 5 4 3 2 1

Library of Congress Cataloging-in-Publication Data

Collinsworth, Millicent.
    Millicent / by Millicent Collinsworth and Jan Winebrenner.
        p.   cm.
    Includes bibliographical references.
    ISBN 1-56796-009-X : $21.95
    1. Collinsworth, Millicent. 2. Psychotherapy patients—Biography.
3. Adult child sexual abuse victims—Biography. 4. Bulimia—Patients—
Biography. 5. Blind—Biography. 6. Manic depressive psychoses—
Patients—Biography. I. Winebrenner, Jan. II. Title.
RC464.C65A3 1993
616.89' 0092—dc20
[B]
                                                                93-11428
                                                                CIP

Jan's Acknowledgments

To Millicent—what a journey! Thank you for letting me share it with you. I wouldn't have missed it for the world. And thank you, Gary, for your quick and ready assistance through long hours and often arduous terrain.

And special thanks to:

Margaret Leary and Terri Johnson for their encouragement and expertise through every mile;

Debra Frazier, whose keen eye helped keep this manuscript on course;

To Carolyn Davidson, who offered humor and distraction at strategic points along the way;

To Matt and Molly, who never fail to remind me that "home" is the sweetest of all words.

And especially to Ken, whose love steadies me every step of the way.

Millicent's Acknowledgments

I would like to thank:

My mother, Pauline Price Collinsworth, for her strength, her wisdom, and her example.

Jackson Mobley Collinsworth, family historian and master storyteller.

Lisa Gaeta and Al Potash, my friends and instructors at Impact.

The women of WRS Publishing: Terri Johnson, Margaret Leary, and Sherry Claypool.

Jan Winebrenner, for weaving power and poetry into a saga that granted us dignity and grace.

My husband, Gary Krantz, whose firm belief in unconditional love sustained me; whose direction, creative input, research, and editing skills were essential. And whose emotional support and encouragement allowed me to tell my story uncensored.

Dedication

*To Laddie, who became the father he never had
and the hero he never knew.*

Chapter 1

My blindness came slowly. I watched it descend like a heavy curtain, gently lowered upon a waiting stage. And with it came the realization that I was well-accustomed to darkness. Though I once considered its presence a shroud, time has convinced me that it is in many ways a gift. Against its background I can see more clearly the rich, treasured times of my life.

Like diamonds displayed upon black velvet, so are the bright moments. They are precious gems of exquisite value because, for so many years, they were rare and carefully mined out of a dark place too often haunted by fear and sadness.

The year I was born, my mother learned that my father was mentally ill.

"He is manic-depressive," the doctor told Mama, giving a name to the demon that would take hold of her husband, pulling him into his own invisible world of horrors. At times his disease would cause him to withdraw into a secret place so deep inside himself that it seemed he would never find his way back out. At other times he roared at his fears and raged against the confusion that overtook his mind. On these occasions, this almost regal, gentle man became an enemy, assaulting the peace of our tiny kingdom, destroying the bliss of our lives.

The doctor's diagnosis was delivered without hope of a cure. "There is nothing we can do for him," he said.

Shortly after my birth, Mama placed Daddy in a private sanitarium. It was the first of many times he would be hospitalized over the years of his illness. When she went to visit him a few weeks later, bringing with her their baby daughter, Millicent, whose birth he had witnessed, he asked, "Who is the baby? Whose child is she?"

So began my life in the Collinsworth family.

An aristocratic family, our heritage is filled with bigger-than-life heroes whose names can be found in the novels of James

Michener and in textbooks of Tennessee and Texas history. My ancestors fought in the Revolutionary War, survived Indian uprisings, and planted rice and cotton. The family of my maternal grandmother, Hallie Ella Williams, floated on a flatboat from Tennessee to Arkansas, traveling down the White River to the Little Red River, and then covered the last leg of their journey by ox cart. In the shadow of five towering oak trees, they built their homestead and named their property Five Oaks. There over the years, they endured and outlived the horror of the Civil War, deadly epidemics, and natural disasters. And there the Collinsworth family merged with the Williams family when my grandfather, James William Collinsworth, arrived from Tennessee and courted my grandmother, Hallie.

After their wedding, Hallie and James Collinsworth made their home at Five Oaks, and raised their children there. My father, Minor Lafayette Collinsworth, was the youngest of their six sons.

For me, the name Collinsworth was a badge of honor, a medal of valor and chivalry bestowed on me by my father. For him, it became a Purple Heart.

Never was a man more ill-suited to madness than my father. He began life on the family homestead where the stately oaks stood like time-worn sentries, the guardians of tradition and pride. Shy and quiet as a child, my father often disappeared for hours at a time, walking into woods filled with oaks and dogwoods, his hunting dog his only companion. Frequently, he returned home long after the house was silent and dark for the night.

After their marriage, Daddy and Mama bought a fine, old brick house on Center Street in Searcy, Arkansas, about half an hour's drive from Five Oaks. But Daddy always seemed happiest when he was back at his old family home. On weekends when the weather was fair and the roads dry, our family often drove out to the acreage and walked for hours, savoring the beauty and tranquillity of the country, recalling the stories of our ancestors.

Daddy had grown up listening to the stories of earlier generations of Collinsworths and Williams. I grew up listening to the retelling of them. I remember walking through the fields with my father, reveling in his good nature, celebrating the joy of hearing his voice as he told about the Five Oaks of an earlier century, in the days when it had been a working plantation.

"See, Mitty, over there is where the cotton gin used to be," he said, his soft, deep voice rich with the rhythm of the South. "And there is where the sawmill stood."

The romance of Five Oaks lived on in its name, if not in the deteriorating house and outbuildings which remained. The former glory had faded, leaving only memories of what had once been a gracious estate. The main house, a two-story, white wood frame with large, green shutters, had long since lost its grandeur. Like a once-lovely gown grown tattered through years of wear, it appeared soiled and worn. Only a vestige of its dignity and style remained. But when my father spoke of it, telling the stories of his boyhood and the accounts of his colorful ancestors, the old place regained its splendor, if only in my imagination. And my father's voice became lively and resonant, and his too-often expressionless face became animated.

At Five Oaks, Daddy seemed to become again the hero I believed him to be. With strong strides, he walked the acreage, pointing out the dogwood trees and occasionally stooping to find ferns that grew in shadowed places. I skipped along beside him, holding his hand tightly, as if my grip could keep this proud, charming man beside me forever; as if I could prevent his departure into that other tortured man who, at that moment, seemed so very far away.

It seemed Daddy could connect with the great trees and the earth smells of Five Oaks. For him, the woods and tall grasses were a place of rebirth; he could return there and touch life and feel whole for a little while. It would be so for him until his disease finally dragged him to a place so distant that no roads would ever lead him back home.

But on the good days, the days when he could touch life and hand it to me, he often said, "Mitty, you have to honor the past if you want to pursue the future."

Those halcyon days of my childhood found me uncaring about the future. And the past had meaning for me only because I could put flesh to it. Most of the time, that flesh belonged to Old John.

Old John was white-haired and well past eighty when I was born. He was blind and ancient by the time I knew him. I was fascinated by the fact that he was the son of slaves. When his family were freed, they had stayed at Five Oaks to work and make their home on the property.

Old John's mother, Aunt Sarey, was the Williams family wet nurse. When malaria swept the plantation, killing all the adults and making orphans of the three children of the white family in the big house, Aunt Sarey became their mother. She moved into the big house and became the matriarch of Five Oaks, meting out discipline, love, and good humor to my grandmother, Hallie, my great-aunt, Mattie Sue, and my great-uncle, Minor, making no distinctions between them and her own young son, John.

John and Minor grew up as brothers, suckling together at Aunt Sarey's breast, sharing toys and games and childhood escapades. They were inseparable. Only when Minor reached school age were the boys forced to be apart. Only then did they become aware of the differences between them—and only then did they learn that the rest of the world did not see them as equals.

Uncle Minor became enraged when Aunt Sarey told him that John could not attend school with him because of his color.

"If John can't go, I won't go!" Minor shouted, refusing to take one step toward the schoolhouse.

"But that's the way of things," Aunt Sarey explained, trying to make Minor understand, hoping he would give up his fight and go on to school with the other children.

Minor remained adamant in his stand. Aunt Sarey finally agreed to send John to school with Minor.

John and Uncle Minor fought their way to and from the one-room schoolhouse every day amid taunts of "Nigger!" and "Nigger lover!" But every day both boys walked to school. Uncle Minor sat at a desk in the classroom, while John sat outside under a tree in the yard.

Minor did not easily accept this injustice, and he did daily battle with his teacher over John's status in the schoolyard, finally refusing to return to school at all unless she would teach John too. The teacher agreed to a compromise: If Minor would continue to come to school, she would teach John—but outside under the trees, and only during recess. It was the best deal Minor was going to get. He agreed.

Uncle Minor finished his education and became a well-respected physician. John attended the first black college in Arkansas, where he earned his degree and became one of the first black preachers in the state. He would establish numerous churches in his lifetime, becoming one of the most respected and influential black men in the region. His influence on Uncle Minor, however, at least in matters of lifestyle and decorum, was not always as powerful.

Although Uncle Minor took his exceptional medical skills to Texas, it was his reputation as a womanizer that made him famous. On more than one occasion, he faced the possibility of a duel with a jealous lover. Once, while visiting in Little Rock, Uncle Minor, desperate with fear after some messy escapade, wired John. John walked more than fifty miles to help out the man who was as much his brother as his friend.

Old John was there when Hallie Williams spoke her vows to James Collinsworth. He was there for the birth of their children and their grandchildren.

To me, Old John's presence in our family was the living embodiment of my father's admonition to honor the past. He linked us to earlier generations that were noble, colorful, and courageous. His friendship was a precious gift, not only because of his ties with my ancestors, but also because I sensed in Old John a special love for my daddy, who was the nephew of John's dearest friend, my great-uncle Minor.

Old John called Daddy "the young man." He understood and loved Daddy as few other people ever would. He had lived nearby with his own family while Daddy was growing up on Five Oaks. He had known the quiet boy my daddy had been. He had watched him grow into a strong young man, too often silent and brooding, already manifesting his private tortures.

Old John had been there to celebrate my daddy's victories as a track star, both in high school and in college. He had cheered proudly for young Minor, the town's favorite football hero. He understood my father's country-gentleman ways and his love of the trees and land that comprised Five Oaks. He applauded "the young man's" brilliant mind and courtly manners. But perhaps more than anything, Old John knew and pitied my father's unspoken horrors. In an era when mental illness was considered a humiliation, he accepted my father's illness without judgment or censure. And he loved my daddy fiercely.

I remember one particular visit to Five Oaks in the springtime when I was a very small child. We invited Old John to come along with us for the day. Never before had the old home place looked so beautiful; never since has a day seemed so magical.

The leaves on the oak trees were vibrant green, soft with the moisture of recent rains. White blossoms decorated the branches of the dogwood trees. Azaleas bloomed in hidden places, peeking out at us with their pink and red and white flowers. I remember walking under the green canopy of branches, smelling the rich scent of wet earth and crushed leaves underfoot, my hand clasped tightly in Old John's. Though we made the trip often, this day was especially sweet because of the presence of Old John.

Together with my brother, Laddie, and Mama and Daddy, we walked to the base of a large oak and joined hands, circling the vast tree trunk. There we stood, an unlikely sight in the South of the 1950s: an old, black man and a young, white family, our hands gripping each others' in silent union, each a reverent part of a beloved whole. And then, childlike, Laddie and I, no longer able to stand still and quiet, burst into laughter and ran away to chase each other among the shadows.

I remember seeing Old John that day standing next to one of the huge oaks. I watched my mama take his hands in her own and place them on the rough bark of the tree trunk. I watched him gently caress the life-skin of the tree, his fingers moving across the bark like a pianist's fingers across a keyboard, playing for him old memories like songs that cannot be forgotten. I watched his kind face smile and his great, white head nod as he accepted from the tree a kind of private symphony only he could hear.

In my childish reverie, I never imagined that I, too, would one day be led by the hand to the place where the great oaks grow. That I, too, blind and unsure of my footing, would be carefully guided to the base of the tree, my hands placed against the bark to play back the songs of days gone by. There, many years later, I would hear my own private symphony of memories. There I, too, would touch the past and draw strength to face my future.

Chapter 2

If my gentle, aristocratic father was ill-suited to madness, my Southern-bred mother was equally undeserving of its accompanying humiliation and hopelessness. Nothing in her genteel breeding, however, prepared her to acquiesce to Daddy's illness.

Mama's upbringing instilled in her a natural instinct to fight for her way of life—the Southern way of life. Her weapons were dignity, denial, and a stubborn but brightly burning vision of the way things ought to be. Her victories were seldom the obvious kind. She triumphed in the realm of the spirit, if not in the realm of the mind.

As a young woman, Pauline Price was tall and beautiful, with luscious, flaming-red hair, alabaster skin, and gray eyes of such exotic beauty that they invited stares. In one eye, it looked as though an artist had brushed a golden-brown splash against the background of gray iris. If she had lived three hundred years earlier, her unusual eyes might have incurred charges of witchcraft instead of admiration.

Mama's father was the son of a wealthy plantation owner in Itawamba, Mississippi. He was six years old when the Civil War erupted, and he never forgave the South for losing. Robbed of the European education planned for him by his father and destitute at the end of the war, he reluctantly settled for the life of a dirt farmer—never forgetting that he should have been a gentleman planter—making his home in Sidon, Arkansas.

Papa's first wife died after bearing him six children. His second wife gave him seven more. My mother was the last of the thirteen children Papa would raise, born when he was nearly sixty years old.

Mama's life was filled with reminders of the greatness that once had been, of the grandeur that should have been. Abject poverty was no reason for shame, she learned. Dignity sprang from one's roots, Papa said, and her roots were sunk deep in Southern splendor. That they slept four to a bed did not negate the richness of her heritage. Her ancestors had paid dearly in the fight for their way of life, Papa told her. Though they lost it all, they had fought well, and they never forgot the glory of the former days. She must never forget either.

And so it was that Mama's poverty did nothing to dim her vision of the ideal nor detract from her sense of how things ought to be. Even with a sack of cotton hung on her back, Mama walked proudly. She worked alongside her brothers and sisters during picking season, learning to adjust her body to support her burden. During elementary school she often walked barefoot to school, her shoes tied together and slung around her neck to save on wear and tear.

When Mama graduated from the one-room elementary school in Sidon, she had to move to Searcy, the county seat, to attend high school. She and her sister, Lucy, rented a tiny duplex apartment on Center Street.

Mama often sat and gazed at the fine, old, brick house across the street from the little place she shared with Aunt Lucy. She admired the four white columns and the gracious wide porch, the wrought-iron balcony on the second story, and the tall willow oak in the front yard. She thought about the small, "dogtrot" farmhouse she had grown up in back in Sidon. With its wide-open breezeway, its tin roof and weathered gray clapboards, it was well-kept and neat, but it wasn't splendid at all, nothing like the impressive brick house that seemed to reign over the neighborhood with an air of regal grace.

"Someday," she vowed, "I'll live in a big brick house, just like that one."

Just like the old brick house on Center Street.

Mama's studies were easy for her. She excelled in every class. Especially gifted in music and theater, Mama was the pride of her family. She learned well from her Papa that there was another way of life for those who could achieve it, for those who could hold onto it against all odds. She would be one of the achievers. And she would hold on with all her might.

Mama met Daddy shortly after high school graduation, when she was eighteen and he was twenty-six. She was attending classes at Central College and working as a secretary at Robbins-Sanford Mercantile Company, where Daddy was an accountant. For my father, it was love at first sight. For my mother, however, it would be years before she would know her heart.

A serious, quiet young man of unimpeachable manners and perfect breeding, Minor Collinsworth was considered the "catch of the county." His family holdings, though not as elegant as they once had been, still evidenced the prestige and stature of the Collinsworth name. He had moved into Searcy and rented a room at the Robinson's house, but he was still recognized as one of the Collinsworths of Five Oaks.

Minor Lafayette Collinsworth knew his courtship of Pauline Price was one of many—she was not only the campus beauty but the most popular girl in town as well. Although she was appreciative of his family's importance in the county and more than a little impressed with his courtly manners, she was not ready for marriage. Minor decided patience would be his greatest ally in this pursuit. He knew she was enjoying the idea of courtship while at the same time feeling unwilling to commit to marriage. He felt certain her other beaus would grow discouraged in time and give up their suit. When they did, he would be waiting. By then, she would be ready to say yes. He wouldn't give up until she became his wife.

Vivacious and intrepid, Mama was the perfect foil for Daddy's somber and reserved manners. With his thick black hair and blue-green eyes, he was placid and cool; she, with her vivid red hair and untamed spirit, was all fire and heat. He was aristocracy and gentility; she was ferocious pride and fervent independence. She admired his genteel manners and his aristocratic ways and, being Southern to the core, she knew the value of a good name and established property holdings. But she wasn't ready to lay aside her dreams of adventure.

The year 1933 found Mama, with an associate arts degree in hand, teaching school in the small mountain town of Shirley, Arkansas, many miles away from Searcy and Minor Collinsworth. The government had no money to pay teachers, but President Roosevelt had initiated "warrants," hoping to shore up the sagging ranks of teachers in America. Mama, ever in search of excitement, found ample doses of it in that tiny country town peopled with lumberjacks, merchants, and dirt farmers—all uncertain of the source of their next meal.

The one-room schoolhouse was small and dingy and smelled of urine and unwashed bodies. In winter, it was freezing. Mama assigned wood-chopping chores to the biggest boys in her class so there would be enough fuel for the stove in the center of the room to generate sufficient heat to still the children's shivering. She asked each student to bring a cup of milk to school every day, then she added her own ration of sugar and cocoa to the

milk and kept a pot of hot chocolate on the stove all day to warm
the children.

Mama won the children's hearts and the respect of their parents,
along with the title "prettiest girl" at the city's annual box supper.
And before her first year of teaching was over, she also won a
reprimand from the school board, along with their grudging
appreciation for her unusual audacity.

This is Mama's version of the story. Her lodgings in Shirley
consisted of a tiny room in a house at the bottom of a hill. Atop
the hill sat the schoolhouse. Every day her route to the school led
up the hill through the town's main street. Her morning walk to
class was peaceful and enjoyable. But she soon began to dread the
walk home after school.

By late afternoon, the town rowdies—out-of-work men, young
and old, who had nothing better to do than watch and whistle at
pretty girls—gathered along the main street and shouted coarse
comments at Mama as she walked down the hill toward the
boardinghouse. Mama grew tired of their unwanted attention
and decided to find another way home from school.

The only alternate route she could find detoured off the main
road to a narrow street barricaded by a wooden fence. Mama was
undaunted. She took off her shoes, hiked up her skirt, pulled the
pins out of her hair, and began running, gaining speed and
momentum on the downhill slope so that she sailed easily up
and over the fence in a single, powerful leap.

Every day Mama ran the same hurdle course, arriving at the
bottom of the hill unkempt and out of breath. She had no idea
that a shopkeeper had seen her downhill sprint and high jump.
The story of the flight of the beautiful redhead traveled through
the small town quickly. Soon Mama's audience from the main
street followed her, watching silently from behind buildings, seeing
her red hair streaming behind her, seeing her graceful flight over
the wooden fence. She had no idea that her daily "track meet"
was the talk of the town until she was called in front of the
school board and advised that her behavior was unsuitable, that
she was setting a poor example of decorum for the city's children.

In addition to her "unladylike behavior," the school board
chastised Mama for using school time for chopping wood and
making hot chocolate for the children. Surely the time she was
spending to feed and warm the children could be better spent on
the three "Rs," they said.

"I agree," Mama answered. "Chopping wood is hard work for the children, but the schoolhouse is quite cold. If any of you men would like to come by every morning to chop and stack wood for us, we would be glad to have your help."

The gentlemen in their suits and vests harrumphed and looked abashed, but every morning thereafter, a school board member arrived to chop the wood.

Mama's year in Shirley convinced her she was not well-suited to life in a small lumber town. She returned to Searcy for a while before deciding to continue her education at Oachita College in Arkadelphia. She earned her degree in English and was initiated into Delta Psi Omega, a national honorary dramatic society. She and Daddy renewed their friendship, but she still refused to commit to marriage. She studied for her graduate degree in physical education and health at Louisiana State University and then returned to Oachita College as a teacher. Daddy continued to pursue an advanced business degree at Chillicothe Business College in Missouri.

Finally, in 1937, Daddy's patience was rewarded. On September 5, he married Pauline Price. The Depression complicated their plans—Mama would continue to teach for a year at Oachita and Daddy would live in Tuckerman, where he had found work as an accountant—but they would be able to spend weekends together. They consoled themselves with the knowledge that this separation would last only one year. Their marriage took place in a minister's office in Padukah, Kentucky, with one family member present. Their only wedding gifts were a crystal bowl and crystal candleholders.

As a little girl, I listened to Mama tell the stories of her college days and her romantic escapades, and I found it easy to believe that this beautiful and graceful woman had once been engaged to three men at the same time. I found it easy to believe that Daddy had been willing to wait for her. Years later, I would grab hold of those stories, trying to convince myself that the man and woman I called Mama and Daddy *had* once known joy and love and good times. Their lives *had* once been spiced with romance and passion, even though not even a tattered remnant of it remained.

Years later, I would touch the crystal bowl and candleholders that commemorated my parents' wedding, letting my fingers travel over the cool glass. And I would read the volume of poems Daddy had given Mama as an engagement gift, memorizing the stanzas she had underlined. I would treasure that thin book and the sparkling crystal as priceless relics of a once-golden age, an era of grace and sweetness that disappeared suddenly when the demons of my father's disease were turned loose in our home.

Daddy never quite forgave himself for not serving in the army during World War II. While his friends and relatives shipped out to Europe and the Pacific, he was left at home, too old at thirty-six to be drafted. Even if he had been under the age limit, however, he would never have been allowed to serve because of his eyesight.

I'm sure I inherited my poor vision from my daddy. He wore trifocal glasses, and, even when he wore them, his vision could not be corrected to twenty-twenty. However, he considered his sight and his age to be negligible concerns. He insisted he was as fit to serve his country as any man alive. He was the first to line up whenever a draft office opened its doors.

So desperate was Daddy to pass the army physical that he coerced Mama into going with him to the recruiter's office to help him memorize the eye charts just minutes before the exam. He memorized each chart perfectly and recited the letters exactly as they appeared. His ruse was discovered when he "read" the wrong charts.

Finally, Daddy had to accept the fact that Uncle Sam did not want him. He spent the war years managing a plantation shipping center that distributed supplies for the war effort. Mama spent them teaching, first at Oachita College, where she was promoted to assistant dean of women, and later in high school and elementary school, proving herself to be a talented and creative teacher for students of any age.

Mama and Daddy were married for eight years and had all but despaired of ever having children before my brother, Minor Lafayette Collinsworth II—nicknamed Laddie—was born in 1945. Then, two years and one day later, I was born, on September 13, 1947, in a little river town called Newport, Arkansas. A year and a half later, our family moved back to Searcy, and Daddy bought Mama the splendid, old brick house on Center Street that she had admired from her tiny duplex on the other side of the street.

My parents were ecstatic over their little family. They had a son who promised to be handsome, courteous, and heroic, as is the destiny of all Southern sons. And they had a daughter who would be beautiful and ladylike and accomplished in all things feminine. Mama's total delight in her family was, however, quickly marred by two factors she had not reckoned on. The first, of course, was my father's illness. The second was my lack of beauty.

"Mitty," Mama told me when I was very small, "You are not a pretty child, but you have character."

Character, to Mama, was almost as good as beauty, but not quite. And beauty, she believed, could be achieved if one worked hard enough at it. For me, it would become an obsession.

I was two years old when I caught chickenpox and mumps at the same time and became extremely ill. A very high fever was blamed for damage to my eyes that weakened them and caused them to cross. When I was just a toddler, I was fitted with thick, bifocal glasses.

My hair, unlike Mama's rich, red tresses and Daddy's coal-black hair, was an insipid dishwater brown. My crossed eyes, huge behind the thick lenses, were an extraordinary blue-green, but their color and size seemed to overwhelm my small face, making me look older than my years and giving me the forlorn appearance of a child possessed of an ancient, weary spirit.

Anemic and pale-looking, I showed little promise of ever becoming the beauty Mama hoped I would be. Every day she brushed my hair until it shone, sprinkled my forehead with thick bangs, and then plaited long French braids down my back, trying, I'm sure, to compensate in some small way for the rest of my inadequacies. It was, however, not nearly enough.

The search for an ophthalmologist who could operate on my eyes and correct them became my mother's consuming quest. When doctor after doctor told her it couldn't be done, she still refused to give up. Someday she would find a surgeon who could make me pretty. Someday…

Mama was consumed with devotion for her two children. When Laddie and I approached school age, she determined that she would not allow anyone else to take her place in our lives. We were her miracles—the children born after so many years of waiting and hoping. She would not send us off to be taught and cared for by strangers. She would teach us herself.

Already state-certified, Mama was every bit as qualified as the other teachers in the town of Searcy. Her credentials quickly gained her state approval to form an accredited school in her home. And so, with little difficulty, Mama established the Collinsworth's Little Red School House, a registered school for children of nursery-school age through third grade. And every day, Laddie and I attended classes in our home with our mother as our teacher.

Even before she opened the Collinsworth's Little Red School

House, Mama had been busy about the task of teaching us all that our tiny minds could contain. Every routine act was an opportunity for lessons. Before we were big enough to run by ourselves, Mama had begun taking us exploring, "adventuring," as she liked to call it, exposing us to the wonders of the world.

While other young mothers in our neighborhood fussed over soiled clothes and muddy shoes, our mother dressed us in overalls for our outdoor excursions. She tied brown shoes on our feet so scuffs would not show, and then she pushed us about the town in a huge perambulator, introducing us to dandelions that were really fallen stars and toadstools that were chairs for the fairies.

"See, children," she said, her rich, contralto voice filling us with awe, "the fairies danced here last night! They left their little chairs!"

And Laddie and I exclaimed over the sights and sounds and smells of the world, content to take our lessons from our beautiful, fascinating mama. The wind was God's whisper and the rain, His tears. Snow was Heaven's blanket, and when autumn turned the Ozark Mountains into a blaze of color, she declared that this was the place where God cleaned His paintbrushes.

Through Mama, all the world was a poem. She lavished laughter and love on us, and we learned to love in return and to laugh and dream as only carefree children can. Our lives were like a fairy tale.

Mama insisted that her children's day begin gently; we were never to be startled from our sleep. Accordingly, every morning a black maid climbed the stairs to our bedrooms and wakened us with a warm, wet cloth on our faces. I remember lying in my huge, antique bed, watching while the maid, in her starched uniform, swung open the doors of a large armoire to reveal dozens of lovely, pressed, frilly dresses. I would lie there, indulged and pampered, like a princess in a storybook, and point to the dress I wanted to wear for the day.

The image of beauty and perfection blurred slightly when I entered the dining room for breakfast in the morning. My eyes quickly darted to my father's hands. Were they still? Did they move with deliberateness or tremble as they gripped the heavy silver pieces that adorned the breakfast table? Were his movements graceful or agitated with uncontrolled tremors? The sound of clattering flatware warned me before I entered the dining room. The trembling hands alerted me that today would be a bad day for my family.

The trembling meant Daddy's condition was manic, and his

otherwise gentle persona would be angry and verbose. His temper would rage over small, insignificant occurrences, and he would attack things—but never people. He hurled books, dishes, inanimate objects that didn't bleed when broken. And when the raging had spent itself, he would retreat to that solitary place inside his soul. Sometimes he retreated to distant locales for days at a time.

Mama learned to accept Daddy's sudden and prolonged absences from home, but not without some fear. I learned many years later that, on those occasions when he left with his hunting gun, she wondered if he would find a hidden place of solace in the woods and shoot himself. At times she was frantic until he returned home. Often, he had gone to his hunting club or to the woods at Five Oaks, or to the kennels where he raised champion hunting dogs. At other times, he had driven as far away as Louisiana and Missouri in search of an illusive peace.

I learned very early to recognize the dangerous hidden currents that lay just beneath the surface of our placid pool. Before I was six, I knew how to maneuver through the waters without upsetting my little vessel, without drowning.

When I was awakened late at night by the sound of my father's nocturnal prowlings through the house, his feet padding across the floor like the paws of a lion in its cage, back and forth, back and forth, behind the bars of his illness, I would crawl into Laddie's bed next to mine in the room we shared. There, I would cling to my brother and huddle down in the warmth of the blankets, hoping the sound of his breathing near my ear would drown out the sound of Daddy's pacing.

Our family life was like a fantastic tragi-comedy enacted on a stage whose background had been painted by some mad surrealist. Behind the lovely characters, with their poise and well-spoken lines, hung terrifying specters. Only Mama's powerful presence could divert Laddie's and my attention from the awful images that formed the backdrop of our lives.

On the good days, Daddy went to his accounting job at White County Motor Company. "Whitey," the owner of the firm, became a co-conspirator with Mama to protect Daddy from the ignominy of his illness. He paid Daddy a generous salary and asked no questions on the days when Mama called to say Daddy would not be able to come to work. Whitey knew of Daddy's unexplainable disappearances. And he knew the occasions when Daddy's illness made him uncontrollable, and Mama had to commit him to a private sanitarium for treatment. He knew, but he never shared his knowledge with the rest of the townspeople.

Whitey believed a man should always stand by his heroes, and he considered Daddy the genuine article. In a town enthralled with football, the name Minor Collinsworth was legend. Whitey would never forget my daddy's prowess on the football field, nor his accomplishments in track and field. He would never forget my father's contribution to the town's prestige. And he would never turn his back on a fellow Mason and Kiwanis Club member. My mother came to depend heavily on Whitey's kindness and his discretion in a town uncomfortable with mental illness.

During those times when Daddy was in the hospital, our home was peaceful, restful. Every day was a delight. I skipped down to breakfast and hurried through my meal, anxious to enter the classroom where Mama waited with fascinating stories.

In a short time, the Collinsworth's Little Red School House became the town's most prestigious private school. The faculty grew to include special tutors, private art instructors, and music teachers. As young as I was, I held an important place in the school. I felt needed. I offered guided tours of the back-yard playground for potential students and their families, making sure the guests saw all the wonders of the schoolhouse, smiling and offering the gracious welcome that is always due a guest in a small Southern town.

I was six years old, a child extraordinaire. I had already learned that good public relations is a key to the success of any endeavor. I had learned that charm is a skill that even the youngest female can perfect, whether she is beautiful or not. And I had learned that it was essential that our clients be happy, that they continue to pay their tuition, because our family's fortune was nearly gone.

The fairy-tale existence of the Collinsworth children in the old brick house on Center Street was quickly coming to an end. Daddy's bad days began to outnumber the good ones. The cost of private hospitals for him, some as far away as Memphis, drained our family bank account. He was able to spend less and less time at his job and, although Whitey continued to be sympathetic and kind, Daddy couldn't continue to be paid for work someone else was now doing. Whitey's loyalty remained steady; his balance sheet, however, indicated he would soon have to replace Daddy.

Gone were the gracious days of gardeners, maids, morning and afternoon cooks, and luxurious family vacations to exclusive hotels and resorts in New Orleans and Natchez and Hot Springs.

Daddy's illness was growing worse, and Mama was running out of money. The income from the school was our only resource, Mama our only support. She shouldered the responsibility of trying to maintain the lifestyle she considered worthy of the Collinsworth name.

Mama's effort to create and maintain a life of beauty and grace in the face of our diminishing resources was superhuman. She determined that, no matter how dire our circumstances became, certain essentials would not be removed from our lives. She was a master of denial, a genius at creating illusion. At certain times, she even managed to transform illusion into reality. Her magic was especially powerful at twilight.

At the close of every day, the simple, sweet moments of early evening passed with Laddie and me snuggled against Mama, rocking in the garden swing when the weather allowed, listening to her read us stories. We devoured the books that came every month from our book club, and we anxiously awaited that hour each night when Mama would read a chapter to us. If Daddy was at home with us, and his graceful, artistic hands were calm and steady on his pipe stem, his presence in the garden with us was a gift.

Daddy would sit at a distance, just outside the circle of our family. I sensed he was listening to Mama's voice, but he seldom made any response. He sat quietly, sometimes smoking his pipe, always silent and shrouded in shadow, while Mama's rich, carefully modulated voice spun tales of fascinating places and people.

Twilight time became for me the best time of day. All the terrifying dragons had been driven back into their lairs, and all weapons were sheathed. Daddy had accepted the terms of a limited peace, and Mama honored its signing with a benediction read from a child's storybook.

I wanted the peace of twilight and the warmth of my mother's arms and the sound of my brother's laughter to be always there for me. I wanted my father to be happy and healthy, and I wanted to know for sure that he loved me. More than anything else in the world, I wanted to hear my daddy say, "I love you, Mitty."

The cyclical nature of his illness kept my father always traveling at a distance from me. In my mind, I saw him revolving around me in an elliptical orbit, at one time coming almost close enough for me to touch him, then spinning away again just before I could grasp hold. Only once did I find myself wrapped in his arms, held against his chest. The memory of it is bolted down in my mind so that nothing can ever rob me of it.

I was a tiny child, but already used to Daddy's silent, shadowed presence in our home. I watched him move quietly about the periphery of the family, seldom speaking, never aware of my childish gestures of love. I often crept into his library at night, hiding under a lamp table or behind a sofa, sitting silent and still, inhaling the smell of peppermints in the dish on his desk and the scent of the pipe he smoked every evening. His face became a burnished bronze in the flickering light of the room's immense fireplace. I thought he was handsome and brave and wonderful.

On some level, I knew he was aware that I sat hidden in the shadows, observing him. Most of the time he sat in silence, allowing me to watch him, but not acknowledging my presence. I sensed that, in that richly scented room, I was like a hunter who had come upon a great and glorious stag, a wild animal that had chosen for just a moment to stand still and let me admire him. Then, in an instant, the moment would pass and the stag would dart away, leaving me thrilled by the grandeur of his fleeting presence. So it was with my daddy. He was comfortable with my presence for only a few moments, and then his fear would overtake him and he would retreat, unable to let me come close.

But on that wonderful night I will never forget, I summoned all the courage of the Collinsworths and walked over to stand near the chair where he sat. For several long moments he seemed to ignore my presence, and then he lifted his eyes from his *American Field* and found me staring at him. Mesmerized by his gaze, I froze, waiting, wondering. But with a nod that was almost imperceptible, he laid aside the magazine, picked me up, and placed me on his lap.

Blinking, I tried to calm my pounding heart, to quiet my excitement lest I suddenly earn banishment instead of this tentative welcome. I sat as still as I could while he picked up his magazine again, holding it in front of us both, allowing me to read along with him.

For what seemed like hours, I sat stiffly, afraid to breathe, afraid to relax and lean back against his chest, afraid that if I accepted too much from him, he would be quickly depleted and I would have to leave him. Finally, I let myself lean against him, feeling the starch of his white shirt on my neck and smelling his spicy after-shave mingled with the scent of tobacco. He rested his cheek against the side of my head, and I felt the roughness of his evening growth of beard. Enfolded between his arms and the magazine, I felt a euphoria I had never felt before. Listening to the creak of the rocking chair as we sat together, moving back and forth, I thought life was perfect.

The moment ended too quickly. Daddy stopped the motion of his chair and lifted me down from his lap. I walked out, glancing back over my shoulder to see him resume his lonely vigil. Somehow, I knew I had just tasted one of the sweetest moments life would offer me.

The dichotomy of our family's life in the old brick house on Center Street never fails to amaze me. Mama poured all her energy into the effort of maintaining the appearance of gentility. A stranger peering in at us through a window would have seen no hint of the reality that lay behind the fragile facade.

Evening meals continued to be served in the formal dining room, using the best china and silver. Colorful floral centerpieces still graced the center of the long, antique table. Mama sat at one end and Daddy at the other, while Laddie and I sat stiff and erect in our side chairs, bathed and dressed in our Sunday best for this formal hour of the day. There, with the tinkling sounds of Mama's antique music box playing Strauss and Tschaikowsky in the background, Laddie and I practiced proper etiquette for proper, young Southern ladies and gentlemen. Mama directed our conversations toward culture and intellectual topics, and she pretended all was well and prosperous in the Collinsworth family.

The only indicators of change were the missing antiques Mama sold to help pay the exorbitant costs of private hospital care for Daddy. Valuable antiques—huge pieces of furniture—disappeared mysteriously from our household, leaving gaping holes in the decor that Mama tried to fill by rearranging the furniture left in the room. Later I would learn she had sold expensive farm equipment and acres of farmland before she had let go of pieces from her treasured collection.

Only a few of Searcy's citizenry knew how we lived behind the wall of dignity my mother built around us. Few ever crossed the threshold into our private hell. But once, just once, while Laddie and I were babies, a stranger ventured into forbidden territory and left a message for my mother, a warning she couldn't ignore.

Laddie and I were about four and two at the time. Mama left us with Daddy for an entire day while she drove to the country club in Newport to coordinate the wedding reception of the daughter of old family friends. She was checking rooms and table service when her friend's softly spoken words caused her to freeze.

"You know, Pauline," the woman whispered to her, "it's not

wise of you to leave the children alone with Minor."

Mama was stunned, confused.

"What do you mean?" she asked.

The woman looked embarrassed, uncertain. She dropped her eyes, and murmured, "Well, of course it would probably never happen, but you never know... "

And then Mama began to comprehend. This woman was suggesting that Daddy was capable of harming his own children. Mama was appalled and angry, offended not only by the fantastic suggestion but also by the unforgivable intrusion into her privacy. And then, because she had not yet perfected the art of denial, because she was still an apprentice at it, she felt doubt begin to travel through her veins. Was it possible that her husband would do violence to his own children?

She was shaken. Alarmed, she acknowledged the remote possibility that, even though she had never felt threatened before, her husband *could* conceivably harm his children if he were overtaken by a manic bout. He wouldn't want to hurt us; he wouldn't intend for it to happen, but she had to admit it *could* happen.

Mama left the country club immediately, arriving home to find the house dark and empty. She ran through the rooms and up the stairs calling our names, fearing the unspeakable, refusing to imagine the unimaginable. Panicked, she finally opened the door on a room at the back of the house. She found us sitting in the farthest corner of the room, swathed in darkness. Daddy held me on his lap and sat staring blankly. Laddie sat next to him, his legs, cold and numb, dangling from a chair much too large for him. Immobilized by fear, both Laddie and I whimpered when Mama picked us up. We clung to her as she carried us out of the dark room and into the light.

Mama would never know how long we had been sitting in the darkness with our silent, staring father. She did know, however, that she would never again be able to leave us alone with him.

Chapter 3

The night my childhood ended lives in my memory like a scene out of a Gothic novel, complete with storm clouds, crashing thunder, and torrential rains pelting my bedroom window. Trees swayed and branches broke off under the gale force of the winds. I awoke to the sounds of the storm and muffled voices downstairs. I left my bed and crept to the banister to peer down into the entryway where Mama stood, wrapped in her dressing gown, talking with our family doctor.

The day had begun badly, with Whitey calling Mama to say that Daddy had left the office visibly agitated.

"Has he come home, Pauline?" Whitey asked.

"No, he's not here," Mama answered, feeling the first gnawing of fear. "Did something happen to upset him?"

"It wasn't anything serious, really, but yes, he did seem disturbed over the books. He left for the bank to check on things and then never came back... " Whitey's voice trailed off. He waited for Mama's response.

Her voice steady and soothing, Mama answered, "Thank you for calling, Whitey. I'll make a few calls and see if he's gone out to the property. Don't worry. He'll probably be home soon."

Mama hung up the phone and glanced out the front window. Dark storm clouds hung low and heavy overhead. The air was still, as if biding its time, awaiting the signal to erupt in violence. Mama knew she had to find Daddy before the storm struck. How much time did she have? She drew a deep breath and willed herself to remain calm. She forced herself to smile at the schoolchildren milling around her, waiting for their teacher to resume their lessons. She couldn't let her distress upset them.

Always the great actress, Mama directed the children in class activities, distracting us from this sudden and unusual interruption. When she could see we were absorbed in our projects, she slipped away to telephone all the places Daddy might have gone, but no one had seen him. No one knew where he could be. By the time she dismissed school for the day, Mama was nearly frantic with worry.

By late afternoon, when the rain began to pelt the windows, Mama grew even more agitated. She had called every place she could think of, and there was no sign of Daddy. Her fear escalated into near panic.

I remember Mama sending Laddie and me upstairs to play, hoping to distract us from the swirl of fear surrounding her. We entertained ourselves with books and games while Mama maintained her vigil downstairs near the telephone.

Years later, Mama told me the details of that day. As the afternoon stretched toward evening, her fears for Daddy increased. She was nearly crazy with the thought that he might have killed himself. Desperate for help, she asked a relative to go search for him. The familiar places, the places Daddy always sought when he needed solace, gave no evidence that he had been there. He had disappeared.

A few hours later, over the roar of the storm, Mama heard the sound of a car out front. She hurried outside and found my father slumped over the steering wheel, his clothes soaked and bloody, his wrists bandaged. I watched them from the doorway as she put her arms around him and helped him into the house.

"Children, go upstairs," she ordered tersely. Laddie and I gripped each other's hands and climbed the stairs slowly, looking back to see Daddy leaning heavily on Mama's shoulder.

The family doctor arrived as Mama was helping Daddy into bed. Laddie and I crawled into our own beds and fell asleep to the muffled sounds of doors opening and closing and the ringing of the telephone.

I learned many years later that Daddy had driven to the White River in Newport, slashed his wrists, and jumped into the muddy waters. A passerby, oddly enough a former business partner, noticed the car parked near the riverbank. Looking closer, he saw a man in the murky, swirling waters, and he rushed in and pulled my father to safety. Then he took Daddy to have his wrists stitched and bandaged.

The ringing phone that night was Brother Wilkins, my parents' former pastor from Newport.

"Did a frightened, desperate young man come to your house this afternoon?" he asked, when my mother's voice answered his call.

"Yes," Mama told him, confused by the way he phrased the question. And then the clicking sound in the phone reminded her she was on a party line. To prevent everyone in Searcy from learning of her husband's suicide attempt, Brother Wilkins had asked his question "in code." Gratitude swept over her. She would never forget his kindness.

Laddie and I were asleep much later that night when the violence of the storm shook the house and the wind brushed tree branches against the windows. I awoke feeling frightened and displaced. The sounds of the voices drew me to the banister.

Dr. Edwards and Mama stood in the entryway near the front door. They spoke in urgent, hushed tones. I remember feeling exhilarated by the sense of mystery and excitement. By morning the exhilaration had ended, replaced by an overpowering sense of disturbance. Intuitively, I understood that the passing of the night had taken with it something of my innocence.

Throughout the next few days, Mama instructed Laddie and me to be very quiet. We walked cautiously through the large rooms of our home, speaking softly, careful not to slam doors or make any loud noises.

"Daddy is resting," Mama told us. "He's not feeling well."

Then one morning, Daddy emerged from his room looking gaunt but elegant in his burgundy robe. I met him in the library and looked up at him curiously. Then my eyes automatically shifted to his hands. The edge of stark-white, gauze bandages showed beneath the velvet cuffs of his robe.

"What happened to your wrists, Daddy?" I asked.

"I cut them," he answered.

From that time on, my mother's beauty began to wane. The vivacious woman she had once been disappeared, to be replaced by a somber, exhausted woman. Her eyes lost their look of wise amusement. The vibrant sheen of her hair faded. Her mouth, which had always been quick to turn up in laughter, became a thin line, drawn tight against a face etched with worry and despair.

My father's elegance faded too. His aristocratic profile was marred by sunken cheeks and a downturned mouth. His eyes bore the look of a man lost and afraid. I wondered what it was he feared. I wished I could take him by the hand and lead him to a place of safety. I wished I could make him happy.

Our family's wounds were deep and painful. However, I learned, as children do, that when I was good, when I did the things I was supposed to do, and when I excelled at a task or performed well in any setting, there were momentary, if fleeting, sensations of joy that made me forget my pain. I sensed Mama's pleasure in me and convinced myself that Daddy was also pleased. I began to believe, quite unknowingly at first, that the power to heal our family lay with me.

It was a grandiose scheme for a seven-year-old, but I never considered failure. I would have to be very, very good, but I would try very, very hard. I would practice my music lessons and do my class work diligently and commit myself to being the best at everything I was given to do, and somehow I would be able to bring back the luster to my father's eyes. I would make him smile and laugh. I would make him whole.

It was a monumental undertaking for one so young, but I believed I could do it. I had already learned from Mama that there was no greater sin than mediocrity, that she believed her children were destined for greatness, that she was certain Laddie and I ranked above anything that could be termed ordinary. With her vision as the fuel for my journey, I could travel to dizzying heights of perfection and thereby heal my father and restore my mother's joy and beauty.

Mama really believed that Laddie and I were extraordinary. Through the Collinsworth's Little Red School House, she was able to route all available resources toward equipping us for greatness. Every small talent we exhibited was examined and probed for signs of genius. The great irony, I realized many years later, was that I was really a less-than-exceptional child in every respect.

Neither Laddie nor I resembled the stereotype of Southern children. He was neither heroic nor athletic by our parents' standards, and I was neither beautiful nor especially gifted. We were intelligent children, quick and ready to learn anything Mama wanted to teach us, but we were quite different from the children she and Daddy had expected to produce.

Unlike Daddy's quiet demeanor, Laddie's was exuberant. Laughter spilled from him as naturally as water spilled from a fountain. He lacked Daddy's interest in hunting and sports—he was more at home with a book of poems than with a rifle or a football—but that didn't matter to Mama. She stepped easily into the role of coach.

I remember Mama in the front yard with Laddie, teaching him how to punt a football. Laddie, with a helmet that kept falling over his eyes, ran toward the ball while Mama held it steady. I remember Mama tossing him the ball across the yard and Laddie catching it and falling to the ground in laughter. When he missed the toss, he fell down crying. Mama, ever patient but determined, drilled my brother in the skills my father had perfected, while my father's chair rocked to and fro in the library.

A gentle, affectionate boy, Laddie was my dearest friend. He had inherited Daddy's beauty, if not his athletic talent, and I loved him fiercely. I envied him his thick black hair and wide, clear-blue eyes. I wished my own eyes didn't have to be hidden behind thick glasses. I wished my drab, limp hair was as beautiful as his. And I listened continually for Mama's convincing words that focused not on my liabilities, but on my assets.

"You have lovely posture, Mitty," my mother told me. The mirror told me I was lanky, but Mama's vision of me was graceful. I learned to see myself through her eyes.

"You have a lovely voice, Mitty, not like other children's. Yours is low and well-modulated. That will be very valuable to you. Always speak as you do now... Yes, like that..." she would say when I dropped my voice down, making its tones mellow and rich.

When Mama brought music teachers into the Little Red School House, I attacked my lessons with enthusiasm, reaping less than spectacular rewards. Mama, however, assured me my gifts were remarkable. I played "She'll Be Comin' Round the Mountain" at my first piano recital, and Mama's serene pride engulfed me. Dressed in a little-girl formal with ruffles and ribbons, I basked in the joy of my mama who smiled at me from her seat in the pew of the First Methodist Church of Searcy. The sanctuary was filled with nervous parents of nervous children. Only my mama was calm, certain of her child's ability to perform with excellence.

Though my talents were mediocre, I was sustained by the force of Mama's powerful will, and I believed I was brilliant, gifted, and, if not beautiful, at least significant. She worked her magic on Laddie too, and we both accepted her assurances that we were exceptional. In her eyes I really was a concert pianist and Laddie an all-American. No matter the degree of our talent, Mama's will compelled us to transcend our own limitations. Laddie, I believe, had not so far to climb.

To say that I loved my brother is inadequate. I adored him, idolized him, wished with all my heart I could be just like him. Nothing pleased me as much as when Mama dressed me in striped jerseys and cowboy boots just like his. We were close in age and nearly the same size, so strangers occasionally mistook us for twins. This delighted me. Although he never became the all-star

athlete Mama expected, he never disappointed me. I wasn't
concerned with his abilities in sports. He was my brother, and I
loved him with all my heart.

While I never really earned the adjective "beautiful," Mama
did credit me with something she called "presence." I could enter
a room and exude a charisma that would draw people to me. I
could speak with children and adults alike, putting them at ease,
showing a maturity and poise far beyond my years. I was becoming
the great actress Mama had once been. I was not so much suited
for it as thrust into it. I had already begun to find the reality of
my life a thing to be escaped.

Not long after Daddy's suicide attempt, Mama instructed Laddie
and me to help her find and remove anything in the house that
could be used as a weapon. She sent us into the kitchen to gather
up knives, letter openers, anything sharp, while she gathered all
Daddy's guns and took them away. We carried out our macabre
task in a matter-of-fact way, much as we might have carried out
any normal household chore.

I found my solace in those early years in an imaginary friend I
named Bad Girl. She was responsible for anything I did that
might be considered naughty. She made the little noises that
irritated others. She, not I, could be blamed if Millicent participated
in a school-yard squabble with the other children. Bad Girl was
the one who occasionally caused minor strife on the playground
or favored one child over another. Millicent wasn't allowed that
luxury. As the teacher's child, I had always to be friendly with all
the children, never choosing one for a best friend. On those
occasions when Bad Girl forgot her role in the Collinsworth's Little
Red School House, Millicent watched aghast as Mama scolded her.

I waited impatiently every day for the newspaper so I could
read my favorite comic strip, "Rex Morgan, M.D.," and I fantasized
that he was my daddy. He was strong and wise and kind. His
hands didn't tremble and slosh his coffee—his hands held the
power to heal. His eyes were not vacant one day and angry and
tortured the next. Rex Morgan was perfect, whole, and, in my
mind, he loved me. He spoke the words I would never hear my
real father say. I pretended Rex Morgan told me every day, many
times each day, "I love you, Mitty, I love you."

My fantasies, while colorful and consoling in some measure,
could not protect me from the pathetic events that were part of
everyday life in the old brick house on Center Street. I had no

choice but to walk through them, conscious and alert, deflecting the pain when possible, accepting it only when I had no other option.

One night when Daddy was overtaken by a manic bout, he began crashing dishes and screaming at Mama. Laddie and I heard the commotion and ran to the doorway of the library to watch in stunned silence as Daddy roared out of control.

"You love that dog more than you love your children!" Mama shouted, pointing at the oil painting of Daddy's championship dog that hung on the library wall.

Daddy shouted back an angry retort.

It was an old argument and one Laddie and I would hear again many times. Mama had set aside money to have a portrait of Laddie and me painted. Daddy had instead commissioned a portrait of his favorite hunting dog. Mama would never forgive him.

Mama saw Laddie and me standing in the doorway, listening to their explosion. She quickly closed the door. Laddie and I held hands and stood nearby, listening to the sounds of splintering wood and breaking glass. The voices in the library rose to a crescendo; angry words tumbled about, threatening, jabbing, drawing blood. Through the hysteria, one word traveled through the walls and into the living room where Laddie and I stood. Only the word "divorce" penetrated our horror.

I didn't fully understand its meaning, but I knew that "divorce" was a terrible thing. I couldn't let it happen. I rushed into the library, sobbing in terror.

"Please don't divorce," I begged. "Please, Mama, don't divorce Daddy!"

"Mitty, Laddie, go upstairs," Mama commanded.

"Mama, please," I cried, "if you divorce Daddy, I'll go live with him!"

"Good," Mama answered, her voice tight with fury. "Then you can take care of him."

I froze there, silent. Laddie took my hand and pulled me away from the library and toward the stairs. I walked up to our bedroom, shaken. Later that evening, I heard my mother sobbing in the bathroom, her tears spilling into her bath water. I had to do something, anything, to mend the tear in our family.

"I'll write Mama a love note and sign it from Daddy," I said aloud with resolve, certain that this would be a miracle cure for our family's heartbreak.

With a child's deliberate care, I printed a note to Mama and signed it, "Love, Daddy." Walking into the bathroom, I handed the note to Mama.

I felt absolutely in control, omnipotent! I could be good, do good things, and Mama and Daddy would love each other, and they would love Laddie and me. This was just the beginning of what I would do to heal our family. I waited, holding my breath, watching to see what would happen next.

Mama, her face swollen from crying, reached out with dripping-wet hands and reverently accepted the piece of paper that bore the message printed in my childish script. She read silently, and then, wearing dignity like the mantle of a queen, she said, "Thank you, Mitty. I feel so much better now, knowing how much Daddy loves me."

I walked out of the bathroom feeling triumphant.

In that moment, Mama became my accomplice in a dangerous game of denial and pretense. In time, we would both be world-class players.

Sometimes it seemed as if nature mirrored the goings-on in the Collinsworth home on Center Street. The storms that assaulted our region of Arkansas were a metaphor of our family life. I remember one spring day when a tornado warning sent us scurrying about the house, gathering up clothes and belongings to take with us to our aunt's farm where we would take shelter in her storm cellar.

"Mama, Mama!" I cried, tugging on her skirt as she hurried through the house grabbing items to pack and take with us. "You're not going to leave Daddy here alone, are you?"

I could see Laddie's and my things neatly packed and ready to take with us. I saw Mama's purse and a large bag by the door. But where were Daddy's things?

I ran into Daddy's room and pulled out sweaters and slippers, his pipe and his robe, frantically trying to pack the things I thought he would need. If Mama wasn't going to take care of him, I would. I wouldn't allow him to be left behind in the storm.

The day of the tornado was, in a way, a day of beginnings for me. Although I had already determined that it was up to me to make our family whole, I now decided that it was also my responsibility to look after Daddy. I had been doing it already, in subtler ways, but my efforts increased and became more deliberate.

I had learned that sometimes I had the power to quiet Daddy when he began to rage. Even when in the throes of a manic bout, he seemed able to hear my voice, to respond to my soothing. His hand would stop in mid-air when I spoke to him, stilling him before he could slam books to the floor or crash dishes against the wall. I lived with my senses tuned to his moods. I learned to gauge his state of mind quickly. I watched at all times for the danger that lay beneath the surface. I became the storm forecaster, the animal tamer, and the resident peacemaker in the war zone. It was much to ask of a seven-year-old girl.

I slipped into a role, playing go-between for my weary mother and my distant father. Estranged from each other by their own private miseries, they inhabited different worlds that were light-years apart. I tried hard to bring them together, but neither of them was capable of making the long journey.

I wondered often what had happened to my parents, what had happened to the love I thought was supposed to exist between them. I wanted so badly to restore it. I told Mama about Daddy's condition every day, giving her updates, hoping something I said would give her hope. Instead, my chats with Mama opened the door for her to confide in me, loading my fragile psyche with knowledge much too heavy for me to carry.

"Daddy never wanted children, you know," she said one day. "I was the one who wanted children."

Please don't tell me this, I begged silently. Please, Mama, I'm only a little girl...

Mama was a great storyteller. With her lovely voice and her rich vocabulary, she told me stories that would haunt me all my life. I know now she spoke out of desperation, so great was her need to tell someone, *anyone*, the things that were corroding her heart. And I was there, trying hard to help ease her pain.

"You were very small, Mitty," she told me, speaking in her lovely voice as she sat at the antique dressing table in her upstairs bedroom. "Daddy was very sick, and I had to take him to the hospital in Memphis. But I took you and Laddie to visit him whenever I could."

Mama studied her face in the mirror as if she hadn't seen it for a long time. With graceful fingers she traced the lines near her mouth, and for a moment, I thought she had forgotten I was standing next to her. Then she blinked and looked down at me and shook her head.

"It was a very expensive place, Mitty. They were trying to help Daddy. But he didn't seem to be getting much better." She reached out to touch my hair. "When I took you and Laddie to visit, we went out into the yard with Daddy. He sat on a swing and tried to pick you up, but his arms were too bruised."

I tried to imagine myself standing near him, my arms outstretched, begging to be held, and his poor arms too weak and injured to pick me up.

"You cried and cried, but he didn't have the strength to pick you up."

I never understood why Daddy's arms were bruised. Had someone hurt him, or was it part of his treatment? No one ever told me. But the image of his bruised and purple arms reaching toward mine is imprinted in my mind for all time. And the feeling of emptiness in my own outstretched arms is ever-present.

Only now, years later, can I begin to imagine the awful emptiness my mama must have experienced. How her heart must have ached for the beauty and elegance she and Daddy once shared. In every room of our house stood reminders of how they used to live.

A tall trophy case in Daddy's library was filled with ribbons and trophies won in athletic competitions and field trials with his championship hunting dogs. The walls were covered with photos and paintings of his favorites, one of them a national champion whose name was entered into the American Field Hall of Fame. In better times, Mama and Daddy had ridden horseback together— Mama on a white stallion, Daddy on a large bay—as spectators at the prestigious field trials, where Daddy's prized English setters took the highest honors. I remember our family spending weekends at the homes of wealthy friends, in mansions built on plantations and in lovely, old hunting lodges.

Laddie and I spent long, carefree hours with the other guests' children, cared for by a bevy of servants, playing games on manicured lawns. When the riders and the dogs and the handlers returned from the field trials or from a quail hunt, we joined them for a buffet served on long, white-draped tables on the lawn. The memories are scented with the smell of green grasses, morning breezes, and steaming horseflesh. But the Camelot-like days passed all too quickly, taking with them both the material and spiritual evidences of better times.

Mama tried not to show her grief as she watched the beautiful antiques she had collected removed from her home, sold to pay bills that were past due. She stood stiffly in the doorway as men in overalls carried out the Chippendale pieces and the Louis XVI pieces, refusing to allow herself to grieve outwardly. Her private pain resided someplace inside her.

I don't know when Mama stopped believing that Daddy would get well, but I remember the day when the money for private hospitals ran out. I remember the day she made the desperate decision to have Daddy committed to the state mental institution.

Mama called me into her room. I watched as she brushed her long red hair. Her arms reached up to pin her curls into place, and she spoke softly, glancing sideways at me, her hands busy all the while. She spoke in very grown-up tones, although I was only seven years old.

"Mitty," she said, "We've got to take your daddy to the state hospital. He is out of control, and it's going to be up to you to keep him quiet in the car."

Mama turned her head at an angle to study her image in the mirror. She drew a deep breath and swallowed before continuing.

"Mitty, we can't let Daddy know where he's going. He'll get too upset. He could kill us all. You've got to keep him still. Do you understand, Mitty?"

Mama turned from the mirror to look at me. Her eyes were intense, her face taut.

"It's your responsibility to keep Daddy calm on the drive to Little Rock. You can do that, can't you, Mitty?"

"Yes, Mama," I answered.

Little Rock was fifty miles from Searcy. The trip would take about half a day because of the poor condition of the highway. I would have to be sure nothing was said or done that would upset Daddy. Mama had to concentrate on driving. I would concentrate on Daddy. Laddie's job was to do anything I deemed necessary to help keep Daddy quiet.

The trip began with Mama behind the steering wheel, Daddy sitting next to her in the front seat, Laddie and I in the back. For the entire length of the journey, I stood up on the back seat and leaned forward to wrap my little arms around Daddy's neck. I sang songs for him, whispered stories in his ear, and stroked his cheek with my fingers. He sat silent, almost catatonic, throughout the drive.

Always present in my thoughts was the knowledge that I had to keep Daddy under control. If he became frightened or upset, he could grab the steering wheel and send us veering off the road and into a tree or a ravine. My family's safety was in my hands. The trip passed slowly, haunted at all times by the sense of danger.

As we approached the grounds of the state mental hospital, Daddy roused from his silent state and fear registered in his eyes. He pulled away from my arms and looked at Mama and then back at me, then at the gates ahead. And then, from somewhere deep inside him, an eerie, animal-like wail gushed forth.

"No... no, Pauline, please no... "

Daddy began to cry like a baby. Great, huge sobs erupted from his body. His shoulders shook with the force of his sobbing. I tried to sing to him, but he shook his head, refusing to listen.

"It's the best thing for you, Daddy," I said, over and over, reaching out to caress his face.

"No... no! Don't do this, please don't leave me!"

Daddy's words got tangled in his tears. He choked and coughed and begged while Mama sat silent and still, holding onto something inside her that kept her from flying apart into a million tiny, broken pieces. I could only croon and cry in my gentlest voice, "It's the best thing for you, Daddy, it's the best thing... "

Attendants in white coats opened the car door and pulled Daddy out of the seat. I scrambled out to be close to him, to try to comfort him one last time. Daddy's hands closed over my arms and he held on as if I were a lifeline and he a drowning man. The attendants pulled him and coaxed him, but he would not let go of me. I stood there, feeling my limbs straining against the pull of the white-coated men who were trying to tear my father away from me. And I believed that my heart was, in that moment, torn into shreds.

In that instant, I knew I had betrayed my father. He feared nothing more than being institutionalized. And I, Judas-like, had kissed him and caressed him throughout the journey that took him to the most dreaded of places: the state mental hospital.

Guilt oozed out of me like a festering sore as I watched my proud, aristocratic father struggle against the restraints of the hospital attendants. I vowed that, no matter whatever else happened in my life, I would never allow this to happen to my daddy again. And I would never allow this to happen to me.

I resolved again to be good, to be better than I'd ever been. I resolved to be perfect, as if that would somehow make up for the fact that my father had been robbed of his dignity. I would make it up to him for my betrayal, I promised myself. I would find a way to garner enough honor in my life so that I could restore it to him and to the family name.

On the long drive home we were each silent in our own private reverie, trying to decide where to relegate the horror we had just experienced. Each of us would assign this nightmare to a secret place inside ourselves and draw it out again and again throughout our lifetimes, never quite able to render a final reckoning of it.

During the months that followed, Mama took us often to Five Oaks to visit our grandmother. There, beneath the huge oaks and dogwoods, Laddie and I ran and played, forgetting the agony of our lives, attentive only to the beauty of the flowing grasses and tall trees. The old home place had a mystical power that healed our wounds, if only temporarily. It was as if the courage of past generations sustained us.

Mama took us regularly to visit Daddy at the state hospital. She tried to make our trips to Little Rock into adventurous excursions, packing a large picnic for us to eat under a tree along the way, and always bringing some special delicacy for Daddy. But the festive air of the trip dissipated as we drove onto the hospital grounds. All sense of pleasant expectation fell away the moment I first glimpsed the dark, steel bars on the windows.

The stench of stale cigarettes and urine stung my nose the instant we entered the corridors of the hospital. In the hallways, inert bodies lay on gurneys, sometimes fouled by their own feces. Small as I was, I walked the hallways nose-level with the bowels of humanity. The sweet scent of springtime never penetrated the walls of the state institution for the mentally ill.

Our visits with Daddy took place in a small, gray room decorated with the hideous apparatus used for administering electric shock treatments. When Daddy came into the room, I could see the burn marks left on his forehead and temples, evidence of the desperate measures used to try to shock him into a level of sanity.

I searched his face for some sign of wellness, some reason for hope. I studied his hands and legs, looking for the telltale tremors. And on the way home from each hospital visit, Mama and Laddie and I talked about Daddy's condition, comparing notes, assuring each other that he seemed better, assuring ourselves that someday soon he would come home well.

Sometimes our hopes seemed terribly far-fetched. On one visit we found Daddy badly bruised, his face cut, and his glasses taped together where they had been broken. Mama was terribly upset. She learned that a riot had broken out in his ward and he had been knocked unconscious. He had been too drugged to take part in the violence, but he had become a victim of it, nonetheless.

At other times, Daddy seemed better, almost jovial. On those days, we spent our visiting hours in the hospital yard. Daddy introduced us to families visiting other patients, and he seemed to exude some of the old Collinsworth pride. We gathered a fragile curtain of dignity about ourselves and allowed ourselves to feel a new surge of hope for our family. On those rare days, for those few moments, we bonded, capturing only the fleeting essence of what we desperately wished to be: a normal family sharing the sunshine of a lovely day.

When Daddy was finally released and sent home, Mama began to think about moving away from Arkansas. Our finances had dwindled to near poverty level. Family members found us an embarrassment. Daddy was no longer able to work, and Mama knew the Collinsworth's Little Red School House could not continue to operate indefinitely with him present in the house. The time had come to consider other options. She began sending out resumés to school districts in California and Florida, states where the beginning pay scale would support us. She began preparing Laddie and me to say goodbye to everything that was familiar to us; she began spinning wonderful stories about the mysteries and wonders found in the regions where palm trees grow.

If Mama was at first ambivalent about finding a job in another state, she began the search in earnest after Daddy's next serious manic bout. It began one night shortly after dark. We had seen his trembling earlier in the day and had watched his face change from vacant to ferocious. By afternoon, his growing agitation sent him charging from one room to another, shouting, "I'm coming, I'm coming!"

I chased him, crying, "Daddy, there's no one here! Come with me, Daddy... Daddy, it's all right."

Daddy couldn't hear anything but the voices inside his head urging him to come downstairs and outside. He ran to the second-story balcony that opened onto the front of the house and overlooked the street. His body rocked against the wrought-iron railing, and he yelled to the ghosts who beckoned him, "I'm coming, I'll be down soon... I've got to take care of business... "

He swung around, bumping into me, and hurried down the

hallway. His body taut with urgency, he clambered about the house, hurling himself into one room after another, and then back onto the balcony. He flung himself against the iron railing, shouting loudly, his voice carrying throughout the quiet neighborhood. Mama and I ran behind him, pulling on him, using all our strength to draw him inside before he could pitch himself from the second story of the house.

"Sing to him, Mitty," Mama commanded, running downstairs. "Try to distract him! We can't let him throw himself off the balcony! I'm going to call the police!"

Daddy would not be distracted. Delusional, he was aware only of the faces and voices of those coaxing him to come outside to "take care of business." His hallucinations were stronger than the reality of my presence. Nothing I said could convince him there were no other voices. The best I could do was entice him away from danger. Mama ran upstairs and locked the door to the balcony to be sure Daddy couldn't run back out and fling himself against the low railing. The drop onto the wide front steps below would certainly kill him.

Laddie sat on the curb in front of the house like a sentry, watching for the police car. Mama and I, ever the efficient soldiers, packed Daddy's clothes for the trip back to the state hospital. Moments later, a squad car arrived and two policemen, one on each side, forced Daddy into the back seat of the car.

Mama, Laddie, and I watched silently as the car drove away. Daddy's howling voice echoed in our ears long after the police car was out of sight.

A few days later, the Collinsworth's Little Red School House closed its doors. Laddie, already beyond Mama's third-grade curriculum, was in public school by this time, so for him there was little sense of loss. But for me, it was a time of terrible mourning. I continued to take my lessons from Mama, but school would never again be the same for me.

Mama's search for a teaching position brought her offers from schools in both Florida and California. During one of Daddy's more lucid moments in the hospital, she told him of her decision to leave Arkansas. "If we have to leave our home," Daddy answered, "let's go as far away as possible."

And so it was that the decision was made for the Collinsworths to move to California.

The day of our departure, boxes were stacked throughout the house, cluttering every room, blocking the doorways. Daddy sat silently rocking in his chair while Mama, Laddie, and I looked into every room, checking to be sure we'd left nothing behind. Movers would store most of the furniture we had left—we would be back in one year, two at the most. That knowledge was the strong cord that kept me from falling headlong into despair. That, and the magnificent stories Mama kept telling about the palm trees and California's Pacific Ocean.

It was mid-morning. I was sitting near the front window, thinking about the train that would take us across the country, when I saw a car pull up in front of the house. Old John had come to say goodbye to "the young man." His grandson led him up the walk to our front door. Neighbors watching from their doorways and windows gasped.

In Searcy, Arkansas, as in all Southern towns, any dealings a black man had at the home of a white family were transacted at the back door. But this was spring, 1956, and the rumblings of change had begun to vibrate throughout the South. The railroad tracks that separated the town into color zones no longer had the power to contain men and women. There were obvious, if subtle, signs that the strict rules of segregation were disintegrating in the downtown area, but had change now reached the boundaries of this quiet neighborhood?

Old John, now nearing ninety, his blind eyes closed and his regal white head held proud, crossed the forbidden zone and raised his huge, gnarled hand to knock on our front door. I ran to open it.

Old John nodded and smiled. "Mornin', chile," he said. "Is your mama home?" His grandson fidgeted nervously in the doorway, looking uncomfortable.

I found Mama among the boxes in the library and told her Old John was here. Mama greeted him at the front door and invited him into the house.

"I'm sorry, Miss Polly," Old John's grandson said. "He wouldn't let me take him 'round back... "

The boy was appalled, frightened.

"There's no need to apologize," Mama said, gripping Old John's hand in hers. "John and his family are welcome at any door in this house."

Mama led Old John to the sofa that still remained in the living room and invited him to sit down. She took his black hat, which he was never without, placed it reverently on a box, and sent Laddie and me upstairs to get Daddy.

It was a good day for Daddy. He had dressed in a navy-blue suit and starched, white shirt; his dark club tie was perfectly knotted. He looked handsome and dignified when he greeted Old John. Together we all sat down amid the boxes and clutter of the family living room. And then Old John began to speak, his words uttered slowly, his voice sounding as if it had to scrape over rough gravel to leave his throat.

"I understand y'all have decided to go to California,"'he said. Mama nodded. "That's right, John."

"Well, come to think of it," he answered, tilting his head to one side, "that's probably the best thing y'all could do."

Mama pressed her lips together and closed her eyes tightly for just an instant. She drew a deep breath, as if steeling herself against the rush of emotions evoked by Old John's tenderness.

"Y'all wouldn't mind if we just prayed together for a minute or two before y'all go now, would you?"

"That would be nice, John," Mama answered, and her mouth softened in a small smile.

Laddie and I bowed our heads and listened as Old John's voice beseeched God's blessing and guidance for our little family. He praised God for His "bountiful goodness" and asked for mercy and strength for "Miss Pauline and the children and the young man."

"Amen," his great voice rumbled.

"Amen," Laddie and I said in unison.

"Amen. And thank you, John," Mama said. "Now, children, let's let John and Daddy visit for a few minutes."

Old John and Daddy sat together in the living room for a long while. I couldn't hear their words, but Old John's deep, bass voice flowed out of the room like music. I knew in my heart that his coming to our home that day was a gift, a special miracle our family needed as desperately as a leper needs cleansing.

For weeks, no visitors had ventured into our home. No one wanted to walk up to our front door, but the issue was hardly skin color. Instead, the taboos associated with the stigma of mental illness quarantined us. Family members withdrew from us, afraid to associate with our pain, uncertain how to act, afraid of contracting some of our shame. Only Old John had courage and compassion enough to cross the threshold into our grief and lend us comfort.

No one else came to say goodbye on the day we left the old brick house on Center Street. Our relatives had agreed with us that it was a good idea for us to leave Searcy and, as much as they were able, they wished us well. But they were glad to be rid of the humiliation of my father's illness. They exhaled a group sigh of relief that we were going to California. Only Old John picked his way among the boxes and clutter to reach out to us in the midst of our chaotic flight.

A kindly neighbor offered to drive us to the train station. Mama gratefully accepted. I remember sitting on my knees in the back seat of the car, my face peering out the back window, watching as the old brick house grew smaller and smaller as we drove down Center Street.

It was a quiet street, made up of old houses, old women, and old friends. My life had been bordered by its hedges and tall trees and driveways overgrown with grass in need of mowing. I watched with sadness as the view of lavender bushes and lilacs faded into a distant purple blur.

Regardless of the fact that danger and sadness had seemed to reside within its rooms, I could never blame the old brick house on Center Street for our family's despair. Instead, I would always view it as a wonderful palace which just happened to be ruled by an ill-fated monarch. Who could fault the castle for the kingdom's demise?

More than a hundred years old, the house on Center Street stood on a lot that was part of the original land grant given by the King of France at the time of the Louisiana Purchase. Its architect had presented the house to his bride as a wedding gift and named it "The Oaks," in honor of the stand of trees that shaded the original property.

Built of dusty, gray-pink handmade bricks, the house was graced by a wide porch and four large white columns. Panels of stained glass outlined the massive front door which was carved out of golden oak. On the second story, just above the front door, a wrought-iron balcony faced the street.

Mama loved the brick walkways, laid in herringbone pattern, that led to the side yards where daffodils, tulips, hyacinths, and crocuses bloomed in formal bulb gardens. In the backyard, she had converted the old carriage house into the main building for the Collinsworth's Little Red School House. She had built a tower to house the bell once used at Five Oaks to summon workers in from the fields. And the old well she had filled in to make a wading pool for Laddie and me. On lazy summer days, we had splashed our feet in its cool, shallow waters, and sailed handmade boats across its width.

Swings and other playground equipment stood on the back lawn between the carriage house and the main house. Mama's students ran back and forth between both buildings, learning songs in the family dining room and washing their paintbrushes in the huge sink installed in the kitchen. Mama had opened our house to all the children and taught them the joy of learning.

I had reveled in all the sights and scents offered by my home. In winter, when the flowers had hibernated beneath the snow, the house had had a special kind of comfort and warmth for me. It had no central heating, so every room had its own brick fireplace. I had loved dressing in my pajamas in front of the crackling fire, smelling the scent of burning pine, and then cuddling close to Mama while she read aloud to Laddie and me.

At dusk, I had often stood on the stairs to watch as the setting sun poured through a rose-patterned, stained-glass window set in the wall just above the first landing. Multicolored prisms would sparkle in the air, creating rainbows on golden particles of dust. I used to whirl and spin, trying to wear the rainbows, dancing to a secret accompaniment only I could hear.

Within the lovely rooms of the old brick house on Center Street my innocence had been snatched from me before I was ready to be rid of it. But I had experienced sweet and simple pleasures there as well. My father's tortured howlings could not drown the eloquence of my childhood. There had been days of laughter to be cherished where honeysuckle and thyme edged my memories. As we drove away, I knew the only thing I would miss as much as the old brick house was my father's property at Five Oaks.

At Five Oaks I had heard my father's laughter for the first time. If I try very hard, I can still remember the happy sound of it vibrating deep in his chest. Daddy and Mama had taken Laddie and me out to the property to teach us to fire a rifle. I remember putting the gun up against my shoulder, siting the target, and squeezing the trigger, just as Daddy had told me to do. And I remember the kick of the rifle smacking against me and knocking me to the ground.

Daddy's laughter had rumbled about the clearing in the woods as he picked me up and stood me on my feet. With gentle, long-fingered hands he had brushed the dust from my overalls and patted my face, his own handsome with the look of humor. His smile made crinkles at the corners of his eyes, and the linger of his touch stayed with me long after he picked up his rifle and strode off into the woods. I heard his laughter echo through the forest, held aloft by the branches of giant oak trees.

All these things I remembered as I fell asleep on the train that night, listening to the clack-clack of wheels on the track. My dreams were filled with great oak trees and sweet-scented honeysuckle bushes, with Old John's gentle voice and my father's laughter—all the things that for too long would be missing from my life, some never to be experienced again.

Chapter 4

Mama was right about California. Tall, skinny palm trees lined the roadways, their bushy fronds hanging high overhead, making strange shadows on the concrete surfaces that seemed to cover every inch of space found in Los Angeles. Unaccustomed noises assaulted my ears. The sounds of coughing auto engines, wailing sirens, and screeching tires were an unending cacophony in the rough barrio neighborhood where we found a small house we could afford to rent.

It was a tiny stucco house, with a small yard trying to produce a few pathetic strands of green grass. Inside, the bedrooms were shoe-box size. A narrow hallway connected the rooms and led to a cramped living room. The kitchen was small and utilitarian.

Outside, scores of Hispanic children ran and played, shouting to each other in a language I couldn't understand. My own Southern brand of English sounded foreign to them as well. I huddled inside for days, afraid to venture outside, afraid to face this new world to which Mama had brought us, unable to grasp the sense of adventure she had tried to instill in me.

I tried to imagine life back in Searcy. It was springtime, and the blossoming dogwoods would be beautiful. The property at Five Oaks would be vibrant with their pink and white blooms. I remember walking down the narrow hall of our cramped house and standing in the doorway of Daddy's room, watching him rock to and fro, wondering if he was thinking of Five Oaks too.

Remember the dogwood story, Daddy? I thought. Remember the legend?

It seemed Daddy couldn't remember anything during those first days of adjustment to life in California. But how well I remembered him telling me the story of the dogwoods, the story of new beginnings, of second chances. The telling of it had become a ritual with me. Every time I heard it was like the first. It filled me with awe and defiant hope.

Every spring, if Daddy were well enough, he used to take me

with him out to Five Oaks where we hailed the coming of the
new season with our own grand ritual of renewal. I'd stand on
the porch of the old house, my grandmother rocking in her chair
next to me, while Daddy walked off across the wide lawn to the
fields beyond. I'd watch him crouch down to examine the crops,
touching the sprouting leaves and filtering the soil through his
fingers. Then he'd turn and walk toward Dogwood Creek. Shading
his eyes from the sun, he'd then look back to the house where I
watched from the porch, awaiting his signal, and he'd shout,
"Come quick, Mitty!"

It was always the same. I'd leap off the porch and run as fast as
I could to meet him on the creek bank. He'd smile at me and
reach up high above my head to break off a dogwood branch.
He'd lay it in my outstretched arms, and I'd finger the blossoms
and listen as he spoke, his deep voice softened, as if muffled by a
mantle of emotion.

"Always remember the legend, Mitty... how the dogwood tree
was cut down and used to make the cross on which our Lord was
crucified. Because of this infamous deed, the tree was cursed,
never ever to bloom again."

He'd always pause and gaze out into the dense forest of oaks
and pines and dogwoods that comprised Five Oaks. Then he'd
pull himself back into the story.

"But a miracle occurred," he would say, smiling, his eyes wide
with new wonder every time he told the legend. "God gave the
tree a second chance. He allowed it to bloom again, giving it a
blossom of four petals, arranged in the shape of a cross."

I would peer down at the blossoms in my arms. Each flower
was shaped like a cross.

Daddy's voice continued, "And on the tip of each petal God
put a blood-red stain, to remind us that the ends of the cross were
stained with Christ's blood."

Sure enough, the outer tips of each petal had tiny red stains. On
some of the petals, it looked as though an artist had dripped blood-
red paint across them before finally placing the tiny droplet on the
delicate, rounded ends. I would hold my breath in awe as I touched
the fragile flowers so perfectly marked with the look of a bloodstain.

"The dogwood bears its scars with dignity and grace, Mitty,"
Daddy told me many times. "It is a symbol of God's promise of
new beginnings. Every spring the dogwood blooms to remind us
of the miracle of second chances."

Second chances. A second chance was just what this family

needed. But would we find it here, in this city of asphalt, where the air smelled of exhaust fumes and garbage?

No dogwood trees stood nearby to remind us of new beginnings. I saw no blood-tipped white or pink blossoms to prove to me that joy could arise out of horror and pain. I saw only palm trees and tiny tract houses with dusty yards where sparse grass tried to grow. I saw narrow streets busy with the traffic of wheezing vehicles. But I saw no proof of miracles.

"Life can be hard, Mitty," Daddy used to say. "But we Collinsworths accept hardship with dignity and grace. Never forget the promise of new beginnings, Mitty. You must never forget that spring will always come."

Spring had already arrived in southern California, but for me, there was little reason for hope. I was eight and a half years old, and all I felt was revulsion and fear.

"We'll be here for only one year," Mama assured me. "Two at the most. Daddy will get better soon and we'll go back to the old brick house on Center Street."

Mama's promise sustained me throughout that first summer in California.

Soon after we arrived in the tightknit Hispanic neighborhood, I realized that the magical lessons learned at the Collinsworth's Little Red School House were not going to be sufficient for my survival in the streets. That first summer was spent listening and learning, and getting in and out of trouble, and by the time school started, I was savvy in ways my mother had never imagined.

In September, I started fourth grade and turned nine years old, entering the world of public education for the first time in my life. I was unprepared for the impact I would have on my teachers and fellow students.

In the first week of school I read every textbook. I was used to Mama's curriculum, where a student progressed at his or her own level. Once a book was finished, I picked up another one, never imagining I was supposed to wait for the teacher or the rest of the class. I worked through the math books, read the history assignments, and moved on to the next. I had no concept of stopping just because I came to the end of a chapter. My teachers didn't know what to do with me.

Other teachers began to take notice of the little girl from Arkansas with the thick glasses and long French braids and the funny accent. They began using me to help tutor the children in the lower reading groups.

It was a natural task for me. I had done much the same thing in Mama's school, so it wasn't anything unusual. The difficulty arose, however, when I began to draw the hostility of the other students. They taunted me because of my Southern drawl and made me feel foolish for being such a favorite with the teachers. And in the sixth-grade class down the hall, Laddie faced his battles as well.

Both Laddie and I had to prove that we could pass muster in the city. We both came home from school with our clothes torn, our limbs and faces bleeding. I proudly told Mama one day that I could beat up all the girls in the fourth grade and almost all the boys. Mama was appalled.

"Mitty," she said, her sharp intake of breath nearly knocking her over, "I do not consider that proper behavior for a young lady." She shook her head, reaching out a tentative hand to untangle my hair ribbons and push my glasses back up on my nose. "You mustn't make a habit of this kind of thing."

Laddie and I tried to curb our fighting ways, and we remained on the outside of the neighborhood cliques, looking in, ostracized because we were so different from the other children in our speech, our manners, and in our skin color. Often, we were the brunt of malicious teasing. One morning, we stepped outdoors to find a chalk drawing on our front walk depicting a large, black "Aunt Jemima" character. Scrawled under it were the words, "This must be your Mama."

Neither Laddie nor I knew what to make of this kind of deliberate taunting. Discrimination and intolerance were something with which we had had much experience back home in Arkansas, but we had never before been singled out as the targets.

As white children of the South, we had absorbed and expressed toward others the irrational bigotry of our ancestors, almost completely without thought. With the singular exception of Old John, we had had little contact with the black community outside of the context of service. Young black girls in starched white uniforms had cleaned our house and washed our clothes; a black man had tended Mama's garden and cared for our lawn and any household repairs that needed doing. Our cooks, Corinne and Ruby Jean, had hugged me and laughed with me and drawn from me the same warm feelings of love and friendship I felt for Old John. But still, I saw a dividing line as clearly as if it had been printed in indelible ink.

I was acutely aware of that rigid line of demarcation even when I was very small. Every weekend, one of our maids took Laddie and me by the hand and walked us through downtown Searcy to the Saturday afternoon matinee at the Rialto Theater. We gripped her hands tightly, giggling and skipping, excited to be on the way to see the latest Roy Rogers and Dale Evans movie. Once inside, we joined the other white children seated in the front rows of the theater, while our maid climbed the stairs to the balcony where she and the other black women were forced to sit. I wondered why it was acceptable for me to hold hands with this young woman in the light of day on a downtown street, but I couldn't sit next to her and share the fun of the matinee with my shoulder bumping against hers in the darkness of the theater.

I wondered, but I never spoke of it.

I remember once, riding in the car with Mama while she drove Ruby Jean home to her shanty in the poor black neighborhood. Crossing the railroad tracks and seeing for the first time the tumbling-down shacks and the dilapidated cars that lined Pleasure Street, I asked, "Mama, why are colored people so poor?"

"They were born that way, Mitty," she said.

To Mama, it was enough of an explanation.

Submerged in a culture that bred bigotry, I accepted her answer. And for a time, I was able to insulate myself against the pain that greater knowledge of the subject might inflict. Until I became a target of a California barrio.

It was the beginning of a slow awakening. Without any grand sense of enlightenment, I did begin to sense the wrongness of racial intolerance and bigotry. My childish logic concluded that discrimination was active in many places, not only in the South, and not only against blacks. It could be directed in varying degrees at children and adults of any color.

Prejudice, unthinkingly handed down from generation to generation, was now no longer a thing I would be able to accept mindlessly. I felt the first tiny pangs of guilt for my own ignorant actions of discrimination, made sharper and more painful because I now knew firsthand the kind of injury I had inflicted upon others.

It was autumn 1956, and many loud voices had joined together to cry out against the irrational racial biases that ruled our country. As a nation we were moving closer to a violent and bloody showdown with our long-held notions of discrimination and segregation. The racial confrontation on the front steps of Little

Rock's Central High School waited only one year in the future. Compared to the larger wars that had yet to be fought, my own small skirmishes were of no significance. My tiny wounds were nothing compared to the injuries suffered by an entire race of people for centuries, but my own slight discomfort had at least brought me awareness. And in time, awareness would beget a desire for justice.

That fall of 1956 found the Collinsworth family rallying a little, nudged by outside forces to pull itself together. Daddy, though very frail, gained some small amount of strength and seemed better than he had been in a long while. He found a job as an accountant with a car dealer, and for a time it seemed as though our family's wounds might be healing. We functioned, although just barely.

Mama's teaching job required every ounce of energy she had and then quickly drained her reserves as well. She enrolled in night classes so she could move up the pay scale as quickly as possible. Her workday was usually fourteen to sixteen hours long.

We felt little of the season's "good cheer" that first Christmas in the barrio. No brightly wrapped packages hid in the closets for Laddie and me to discover. No garlands hung above the front door. We had no money for such frivolities. A couple of days before Christmas, Daddy bought a tiny tree so scraggly and limp that no one else would buy it. He placed it on the wobbly card table that served as a dining table in one corner of our small living room, and we stood together, silent and staring, remembering the glories of Christmases past.

Laddie was the first to break the silence. "Oh, Mama," he exclaimed, "If we ever have money again to live in a house with a real dining room and a real dining-room table, I promise I'll set the table and clean up every night, and I'll never complain."

Mama's eyes filled with tears as she hugged Laddie.

"Don't worry, Laddie," she whispered fiercely, "We will have it all again someday. We will have it all again."

I tried not to grieve too much for our home in Arkansas, at least on a conscious level. But in my dreams, I traveled back to Five Oaks often. I awoke many mornings with an ache in my heart when I realized I was two thousand miles away from Dogwood Creek. I covered my head with my pillow to close out the harsh city noises of sirens wailing and cars backfiring. I had to content myself with dreams of the gentle sounds of a small Southern town.

Mama hadn't been in California long before she enrolled me in the University of the Dance, where Burch Holzman was the chief choreographer. She worked with such famous children as Disney's Mouseketeers, and Mama was certain that under her tutelage I would become the prima ballerina Mama knew I could be.

Next on Mama's agenda was finding a surgeon who could operate on my eyes and make me pretty. Though she had not been able to find a doctor in Arkansas, Mama had never given up her quest. After multiple examinations and closed-door consultations with numerous doctors, Mama finally announced that she had found one who would operate on my eyes. He was sure he could make my eyes straight. Now I could put away my glasses and be pretty.

Mama had always hated my glasses. She insisted that they be removed whenever my picture was taken. Then she would position me at an angle to the camera so that my crossed eyes were not obvious. And if anyone happened to snap a picture of me facing forward, so that my flaw was visible, she destroyed the photo quickly. I knew she was obsessive about correcting what she viewed as a major imperfection in my looks. I was obsessive about making Mama happy.

The day before I was admitted to the hospital for surgery, Mama took me shopping to pick out new pajamas. She put new ribbons in my hair, packed my favorite rag dolls, and told me this was going to be a grand adventure. At the hospital, Mama walked with me to the admissions desk. She stayed with me throughout the routine tests, escorted me to the pediatric ward, and helped me into my new pajamas.

"Up, Mitty," she said, as she boosted me into the crib-like bed in the pediatric ward. I watched as she lifted the bars on the sides and clicked them into place.

"I have to go to work now," Mama said.

Yes, that sounded right to me. She had to take care of Daddy and Laddie, and she had her job and night school. So I kissed her goodbye and let her walk away, never imagining what lay ahead for me in the next hours, the next days.

A short while after Mama left, hospital attendants and nurses came in and out of the ward, occupied with the needs of children around me. I watched, waited, and wondered what would happen next. The evening passed slowly, and I fell into a restless sleep, to be awakened early the next morning when masked forms in green uniforms scooped me up and carried me out of the ward.

I felt myself placed on a flat surface in a brightly lit room. Faces of strangers stared down at me, and I was startled by a sudden sensation of pain as a needle was inserted into my arm. I was afraid to cry in front of these strangers, but the pain increased as ungentle hands probed for a vein. When a mask was lowered over my face, I began to struggle.

"Mama... Mama... " I cried out. Then, silently, I thought, "Is this what you meant by making me pretty?"

An awful roaring filled my ears. My next thought was, "I don't want to be pretty... "

And then blackness smothered me.

I awoke in total darkness. My head throbbed and sharp pain stabbed my eyes. My stomach suddenly revolted and I turned my head to the side to spew vomit all over my bed. I kept calling for Mama, but she wasn't there. I tried to raise my hands to touch my eyes, but to my horror I discovered my hands were tied down to the bed. I couldn't rise to turn over or lift my head more than a few inches. I could only lie there, terrified and in pain.

Mama came to be with me sometime later that day, but she was only able to stay a few minutes. I learned that the restraints that held me down were for my own protection, to keep me from removing the bandages and to prevent me from hurting myself by thrashing about in bed. There weren't enough nurses in pediatrics to watch all the children, so tying them down after surgery was a common practice. Time would prove it was also damaging, increasing the trauma and intensifying the terror felt by small children rendered helpless in a dark and foreign place. From that moment on, the dark became a terrifying place for me. For years afterward, I couldn't sleep in a room without a light on, so great was my fear.

Days passed, and Mama came and went, visiting a few minutes and then leaving for work or night school. Finally, it was time to remove the bandages from my eyes. Mama stood by, watching, waiting. My eyes felt heavy and my head ached. Weakness made me nauseous. I couldn't turn my eyes without excruciating pain. I rotated my whole body to change the direction of my gaze.

"She's had a bad time of it," the doctor told Mama. "Take her home and put her to bed in a darkened room. It will be a few weeks before her eyes are completely healed."

The mirror showed me a bruised face and eyes that were swollen and circled in dark purple. The whites of my eyes were red and pulpy from the surgery. Mama had eye drops that would help my eyes heal, but it would be many days before the ugliness went away. Beauty still eluded me.

When the doctor left the room, Mama pulled my pajamas off me and began dressing me.

"You have a commitment, you know, Mitty," she said. "The dance recital was scheduled long before the surgery, and today's rehearsal is mandatory." She pushed my arms into the sleeves of a leotard and turned me around to brush my hair and braid it.

"I know you don't feel your best today, sweetheart, but you have a commitment. If you don't show up for rehearsal, you will be replaced in the program."

My head ached and my eyes throbbed under the bright sunlight pouring into the hospital room.

"You don't want to miss the performance, do you, Mitty?"

I really didn't want to miss the performance, but more importantly, I didn't want to disappoint Mama.

We arrived at the rehearsal hall and I thought I was going to be sick. I must have looked awful because the dance captain asked Mama if I should be there.

"She'll be fine," Mama answered.

And so I would.

I spun into action, unaware of everything but the pain in my eyes, unable to turn my eyes to the right or the left to gauge my distance from the other dancers on the stage. I listened to the music, trying to determine where I should be and what I should be doing without having to turn and look.

Oh, yes, this is where I run and take a pose... and so I did, blindly, and collided headfirst with another dancer. Our skulls hit with such a force the snap of it echoed throughout the large hall. I screamed and dropped to my knees in agony.

I tried to stop crying, but the pain was too great. I sniffed and willed myself to regain some sense of dignity. And then I tried to finish the rehearsal. I went home exhausted, soaked in perspiration, aching from head to foot. I lay in my bed and wondered if this was what being pretty was all about.

My eyes healed slowly, but within a few weeks I was as good as new—better, in fact. I didn't have to wear my glasses all the time anymore. I wore them only for reading, and I began to feel pretty for the first time in my life.

I noticed glances coming my way that before had gone only to the "beautiful" girls. I grew taller and slimmer. My hair, once limp and fine, took on new texture and the color deepened to a rich auburn brown. People treated me differently than they had when I'd been a gangly, bespectacled little girl with glasses and French braids. I didn't know quite what to make of the sudden attention, but I knew it pleased Mama, and that was all that mattered.

The months passed slowly for our family. Daddy's health, which had seemed to improve for a while, began to deteriorate. He caught a serious case of the flu and couldn't seem to recover from it. Weak and disoriented, he soon lost his job, and the full support of the family fell to Mama again. It was up to Laddie and me to look after Daddy, but his needs far exceeded our abilities. We all felt overpowered, overwhelmed, and undone.

While we had fled to California to spare our family the humiliation of mental illness, we had also left behind a helpful support system that had protected us from further shame and helped Mama to deal with the many horrific aspects of Daddy's disease. Dear Dr. Edwards, the family doctor, had understood and offered help to Mama when others had turned away. Having a relative who also suffered from manic depression, Dr. Edwards knew that much of Daddy's memory had been destroyed by the eighty electric shock treatments he had endured. Dr. Edwards understood the disorientation and confusion Daddy suffered. And he knew what Mama had to go through to convince Daddy to take his medications. Kindly and with great patience, he had made many visits to our home on Center Street to make sure Daddy took the powerful tranquilizers and antidepressants that helped control his behavior.

Searcy's pharmacist also knew and understood the agony that was present in the house on Center Street. He, too, had a family member who suffered from mental illness. Without question or censure, he quickly filled and delivered the expensive prescriptions called in by Dr. Edwards. Along with Daddy's friend, Whitey, these two gentlemen offered Mama support and upheld the code of secrecy that is the cornerstone of small Southern towns.

Mama found no such support in California. Alone, she bore the full weight of our circumstances. Daddy grew more and more sluggish, almost vegetative, his condition worsening as a result of the powerful and toxic drugs—fourteen different prescriptions in all. Years earlier, when he was hospitalized, doctors had tried to treat his illness by deliberately inducing insulin shock; then they injected him with insulin to bring him out of a comatose state.

While the doctors mistakenly believed this procedure might somehow "startle" Daddy into lucidity, it proved to be not only terribly dangerous but damaging as well. This, in addition to the awful side effects of many medications taken over the years, contributed to Daddy's kidney and liver damage. He was ill, confused, and, when not withdrawn and catatonic, he was angry. And, as he had done before, he began to stubbornly refuse to take his medication.

Often Mama discovered that Daddy had thrown away bottles of costly medication. Sometimes she caught him flushing pills down the toilet. She was tempted to hide his medicines in his food to be sure he took the prescribed dosage, but his growing sense of paranoia convinced her not to try it.

She wondered what would happen if he became obsessive about someone trying to poison him. She was sure his fears would be aggravated if he found a foreign substance in his food. So Mama vowed not to do anything to increase his agitation. She finally gave up all attempts to medicate him.

Frightened, weary, and brokenhearted, Mama had no energy left for fighting. She declared a unilateral peace, reconciling herself to live with the symptoms of Daddy's disease, refusing to do battle with him anymore. And so it was that, in the early months after our move to California, all medical treatment for Daddy ceased. He was never again committed to an institution for the mentally ill. The intervention of medical science had offered neither healing nor hope, and so Mama determined to live with him for better or worse, in sickness and in health. It was a decision with far-reaching and damning consequences.

Mama had gambled on California being a remedy for our ills, but by the end of our first year there she knew that the move had only added more complications to our already miserable existence. Laddie and I had made no friends in the neighborhood. We were misfits at school. We would never "belong" in the barrio. It seemed the only thing we could do was move again.

Again, Mama gambled that a change of location would offer some small measure of healing. She found a little brown-shingled bungalow in Covina, not far from my ophthalmologist and the hospital where I'd had my first surgery. Laddie and I could walk to school and I to my checkups with the eye surgeon, but the move put Mama even farther away from her teaching job and the college where she took night classes. The length of her workday increased with the added travel time, but Mama was determined to do anything she could to increase our chances of survival in this strange new environment. It was one more gamble—a gamble that, for me, would be very costly.

I was ten years old and beginning to adjust to the adjective "pretty." I had made peace with public school and was even beginning to appreciate California's unique beauty. My life was busy with dance classes, homework, and the care of my father, when a routine checkup with the ophthalmologist told Mama we had been a bit premature in our celebration of my beauty. My eyes had begun to cross again. The doctor fitted me with a black patch over one eye to control the movement of my vision and scheduled another surgery in the coming months. I walked out of his office feeling as if I had just taken a knockout punch.

At home, I studied my appearance in the mirror. How long would it take the children at school to dub me "one-eyed Pete" or some other awful name? Not long, I discovered, the very next day.

I tried to tip my face toward the ground when I walked so that my black patch wasn't immediately seen, but I couldn't hide it from the children on the playground. They teased and taunted and called me names, and there was nothing I could do to stop it. In class, I had to put my glasses on over the patch so I could read. My embarrassment was compounded by the fact that I had grown to be the tallest girl in the class. There was no end to the teasing from the other children. And there was no place for me to hide. Only in our little house could I find respite from cruelty and embarrassment. Soon, however, that house became not a refuge but the scene of unspeakable horrors.

It was the first week of December. Laddie and I were twelve and ten, and in spite of our family's poverty, our hearts were still susceptible to the delicious feelings of holiday anticipation. Mama brought home a Christmas tree, trying to relieve the austerity of our tiny, unlovely bungalow. Christmas carols played on the radio, drowning the sound of Daddy's rocking chair down the hall. Laddie and I were laughing together, busily decorating the tree in the living room when our landlord, Mr. Simpson, came over to the house. His son, a man in his forties, went into the kitchen to discuss something with Mama, and the elderly Mr. Simpson stood watching Laddie and me.

Old Mr. Simpson admired our work on the spindly little tree that was fast dropping its needles on the hardwood floor. Stockily built and gray-haired, Mr. Simpson reminded me a little of the folks back home in Searcy. He made me think of family and old friends. I smiled at him and grabbed his hand, pulling him toward the tree so he could better admire our handiwork.

Laddie stood on a chair so he could reach the highest branches. I walked ahead of Mr. Simpson, pulling him along behind me. Suddenly, he released my fingers and grabbed my shoulders in a tight grip. He closed the small distance between us and pressed his body against my back, his hand on my breast. I could feel his buckle against my back and his hand touching me as no other hand had ever done. I began to tremble and my face burned hot as fire.

Panic filled me. I felt pinned against him, his groin rising and rubbing against my back. I struggled, but his hold on me was too strong. Just when I thought I would choke, Mama's voice entered the room ahead of her, and Mr. Simpson let go of me.

I ran behind Laddie's chair, wrapping my arms around his legs and peeking out from the side, shaking and fighting for breath. A few minutes later Mr. Simpson left with his son, but the sickening feel of his hands stayed long after he was gone.

Terror rocked me to sleep that night. I tossed about on my bed, wondering what to do.

He shouldn't have done that, I kept telling myself, he shouldn't have done that to me...

Something came apart inside me that night, and I didn't have the tools to reassemble it. And I didn't know how to ask for help.

Help was the one commodity all of the Collinsworths were in desperate need of in those days, but none of us was capable of asking for it. The Collinsworth pride ruled. We took care of our own. We bore our scars with dignity and grace. And we waited for miracles that never came.

Daddy's condition worsened steadily throughout the holiday season. Laddie and I listened to the sound of his tormented howling during the night. Sometimes his pacing to and fro throughout the tiny house kept us awake. He prowled like a wild animal unable to bear the confines of his cage. Always he made that low, keening sound in his throat, the sound of desperate, inarticulate yearning. I remember wakening in the night to find him standing in the doorway of my room, staring at me with vacant eyes. My terror of the darkness increased along with my terror for my father.

Because Mama usually left for work before dawn, Laddie and I had to care for Daddy before we went to school. We did little more than just be there with him—most days he was like an inanimate object in the house—but Mama didn't want him to be left alone any longer than was absolutely necessary. So we stayed with him until time for school, checking on him before we left. Then we went our separate ways, Laddie to junior high and I to fifth grade.

Mama worked late, staying long hours after school to grade papers and plan her lessons. Laddie's school day ended an hour later than mine, and because of his after-school activities, he seldom came home much before Mama. So every afternoon I went home alone to be there with Daddy, and every day it was the same. I found Daddy, worn out from his pacing or finally, after hours of violent trembling, sitting in the rocking chair in his room. Back and forth he rocked, the creaking of his chair making strange harmony with the weary sound of his moan.

It was during that hideous gap of time while I was home alone with Daddy, that Old Mr. Simpson began coming to the house.

He was there when I came home from school one day, only a few days after the incident when he had first grabbed me. He was waiting for me, seated in a chair near the Christmas tree in the living room. I froze with terror when I saw him.

"You mustn't tell anyone," Mr. Simpson said, as his hands moved over my body, fondling me and pressing against me. "This has to be our secret, just between you and me. I'm your landlord, you know, and if you tell, I'll take your house away from you.

"I could have all your things put out of the house," he droned on, using the advantage of strength and fear to hold me captive against him. "Your mama would come home and find everything in the front yard. What would your daddy do, Mitty? What about your daddy? Shall I put his rocking chair out in the front yard?"

With his taunts ringing in my ears, I entered my house every day after school, not knowing where else to go, not knowing what else to do. Mama expected me to go home and look after Daddy—I had been charged with his care. But did that charge require me to endure Mr. Simpson's horrid assaults? I didn't know the answer to that question. I only knew I had to protect my family.

When school was dismissed for the holidays, Mr. Simpson watched for an opportunity when Mama and Laddie would be out of the house. He entered with his own house key and found me alone with Daddy, hollow and mute with terror.

Picking me up like a sack of flour, Mr. Simpson carried me into the back bedroom and threw me onto the bed. The awful weight of his body pressed down on me as he covered my face with a pillow to stifle the sounds of my terror. There, as I listened to the creaking of my father's rocking chair in the room down the hall, Mr. Simpson raped me.

I had no means of describing the horror of what was happening to me. I had no frame of reference for this cruelty. Day after day it continued, and I was helpless to stop it. I tried to drown myself in thoughts of the coming holiday, holding tightly to childish hopes and dreams of Christmas magic.

The magic happened for me one night during the week of Christmas.

We attended the First Baptist Church of Covina, a huge church that presented the community with a living Nativity every year. Laddie's Sunday school class made up the cast. Every night during the week before Christmas, the children came to hold their silent vigil on the church lawn. Angels, shepherds, Mary and Joseph, each dressed in a bathrobe, took their places among the wooden livestock—a donkey, a few sheep, and a cow. I stood in awe the first time I saw them bathed in floodlights.

On the second night of the Nativity, we arrived with Laddie to find that the angel Gabriel was sick. Parents and teachers scurried about frantically, worried that there would be no archangel unless they could find someone tall enough to wear the snowy-white costume. For the first time, I was thankful for my height. The costume fit perfectly, and I took my place on top of the makeshift stable, standing tall, my arms upraised in angelic worship.

Looking down, I saw Laddie's face full of earnest wonder. His wide, round eyes, fringed with thick lashes, kept careful watch over his flock of wooden sheep. No wolves would come close to this shepherd—not as long as he stood guard with his broomstick staff. To me, he looked ethereal. His cheeks were rosy from the excitement and the night's winter cold. His spiked crew cut peeked out from beneath a towel turban. I gazed at him out of my one good eye, and suddenly, I, too, felt beautiful.

Garbed in my white, crepe-paper costume with its chicken-wire wings, and a halo that kept sliding down across my black eye patch, I concentrated on my solemn charge. Below me, pretend wise men and shepherds in chenille bathrobes knelt on brown winter grass to worship the baby doll lying in the manger. A tiny Mary and Joseph leaned toward him, offering protection and adoration. As I stood there, swathed in the chilled, damp air, the make-believe scene came to life for me, bathing me in comfort that, for those few moments, cleansed me of the awful touch of Mr. Simpson.

I remember thinking about the plight of the Holy Family, how they, too, had been forced to flee their home for the promise of a new beginning. My ten-year-old heart ached for Mary and Joseph, first uprooted from Nazareth, then fleeing with their tiny child to faraway Egypt to escape Herod's cruelty.

But God let them return home eventually, I thought.

And so it would be for the Collinsworths. The little town of Searcy, Arkansas, was our Nazareth. And when all this cruelty was over, we would return home too, with the promise of a new beginning.

Christmas passed, and the Nativity scene was dismantled. But long after the costumes were packed away and the wooden animals returned to storage, I continued to cling to my childlike belief that somehow, some way, we would find our way back home.

And Mr. Simpson continued his daily assaults.

I could not communicate in words the horror of what awaited me every day after school, but my teachers began to sense that something was terribly wrong with me. My schoolwork deteriorated until I was failing most of my classes. I had no energy or enthusiasm for anything. Dark circles hung beneath my eyes. Everything about me suggested I was suffering from severe trauma. Finally, a teacher sent me to the school nurse, who then sent me to the school psychologist, but I had nothing to say to either of them.

A few days later, Mama arrived at the school early to pick me up. Surprised, I was thankful for another respite from Mr. Simpson. I hoped for a pleasant interlude. Instead, it became an inquisition.

"Mitty," Mama said, her voice low and intense with anger, "what is wrong with you?"

"Nothing, Mama," I answered, feeling fear pour over me like scalding water.

"The school nurse called me, and she and the school psychologist say you are emotionally disturbed. What do you have to say to that?"

Again, I answered, "Nothing, Mama."

"Listen well, Mitty, and understand. I don't have time for this. I have to worry about your father and about keeping a roof over our heads. I do not have the strength to worry about you or your problems."

"Yes, Mama," I answered.

Guilt and shame made my heart pound as if it would break through my chest and explode.

I've upset Mama, I thought.

I remember looking at her profile as she drove through the traffic to our house. Her mouth was set in a grim line, her eyes squinting against the afternoon sun. She gripped the steering wheel so tightly her knuckles shone like snowcapped mountain peaks.

How could I tell her? I thought. What if it's all my fault? What if I am really a *bad* girl?

Bad Girl. She had been my imaginary friend, the one who accepted the blame when things went wrong, allowing Mitty to escape unscathed. But now, it seemed, Bad Girl and Mitty were no longer separate entities. They had merged into one. My imaginary friend had turned enemy to consume me and soil me. And it was Mr. Simpson who provided the catalyst for this deadly metamorphosis.

Mama may have said she didn't have time for my problems, but when she learned that I had been removed from all my regular classes and placed with a remedial group, she made time for me. Determined to prove that I was brilliant, that I didn't belong in any remedial classes, she brought IQ tests from her district and tested me at home. I was so emotionally dysfunctional and overwhelmed by Mama's rage that I tested poorly. Mama wouldn't give up. She tested me three times, and I tested lower each time. Her rage increased with each test result.

Meantime, my confusion and hurt swelled until there was no controlling it. I loathed my body. In my mind it became synonymous with Mr. Simpson's stench. I began layering my clothes to cover up the smell and the feel of him. I went to school wearing piles of clothing, not daring to reveal an inch of skin that bore the mark of Mr. Simpson.

At dance class, I wore heavy sweaters over my leotards and tights to prevent anyone from seeing the source of my humiliation. My dance coach, an intense, creative man who demanded perfection, was completely undone by my bizarre behavior. Screaming and striking the floor with his cane, he hauled me up to the front of the class to mock what he called my "costume."

"She is the worst student I have," he bellowed to Mama. "Look at her! She is too tall! See? Look at this!" he screeched, pointing at the line of dancers. "She ruins the overall look of my choreography!"

With his cane tapping loudly on the hardwood floor, he leaned toward Mama and hissed, "I don't want her to dance in my recital."

It was the first shot in what became an ongoing battle over whether or not I would be allowed to dance in the annual recital. Mama won every skirmish. Week after week she fought with the temperamental dance instructor. Week after week his cane pounded the floor, accompanying his shrieks of anger. And week after week I caught the damage in the cross-fire. But my lessons continued. I danced and endured the frustrated teacher's barbs and shrank from the feel of my own loathsome body. I was unable to concentrate, and I danced without energy or passion.

I no longer looked forward to the afternoon classes as I had before. While it was true that any opportunity to be away from the house afforded me respite from Mr. Simpson, it seemed I had traded one agony for another.

My life was out of control.

"You mustn't ever tell anyone... " Mr. Simpson's threat echoed in my throbbing head day and night. "I'll see your family thrown out of this house... you don't have any place to go... think of your mama... "

What if Mr. Simpson really did put us out of the house? Would it be my fault? And where would we go? What would we do?

At ten years old, I had no answers, only more questions. Questions that would take a lifetime to answer.

Chapter 5

Ours was a house of the damned.

It had not always been so.

I could remember days of laughter and celebration, days filled with delight. But they seemed long, long ago and far away.

In the old brick house on Center Street, I had lived in a mystical, magical kingdom. Although assaulted at times by the cruelty of my father's illness, our family had known a measure of safety, secured by the powerful moat of dignity and privacy my mother maintained around us.

Within the castle walls, in the presence of my brother, Laddie, I had felt safe. He was my champion, the knight of the realm. When he was with me I was content. He slew the dragons that haunted my dreams, and he filled my childhood with games and laughter.

It didn't matter to me that he wouldn't be an all-American track star, or that he couldn't catch a football with any consistency. Laddie would always be my hero. Once, at a party in Searcy's Spring Park, I saw him tackle a small child whose clothes had caught fire, and together they rolled in the dust until the flames were extinguished. To me, he was chivalry personified, the epitome of all the great characters Mama read about when we snuggled close to her, listening to her at twilight time. Laddie was charming and gallant and filled with laughter.

Warm, humid summer days had found us running in the yard on Center Street, trying not to step on the flowers that spilled out of their garden beds and onto the lawn. He chased me tirelessly. Dressed in an exact replica of a Confederate general, he wore butternut pants, a gray coat, and a plumed hat which bobbed on his head while he ran after me—"the Yank"—until I finally fell down dead, slain by his make-believe sword. Then Laddie would fall down beside me and together we would roll in the grass and roar with laughter. It was ages before I learned the truth about the Civil War—that the Yankees had defeated the Rebs! I'll never forget the shock of it.

It was a good day for Daddy. We were driving out to Five Oaks for the afternoon. I was in the back seat with Laddie, listening to my parents' conversation in the front.

"You know, Minor," Mama said with a teasing laugh, "things would have been a lot different if we had won The War."

"What do you mean, '*if* we had won The War?'" I demanded.

For as long as I could remember I had heard about The War. I couldn't count all the times I had gone with Mama to the courthouse in downtown Searcy and visited with the old men in overalls who sat on benches in the marble hallways. I'd watched them spit tobacco into brass cuspidors and listened to their stories about The War. I'd never imagined we hadn't won it.

"The South lost The War, Mitty," Mama told me. "The Yankees won." Her voice carried a hint of wistfulness.

I was stunned. Then, gasping, I turned on Laddie. "The Yanks won!" I shouted. "The Yanks won! Next time we play 'Johnny Reb and Billy Yank,' I get to kill you!"

When we tired of "Yankee and Reb," we played "Preacher and Sinner." Laddie preached while I sinned. He raised his voice in mock severity and condemned me to everlasting fire. And together we dug deep holes in the back yard, searching for the flames of hell. Never in our wildest imaginings did we expect to find it located above ground, within the walls of a small brown bungalow in California, within the walls of our individual psyches.

Laddie's laughter died not long after we left Center Street. His academic career, which had begun with such promise, spiraled downward, removing him farther and farther from the goal of greatness Mama had once set for him. Silent and tortured, his gallantry was all but used up in the mere effort to keep on living— to simply survive.

I could not burden him with my own horrors. I could not tell him of Mr. Simpson's daily assaults. I could not ask him to take on a dragon of such size and strength.

"This is our secret, Mitty," Mr. Simpson whispered to me every afternoon. "You won't tell anyone, will you? I know you don't want anything to happen to your family."

With every assault, the threats increased.

"You wouldn't want your poor mama to find herself without a house, would you?" he said. "She looks so tired... Think about it—what if she came home and found out you'd lost your house?"

"Your daddy is very sick. He can't do anything to help out. It's just your mama. She's got to take care of everything. You don't want to make things harder for her, do you? I know you'll keep our little secret."

And so I kept the secret of Mr. Simpson's abuse. How could I become the cause of more pain for my already overburdened mama? How could I allow us to be tossed out of this house? I had no choice but to keep silent. I had no choice but to protect my family.

At night, when she returned late from her evening classes, I studied Mama's face. Where had her beauty gone? I wondered. Once vibrant and full of excitement, she had been like a gaily wrapped package at Christmas. On the outside, she had sparkled with a beauty and elegance that beckoned us to come closer, to peer into her heart and see the delightful adventures she offered. Now, as though torn apart by unkind hands, she seemed empty of all her lively promises, her beauty discarded like yesterday's used and damaged gift wrapping.

There had been a time when Mama was acutely aware of every nuance of feeling that exuded from her children. She had known our hearts. She had understood. She had seemed especially attuned to Laddie's torment over our father's illness. At times, she had sensed that Laddie would explode with silent rage, and on those days she had loaded us into the car and driven through Searcy to my Aunt Jo's house in the country. As soon as the car stopped, Laddie would jerk the door open and run into the vegetable garden. Standing there among the cabbages, he would scream his anger to the sky, bellowing like an injured animal caught in a trap, begging to be freed. Finally, emptied of his rage for the moment, he would walk back to the house and Mama would drive us home to Center Street.

California was a long way from Aunt Jo's vegetable garden. In the crowded suburb where we lived, there was no place to stand and scream at the world.

I understand now that Mama's own pain had cauterized her senses, making her numb to the troubled vibrations both her children were emitting. She was oblivious to our anguish, so damaged was she by her own injuries. We had become a family of strangers, each harboring our secret pain, each moving alone, forging a desperate path through hostile terrain.

To add to Mama's troubles, the condition of my eyes continually worsened. She had been deeply disturbed by the fact that the first surgery had been a failure, but she was even more disturbed to notice that my eyes were now actually worse than before. Before, both eyes had strayed toward my nose, but now, after surgery, one eye strayed outward and the other strayed inward.

I entered the hospital for surgery a second time. Again, Mama packed my favorite dolls and a new pair of pajamas. She stayed with me until all the paperwork was done and the tests were completed, and then she returned to work. I knew what to expect this time, and I was terrified. As the anesthetist placed the mask over my face, I cried silently, I don't want to be pretty... I don't want to be pretty...

I awoke to pain and darkness, as before, and the nurse's voice commanding, "Don't cry, Mitty. You mustn't cry."

When the bandages came off, it appeared as though the operation had been a success, but as the weeks passed, we were again disappointed. The second surgery was yet another futile effort to make me beautiful.

Mama was not willing to give up. Her search for a cure for me took her to Pasadena, where she located a doctor who specialized in training children's eyes to function together, with fusion.

I looked forward to the frequent after-school trips across the city to Pasadena, because they offered me respite from Mr. Simpson. Mama pointed out the route of the Rose Parade and told me, "Mitty, someday when you're all grown up and pretty, you're going to be the Rose Queen."

Perhaps nothing is so telling of Mama's Southern heritage than her dream that I would someday become a beauty queen. The quintessential Southern Belle, she understood, as do all daughters of fine Southern families who have won titles and worn crowns, that it was her duty to pass that honor down to her daughter. Mama's beauty had won her the title of "prettiest girl" in Shirley, Arkansas, and in college she had amassed trophies and medals for her talent in speech and drama and music. She considered it her right, her responsibility, to designate me as her heir to these honors. Her voice, so sure and confident, promised me success.

As a tall, gangly, ten-year-old with a black pirate's patch over one eye, the idea of my becoming a beauty queen was incomprehensible to me. And yet, who was I to argue with fate? Had not my father chosen that honor for me, too? Many years earlier, in my baby book, under the picture of a cherub wearing a ribbon and a crown, Daddy had written "Miss America 1967." He, too, coveted a beauty title for me.

Daddy wants this for me, I thought, as I looked out the window at the parade route. This is what I have to do, to garner the prize, to heal my family...

I had never forgotten the promise I made to Daddy on the day I had betrayed him into the hands of the attendants at the Arkansas mental institution. I had not freed myself from the bonds of the vow. I was still determined to restore my family's pride and my father's dignity. Only when I felt Mr. Simpson's hands on me did I wonder if it was within my power to bring healing to my family. Then I wondered if I could ever heal myself.

In the ongoing pursuit of beauty, we continued regular checkups with the eye surgeon in Covina, and one day as I walked down the street toward his office, I noticed a picture hanging in the window of a nearby realtor's office. It was a picture of an old house. Something about it reminded me of the house on Center Street.

This is it, I thought, this is the answer to all our family's problems!

"Mama, Mama," I shouted, racing into our bungalow after my doctor's appointment, "you have to see it, you have to see it!"

"Mitty, what is it?" Mama called.

"Mama, the house in the picture in the realtor's office!" I shouted, nearly colliding with her as I hurried into the kitchen. "It looks just like the old brick house on Center Street... Well, not exactly like it, but it's old and it's two stories and... "

"Mitty," Mama said, her voice sounding fatigued, as usual, "you know we can't afford to buy a house."

She wiped her hands on her apron and reached into a cabinet.

"But Mama, you have to look at it, at least. You'll love it. It looks old, and there are trees... "

My voice trailed off, lost in thoughts of antiquity. I had never been able to accept the newness of California. I longed for large, old houses where overgrown vines hugged the walls like friendly arms.

"Mama, if you see it, you'll understand. It's beautiful."

The next day, Mama and I returned to the realtor's office. I pressed my face against the window and studied the picture of the old house. It was located in a rural community called Charter Oak, and I was sure destiny had led us to it.

"This old place has been on the market for a long time. But no interested buyers... We've been expecting it to be torn down and the land rezoned commercial," the realtor told us. "But if you'd like to see it, I'd be glad to show it to you."

"What do you think, Mama?" I asked, holding my breath.

"It's beautiful, all right," she answered, studying the photo of the white, stucco, two-story house.

And it was. In the picture.

We made an appointment to drive out the next afternoon.

Charter Oak was about ten minutes away from Covina, in a rural area carved out of acres of citrus groves. We drove through narrow roadways lined with orange trees. Winter was nearly over, but the warning of unseasonable cold had brought smudge pots out among the rows of trees. The smell of smoke mingled with the pungent scent of damp earth. I was enchanted by the sight of trees—vegetation! Something besides skinny palm trees did grow in California!

And then I saw the weeds. As tall as I was, they were even taller, filling the yard of the house I hoped would be our Shangri-La. A sharp machete would have made our trek to the front door easier, but Mama thrust her way through the forest of thistles and tall grass, finally stepping up onto the wide, columned porch of the old house.

Built in 1910, it was a manor house designed for a wealthy San Francisco woman who at that time owned the vast citrus groves in the area. The elegant, spacious house had been her summer villa, but since her death many years earlier, it had stood empty. Most of the acreage surrounding the house had been sold off to developers, but its present yard was still generous. Several large trees shaded the porch, and nearby, overgrown rose bushes clung tenaciously to life.

Mama stepped into the large living room, and in a single instant, she established a rapport with every plank of wood and every brick and every floorboard in the old house.

It had once been a very grand home. Not unlike the Collinsworth family, it had fallen on hard times, but something of the stateliness it had once possessed was still present. An immediate kinship between this falling-apart house and this sad, falling-apart family sprang to life.

The $14,500 selling price of the house was cheap by most standards, but for our family it was exorbitant. The down payment alone was out of reach. But Mama was undeterred. She began negotiating with the agent, and by spring, the house was ours. Rental income from the old brick house on Center Street would help some toward the monthly mortgage payments, and the rest Mama would budget out of her teaching salary.

I understand now that Mama viewed the house as an investment. With her eye for architecture and fine construction, she could see what other buyers had not been able to see. From the exquisite rosewood paneling to the hardwood floors, from the hand-tooled banisters to the stained-glass windows, the house was a treasure. It deserved better than a bulldozer's blade. In time, Mama speculated, the house would be worth far more than the price she had paid for it.

And in time, Mama determined, she would be able to fill this house with antiques and beautiful things, as she had the house on Center Street. She would restore this villa among the citrus groves to its former glory, and, perhaps, in the process she could infuse her family with some small measure of its former glory as well. The house was well-suited for both endeavors.

It was a risky gamble, buying the manor house, but Mama never looked back. Once the decision was made, she focused only on the future benefits, turning her face away from the huge liabilities that lay at her front door. She had two young children, a husband too ill to work, and a pitifully low income. But she believed that this house could become an essential element in her plan to redeem our family. She believed its restoration could preface our own return to grace and dignity.

I believe it was at that time that Mama gave up her dream of ever returning to Arkansas. Two years had passed since we had retreated from our embattled kingdom, defeated by the shame of Daddy's illness. We had no reason to believe it was safe to return now. Our family and friends had been unable to understand his disease before, and now, two years later, he was much worse. His sometimes catatonic, sometimes raving-prowling-moaning behavior, was difficult for us, his closest family members, to cope with. How could we expect relatives and casual acquaintances to be able to understand?

Moving day was another great adventure. Laddie and I carried boxes into the house while Mama unpacked them and filled cabinets and drawers. Daddy's chair rocked back and forth in an upstairs bedroom while we worked around him, tossing linens onto beds, arranging rugs on the hardwood floors, and sweeping dust and dirt off the wide porches that spanned the front and back of the house.

Gangs had used the house as a gathering place, and we found old slot machines and discarded liquor bottles in the basement. Streamers of peeling paint hung from the walls and ceilings. In some rooms, water-damaged plaster reeked of mildew, but nothing could dampen Mama's enthusiasm for the place. She scraped at gray patches of mold and scrubbed the thick, sticky layers of dirt that hid in the corners of the kitchen and bathrooms. With each swipe of her cloth and each sweep of the broom, she planned every phase of the house's rebirth.

"A fresh coat of paint will do wonders, Mitty," Mama said, putting a paintbrush into my hands.

Together we began to paint the dirty walls. The first coat, smeared and messy, looked like the job of an amateur, but we admired our work with the pride of Picasso. We polished the rich rosewood paneling and the banisters and oiled and buffed the floors. Mama placed our few pieces of furniture about the house and then stepped back to admire her work. We had so few pieces that the large rooms still looked vacant, but the old house was clean, and it was ours.

The move had been a huge undertaking for a crew of two children and one woman, but we found new energy in the doing of the tasks. After several days, the house itself seemed to preen with pride as if it, too, could recall its former grandeur. If not exactly beautiful, the house did at least look respectable.

I knew Mama was pleased when she unpacked the crystal wedding bowl, the candleholders, and the book of poems my father had given her years ago. She had not bothered to unpack them since the day they'd been carted out of the old brick house on Center Street. Now, she made a place for them in this home, filling its open, uncluttered spaces with new hope. To me, it was a gesture of acceptance, of permanence.

Mama enrolled Laddie and me in our new schools. It was late in the spring semester, and the change, for Laddie, appeared to be a good thing. Suddenly, he began to make new friends. His grades improved and some of his old humor sparked into life. I watched him with envy. The move had done nothing to alleviate my sense of misery and self-loathing. I continued to live as though dead inside.

Mr. Simpson followed me to Charter Oak. Every week he found reasons to visit us in our new home. Mama, completely unaware of his perversion, welcomed his gestures of friendship. He presented himself to her as a caring and thoughtful old gentleman, generously offering to help her with many of her refurbishing projects. So she often drove to Covina to pick him up and bring him out to the old manor house. And there, whenever he could catch me alone, he committed his heinous crimes.

The villa among the citrus trees was, for Mama, the promise of refuge and redemption, but for me it was a house of horrors. It could not afford me the privacy and protection I had found within the old brick house on Center Street. With bitter disappointment, I discovered that its walls could not withstand Mr. Simpson's assaults.

While I did not share Mama's warm feelings for our new home, I was glad to be out of the subdivision in Covina and away from the tiny tract houses that all looked alike. I adored the quiet setting among the citrus trees and the music that awakened me in the mornings when the migrant workers arrived in the nearby orchards singing lively tunes. I loved the sweet smell of orange blossoms that filled my room when the breeze lifted the curtains at my open window. And I felt strangely drawn to the young families that came to call on us shortly after moving day.

A Baptist seminary in the area had been using the manor house's parlor and dining room as makeshift classrooms for their student preachers before we moved in. For months, they had held Sunday school classes in the downstairs, operating a tiny mission church on Sundays. Mama told them they could continue to hold church services there on Sundays, and soon Mama, Laddie, and I joined in with the worship. Mama sang with the choir, and Laddie and I sat in Sunday school classes.

We established a quick and easy rapport with the young seminarians and their wives. They came and went in the big old manor house, bringing their children and their songs and their big, black Bibles. Loving and friendly and just as poor as we were, they offered a sweet and healing touch to our spirits. When the seminary moved to other facilities, we were sorry to see them go.

With the departure of the seminary, we began attending a little Baptist church near our home. Mama placed Laddie and me in Sunday school classes, and she found her place in the choir.

What a strange dichotomy existed in our lives. Our father's bizarre and tormenting behavior haunted the shadowy corners of our home. His moaning filled the night hours and his rocking, creaking motion lent a macabre rhythm to our everyday routine. And yet, at the same time, there were moments when normalcy walked upright among us. For me, its presence was especially poignant on Sunday mornings.

On Sunday, we fled the darkness and entered the light.

On Sunday, each of us donned our own invisible armor to

hide our invisible wounds, and together we basked in the warmth of the solemn and the predictable. Our weapons of defense were at the ready, but we carried them in secret, entering the church looking like any other small-town family, poised and ready for weekly worship. There, in the sanctuary, among the hymns and prayers and the simple sermons, we experienced sweet moments of solace.

For me, such moments were fragile and short-lived. Like wisps of pink cotton candy that dissolved before I could savor it, they dissolved in an instant when exposed to the memory of Mr. Simpson.

I remember one particular day when he came to the house, entering with friendly greetings, bringing Mama his offers of unselfish assistance on her latest project. As soon as he was able, he cornered me in my room upstairs. I struggled to pull away from him, but he grabbed my arms and pulled me against him. His face was so close to mine that the stubble of his beard scratched my cheek. His breath was hot and putrid when he whispered, "You mustn't tell anyone... This is our secret... You don't want anything to happen to your mama, do you, Mitty?"

I wrenched out of his grasp and ran out the door of my bedroom and onto the verandah that ran the length of the back of the house. He tried to corner me, but I ducked and ran past him and down the stairs. Later that day, when he had done what he came to do, he asked Mama to drive him home.

Mr. Simpson sat up front in the passenger's seat next to Mama. I sat in the back seat. Throughout the drive back to Covina, Mr. Simpson rode with his arm over the seat, reaching back to grope at me. I moved from one side of the back seat to the other, trying to stay beyond his reach. He stretched and finally grabbed my knees, holding me in a vice-like grip until we reached his house. All the while, Mama drove on, her back ramrod straight in the seat in front of me, her eyes never turning to the left or the right, never looking back to see why I was scrambling about behind her.

On the drive back home to Charter Oak, Mama said, "Mitty, was Mr. Simpson trying to touch you?"

I answered, "Yes, Mama."

"I thought so," she said, her eyes never leaving the road. "From now on, when Mr. Simpson comes to the house, I want you to hide."

The subject was closed. Mama asked no more questions. I offered no more comment.

It didn't matter that Mr. Simpson was no longer our landlord. His threats still silenced me. His evil had dulled my sense of judgment. I had no logic strong enough to wage war against him. While he could no longer throw us out into the streets, I knew he still possessed the power to injure my family. And so, I maintained my silence.

The summer before I turned eleven was one of great upheaval for me. I was caught unprepared for the changes that puberty would bring. My tall, gangly form became more womanly, more curvaceous. Suddenly, I was more woman than child. Mama, noticing the changes, handed me the booklet, *Growing Up and Liking It.* I read it with childlike curiosity until I came to the part about how babies are made. Appalled and sickened, I ran to Mama.

"Mama, is this really true?" I asked, holding my breath, hoping she would tell me the book was all wrong.

Mama assured me that the book was right. I couldn't believe it. Again, I questioned. And again. Always the same answer.

"That is how it is done, Mitty."

For days I quizzed her on the facts of life, always hoping she would change her story. Always she repeated the same information the book had given. Finally, I had to accept the truth of it.

Shaking my head, I closed my eyes tightly against the dawning realization. I felt bile rise up into my throat. Mr. Simpson's hideous act of violence upon me was the means by which babies were conceived. Terror and revulsion paralyzed me for an instant, and then I ran from Mama's presence, completely undone by the knowledge of what had been forced upon me.

Ironically, the onslaught of puberty proved to be my salvation from Mr. Simpson. He lost interest in me when I left the physical traits of childhood behind. My womanly shape held no attraction for him, and his perverted assaults ceased almost as suddenly as they had begun. The man who had preyed on my innocence and traded on my family's despair disappeared, never to return again, except in my haunted nightmares.

That summer is further marked in my memory as the time when I began to understand how poor we really were. I awakened with shock to the reality of my mother's heavy burden.

A friend in the neighborhood invited me to go swimming with her at the city "plunge." Excitedly, I ran to ask Mama for a dime. She never looked up, she just kept her head down and continued pulling at the stubborn weeds that threatened the flower beds.

"No, Mitty," she told me. "You can't go."

"Mama, please... why not?" I begged.

"Mitty," Mama answered, still digging in the dirt, "I don't have a dime."

At that moment, I allowed myself to be truly a child. I burst into tears and cried, "Mama, what do you mean? It's only a dime!"

Mama stood up and stretched her back. With a weary gesture, she pressed a strand of faded red hair back behind her ear. She stared down into my eyes and said slowly, "I meant what I said, Mitty. I don't have a dime."

I never again asked to go to the city plunge to swim. I tried not to ask for anything that would increase Mama's worries about money.

Mama spent that summer gardening, caring for her family, taking night classes, and studying many hours. She was determined to climb up the California teacher's pay scale, but it was a painful ascent. She made friends with the woman who owned the little country store down the road and arranged to get credit to buy groceries. She also accepted hand-me-down clothes from the woman's daughter, who was several years older than me.

I had never worn another child's clothes before. The too-large clothes were in a more sophisticated style than a girl of my age would have worn, and they hung on my much smaller frame. I stared at myself in the mirror and felt hot with humiliation.

I should be thankful, I thought, feeling shame now coupled with embarrassment.

I remembered the beautiful clothes that had once hung in my closet in the old brick house on Center Street. With the point of a finger, I had selected a frilly dress from among a dozen or more, and, like a pampered princess, I had dressed with the help of a maid. Now I was being offered another child's castoffs.

Injured pride was only one small element to be factored into the misery I felt as I stared at myself in the mirror. I viewed my body as a war zone, a defeated territory that had been looted and desecrated by a vile presence. To me, it was ugly and damaged, and I couldn't bear for others to see my shame. I wanted to fade into shadow, unseen and unwatched, but my height would not allow me even that luxury. The tallest child in my age group, I stood at least a head above the other neighborhood children I played with.

While my height was an embarrassment, it was not nearly as humiliating to me as the fact that I was the only girl my age who had developed breasts. At not quite eleven years old, I was appalled by this. To me, it was the final toll in the death knell of my childhood. At times, I wrapped cloth around my chest to flatten myself, and I continued to layer my clothes to camouflage the despised curves. In spite of the summer heat, I wore shirts on top of shirts and blouses buttoned over dresses, all in a futile attempt to cover up the truth that I was no longer a little girl. That I was different from the other children who ran and played among the citrus groves. That my childhood had ended almost before it had begun.

I yearned to be able to laugh with the kind of carefree abandon I heard from the neighborhood children who ran and played among the citrus trees. I wanted to be a part of that lively knot of children who seemed so secure and happy, but I stood apart from them, removed from their untroubled band by a distance too great to cross.

I was often guilt-ridden about the fact that I could not feel happy. I knew Mama wanted me to be thankful for what we had. But it was so hard to be thankful for the house that had not protected me from Mr. Simpson. It was hard to be thankful for the ugly hand-me-down clothes I wore. I remember buckling the other girl's scuffed shoes on my feet and stumbling in them because they were a size too big. I remember the sting of being the poorest family in the area and being mocked for buying the ugly old house that no one else wanted.

All that was gracious and beautiful in our lives had disintegrated to ashes. After the genteel, "old money" way of life we had known, we were poorly suited to poverty.

Mama let us sleep late every morning that summer. It was not like her at all. In the past, she had insisted that we rise early, eat a good breakfast, and begin the day with order and routine. But that summer of our extreme poverty, she allowed us to sleep very late so she could feed us only two meals a day. It was one more way to save money.

Feeding her family was an ongoing challenge for Mama. She was grateful for the abundant orange trees that surrounded our house and offered us bushels of fresh fruit for salads, for snacks, and for fresh juice. Potatoes became the mainstay of our diet, cooked in every conceivable manner. Once a week, Mama splurged and bought hamburger, and occasionally she treated us to a dollop of ice cream.

When the summer ended and Laddie and I returned to school, it was with the knowledge that our poverty was a fact of life that would not soon change; it was something to which we must adapt. It was not, however, something of which to be ashamed.

"The poorer you are, Mitty," Mama told me, "the more carefully you dress."

Mama's fingers stroked the rich fabric on the bolt in Henshaw's Department Store in Pasadena, instructing me on how to determine the quality of material. It was one of many excursions Mama took me on in her effort to teach me about the things that she knew so well—the things which she was now forced to do without.

I remember being mesmerized by the beauty and the feel of the material in Mama's hands. The dress I wore was faded and out of style, but Mama would not let me act as if I were dishonored by it.

"If you have limited money to spend, always choose classic, understated lines," she said. "Never wear trendy fads, Mitty."

We couldn't afford to buy the beautiful linens and woolens and silks that lined the walls of the fabric stores, but Mama made sure I learned to recognize them. She led me through the couture department of leading clothing stores and taught me style and fashion.

Alone with Mama, exploring the world that she knew so well, I felt rare stirrings of pure joy. I had her total attention during those hours. When we sat together at home and pored over fashion magazines, noting the leading designers and the lines they were presenting for the current season, Mama's face, intelligent and animated, flashed reminders of her former beauty. In her rich voice, she tried to convince me that while, for the present, I couldn't wear the best, I should at least be assured that I deserved it.

"Stand taller, walk prouder," she told me often. "Keep your chin up, shoulders back. You are a Collinsworth, Mitty. Wear your clothes as if you were royalty."

She was already gone in the mornings when I left the house wearing my odd-looking, layered outfits.

My classmates teased me daily about my clothes. The out-of-fashion dresses, too long and oversized, were even more ridiculous with a shirt or sweater worn over the top. In the locker room after physical education classes, I refused to shower for fear of revealing my woman's body among all the other little girls. I suffered their derision and never answered them, never knowing what to say in my defense.

I remember coming home from school one afternoon, devastated by yet another day of playground cruelty. A group of girls had encircled me and yelled taunts about my ugly clothes being too big; worse yet, they had assaulted my mother's character.

"Doesn't your mother ever iron your clothes?" one girl shouted.

The girls all laughed, and another asked snidely, "Is she too lazy? She is! I'm sure she is!"

Their mocking laughter followed me home from school. That night I told Mama I wasn't going back to school ever again.

"Mitty," Mama said, placing her hands on my shoulders and looking intently into my face, "you will go back to school tomorrow, and you will look those girls straight in the eyes, and without flinching, you will tell them they are absolutely right! Your clothes *are* ironed poorly! You have no apologies for that fact. Tell them your mother was not trained to be a laundress, she was trained to be an educator, and she does a damned good job of that."

When my tormentors attacked me at school the next day, I gave them the speech I had practiced all night. They never again ridiculed my clothes or my appearance.

Mama didn't concern herself only with teaching me clothing styles. She was determined to educate me on all the fine things that had once been the normal accoutrements of her gracious lifestyle. We toured the Huntington Library and strolled through its formal gardens. Together, we attended art exhibits and she pointed out the many forms of art, from painting to sculpture to interior design. We wandered through dusty antique stores, examining rare books and studying the beauty and style of period furniture. She taught me how to select fine china, silver, linen, and jewelry. I quickly learned how to discern authentic works from reproductions.

Often, after an outing at Henshaw's Department Store, Mama would drive by the Pasadena Playhouse, where we toured the auditorium and the rooms backstage. With curiosity, I studied the posters advertising the children's theater.

"Someday you'll be a part of this, Mitty," Mama told me.

I wondered how such a thing could come about, but I never doubted Mama's ability to make it so.

My excursions with Mama filled me with an overpowering

sense of her love for me. Alone with her, listening to her voice as she explained and pointed out the wonders of art and nature, I felt completely happy. Like little islands of mercy, those times were like places where paradise could intrude, if only for a little while, into the otherwise bleak landscape of my life. And they enabled me to hope and dream of better times to come. The beauty of those dreams, however, was often dimmed by the harsh reality of our daily lives.

Our financial state remained desperate. Nowhere was it more evident than at mealtimes. I grew tired of potatoes and oranges and the occasional hamburger. I longed for the kind of rich foods I had grown accustomed to in the old brick house on Center Street. I missed the satisfied feelings, the feelings of love and well-being that I associated with good food and a well-stocked kitchen.

I used to try and recall the flavor of Aunt Vera's fried catfish. Along with the wonderful tastes and the piquant aromas of the other picnic dishes, I remembered the great crowds of cousins and aunts and uncles who gathered for the annual fish fry at Mama's sister's house. With great food came a wonderful sense of belonging, of being loved.

And then there was the yearly watermelon feast at Aunt Belma's farm, when all the uncles would go into the field and harvest the melons we would devour out under the steamy summer night sky. We would eat watermelon until we thought we would burst. Then, when we could eat no more, we would sing together. Mama and her sisters would harmonize on the old familiar songs, and I would fall asleep listening to their voices, my head resting on Mama's lap, my fingers sticky with the juice of the watermelons.

I fantasized about the three-layered coconut cake Aunt Carrie brought to every family dinner. She carried it in on a clear glass cake plate and set it down on a table near where I stood, making me exactly eye level with her thick, white frosting doused in fresh-grated coconut. I could hardly control the temptation to swipe a finger through that luscious creation.

I could make my mouth water just thinking about Grandmother Collinsworth's cinnamon rolls. To me, they were the expression of her love. Reserved, stolid, and intimidating, she spoke little of her feelings, but she expressed them eloquently in the cinnamon rolls she baked when she knew we were coming to visit. I could remember rolling down the car window to catch the scent of yeast bread as Daddy drove up the road toward Five Oaks.

All the good times, all the wonderful family times I had enjoyed, where fun and laughter and love had been in abundance—all these I associated with food. It is easy to see where I made the connection between good food and good feelings. It is easy to see, now, how food became my secret passion.

I could never eat enough to satisfy the emptiness I felt. Every morning I awakened hungry. Throughout the day I fantasized about food, pledging that when I grew up I would eat everything I wanted, anytime I wanted it. After school, I walked home thinking about a kitchen filled with the smell of roast beef in the oven, of fresh homemade cookies waiting for me on the table. The fantasy ended abruptly as I set foot on the threshold of the manor house.

Standing there, gripping the brass handle on the heavy wooden front door, I forced myself to run through my mental checklist before I stepped inside the house. Today could be the day I would find Daddy's lifeless body dangling from a rope in the basement. Perhaps he would be dead in his bed from an overdose of pills. Had he slashed his wrists while I was at school? Would I find him with his brains blown out?

Each afternoon I braced myself to find my father dead by his own hand. I drew a deep steadying breath before I opened the front door, praying as I walked in that he would be as we had left him, alive, although lifeless.

Once I was assured that Daddy was unharmed, I would go into the dining room, drop my books on the floor, and settle myself at the table to wait for Mama. It was a lovely old dining table, with side and end chairs to match, and it was much too grand for our budget. Mama had bought it from a neighbor who had no interest in antiques and who had no idea of the value of the pieces she was planning to throw away. To her, they were nothing more than junk. So, for only a few dollars, Mama bought the set.

Every day when I entered the dining room, I let my thoughts drift back to the old brick house on Center Street. I sent my mind into the kitchen where Corinne and Ruby Jean sang and cooked and played games with Laddie and me. Like proud African queens, Corinne and Ruby Jean reigned over my memories, summoning up all the good feelings that went with the sweet treats they offered every afternoon. Ruby Jean would lift me up onto a high stool and greet me with a crushing hug.

Corinne, her skin the color of coffee with cream, was tall and slender and breathtakingly beautiful. She had high cheekbones and slightly almond-shaped black eyes, and she carried herself with unhurried regal dignity. I loved the sound of her voice when she taught Laddie and me spirituals and ballads from her own childhood.

In my own immature way, I had loved Ruby Jean and Corinne fiercely. It was an ignorant, contradictory love, defined by the dogma of the South, but it was strong and protective. I would have done anything for them, anything to please them and to solicit their laughter and music. I wondered often, from the dining room two thousand miles away, if they were well, if they were happy. I wondered what their lives were like now.

It was 1958. A year had come and gone since the confrontation on the front steps of Little Rock's Central High School between the governor's troops and the black families trying to send their children to school. President Eisenhower had vowed to take any necessary measures against the Arkansas governor to keep the school open to students of any color. Throughout the South, segregation writhed in the throes of death. Change marched across the country with the surety of step that has always accompanied a righteous cause.

I listened to news stories on the radio and I heard Mama speak of the civil rights demonstrations that were occurring in every major city in the United States. The accounts of violent upheaval frightened and confused me because I was still such a child of the South, but at the same time it all seemed very distant to me. Distant, that is, until Old John died.

Daddy's family wrote to tell us of Old John's death that fall of 1958. With his death, all the changes that had seemed so vague and distant suddenly took on form and dimension. The only living remnant of the old ways, of our family's history, Old John took with him my touchstone to the past and to a former way of life. It all died with him. Everything familiar passed out of my life. I felt bereft and more lonely than I had ever felt before.

I kept my silent, solitary vigil in the dining room every afternoon after school, waiting for Mama to come home from work. I turned on the lights to be sure she didn't come into a dark house. Most days I fell asleep, awakening when she came in, finding her exhausted and strained after a long day of teaching and night school.

It was an instinctive if unspoken thing that alerted me to Mama's fear of the darkness. It was a shared fear that neither of us would tell the other, but in silent agreement we each made certain that lights were turned on in the house before the dusk could throw us into the shadows.

Laddie's fears manifested themselves in other ways. He began sleepwalking. Every night Mama barricaded the second-floor stairwell so he would not fall down it during his nightly wanderings. One night, in a deep trance, he walked into my bedroom and began punching me, throwing all his weight into every slug. I awakened terrified, and screamed for Mama. She rushed into my room and hauled Laddie off me. He awoke disoriented and confused, with no memory of attacking me. Embarrassed and apologetic, he returned to his own room.

I wasn't old enough to understand the psychology of Laddie's behavior, and so it troubled me. For months, we had been estranged, ever since he and his few friends had decided they hated girls. It was required behavior according to the code of his newly formed "Wolfett Club." As his little sister, I was a pariah.

I was no longer welcome to go with him when he set off on his grand adventures in the orange groves. The first requirement for admission to the Wolfett Club automatically disqualified me— all members had to be boys. The second one—all members must kill four hundred snails—wouldn't have been a problem for me, but the third rule required Wolfetts to hate all girls. I finally had to concede that I wasn't destined to become a Wolfett.

I missed the camaraderie Laddie and I had shared when we were smaller. I ached for the friendship that had been so precious to me. On those rare occasions when he forgot his pledge to hate girls, I was almost euphoric with joy. We played "Zorro" together, searching the closets and hallways of the old house, looking for secret passages. The balcony was the setting for our sword fights and for dramatic, slow death scenes. Once, we dared each other to dig up the grave of a neighborhood cat, to see if it had gone to Heaven, as the adults had said. I lost the dare and began digging. Hours later, I put down the shovel and concluded that yes, cats really did go to Heaven.

Those special times with my brother did more than just offer me companionship. They gave me the chance to feel like a child again. To Laddie, it didn't matter how tall I was or whether or not I had breasts; to him, I was just his little sister. When I played games with Laddie and climbed the trees in the orchards, hiding from him among the thickest branches, I was able to recapture the sweet moments of childhood that had been stolen from me.

The good times at Charter Oak were scarce. The old manor house failed to yield the peace and serenity we had hoped for. While Laddie had shown some early signs of adapting and adjusting, the increasing cruelty of the neighborhood children began to encroach on his fragile peace. We both became the brunt of jokes because we were the poorest kids in the area. Children continued to taunt us for living in the ugly old house that no one else would buy. Even Laddie's "Wolfetts" joined in the harassment. He stood up to the tauntings as best he could, and I learned to endure. My black eye patch, the old house, the ugly, old-fashioned hand-me-downs I wore, all were reasons for ridicule. And when word of Daddy's mental illness circulated through the neighborhood, his condition became the source of many cruel jokes and comments. I thought I would die of humiliation.

The assaults pushed Mama, Laddie, and me into a tight circle where we held onto one another, protecting Daddy in the center, not allowing anyone to come close. We moved as though we had one heartbeat, one thought—to endure, to survive. We each understood the unspoken order of the day: circle, join hands, square your shoulders, and adjust the load. One more hour. One more day.

Christmas that year was bleak. Mama bought a tree, wood for the fireplace, a box of six ornaments, and then she splurged on the one luxury she knew we would all enjoy. On the stairway landing stood a bronze statue of the explorer, Cortez, holding a small lamp in his upraised hand. Laddie and I loved that statue and nicknamed him "George." We talked about him as if he were a family member. That Christmas, Mama took some of our precious few dollars and had "George" wired. The lamp in his palm lit the dark shadows of the stairway.

Laddie and I squealed with delight as the bright light flooded the steps. Then we hurried into the corner of the living room where our little tree stood, and placed the six shiny new ornaments on its branches. I tried to stifle the feelings of disappointment that overcame me when I studied the skinny, woeful-looking tree that was overpowered by the large, otherwise unfurnished room.

Memories of the magic of Christmases past flooded my mind. Every December, Mama had transformed the old brick house on Center Street into a scene from *The Nutcracker Suite*. I would play the part of Clara, if only in my imagination. Twirling in my velvet and lace dress, I would dance through the house, touching the boughs on the huge Christmas tree that nearly reached the ceiling. Fingering the elegant, Victorian ornaments that hung on every branch, I would coyly peek at the brightly wrapped packages stacked knee-deep beneath the tree. The scents of candles and sweetbreads and pine garlands permeated the air. Pots of poinsettias decked the stairway and the mantles and the table tops.

Traditional carollers would arrive every Christmas Eve, standing on our wide front porch and singing all our favorite songs. Mama would invite them in for steaming mugs of hot chocolate and homemade bread and cookies. Then, dressed in matching Christmas pajamas, Laddie and I would throw ourselves into the task of opening the scores of presents that had tempted us from under the tree for so many days. Nothing that money could buy was denied the Collinsworth children.

On Christmas morning, we would open our eyes to discover more gifts, brought in the night by Old Santa. Chasing each other downstairs, Laddie and I would find stockings overflowing with toys and fruit and more delights than a child could count.

Mama would preside over Christmas breakfast in the dining room. The table, heavy with the best china and silver and crystal, offered the most elegant dishes our cooks could prepare. On the mantle above the fireplace, sparkling under the light of a crystal chandelier, stood a miniature winter village, complete with a church and spire in the center. It was a charming, magical scene with columns of angels whose tiny hands held fresh flowers.

Every room in the house on Center Street matched the beauty of a Currier and Ives painting. But in the old manor house in Charter Oak, I saw little charm and felt none of the warmth that should have been present at this holiday season. Instead, I felt only loneliness.

There would be no visits to aunts and uncles on this Christmas Day, as there had been in years past. We would not be spending the day with our jovial relatives at Five Oaks, watching the men in their hunting clothes walk off into the woods, rifles gleaming against their shoulders. This year, there would be no laughter and games with cousins while the women worked their mysterious, aromatic wonders in Grandmother's kitchen.

Two thousand miles away, in Arkansas, the rest of the Collinsworths would be together at Five Oaks in the dining room, with our grandmother seated at the head of the table presiding over a feast. I could see them all now, gathered together, laughing and retelling the stories of family heroics that were told every

year. As darkness fell, the aunts and uncles would wave goodbye
and drive home, the children asleep in the back seat before they'd
driven as far as Dogwood Creek.

It had been the same every year. For generations the
Collinsworths had gathered together to celebrate the holiday. I
walked through the memory as if it were a literal event, finishing
the day with our last ritual—the visit to Aunt Lucy's neat white
cottage on the way home. Awaiting us would be a child's tea
party. We would drink out of delicate china cups and eat sweet
treats on prim lace doilies. Finally, stuffed and sleepy, we would
be carried by Mama and Daddy to the car for the ride home to
Center Street.

I closed my eyes and drank from the sweet memories. How
different it was on this our third Christmas in California. Daddy
was too ill to come downstairs, and Mama talked a lot about
dignity and pride and something she called "presence."

There was no doubt Mama had presence, and pride and dignity
enough for us all. She reigned over Christmas dinner like a queen
holding court in a palace. The rose-paneled dining room seemed
to reach out and embrace the newly acquired antique dining
table. The meal, though sparse, looked elegant and elaborate,
served on the fine china and silver pieces brought from Center
Street. Mama used the special occasion to remind Laddie and me
that we were Collinsworths.

"Never forget that, children," she said, patting her lips with a
linen napkin. The strains of a Strauss waltz played in the
background on her music box. Gracefully, she sipped tea from a
china cup and then continued. "Maybe we are poor," she said,
"but we are rich in family pride. The Collinsworths have lost
many things through the years, but we have never lost our
dignity."

Throughout the next months, we heard often about dignity
and family pride. It was as though Mama knew we had nothing
else to hold on to. She reminded us often of the legend of the
dogwood, telling us that no matter how difficult things might
get, spring would always come. The dogwoods would bloom again,
and we could expect our miracle as well. As Daddy's condition
worsened, she increased the recitation of the family mantra—just
hold on until spring... hold on until spring...

One day she brought home a parchment card decorated with
hand-painted dogwood branches heavy with white, blood-tipped

blossoms. Printed on the other side was the legend. Many times, we sat together and read the story, reminding each other that miracles can still occur, that second chances really do happen.

Maybe Mama believed I was the key to our family's chance at happiness. Maybe she believed that I was capable of restoring the family to a place of honor. I don't know what drove her, but in the midst of our poverty, she continued to take me to dance lessons. It was the only luxury we afforded. She refused to give up her dream that I become a prima ballerina. She continued to push me in dance until her determination overrode my mediocre talent. To my surprise, I actually began to excel. And she grew obsessive about me, to the neglect of my brother, Laddie.

Mama adored Laddie, I knew that. But he had withdrawn so deeply into himself that she gave up her efforts at promoting him to greatness. On some level, she must have sensed that the trauma of our family life had stolen from him the seeds necessary to grow him into a strong, aggressive man who would be able to succeed against all odds. And so she focused all her energy and attention on me. I hated the fact that the cost of expensive dance coaches for me deprived Laddie of the things young boys crave. And yet, I could not stand up to the force of Mama's will.

Finally, to my mother's great joy, a third operation on my eyes succeeded, at least cosmetically. My eyes no longer strayed. I did not have fusion, as the doctor had hoped—my right eye did all the work—but I was able to take off my glasses, never to wear them again. Mama was satisfied, at least on that issue. Now I would be not only a great dancer but a beautiful one as well. And she embarked on the next phase of my development.

Mama enrolled both Laddie and me in Cotillion, hoping to put the final deft touches on our already highly polished manners. How ironic it all seems to me now. We lived below the poverty level, but Mama sacrificed to pay for dance and etiquette classes for us. In her mind, she believed our greater need was not for basic essentials, but for training in proper conduct. She was willing to do anything to prepare us to face the world with the manners of an aristocrat, as if that would make up for any of life's other deficits.

True to her Southern upbringing, Mama believed with all her heart that dignity, intelligence, manners, and poise would equip us to tackle and overcome even life's greatest obstacles. With Scarlett O'Hara–like determination, she clung to the ways of her ancestors, almost as if the twentieth century had never arrived, and yet, somewhere in her psyche, the present had intruded, bringing with it painful realities. Gripping the past in one hand, she would thrust the future at me with the other.

"Never, ever think you can grow up and depend on a man, Mitty," she would say. "Look at me. I believed your father would be healthy and strong and take care of me forever. Depend only on yourself, Mitty.

"Whatever else I do as your mother, I must make sure you are highly trained and educated to be at the top of whatever profession you desire. If you're the best, you will never end up as I have, and then I'll know I've done everything I could to be a good mother."

I'll never forget the night of the first formal Cotillion dance. I would be the youngest girl there. Mama had enrolled me in Laddie's age group to ensure that he would always have a dance partner—he was too shy to ask anyone to dance—and so I would be the only twelve-year-old in a ballroom full of high school-age young people.

I remember looking at the dress I would wear, thinking it was too old-looking, and too drab. A champagne color, it was designed for a shapely woman, not a child; and yet, much to my humiliation, it fit me well.

Another hand-me-down, I thought, sighing and wishing for a new dress, a dress of my own that would let me look like a girl of twelve.

Suddenly, a memory broke loose from somewhere in my mind, and I saw myself standing at the counter of Searcy's Dairy Queen. With its bright neon sign, the Dairy Queen stood on the edge of the line of demarcation, Park Street. At night, black families with their young children came and stood in the shadows, just out of sight, waiting to make the crossing, as if the distance were a demilitarized zone. There they waited for the white families to buy their treats and leave so they could step up and buy ice cream for their families. I remember looking off into the tree-shaded areas and seeing dark-skinned children whose gaze dropped to the ground as soon as their eyes met mine.

One night, as I stood waiting for my ice cream, I saw a black child about my age standing in the shadows, dressed in a frilly taffeta dress of iridescent blue. It was my dress! I was certain of it! There couldn't be another party dress like that anywhere. And then I realized Mama must have given it to this child's mother when I outgrew it. The little girl was wearing one of my hand-me-downs. And to my horror, her ice cream cone was dripping all over the delicate, tissue-like fabric.

Crystal clear, the memory hovered in my brain, replaying the thoughts I'd had as I stood there, feeling haughty and superior. Why, she doesn't even know that's a party dress! I'd thought. She doesn't know that's not the kind of dress you wear to go out for ice cream.

The memory stung.

With its pain came understanding. The little girl standing in the shadows with her dripping ice cream cone had worn what she had. As I would do this night.

I dressed without enthusiasm.

I viewed myself in the mirror and tried to summon some feelings of anticipation for this, my first formal dance. The dress wasn't ugly, it was just too old-looking for me, and I felt self-conscious. Frothy petticoats covered the lacy garter belt Mama had bought me to hold up my first pair of nylon stockings. Layers of net and chiffon swished as I walked downstairs to take Laddie's arm, as I had been taught to do, and together we climbed into the car. Mama smiled at me over her shoulder as she pulled the car out of the driveway.

"Stay close to Laddie," she instructed me as we approached the doorway of the large hall where scores of young girls and boys stood watching each other. "He may not have any partners, so you will have to dance with him."

"I will, Mama," I answered.

Laddie was too shy to ask anyone to dance, and neither Mama nor I could bear to think of him standing alone like a wallflower. And so we danced together, dazzling the other couples with our style. Laddie and I had partnered each other in all the Cotillion classes, and we had learned to move together like a youthful version of Rogers and Astaire. One distinct difference, however, was that Laddie always expected me to take the lead. So, mimicking Fred and Ginger, we whirled and glided across the dance floor, leaving a gaping crowd in our wake. Soon, a crowd of boys lined up to dance with me, and Laddie did indeed have to stand alone.

It was a new experience for me to be sought out, to be treated as though I were beautiful. No one would have guessed I was only twelve years old. I was uncomfortable with all the fuss, and I was appalled by the fact that the boys' fathers asked me to dance as well. But to Mama, it was a night of triumph. Finally, she had managed to pull me up onto the first rung of the ladder leading to her idea of success. But when the evening was over, I was exhausted and miserable.

The memory of Mr. Simpson's hands on me hung about me like a shroud, robbing me of the innocent joy I should have been able to feel while waltzing with a charming, attentive partner. I was twelve years old, and I longed to be innocent and carefree, but those emotions were lost to me, and I would never be able to reclaim them.

Not long after my transformation from ugly duckling to beautiful swan, Mama contracted pernicious anemia. Both she and her doctors were convinced she was near death. She spent weeks in the hospital, desperately ill. Daddy's full care fell to Laddie and me.

Laddie and I were terrified Mama would die. We prayed and begged God to make her well. Her recovery was slow and frightening. For months, she was too weak and ill to work, but the force of her personality still dominated our family. She determined that it was time to enroll me in finishing school, the best finishing school, and nothing could be said to dissuade her.

We had no money saved and certainly nothing extra for such a superfluous expense, but Mama insisted. Finishing school for her daughter was not a luxury but an essential. Undeterred by the condition of our family finances, she arranged for a bank loan to pay for my tuition at an exclusive modeling and finishing school. From her sick bed, she made all the arrangements, and I could not argue with her.

"You will have the best, Mitty," she told me. "It doesn't matter what else we have to sacrifice, you will have the best. If I don't recover, you must be able to make a living. I can't leave you unless I know I have provided you with every opportunity to excel."

Again, guilt settled on me heavily. What about Laddie? I wondered. I felt so bad I could hardly bear to look at him. Mama's full attention was focused on me. She willingly did without, as did my brother and father, so that there would be enough money for me to learn the proper way to sit, to walk, to stand, to converse at dinner, and to be the perfect hostess. It was all so foolish to me, but I had no voice strong enough to raise against Mama's. I did whatever she instructed me to do.

Always in the back of my mind, fighting with the inequity of Mama's decisions, was the thought that maybe she knew what she was doing. Maybe, after I had been trained and schooled and polished to a high gloss, I would be able to help my father. Maybe I could be the instrument to bring the light back into his eyes. Maybe I could accomplish the impossible... maybe I would be a part of the miracle we so desperately needed.

And, ironically, while I was in finishing school and Mama was so ill, Daddy did seem to get better. Like Rip Van Winkle, he awoke from his long reverie, discovering that he had a wife and children. At that time, I interpreted Daddy's improvement as a response to my blossoming beauty and budding talent. I believed my achievements, small as they might be, did indeed play a part in his healing.

Now, I know differently.

Now, I understand that Daddy suffered from the mental illness defined as manic-depressive disease with psychosis. Shortly after our arrival in California, his illness thrust him into a long period of deep depression that spanned most of those first three years in our new home. So deep was the pit of his depression, so tortured his distant thoughts, we had believed he was incapable of ever emerging from them. And yet, almost as suddenly as he had fallen, he climbed up onto a level plane—or what we believed was a level plane.

Though I secretly claimed the credit for his remarkable "recovery," I know now that the change in Daddy was just another manifestation of his insidious disease. It was not my mild social successes but rather the trauma of my mother's life-threatening illness that triggered a manic phase that proved to be as frightening and destructive—if not more so—than his long, depressed state had been.

In its early stages, however, Daddy's manic phase manifested itself as a kind of miracle. Alert and talkative, where before he had been silent and catatonic, Daddy began to talk about going back to Five Oaks. He began to insist that we travel back together to see the old home place.

Mama wasn't really well enough to travel yet. She was terribly weak. But none of us could resist the idea of going home. It had been so long since we had seen the beloved house on Center Street, and Dogwood Creek, and the great oaks that guarded Grandmother's stately white house with its green shutters. But just as compelling to us was the sight of Daddy's liveliness. It had been so long since he had recognized us or shown any interest in life outside his room. How could any of us deny him his request?

During the first three years of our exile in California, I know of only two occasions when Daddy pulled himself out of the abyss long enough to communicate with his family. The first occurred when Mama showed him a picture she had had taken of Laddie and me. Our family could no longer afford to commission a portrait, as had been the Collinsworth custom for generations. But she had managed to save enough money to pay a professional photographer to take our picture. One day, she walked into Daddy's room and found him sitting in his rocker, staring at the photograph of his children, tears spilling from his eyes.

"What is it, Minor?" Mama asked, touching him tentatively. "Minor? What's wrong?"

Daddy hadn't spoken in a long time, so she was surprised to hear him answer, "Can't you see it, Pauline?"

With his long, aristocratic fingers, Daddy touched our faces in the photo. "Look at our children, Pauline... Look at their eyes... What have we done to our children?"

"I don't know what you're talking about," Mama answered, drawing back as if Daddy had struck her.

"Look at the pain in their eyes," Daddy said. "Can't you see how we have harmed them?"

"Our children are fine," Mama answered firmly.

In the darkness of his madness, Daddy had found a spot of light and lucidity. Gazing through it, he could see what Mama, in her denial, could not or would not see. She took the photograph from his hands, carried it downstairs and returned it to its prominent place in the living room.

On another day, when Daddy seemed too far away to be reached, Mama brought home a stray dog that someone had dumped near her school. It was a mongrel, a beagle and hound mix of reddish color, and it looked a lot like Daddy's childhood dog, Old Gus.

"Minor," Mama said, stepping into Daddy's room and holding out the wriggling bundle, "look what I've brought you."

The dog made a soft sound and Daddy looked up. His eyes focused on the dog and his arms reached out to take it from Mama.

"It's Gus... It's Old Gus... " he said, over and over again, his face bent over the wriggling dog to accept its wet kisses and gentle nibblings.

Mama and Laddie and I stood in the doorway, watching Daddy and "Gus." For years, Old Gus would sit on Daddy's lap and sleep on his bed, never leaving his side, supplying the comfort and companionship Daddy could not accept from any other source.

The picture of Daddy's delight that day had embedded itself in our minds. I think we would have done anything to make him that happy again. As soon as Mama was able to travel, we began the long pilgrimage back to Five Oaks.

It was the summer of 1959. The journey was a terrifying one. Although Mama had given Daddy money to outfit our old used car with new tires, he had bought cheap retreads instead. All four tires blew out before we reached Barstow. Engine problems plagued us every mile of the trip.

Controlled by the manic phase of his illness, Daddy's earlier talkative behavior, which had so delighted us at first, degenerated into restless agitation, quick fury, and an unreasonable, demanding attitude. Throughout the long, hot trip, he refused to stop except for gas and the necessary repairs, driving straight through from California to Arkansas. He drove with maniacal speed, often darting among cars and erratically changing lanes. At times, Mama and Laddie and I were certain we would all be killed in a fiery crash on the highway.

We arrived at Five Oaks totally exhausted—except for Daddy, that is. His trauma-induced manic state empowered him with a sense of exhilaration and feelings of sheer indomitability. He needed neither food nor sleep. As soon as we reached the property, he leaped from the car and hurried across the lawn toward the creek.

The dogwoods had finished blooming already, but the fields were green with the promise of life. The huge oak trees shaded the porch where I had stood and waited for Daddy's summons every spring. I watched as he walked away from us and toward Dogwood Creek, wondering if he would turn and call to me, wondering if he remembered the ritual.

Daddy was intent on only one thing. He had to make contact with the trees and the earth. I stood and watched him disappear into the woods alone.

Mama and Laddie and I visited the old brick house on Center Street. I had to steel myself not to sob openly when I saw the abuse the renters had inflicted on the house we loved so well. The gardens were overgrown with weeds. Deep scratches marred the lovely wood floors, and filthy hand prints stained the walls. Mama walked through the rooms, assessing the damages. She had refused to sell the house when we left, believing we would return soon and live there again. Naively, she had believed that anyone who lived in the house would love it as she had. Never had she imagined it would be treated with such disrespect.

Still, Mama was not ready to sell the house. She arranged for some repairs to be made and walked out with her back stiff and straight, not daring to look back as the door closed behind her.

We returned to California and the manor house in Charter Oak. If I had been disappointed in it before, I now felt a kind of loathing for it. How could I ever have believed it was like the old brick house on Center Street? In spite of the agony endured in our childhood home, we had known some measure of peace and tranquillity there. Not so in the manor house. While there may have been some good times enjoyed within its walls, the stench of Mr. Simpson permeated the air. Echoes of my father's wailing haunted its rooms. I could never love the house built among the citrus groves as I loved the house on Center Street. Perhaps I would never love any house as well.

That summer, after we returned home from Arkansas, Daddy's manic state continued unabated. His belligerent, aggressive, sometimes violent presence, ruled the household. I dubbed the old manor house "Sunnybrook," finding a perverse kind of irony in its comparison to the blithe and congenial farm in the Shirley Temple movie, where all of little Rebecca's dreams came true. For Laddie and me, dreams usually degenerated into nightmares, filled with the sounds of angry, shrill voices and my mother's quiet sobbing.

Still, something of a child's defiant optimism lived deep inside me, despite the ugliness that scarred my hopes. Something within me still clung to the belief that there was such a thing as a second chance. That someday I would find a healing, perhaps even a rebirth.

Chapter 6

My life pivoted oddly after we made the long journey home to Arkansas, to that familiar and well-loved part of the country that had given us our identity. While once that place had been like the strong axis of my spinning existence, it now seemed to do little more than cause a painful, stabbing wound.

The proverbial "poor relations," we had arrived at Five Oaks bringing with us the humiliation that had driven us away three years earlier. Our family had received us with some embarrassment and had sent us on our way again with apologies and the assurance of their continuing prayers.

The journey had given us no balm, no healing. But I could not release myself from the belief that someday, somehow, we would be able to return to our family home and find peace. The old brick house on Center Street was my Mecca, and in my heart I fled there often, expecting it to contain some kind of special miracle for me: a miracle that would restore our family to health and happiness.

I know now that there was never any possibility of healing in the simple act of travel. My father's condition could not be cured by a pilgrimage to the home of his ancestors. Nor should Mama, Laddie, and I, with our own individual injuries, have expected healing to be found in the shade of mighty oak trees or on the wide porch of an old brick house on a quiet street in Searcy, Arkansas.

Healing, for me, would be slow in coming.

In September 1960, I became a teenager and left behind the habit of hiding my body under bulky layers of clothing. Perhaps it was because I noticed that other girls' bodies had begun to develop by then also—I was not the only girl who had arrived at that fateful place called puberty. That, coupled with the influence of Mama, caused me to let go of the compulsion to hide myself. Mama continually assured me that she believed I was beautiful. She told me I was talented and destined to achieve. Finally, I began to believe her.

At the age of thirteen, I embarked on a professional dance career. It all came about rather naturally. Jerry Singer, the owner of the Jerry Singer Studios, saw me dance on several occasions, and, thinking I was probably sixteen or seventeen, asked me to work for him as a teacher for his younger students.

It was a great honor to become associated with such a prestigious chain of dance studios, and Mama, of course, was delighted. She took me to the labor department office to inquire about the child labor laws. I became the only child in my junior high school to have a work permit. School administrators agreed to release me from classes half an hour early each afternoon. A car and driver from the studio arrived at school to pick me up and drive me to one of three different studios located in the San Gabriel Valley. Eventually, I would join Mr. Singer at his Los Angeles studio, working with him to teach the children of the film industry.

For a youngster who had once been the worst student in dance class, it was heady stuff for me to be sought after as a teacher for the respected Jerry Singer Studios. His name had been linked with some of the best dancers in the entertainment business. And now mine would be linked with his.

While it was a step worth celebrating, it was also a step that forced me to face a fact I had been trying to ignore for several months: I would never be the prima ballerina Mama had dreamed I would be. It wasn't for lack of training—my training was the best. It wasn't that I couldn't make the leaps and pirouettes with grace and style—sheer determination sent me soaring. I could technically perform the role of Giselle and the "Dance of the Sugar Plum Fairy" from *The Nutcracker*. I could render a powerful, tragic dying swan from Tschaikowsky's *Swan Lake* ballet. I was more than proficient (some had called me brilliant) as a dancer, and with proficiency had come confidence and the passion that had been lacking in earlier years. And although I had worried about my visual impairment interfering with my eye-hand coordination and depth perception, I had been able to overcome even that obstacle. It was my shape in a tutu that defeated me.

I knew as soon as I saw Margot Fonteyn dance that she had something I would never have: a flat chest. She was reed-thin in her costume the night I watched her dance with Rudolph Nureyev several months after his defection from the Soviet Union. Together, they were exquisite. As soon as Mama heard they were scheduled to appear in Los Angeles, she ordered front-row seats. I sat mesmerized throughout their performance of *Giselle*. Never had I seen such beauty and grace. Never had I seen such perfection.

Later, back in the studio, with the stereo volume turned up, I danced alone, swaying and leaping and turning, trying to imitate Dame Margot's graceful yet electrifying motion. I studied myself in the mirrors on the wall and watched my every step, every movement, as I spun away into the vortex of the music. I tried to mimic her gestures and her look of total absorption in the mystery of the dance. I copied her hairstyle, containing my long, heavy hair in a ballerina's bun on the back of my head. But I couldn't contain my breasts. And prima ballerinas aren't allowed to be buxom.

It's a matter of balance, and I understand that. But oh, how it hurt to have to acknowledge that my own body had betrayed me. After all those years of working to subordinate it, commanding my limbs to obey both mind and music—of stretching and leaping and training until my muscles felt as if they would melt or explode—it was that body which robbed me of my dream (and Mama's) to be a ballerina.

At about that time I began to notice that other dance forms did not require the same rigid body standards as the ballet. Ann-Margret, with her voluptuous figure, was having great success in both Broadway and movie musicals. She had both talent *and* curves, and she represented hope for dancers like me who needed more than a bra with an "A" cup!

Making a quick adjustment in my career goals, I set my sights on Broadway. I decided to become one of Broadway's long-legged "gypsies"—a dancer who moves from show to show. The years I had studied classical ballet didn't go amiss, however. All those lessons with private coaches served as the perfect complement for the jazz and tap and acrobatics that rounded out my dance training. I performed with style and flawless technique. And Mama's years of encouraging creativity of thought and expression proved to be fertile ground for my budding talent as a choreographer.

Putting dance steps to music was, for me, both effortless and satisfying. With the motions of my body I could create a mood or tell a story, and I sensed the unspoken response of audiences. Jerry Singer encouraged me in this talent and entrusted me with several choreography assignments. When I was fourteen, he allowed me to choreograph the production of *Pinocchio* at his Los Angeles Children's Theater.

Such exhilaration I felt during those exciting days at the theater!
I loved teaching. I loved the children. And I loved being a part of
the fantasy world of entertainment. Sometimes I went alone to
the studio and there, surrounded by the mirrors and the barre
and the pulsing sound of the music, I danced until I sent myself
flying off into a secret world. I could hear Mama's voice telling
me to "look at the world through magic eyes," and so that's what
I would do. With the aroma of sweat and alum powder in my
nostrils, I stretched and leaped and whirled until I was too tired
to stand. And I escaped the reality of life at home.

Dance now offered me respite, unlike those earlier years when
it had been a source of pure agony for me. My life began to
change in other ways as well. My schoolwork improved—except
in math and science, where I continued to founder—and I
discovered I had a natural aptitude for speech. This pleased Mama
immensely, as she herself had been such a gifted speech student.

My mother's enthusiasm for fine oratory paralleled a national
interest that seemed reborn in 1960–61, with the emergence of
John F. Kennedy as a presidential candidate. His entrance into
the national political scene brought a new appreciation for
language and rhetoric. For decades, no one had stood and
addressed the country with such eloquence and style. Even those
opposed to his political beliefs had to applaud his oratorical skills.
I'll never forget the day of his inauguration in January 1961.

It was a school day, but Mama kept Laddie and me home to
watch the event on television. "History is being made," she told
us, "and I want you to witness it."

I remember sitting, rapt, in front of the television, completely
charmed by the gray-eyed young man who stood before the nation
with his beautiful wife. He spoke eloquently about honor and
duty:

"Ask not what your country can do for you. Ask what you can
do for your country."

My interest in politics was probably more keen than that of
most thirteen-year-old girls. Since earliest childhood, I had listened
to the stories about "The Honorable James Collinsworth," whose
signature is on the Declaration of Independence of the Republic
of Texas. During his political career he ran for president of the
Republic of Texas, was elected Secretary of State, and was appointed
and served as the first Chief Justice of the Supreme Court of the
Republic of Texas. For generations our family had produced
governors, senators, state representatives, state and county

commissioners, judges, mayors, and legions of lawyers. Politics had long been a popular subject of discussion in the Collinsworth household.

That January day I was fascinated by the pomp and ceremony on the television screen. Mama had taught me the power of words and the importance of what she called "presence," and it seemed to me that John F. Kennedy personified those two qualities. I would never forget the sight of our youngest president standing there on the dais, nor the sound of his voice, nor the strength of his words as he delivered his inaugural address to the nation.

To say Mama took great pride and pleasure in my speech successes is an understatement. She also delighted in taking credit for my talent, believing I had inherited my natural ability from her. With true Mama-like determination, she took me in hand. When it came time to register me for high school in September 1961, she enrolled me in the college preparatory curriculum with an emphasis on speech courses.

With Mama as my coach at home, coupled with the instruction I received at school, I developed rapidly into an able speech competitor, claiming prizes in extemporaneous speech, original oratory, and debate.

Often, I would pull out an old picture of Mama from her college days. Her red hair arranged in soft, fingered waves, she was leaning against a banister, looking beautiful and perfect, like a heroine from an F. Scott Fitzgerald novel. She was the epitome of classic, casual elegance. I envisioned her standing tall and erect behind a podium in an auditorium, delivering her prize-winning speeches in front of a panel of judges who were overwhelmed by her perfection. The idea of following in her footsteps held great appeal for me.

My Southern drawl, which had been such a source of embarrassment to me when we first arrived in California, became a great asset. The years of California living had allowed a bit of a Western accent into my speech, and Mama set out to correct that immediately. She knew somehow that the soft, cultured style of the South carried a special ability to charm. She was right. The judges loved it. I won every contest I entered in my first year of high school. In a very short time, I moved up to compete against students in older age groups.

My life became a blur of activity, with my studies, speech and debate practice, tournaments, and dance filling every minute of each day. Yet it seemed the more that was asked of me, the better

I performed. And, of course, I continued to mistakenly conclude that my father's current lucid, if manic, condition was directly related to my achievements.

Daddy no longer confined himself to his room and his rocking chair. At night, when I returned home from the dance studio laden with that day's homework assignments, I worked with Mama on the speeches I would deliver in the next tournament. And Daddy sat nearby, listening, as Mama commented on my every intonation, corrected my posture, and critiqued every gesture. He never spoke or applauded, but I always looked toward him, hoping for some sign of his approval, some sign of his love.

When I began entering and winning beauty contests during my sophomore year of high school, I found that I had not only my father's approval but also his attention, to an almost obsessive degree.

As many good Southern daughters did, I grew up believing that a tiara, a banner, and a beauty title are among life's essential possessions. I put up no argument when Mama entered me in my first beauty pageant. And as I watched my father's growing interest in my success, I determined to do everything I could to win. Every trophy, every success, was an antidote to Daddy's illness, I believed, as well as the fulfillment of the promise I'd made to him so many years ago on the driveway of the Arkansas mental institution.

With my successes both as a world-class competitor in speech and as a beauty queen, I was single-handedly restoring to him and to our family the dignity that had been lost to us on that awful day years earlier. Every prize I won, every trophy I claimed, went toward settling the huge debt of honor that had been levied against us so long ago when white-shirted hospital attendants had bound my father in restraints and dragged him away from us.

Hiding in my psyche, along with the belief that I was healing my father, was the fear that, if my success started to wane, my father's condition would again deteriorate, spiraling him back down into the darkness of depression. And so I drove myself to achieve, to excel, to win the prize in every endeavor, to keep from losing him again. And he seemed to reward my frenzied efforts by making me the focus of his total attention.

I have only recently begun to assimilate the memories of this period of my life, and to recognize that Daddy was completely lost in psychotic mania during this time. What had begun in the summer of 1959 as a sort of awakening to the reality of his family soon became a full-blown psychotic episode, with all the behavior typical of this phase of the disease.

During this time, Daddy believed he was indomitable. He returned to the workplace, accepting a high-level accounting position with a prestigious auto dealership. Soon he was handling the accounts for several dealerships under one ownership. And he insisted that Mama relinquish all the household finances to him. In time, this would prove to be the most costly decision she would ever make.

Daddy's manic behavior caused him to lose one job after another, but his brilliance as an accountant—and as a manipulator—always enabled him to find another, even more prestigious, position. He continued to climb, spiraling into the upper echelon of the automobile business in Los Angeles, where his pay reflected his high status in the industry.

It should have been a time of financial recovery for our family, but because Daddy's logic and behavior were controlled by his mania, it was instead a period of great strain for my mother. Daddy exercised no judgment in the spending of large sums of money, and became outraged whenever Mama asked him for an accounting of the family's finances. Irritable, unreasonable, and deluded by his own sense of power, Daddy ruled our household with tyrannical force.

Medical science now understands that manic-depressive disease has many sub-categories. Daddy suffered from what has been labeled Bipolar I, the most classic form of manic depression. The symptoms he exhibited throughout his life could have been dictated onto a page in a medical textbook, even to the most shameful and heartbreaking behavior: sexual promiscuity.

In Daddy's manic state, which lasted throughout my high school years, he not only felt invincible, he believed he was accountable to no one—not even his wife and children.

I can forgive Daddy for the pain he inflicted upon us, because I know he had no clear sense of what he was doing. His manic phase gripped him until he was delusional. He went long periods without sleep, finally collapsing in exhaustion, only to awaken to overwhelming agitation and confusion. He ate little, worked as though wired to a nuclear substation, and communicated with his family almost exclusively in terms of rage, abuse, and belligerence.

Until recently, my mind blocked out all of these horrendous memories.

What I chose to remember was that Daddy was there, in both mind and body, throughout my high school years. He was there when I walked the beauty pageant runway, bedecked in banner and tiara. He was there for the speech tournaments and the debates and the awarding of every trophy. He was there to cheer me on, to congratulate me, to carry home the spoils of victory. And I believed my winnings kept him there with me. Without them, I thought, he would descend back into his private hell.

I remember him traveling with me to various pageants throughout the region. In the beginning, he sat near the front during the competitions and watched intently, totally absorbed by my presence on the runway. I loved being the focus of his attention and the source of his pride. Before long, however, his interest became obsessive, and I crossed the runway to find my father seated behind the pageant judges, holding scorecards just like the ones the judges used. He scored me in every category of competition, holding up his card for me to see, telling me in front of the world whether or not he approved of my performance.

What I refused to remember until recently were the episodes of violent quarreling that went on in our home almost continually for nearly four years. In the last few years, when I dug back into the far recesses of my mind, I found painful memories of Daddy's fury and his unreasonable behavior. I found conversations my mind had recorded and then tried to erase, conversations that revealed my father's extreme, delusional psychotic mania. I found memories of abuse heaped on my brother Laddie at a time in his life when what he needed most in the world was a loving, understanding father.

For years, Laddie had allowed me to occupy center stage with Mama, and now I had Daddy's attention as well. Day after day throughout his life, Laddie had spent hours sitting on a hard bench in a dusty dance studio, watching "baby sister" perform. And he rarely complained. Only once, succumbing to extreme frustration, did Laddie shriek at me, "When I grow up, if I ever have a kid who wants to take dance lessons, I will kill it and tell the Lord it died!"

I remember one night Laddie tried to kiss Daddy goodnight. He approached Daddy quietly and leaned forward to embrace him. With a rough push that would have flattened a bear cub, Daddy thrust his son away from him. Then he shouted to Mama, "Damn it, Pauline! Every time I think the little bastard's going to grow up and be a man, he does something sissy like this!"

Laddie, stunned and humiliated, regained his balance and walked quietly into his room, shutting the door behind him. He vowed never to try to get close to Daddy again.

Throughout this time of confusion and abuse within our home, I continued my pursuit of perfection. And Mama aided me. She added voice lessons to my curriculum. I had two coaches: one for classic operatic technique and the other for musical comedy and live theater. Believing that every well-bred young lady should be able to play the harp, she searched for a harp teacher for me as well. (Thank God she never found one!) And when I turned sixteen, she allowed me to begin working as a professional dancer in a dinner theater called the Diamond Horseshoe.

The Diamond Horseshoe scheduled performances Thursday through Sunday, with a matinee, dinner, and late show on Saturdays. The first act was a musical melodrama, set in the Old West. Elaborate stage sets created the scene of an old-time saloon. During intermission, the Old West disappeared and the stage became a 1960s nightclub, complete with psychedelic lighting and blaring music. Dancers performed larger-than-life production numbers and then changed quickly for bawdy, vaudeville blackout skits much like the ones seen on television's "Laugh-In" a few years later.

On stage with other tall, buxom dancers, I was the youngest girl in the chorus line, though no one would have suspected it. At sixteen, I was the baby of the company. And because I was so young, the law required that an official representative from the Child Labor Department be present in the dressing room for all my performances.

Each night, as we dressed for our shows, a somber, conservatively dressed matron mingled backstage among the chattering, stretching, long-limbed dancers. She chaperoned my actions, checked the number of hours I worked, and made certain I was not being corrupted by the atmosphere.

The shows were considered "family" entertainment, but they were still somewhat risqué. In the musical melodrama, I played the part of a saloon girl named "Honey Babe." Dressed in fishnet stockings and a sequined "merry widow," I sang and danced "The Pick-Pocket Waltz." In that number, I was supposed to select a man from the audience, bring him up on stage and sing to him while pulling funny stage props out of his suit pockets and pants. It was a funny, sexy number, and I did it well, using all the feminine wiles that an 1880s dance-hall girl would have used.

And when I took off my costume later, I took off all the mannerisms of a flirtatious dancer, reverting quickly to the little girl I had never had a chance to be.

Confusion reigned in my thoughts throughout those years of dancing and singing and walking the pageant runway. On one hand, I loved the attention and the opportunity to perform. I shivered with excitement in those moments just before the curtain rose on the chorus line at the Diamond Horseshoe. The sound of the first bars of music, the backstage "shh-shh-ing," the last-minute costume check—all this was exhilarating. Even the playful interaction with men in the audience was fun for me. But when it was over, I felt sad and scared.

At no time was this confusion more poignant than on my sixteenth birthday, when I asked for a cake with a ballerina on it. It was more suited to a little girl than a teenager, I knew, but perhaps that was why it appealed to me. When I was alone with my thoughts, I hugged myself and reveled in the fact that I was "sweet sixteen and never been kissed." It was ironic after what I had suffered from Mr. Simpson, but that was the one part of my body he had not violated—my last vestige of innocence.

During my sixteenth year, I began to take special notice of the social and political climate around me. What a fascinating period of time that was! The presence of American troops in a tiny Southeast Asian country was beginning to be questioned; the issue of civil rights roared throughout the country, its voice sounding loudest in the Southern states. Desegregation versus individual states' rights was debated in every forum, from the high school level up to the U.S. Congress.

Being a member of the debate team and competing in original oratory and impromptu speech, I had to study these national issues by the hour. The subject of states' rights and desegregation, I discovered, intrigued me. I could debate either side of the issues adequately, but I was most convincing when I took up the defense of states' rights and opposed desegregation. Passionately attacking the liberal point of view, I became the "Southerner's Southerner," offering brilliant, if misguided, rebuttals to the civil rights movement.

A daughter of the South, I was the great-granddaughter of plantation owners who had worked their land with the sweat of slaves. My mama and daddy had instilled in me a great pride in my Confederate heritage. My kinship with the South bound me to notions that were generations deep, and I found I could not easily dismiss them. Making myself into a caricature of the typical Southern belle, I defended the position of the historic South and drew my own Mason-Dixon line across Southern California. When the television blared with the reports of lunch-counter demonstrations and the arrest of Dr. Martin Luther King in Birmingham, Alabama, I watched unmoved.

I know now that more complex dynamics were in force than just the fact of my heritage. I was angry, unhappy, and confused, as are most individuals who are held in the grip of bigotry. The horror of my home life was a breeding ground for unreasonable hostility and fear. Repressed emotions from home spilled over into the hatred and prejudice I spouted at school. But I understood none of this at the time. I only knew I was angry, and that when I spoke with carefully tutored eloquence, people listened.

I used my power as a thespian and an orator to proclaim my prejudiced views. My peers viewed me as unusual, controversial, outspoken. I reveled in their attention, believing I was "special," but in reality, I was nothing more than a racist. In my heart I knew I was wrong—I had felt the sting of discrimination myself— but I relegated that memory to a distant place. It took the death of the president to startle me into seeing myself as the person I was: the ultimate Southern bigot.

I remember that day in November 1963, when the principal's voice spoke over the intercom system, announcing that the president had been shot. I was in U.S. History class, and my teacher, Mr. Fox, turned to us with a stunned expression on his face. With tears streaming from his eyes, he suggested that we bow our heads and recite the Lord's Prayer together. School was dismissed, and I rushed home and kept vigil in front of the television set for the next three days, watching the funeral and every news report on the assassination.

Unexpected emotions flooded me as I watched our nation mourn its young president. I felt suddenly ashamed of being a Southerner, as though we represented the nation's recalcitrant children, with our noisy temper tantrums over civil rights and desegregation. In my youthful thinking, it seemed to me that we had heartily contributed to our country's violent climate—a climate in which a president could be gunned down in a motorcade on a public roadway on a bright, sunny afternoon in a Southern city.

I remembered a childhood event that I hadn't thought about in years. I remembered standing under the branches of "the whipping tree," where slave owners used to tie their slaves and punish them with the tongue of a whip. The Cole family owned the property where the old tree stood, and their son, Ritchie, a student at the Collinsworth's Little Red School House, took Laddie and me to see the legendary oak that stood alone on the hill behind his home. Together, the three of us had gazed with curious horror at the gnarled old tree.

Legend said that the sap which oozed from it was really the blood of a young slave girl who had been whipped to death by a wicked owner. With my eyes shut tightly, I could imagine her limp body sagging against the rough bark of the tree. Evil seemed to rise up out of the ground in that place. We ran away from it as though demons chased us.

How could I have forgotten that sense of horror and wickedness? I wondered. How could I ever have defended the mindset of the segregationist—a mindset shaped by hatred and racial arrogance? I forced myself to look again at the memory of the whipping tree, and then I looked at myself, and what I saw sickened me.

Guilt bore down on me. I abruptly changed course. I walked away from my role as a bigot and documented my change of heart by writing an essay about the sense of personal guilt and grief I felt over the death of President Kennedy. All my feelings of responsibility and regret spilled onto the page. My viewpoint, as a sixteen-year-old, oversimplified a complex national tragedy, but I truly believed that my inflammatory and insensitive behavior toward others had played a part in the president's death, as if I had symbolically loaded the weapon that killed him. When I turned in the essay to my teacher, he was deeply moved by it and read it at a memorial assembly.

Soon after I joined the dance company at the Diamond Horseshoe, Mama designed a private studio for me in the old manor house. She had one side of the basement transformed into a professional rehearsal hall, complete with barres, mirrors, and state-of-the-art stereo. With my very own rehearsal hall, I could rehearse and create choreography for my dance students at the Jerry Singer Studio.

I loved to create innovative and exciting choreography. I found escape from my own confusion when I lost myself in concentration and focused on the music and dance combinations. My basement studio became my refuge, a place where I could feel in control of my life. Only when I ventured upstairs did I realize how powerless I was, how controlled and utterly helpless I was in the face of the symptoms of my father's disease.

Life at home throbbed with the turbulence of an impending storm at all times. Mama and Daddy fought continually. Their hurtful words seared my heart.

Mama had discovered a delicate, cherry-wood piano in an antique store in Los Angeles. For months, she had admired it and had finally been able to save the amount needed to purchase it. She invited me to drive into Los Angeles with her to buy the piano. Daddy grew very agitated as we prepared to leave.

"I'll go with you," he insisted.

Mama and I looked at each other.

"I said I'll go with you!" he bellowed.

Mama nodded quietly and ushered me toward the car door.

The drive into the city was tense. Daddy spoke little, and Mama and I sat silent and still, as though waiting for his fury to erupt. Not until we reached the store did his unreasonable, deluded temperament explode. With rude, flamboyant behavior, he began bartering with the store owner, refusing to buy the piano for the asking price. Mama and I stood by, watching in embarrassment. We left without the piano.

On the drive home, Daddy began shouting and ridiculing Mama.

"If you insist on owning that damn piano," he rasped, "I'll send over one of the girls from my office to bargain for it. Those are real businesswomen," he said. "They know what they're doing... You're not smart enough to transact a business deal like that... You're too stupid!"

His voice rose, his gestures grew wild, and all the while Mama sat quietly, not defending herself, not arguing with him. When I saw her shoulders shake with silent sobs, I could sit still no longer.

"How dare you talk to Mama like that!" I shouted. "She has been quite capable of taking care of our family and keeping a roof over our heads every time you've been sick and unable to work. I certainly believe she is capable of buying a piano on her own right now!"

Daddy's jaw clenched. His eyes glinted with fury. Spittle gathered at the corners of his mouth. His arm whipped across the seat and he smacked me in the face, slamming me against the back seat of the car.

"Don't get smart with me, you little bitch," he shouted, "or I'll beat the hell out of you both right now!"

Later, Mama learned that the woman Daddy wanted to send to the store to barter for the piano was a woman he had been having an affair with.

This was not my father, I always told myself after an explosion of his abusive wrath. This was not the gentle, aristocratic man I had known as a tiny girl, the man whose long-fingered hands had written so beautifully and lovingly in my baby book; the man whose vivid blue eyes used to peer up into the gnarled oak branches at Five Oaks, his face solemn with pride and pleasure. This was someone else. This was the monster who took over my father's being, crushing the quiet, gentle man inside.

Now, with the knowledge that medical science has been able to provide, I know with certainty that the man who was abusive and angry and delusional in his manic behavior was not my father. And I understand that the meanness and chaos we witnessed in Daddy was not an evidence of his character. These were symptoms of the chemical imbalance in his brain, an imbalance that would never be corrected by medicine or treatment or psychotherapy.

Daddy was not wicked. He was sick.

Ironically, during that painful time of our lives, while Daddy was gripped in the manic phase, with only short, silent wanderings into bouts of depression, medical research was experimenting with a substance that, in time, would bring hope to many individuals with manic-depressive illness. But for Daddy, it would be too late.

In the early 1960s, lithium was being used as an investigational drug, and the psychiatric world was excited about its success in the treatment of manic-depressive disorders. But it was not approved by the Federal Drug Administration, and it could not be legally marketed in the United States at that time.[1]

Lithium had been the focus of some study and experimentation since 1949, when an Australian psychiatrist had inadvertently stumbled upon its ability to affect manic behavior in guinea pigs.[2] The road from experimentation to approved prescription doses for human patients was long and fraught with confusing data, conflicting medical opinions, and long legal delays. Although the American Psychiatric Association presented the results of a well-documented study by the New York State Psychiatric Institute in 1965, lithium would not be approved by the FDA until 1970. It would be yet another year before it would find its way into the daily medical regimen of manic-depressive patients.

While not considered a cure for manic-depressive illness, lithium is effective in controlling the disease in certain patients. Given Daddy's medical history, which indicates that he did not respond to *any* medication, I wonder if lithium would have been effective in his case. And knowing his paranoia, his terror of being medicated at all, I feel certain that he would have refused to take "the little beige pill"[3] that for so many manic-depressive patients has become the means of release from the bondage of their illness.

During the early 1960s, however, there was no option, except that of incarceration. And even that was a limited option. The laws of California allowed a family member to commit another family member to a mental hospital for evaluation, but patients could check themselves out after seventy-two hours. Mama feared that, if she committed him, Daddy would simply walk out of the hospital after the required seventy-two hours. He would disappear into the maze of city streets, never to be seen or heard from again

And so we endured, praying Daddy would slip back into a depressed state. Daddy was more dangerous to himself during deep depression, of course—his tendency toward suicidal behavior made us always wary. But it was our own safety we feared for when Daddy's condition was manic. He slapped away Mama's steady hand on household affairs, and our family tilted oddly off-center. Out of control in every phase of his personality, he moved through the motions of daily routine with dizzying starts and stops. We yearned for the respite afforded by his silent, catatonic state, but it was not to be. His manic phase continued unabated, except for a few short forays into a depressed state.

Good times did dot the landscape of my life during those years. I remember Daddy taking us to the symphony and to an occasional ballgame. These were tantalizing hints of what a "normal" teenager's life might have been, and they were too few, too rare, to ever be forgotten. After each of these special occasions, I would cling tightly to the false idea that Daddy was getting well, that we were going to be all right as a family. And then he would revert to the aggressive, abusive figure I had learned to fear.

I was still very skilled at playing peacemaker. Often I stepped in between Daddy and Mama or Daddy and Laddie, defending my father's unreasonable, outrageous behavior. Sometimes I turned against Mama and Laddie, exhibiting my own viciousness. Without realizing it, my own fragile psyche was slowly but steadily disintegrating. Self-imposed denial was all that was holding me together—that, and the compulsive, now almost obsessive, need to be perfect, to win at all costs.

Winning beauty pageants began to require more and more of me. In the talent category, I was always well-prepared and far ahead of the other contestants. Mama found the means to dress me in winning outfits. But, like the other girls I competed against, I worried incessantly about my weight. I dieted constantly, and if I felt just a bit too heavy as a pageant date approached, I did what all the other girls did: I took diet pills.

It began very innocently, or so I thought at the time. I asked Mama to help me "lose a few pounds." Immediately, she scheduled an appointment with a doctor whose name was mentioned often on the pageant circuit.

Young girls and hovering mothers filled the waiting room at the doctor's office. We all studied each other with wary eyes, knowing we were all present for the same reason: to obtain a prescription for pills that would help us achieve the weight that would enable us to win the upcoming beauty pageant. It was the thing to do.

What a tangled mess of contradictions my life was at that time! I still craved food as a form of comfort, a kind of link with the good times and good feelings that had been absent from my life for so long. Food was still my secret passion. I ate when I was sad, when I was nervous, when I was angry, and when I felt insecure or depressed. Then, guilt-stricken, I would increase my dance regimen to work off the forbidden calories. Diet pills offered an antidote for my compulsive eating habits, and so I ignored the fact that they made me jittery and irritable and unable to sleep at night. The only thing that mattered was that I look good in my gown and swimsuit on the day of the beauty pageant. Regardless of the cost, I had to be thin for the judges.

I battled daily with the bathroom scales. Eventually, those small skirmishes would escalate into a deadly warfare in which I would fight for my very survival.

In so many ways, my whole life was out of sync. I was not allowed to date, and yet a thirty-five-year-old man sent me a written proposal of marriage. He was a producer in the movie industry and had seen me perform. He wanted to marry me and manage my career. College boys from the nearby campus called the house continually, but Mama forbade me to go out with them.

Mama's edict concerning boys and dating did not stop me from enjoying my share of schoolgirl crushes, but I only "worshipped from afar." My experience with Mr. Simpson had left me terrified of any kind of physical contact. And because I had no healthy sphere of reference in the realm of emotional or physical love, I was actually glad of Mama's protection.

John Riggs was the only boy Mama allowed me to spend time with during high school. Because he attended the same Baptist church we attended, I suppose Mama believed he was all right. She let me sit in church with him and hold his hand when he walked me to the car after services. With the exception of the Christmas ball, those few moments with him were the only excursions I made outside of the social isolation Mama enforced.

Meanwhile, my work schedule continued to increase. The high school football coach decided that his team would play better football if they had ballet lessons. He asked me to teach them. The men's gymnastics coach also decided that ballet might contribute a missing ingredient to his budding Olympians, and he, too, asked me to teach a class at the gym.

I became a slave to the calendar and the clock.

Moments of whimsy didn't exist for me. I did not know the meaning of the word "spontaneous." Every hour of my day was obligated to someone, to some activity. Carefree, frivolous times were something I had no knowledge of. I had no time for playing, no time for relaxation, and no time for dating. Just as childhood had been lost to me, so was a normal adolescence. My life was scheduled and monitored by both my professional responsibilities and my formidable mother.

At this time, Laddie began to show some interest in the sports in which my father had excelled, perhaps in an effort to make a small space for himself in my father's heart. He joined the cross-country team and trained faithfully, but he came in dead last or next to last in every race. And Daddy ridiculed him as a failure.

It didn't matter that Laddie won academic honors for his outstanding scholarship, Daddy still berated him as worthless. In Daddy's deluded, manic thinking, there was no compensation for his son's miserable showing as an athlete. But Laddie wouldn't stop running. His defeats piled up, one after another, a growing heap of damning evidence that he was the loser his father said he was. Teammates and classmates added their cruel comments, making Laddie the brunt of their jokes. But still Laddie ran. Up early in the morning, he raced against the sunrise. At night, while I postured in front of the mirror, preparing for yet another walk down the pageant runway, he ran down the country roads that mitred the orange groves.

"He'll never win anything, Pauline," Daddy growled to Mama. Disgust twisted his face into an ugly mask. "You're slow! You're nothing! Give it up!" he shouted as Laddie returned home from races, defeated again and again.

Mama hadn't raised her children to be quitters. "You're Collinsworths," she had said, "and the Collinsworths do not give up!" She had preached it, and we believed it, but suddenly Mama questioned the truth of her own sermon. Is it possible that there are times when it is better to give up and walk away than to be continually knocked down? she wondered.

Every defeat Laddie experienced sent pain into Mama's soul. She shuddered when she thought of his embarrassment as he crossed the finish line last in every race. Was he subjecting himself to humiliation because of her stubborn edict? Did he believe she wouldn't allow him to quit? She finally asked him one day if he would like to consider leaving the team.

"Because the kids make fun of me for losing?" Laddie answered. "Is that what's bothering you—that they joke about me coming in last in every race? That doesn't bother me," he told her. "I'm not ashamed of losing, Mama. When I run, I run only against myself."

And so Laddie continued to run his solitary race into the sunset, and every morning he chased the dawn.

My junior year of high school was a frenzied roller-coaster ride as we rode out the ups and downs of Daddy's disease. For a time, he entered into a "Father Knows Best" phase, and like TV's Robert Young, he became a cheerful, if somewhat frenetic, presence in the house. Charming and verbose, he rekindled his interest in the Masons and accepted a position on the deacon board at the Baptist church we attended. He encouraged Mama to join the Eastern Star, shoved Laddie toward the DeMolays, and pushed me toward Job's Daughters.

During this time, we exhibited many of the outward signs of a healthy family. The many problems that existed were often subtle, barely troubling the surface of our family life. Other conflicts escaped my notice completely until many years later, when I felt compelled to unravel some of the mysteries left from that period.

Once, Daddy announced rather grandiosely that he had to buy an entire new wardrobe. I was delighted that he had taken an interest in his appearance. He would again have that handsome, aristocratic look that had been so attractive when he was younger, before his disease had ravaged him.

I couldn't understand why Mama seemed unduly stressed by Daddy's sudden compulsion to own new clothes. Surely we could afford it. I hadn't any idea of the price tag of a new wardrobe of business suits, but Daddy was working. He had stayed with the same company for some months now and even drove a company car. We had Mama's salary, Laddie worked part time, and I had been almost self-sufficient for nearly two years, with income from the Diamond Horseshoe and the Jerry Singer Studios. It never occurred to me that money might be in short supply. But it was, and I didn't learn the reason for many years.

Absorbed in my own whirl of activities, I hadn't observed the subtle signs of financial distress all around me. I knew Mama hadn't had any new clothes in a long time—the ones she wore were clean and mended, if not stylish—and she had made no large purchases since battling Daddy over the antique cherry-wood piano. But I did not notice anything else amiss. I had no knowledge of my father's spending habits. I would, however, learn soon enough the high cost of his manic delusions.

It was during this time of "normalcy" that my best friend, Kathy Patterson, wanted to move in and live with us. The daughter of divorced parents, Kathy had been bounced between her father in California and her mother in Kansas for as long as I had known her. Her idea of a healthy and normal family was colored by the pain of her own experience. To her, the old manor house looked like a safe haven. When both her mother and her father told her she was no longer welcome in their homes, Mama said we could make room for her in ours.

This wasn't the first time Mama had taken in a child who needed a home. She had always been drawn toward "strays." During the eight years before Laddie was born, when she was struggling with her fear that she might never have a child, she had made a place in her heart for a very different, very needy child, Charles Love.

Mama and Daddy were living in Tuckerman then, and Daddy would leave early every day to drive to his job at the cotton gin and return home late every evening. School was out for the summer, so Mama was home alone each day, passing the time caring for Daddy's championship hunting dog, Dixie, and Dixie's puppies, and working in the yard. One day as she was raking the leaves that fell from the huge magnolia in the front yard, a small black child approached her.

"'Scuse me, ma'am, you be lookin' for a boy to he'p you roun' the yard?" he asked.

"Well, fella," Mama answered, "what kind of work do you think you could do?"

"I could rake leaves, ma'am," the child answered.

Mama studied the little boy. Huge round eyes stared up at her from his thin face. He couldn't have been more than five or six years old. The rake was twice as tall as he was.

"What would your mama say?" Mama asked him.

"She wouldn't keer," he answered. "She be glad to git shut of me."

"What about your daddy?"

"He don' keer none. He be a preacher-man."

Mama told the child to go home and talk with his parents. In a little while, the boy returned, bringing his father with him.

"My boy says you be hirin' him to rake leaves," the father said, gripping the rim of his felt hat in large hands. He wore a suit and a tie, as if he were on his way to a Sunday service.

"I wanted to get your permission first," Mama answered.

"That be fine wid me."

"How long may he stay?" Mama asked.

"His mama ain't right," the man answered. "Keep him all day, 'cuz she hurts him."

And so, for that summer, Mama and Charles spent every day together. He arrived each morning and raked the leaves in the front yard. He played with Dixie's puppies, and in the afternoons Mama brought him into the house for a nap. He climbed into her lap to listen to her read stories until he fell asleep. Sometimes they made ice cream, and it was Charles' job to turn the crank on the freezer. He'd watch for the first spurts of ice cream to shoot up from the container, and then he'd shout, "It's arunnin' over, Miss Polly! It's arunnin' over!"

Mama lost track of Charles after she and Daddy moved from Tuckerman to Newport, but in Newport she found another soul to nourish.

His name was Rayburn Aaron, but Mama and Daddy nicknamed him Sonny. They learned about him from a missionary who visited their church and told a tale about a destitute family of five children. The mother had died of cancer and the father had begun drinking heavily. Four of the five children were living with relatives, but no one had welcomed the oldest, an eleven-year-old boy. Mama said she would take him.

Sonny was due to arrive from Little Rock by train on the same day that Mama had to be at a wedding reception for one of the young women in her Sunday school class. The day's schedule would be tight, but if she left the reception a few minutes early and hurried across town, she could get to the depot just in time to meet Sonny. She did, but arrived to find the train station empty.

Frantically, Mama searched the building for an eleven-year-old boy. Frightened that she had missed him and worried that he might have wandered away alone, she sat down to think about how best to find the child. Across the room, she noticed the top of a man's hat resting against the back of a bench. She walked around to the other side and discovered, under the man's hat, the face of a small, thin boy about eleven years old. Under the brim of the oversized hat, he slept peacefully. Mama's heart was immediately his.

Sonny's clothes were hand-me-downs from a much older boy, and like his hat, they were much too large for him. He was scrawny and underfed and his eyes, when she wakened him, were large and uncertain. In time, Mama would fatten him up and infuse him with the courage of a lion.

She took him home and led him into the room that would be his. She watched as he unpacked the only thing he had brought with him—a small, nearly crumpled box. From it he removed twenty-five cents, a small Bible, and some ribbons and dried flowers that had been part of a bouquet laid on his mother's grave.

For years, Sonny lived with Mama and Daddy. I have vague memories of his presence in our home when I was about two years old. Soon after that he graduated from high school and joined the Air Force. During the Korean conflict he was stationed in Germany, and I remember sending him packages of goodies from the kitchen in the old brick house on Center Street. He contacted Mama once, several years later, to tell her of his impending marriage.

Now, Mama's heart, still large and open for those in need, made room for my friend, Kathy.

I loved sharing my bedroom with Kathy and waiting up for her to return from her dates. We shopped together, drove to school together, and gushed over clothes and music and boys together. A year older than me, Kathy enjoyed privileges that were denied me, but it didn't matter. I wasn't jealous of her, I was just glad to have the presence of a "sister." And, in the beginning, Kathy loved being with us.

Daddy, though still in his manic phase, was generally pleasant and charming during Kathy's time with us. She saw little to disturb her or frighten her. Her own home life had exposed her to so much turmoil that she was not unnerved by the episodes of conflict that erupted in the old manor house. She seemed able to cope with our family's dysfunctional behavior—or perhaps she, too, lived in a state of constant denial. And when times were good, she shared in them like one of the family.

We loved it when Daddy took us to Dodger games with him. We ate "Dodger Dogs" smothered in mustard, and we giggled together and scanned the stadium for good-looking boys while Daddy watched the action on the diamond. Sometimes Daddy took us to the theater, Kathy on one arm, me on the other.

Mama accepted Kathy like a second daughter. Wild and tempestuous, Kathy may have reminded Mama of the girl she used to be. Both were intelligent and a little impulsive; both were creative and ingenuous. And they shared a kindred spirit. Kathy blended in as if she had been born a Collinsworth, joining us on excursions to the ballet, to museums, to art exhibits—to all the events Mama believed young ladies should appreciate and enjoy.

Before Kathy ever moved in with us, Mama explained the system at work in the Collinsworth household. The rules were few and they were simple: Kathy understood that she was expected to do her share of the chores, attend classes, and obey Mama. But Mama didn't understand Kathy's rule: that rules were made to be broken. Kathy made this achingly clear in a hurry, however.

Oh, how I envied Kathy her carefree, adventurous spirit! How surprised I was to learn that she envied me my dance ability and my job at the Diamond Horseshoe. When I mentioned to her that a new dance number in the show was going to require additional dancers, she asked me to work with her and train her—to get her ready for an audition.

While Kathy had some natural talent, she had had no formal training and so she had no technique. It would require lots of hours in the basement studio at the old manor house to ready

Kathy for a professional dance audition. I was willing to commit every spare hour to the task, but Kathy didn't take it quite so seriously. She wanted to practice only when it was "fun." In the end, however, her audition went well, and soon we were both dancing on the stage at the Diamond Horseshoe Theater.

One night, after a strenuous rehearsal, we stopped at a drive-in to get something to eat on the way home. Kathy began flirting with a group of boys nearby. Caught up in the fun, I completely forgot about the time. Suddenly, I realized we were going to arrive home past our curfew. Mama would be furious.

"Kathy, we've got to go," I whispered, trying to distract her attention from the good-looking boy she was making a date with for Saturday night.

"Kathy... Kathy, come on... "

"It's all right, Mitty, your mom will be in bed. She'll never even know what time we came in," Kathy answered.

"She'll know, Kathy!" I answered. "Please, you don't know Mama... "

"It's our first time to be late—she'll let it slide. You worry too much, Mitty," Kathy said, laughing up at the boy whose arm lay draped across her shoulders.

We arrived home a few minutes after midnight. We opened the big front door slowly and peered about the dark room. It was silent and empty. Breathing a sigh of relief, we giggled and headed for the stairs.

"Mitty and Kathy," came my mother's voice from overhead, "come up here immediately."

I gasped. Kathy groaned. Mama grounded us for two weeks.

Kathy wasn't used to restrictions, but she accepted the punishment without too much complaint. The punishment meted out to us a few weeks later, however, was not so easily endured.

It was early spring. Teenagers by the thousands migrated to the beaches in California to soak in the sun, play beach volleyball, and meet other golden-bodied teenagers. Only Kathy and I, it seemed, had responsibilities. We had to be in the theater, rehearsing for weekend performances. It was terribly unfair. And besides the restrictions on our time, our contract with the Diamond Horseshoe forbade us to get a suntan. Under the theater lights, tanned skin looked yellow, and so we had agreed, under contract, to keep out of the sun, to come to work with pale skin. On a brilliant, sunny, weekday morning during spring break, Kathy rebelled.

"Why don't we go to the beach today?" she suggested.

"Kathy! You know we can't do that!" I exclaimed. "We have to be at rehearsal this afternoon! If we show up with a tan—or worse, a sunburn—we could get fired!"

"They wouldn't fire us," Kathy said, reaching for her swimsuit. "Besides, we won't stay long enough to get tanned. We'll just meet some guys, have a little fun, and then go on to the rehearsal. No one will ever know."

Moments before, I'd been appalled by the suggestion, but suddenly it sounded like fun. We could pack our swimsuits in a bag with our leotards and Mama would never suspect... We could drive to the beach, play for a while, and then drive to the theater in time for rehearsal.

"Why not?" I thought.

Kathy and I drove to the beach with nothing but fun and adventure on our minds. For hours, we lay on towels under the bright sun without even a light smear of suntan lotion on our skin. We splashed in the surf and laughed with the boys who tried to convince us to go out with them later that night, and we paid no attention to the fact that our skin was growing pink. By the time we loaded the car and left the beach, we both realized we were seriously sun-scorched.

Kathy and I hurried from the car to the theater, hoping no one would see us before we could get to the dressing room and change into our leotards. Large water blisters had already begun to form on the backs of our legs and across our chests. We felt feverish one minute and shivered with chills the next.

"Don't worry," Kathy whispered to me, shoving me toward the dressing room door.

The director of the show caught us before we could hide under our practice leotards.

"What is this? What have you done!" he shrieked. He marched us in front of the entire cast. "You know I could fire both of you!"

Kathy and I stood mute and miserable, fighting nausea. "You've broken your contracts!" he shouted. Then with a wave of his hand, he dismissed us. "Get dressed, both of you!"

As we moved toward the dressing room door, he bellowed, "Put on your costumes! I'm going to dance you all night. The first one to collapse will be fired."

Costumes, not leotards. Cringing, I looked at Kathy and fought to hold back tears.

There would be no practice tights, no soft cotton or smooth

nylon against our burned skin. Instead, we pulled on tight-fitting fishnet stockings, and the threads dug deep into our blisters. My head ached and a roaring filled my ears. I fought to keep from vomiting while I danced and kicked in the chorus line. Then, as if he hadn't made us suffer enough, the choreographer sent the male dancers up on stage to go through a routine of lifts and tosses. I wanted to scream every time a hand gripped my arm or grasped my leg or circled my waist. I was only vaguely aware when Kathy slumped to the floor, unconscious. Two male dancers carried her off the stage, and she was fired on the spot.

I can't fall over... I can't pass out... I thought.

I flung myself into the music, praying I would be able to keep going.

I'll keep dancing if it kills me... What is Mama going to say?

Kathy and I were in agony when we arrived home later that night. Mama took both of us to the doctor the next day. He treated us with antibiotics for sun poisoning, and for the next few days, we were very sick girls.

It was a painful lesson, but one that I never forgot. Within the professional ranks, there is no room for mercy.

Shortly after the day on the beach, Kathy decided to move out of our home. I was devastated.

Not long after Kathy's departure, Daddy decided to return to Five Oaks for a visit.

It was spring, 1964. It was the time of year when Daddy became nostalgic about the old home place. He had an almost physical need to see the house with its green shutters and to walk through the forest of oak trees; to stand among the fields during planting and feel the pulse of life in the earth. He needed to break off a branch of dogwood and finger the blossoms, reviewing the legend, reminding himself of miracles.

Daddy was excited in the car as we drove him to the airport for his flight to Arkansas. He waved goodbye to us as he climbed the steps into the plane. It was the final gesture of sanity we would observe in him. When he reached Five Oaks a few hours later, his manic condition had begun to intensify to a psychotic level.

We knew something was wrong when Daddy stayed away longer than planned. He had a new job to come home to—all the paperwork was done and a shiny new company car awaited him. All he had to do was show up. But he lingered in Arkansas, watching the spring planting, hiking the shaded forests, while Mama worried and feared the worst.

One night, Aunt Vera called from Searcy. Daddy was completely incoherent. He had begun hallucinating, laughing and talking with people who were not present; walking, then running across Aunt Vera's back porch, gesturing wildly and saying things that made no sense to anyone. With the help of Uncle Hub, Aunt Vera had been able to quiet Daddy, and over the next few days they would try to subdue him enough to get him on a plane for California.

Mama declared a holiday on the day Daddy was due to arrive home. She cooked all his favorite dishes and put Laddie and me to work decorating the house with balloons, crepe-paper streamers, and a "Welcome Home" banner. Mama's party-like air was forced. I sensed a kind of pall hanging over all the festivities, but she kept up the ruse, pretending that this was going to be a wonderful homecoming. In my heart I knew something was terribly wrong. I'd been certain of it when Daddy refused to let us meet his plane at the airport. He wanted to ride the bus home alone.

Hours after he was due to arrive, Daddy walked into the house. With trembling hands, he dropped his bags near the front door beneath a sagging "Welcome Home" banner. Wilted balloons and drooping crepe-paper streamers hung about the house, eloquent, if pathetic, symbols of our deflated spirits. His voice was hollow when he spoke.

"Pauline, sell everything we own in Arkansas," he said. "I'm never going home again."

He turned and walked toward the stairs. Mama watched him in silence. Then, with tired motions, she began clearing away the dishes and the meal that had grown cold on the dining-room table.

Daddy never went to his new job. He never worked again. He never returned to Five Oaks. He never emerged from the deep depression that overtook him in the spring of 1964.

In the fall of that year I began my senior year of high school. It was one of the saddest times of my life.

Daddy's mental state worsened by the day. In some ways, it was a relief to have him depressed instead of manic. He was no longer loud and abusive and aggressive. His habit of leaving the house and returning late, smelling of alcohol, ceased. He no longer left us on Saturdays to "work," or to meet friends. He had no interest outside his upstairs bedroom. His life was contained within the walls of the old manor house.

We were all caged with our long pent-up emotions: Laddie, possessed by a visceral hatred for our father; Mama, controlled and silent, repressing her horror of the present and future; and I, an accomplice with my mother, well-schooled in the fine art of denial.

As the date of my graduation approached, I felt deep stirrings of homesickness. Deliberately ignoring the memory of the empty feelings I had brought back with me after that one visit back, when we had found it all so disappointing, I fancied that if I could only return once again to Five Oaks, I could find healing for my pain. I began to fantasize about moving back into the old brick house. I began to wonder if perhaps, after all this time, we could finally return home. I told Mama.

"We no longer own the house on Center Street," Mama said, flat and emotionless.

I gasped.

"How can that be?" I asked. "Mama, surely you didn't sell it?"

"Yes, Mitty, I sold it."

I couldn't believe it. How could she have done this?

"Mama, you know what the old brick house means to me, to *us*! How could you have sold it?"

"I had to sell it, Mitty, I had no choice."

The house was gone. The house that had been my place of solace, if only in my heart, now belonged to someone else. I felt as though a death had occurred. Deep, soul-shuddering grief settled on me.

"Why? Why did you have to sell it?"

The explanation she offered was too terrible, too heartbreaking. I simply could not allow myself to accept it. A dangerous wall of denial rose up in my consciousness, a wall I hastily constructed in order to keep the truth of her words from destroying me altogether.

For more than two decades, I would deliberately block the painful knowledge that it was my father's illness and his manic behavior that cost us the beloved house of my childhood. For more than twenty years, I would blame my mother for its loss, even though she had carefully described the events that had led to the sale of it. Stoic in manner, she had explained it all to me in great detail.

It had begun four years earlier, when Daddy had appeared to

rally at the beginning of my high school years. Mama had relinquished all financial responsibilities to him; Daddy had proceeded to make several bad business investments. Although the house on Center Street was paid for, Daddy insisted on taking out a mortgage against it to help repay his debts. He convinced Mama that he needed the money to make repairs on the old manor house. He persuaded her that we could use the money to live more comfortably in California. Mama acquiesced.

Daddy borrowed heavily against Five Oaks, too, in order to buy into a partnership and prime farmland in Sidon, Arkansas. Then, unstable and paranoid, Daddy began to accuse his partner of cheating him. Angry, unreasonable, and out of control, he dissolved the partnership before he had had time to recoup his original investment. When creditors and bill collectors began calling the house to insist on payment, Mama wrestled the family accounts away from Daddy and discovered, to her horror, that the savings account was empty, the checking account nearly depleted.

Daddy had used the thousands of dollars he had borrowed, as well as our savings, to finance an affair with another woman. Week after week, Mama had signed over her paychecks to Daddy, never suspecting that he was spending them, without conscience, to pursue an illicit relationship with a woman he worked with. When the note on the house on Center Street came due, there was no money to pay it.

Approaching foreclosure on the old brick house, Mama negotiated the sale of the property to our former neighbors on Center Street, the Huffs. Mr. Huff paid off the outstanding loan at the bank, giving Mama a cash amount to acquire the deed. And so the stately old brick house on Center Street, with its history and its formal gardens and wide porch and tall columns, passed out of our hands for the bargain price of a mere four thousand dollars.

All this Mama told me, but I couldn't bear it. The knowledge of my father's infidelities, his financial irresponsibility—it was too much for me. I simply could not live with the image of my father as a promiscuous, destructive man. I blocked out that which was too painful for me to live with. I denied that my father had played any part in the loss of my childhood home. I relegated all the blame to my mother.

I don't know how Mama was able to meet the payments on the loans against Five Oaks. Somehow, as our financial house crumbled down around us, she was able to salvage our ancestral home. But she could not rescue the house on Center Street from the seller's block.

I can see now, from the vantage of adulthood, that throughout that traumatic time when my father was out of control, my mother functioned behind a large, sturdy structure of denial. She, too, had her well-built wall. When Daddy left the house on Saturday mornings, looking dapper in his new business suit, his jaunty manner energetic, almost electrifying in his manic mode, she would close her eyes and shut her mouth. He often worked late and returned home reeking of alcohol, but Mama's impotent rage simmered silently.

I've learned in recent years that, even as a young bride, Mama had been frightened by Daddy's sudden mood swings and his abrupt, unexplainable, inappropriate behavior. She had wondered, and blamed herself, when she began to suspect that her husband of only a few months was having an affair. She began to construct her protective wall of denial during the early years of her marriage, when she saw the "other" woman driving around town in Daddy's car.

Laddie, too, had built walls to ensure his safety, as do most individuals who have lived with severe emotional trauma. He has few memories of our childhood, and those he retains have been carefully checked for hidden explosives. He has never denied the reality of Daddy's promiscuity, however. By the time he was a young man, he was aware of our father's infidelity. He knew of it, and that knowledge stoked his already burning hatred of our father. He never suspected that Daddy's compulsive, obsessive sexual behavior was yet another of the many destructive symptoms of his manic-depressive disease.

Many of Daddy's actions were expressions of his illness, but we did not know it then. We knew so little of his disease during his lifetime; we had no tools for digging into the mystery of his bizarre and often cruel behavior. We didn't know that both drug and alcohol abuse commonly overtake the manic-depressive. Mama, being the staunch Southern Baptist that she is, deplored the sight of Daddy with his six-packs and his bottles of expensive wine, but Daddy, in his manic mode, could not be stopped. As he carried cases of liquor into our home, Mama could only watch helplessly.

Mama did sense that Daddy's meanness and abusive language

were manifestations of his disease, but that did not make them hurt any less. She suffered for herself and for her children when Daddy unleashed his venom on us. She lived with it, accepted it, only because she felt helpless to control it.

Mama knew, intuitively, that Daddy's true persona, beneath the hideous monster of his disease, was gentle and kind and capable of loving deeply. But as time passed and his condition worsened, it became harder and harder for me to recall that he had ever been anything other than the pathetic, demented creature who inhabited the dark corners of our home.

I graduated from Charter Oak High with the class of 1965 with only Mama and Laddie in attendance. As the strains of "Pomp and Circumstance" floated out over the football field and into the windows of the old manor house half a block away, Daddy ran from room to room in a state of psychotic delusion. He believed he was once again the young football star of Searcy's 1924 high school team. He slid across the polished hardwood floors in his stocking feet, catching imaginary passes and taking "snaps" from a make-believe center under the coffee table. He ran into the dining room to score the final touchdown.

His bizarre behavior, begun days earlier, was both comical and heart-rending. I didn't know whether to laugh or cry when I first saw him leaping into empty air for an invisible ball. And then, as suddenly as it had begun, his insane choreography ended, and we entered a period so dark it resembled a nightmare that will forever haunt me with its pathos.

A terrible stench began to permeate the old manor house. The odor assaulted my nostrils every time I walked in the door. No amount of air freshener would make the odor dissipate. We constantly opened windows to let in a breeze. And then one day Mama discovered the cause of the awful smell. She came downstairs early one morning and discovered that Daddy had turned on the heat, even though it was the middle of summer. She found him in a deep psychotic state, standing over the floor register, humming tunelessly and frantically masturbating. His sperm was spilling out into the floor register.

Lost in his insanity, Daddy was unconscious of where he was and what he was doing. Over the remaining years of his life, this primitive psychotic ritual would occur with great regularity. Our lovely manor house, purchased to be a haven, became an asylum. Once fragrant with the scent of orange blossoms, the villa now reeked with the stench of insanity.

Over the years, I have learned that my father's behavior is common among the most seriously ill mental patients. A single pass down the hallway of a mental institution will offer similar sights of individuals, lost in their psychoses, acting exactly as my father did. I find no comfort in this discovery, only deep sadness for their loss—to themselves and to those who love them.

That summer, Daddy began setting fires in the house—whether consciously or unconsciously, we were never certain. He emptied the ashes of his pipe into waste cans, and we often found smoke spiraling up out of odd places in the house. We went to bed at night hoping and praying he would not burn the house down while we slept. One night he nearly did just that. He fell asleep with his pipe lit, and his bed caught fire and nearly destroyed the upstairs bedroom. Soon after that, Daddy crept downstairs and made his home in the darkest corner of a back bedroom in the basement.

Once handsome and dignified, even a little vain about his appearance, Daddy now grew thick and his face became puffy. He scratched at imagined irritations on his skin until his arms were covered with bloody scabs. His thick, luxurious hair turned gray, and he mindlessly rubbed the front of it until a huge bald spot appeared.

Unable to bear the presence of another human being, Daddy refused to leave the basement, even to eat. We would carry his meals downstairs on a tray which we set down quietly while he watched us from a distance. Later, we would sneak down silently to retrieve his empty dishes.

Days would pass before Daddy would change his clothing. Total warfare erupted if any of us tried to get him to shave or bathe or cut his hair. Mama, Laddie, and I took turns doing battle with him. If we were lucky, we scored a victory about once a week. The ordeal was exhausting and often used up the entire day. I can remember times when the process of getting him cleaned up began early in the morning and lasted until well after midnight.

Daddy refused to use the bathroom in the basement. He defecated like an animal and sometimes flung his feces out a basement window. More often, he left them for us to find, not unlike a dog that has forgotten his housebreaking discipline.

Sometimes, if he felt it was safe, Daddy made furtive forays upstairs into the light. He crept up cautiously, peering around corners, looking very much like "the wild man of Borneo."

Sometimes he went as far as the front porch, where he would urinate off the steps while the traffic on the street passed by. When we found him there, we would gently lure him back into the house, talking to him as though he were a child.

As if Daddy's present ills were not enough to burden Mama, he also suffered recurring problems from a badly botched surgery many years earlier. During a hernia operation eighteen years before, a surgeon had inadvertently tied one of Daddy's testicles. Often, in the following years, infection would occur and result in painful swelling. Daddy lived with chronic pain. By 1965, the original hernia repair had torn loose, and the old hernia pushed itself through the split, hanging from the groin area like a huge distended sack. Daddy was in such excruciating pain that, for the first time in years, he agreed to let Mama take him to a doctor.

The doctor who examined Daddy said it was the worst hernia he had ever seen. After giving Daddy a thorough examination, he also said he was unsure of Daddy's chances of surviving surgery. His was the first sympathetic voice Mama had heard in a long time. He agreed with her that Daddy's illness was severe enough to qualify him for permanent disability.

In Daddy's confused state of mind, he believed that being classified as permanently disabled condemned him to life in an institution. He panicked. Refusing to discuss the application process with Mama, he balked at all the paperwork. There were forms to be filled out and signatures required. Daddy was too upset to hold a pen or to write his own name.

Mama gave up. She called the Social Security office and explained that she had decided against filing for permanent disability. Her husband was too upset to go through the filing process, she said. In a matter of weeks, personnel at the Social Security office completed the paperwork on their own, using the compelling evidence from both Mama and the doctor's report as evidence of need. A social worker called Mama and told her that checks were waiting for her at the office. Laddie and I received Social Security checks, retroactively, as dependents of a permanently disabled person, until we were twenty-one. Daddy would receive them until he died, but he would never forgive Mama for telling the world he was disabled.

Ironically, in his rare moments of lucidity, Daddy considered it a humiliation to be classified "disabled." Even in his dementia, he maintained a sense of arrogance bred from his earliest understanding of his identity as a member of the "landed gentry."

Much like Mama's, his value system remained entrenched in the nineteenth century. He was the one who cared for the less fortunate. He was not the one in need of care.

I remember Daddy slipping back into the role of the country gentleman during our extreme poverty. Lucid at times, he was aware of the migrant workers who labored in the groves near the old manor house. When there were no oranges for picking, they earned money for their families by chopping and selling cords of firewood. Every day, Mama would come home from school to find our woodpile near the house had grown larger. When it stood over twelve feet high, she chided Daddy.

"Minor, you simply must stop buying all this firewood. We could live here a lifetime and not use it all."

Daddy whirled toward Mama, amazement on his face. Standing in the side yard, his face flushed, feet spread and chest heaving, Daddy thundered, "Pauline, how dare you be so cruel! It is our duty to take care of these people!"

Mama, her eyes snapping defiantly, answered back, "Minor, why is it that our blood is so blue that we must take care of others and starve in the process?"

She asked, but she knew the answer. In Daddy's mind, he was the benevolent benefactor of those less fortunate. He had inherited his patriarchal view from generations of Southerners who considered those of color, any color, to be dependent. Deluded by his disease and held captive by an old-fashioned mindset, he concluded that the Mexican workers near his property were his responsibility. And so he bought their wood when the trucks pulled into the driveway. And the woodpile grew larger and spilled out into the yard. After his death, Mama had to hire men to come and haul it away.

On the first of every month, for as long as he was aware and able, Daddy staged his own kind of rebellion against accepting the government's responsibility for him. He checked the mailbox and confiscated the checks, hiding them in his pockets. Mama couldn't understand why the checks didn't arrive, and the Social Security officials were puzzled over why the checks weren't being cashed. Then, one day, while folding the laundry, Mama found the checks, water-stained and crumpled, in Daddy's pockets.

Daddy survived the hernia operation, but he was weak and delusional during the days that followed. When Mama visited him in the hospital, he ignored her.

"Minor, please, will you listen to me?" she said. He lay with his back toward her, staring blankly at the window in the wall.

"You've got to try to pull yourself together," Mama told him. "You'll be leaving here soon."

Daddy rolled over and, with panic in his eyes, he asked, "But Pauline, where will I be going?"

In a quiet voice, Mama assured him, "You'll be coming home to me and the children."

Perhaps my father understood her words. Perhaps, to him, at that moment, home was wherever Pauline was. But for me, home was and always would be the old brick house on Center Street. The house my mother had sold.

That summer, Mama had a swimming pool built in the back yard of the old manor house. It was the quintessential California gesture, a final wave of goodbye to all that the old brick house on Center Street had represented.

A fire of anger began to burn inside me, anger toward the old manor house, which now held such an esteemed place in my mother's heart, a place I would never believe it deserved—and raging anger toward the family that inhabited it. It would be many years before that fire would be quenched.

1. Patty Duke and Gloria Hockman, *A Brilliant Madness*
       (New York: Bantam, 1992, p. 121)
2. Ibid, p. 120
3. Ibid, p. 99

Chapter 7

Mount San Antonio Junior College, located in Walnut, California, just a few miles from my home in Charter Oak, could have been ten thousand miles away, so distant was it from high school life. And I wished often that it *were* ten thousand miles away. I wanted to put as much distance as possible between me and my troubled family.

After only a few days in the college classroom, I realized that my academic career was going to be less than brilliant. Throughout high school, my speech and debate coaches, along with school administrators, had placed me in "dummy" courses, trying to keep my workload light so I could spend time preparing for speech and debate tournaments. By the time I graduated from high school with a "college prep" course of study, I had taken only general math, no algebra or geometry, and no chemistry or physical science, although my official transcript credited me with all those required courses. I entered college poorly prepared for college-level math and science, although I excelled in fine arts courses.

I found distraction from the miseries of home by staying busy—busier than I had ever been before. In addition to my schoolwork, I continued teaching at the Jerry Singer Studios. I kept my job at the Diamond Horseshoe and continued to study dance and voice with private instructors as well. When I learned I'd been awarded a small performing arts scholarship, I applied it toward classes three days a week at the American School of Dance.

Housed in a building that had been condemned in 1947, the American School of Dance on Hollywood Boulevard refused to give in to its crumbling visage. Like many of the legendary dancers who still came and went through its poorly lit hallways, the markings of age gave it a kind of mystique that other, more modern buildings, would never possess. Huge cracks, like large, ugly varicose veins, crawled across the basement walls where the dancers stretched and practiced, but the beauty of motion and music lent the place an air of regal dignity. Many mornings I arrived to find Mary Tyler Moore standing in front of me at the barre in a rehearsal room. Sometimes I worked alongside George Chakaris and Juliet Prowse. Cyd Charisse was a regular in the room across the hall.

The building had no air conditioning and the small windows in the rehearsal rooms offered no cross ventilation. In the summer, when the temperature soared, the rooms radiated heat like convection ovens. In winter, cold, damp air seeped in through the cracked concrete walls. In the main rehearsal hall, where large chunks of flooring had buckled, dancers maneuvered carefully around ragged, gaping holes, never missing a step. And no one ever complained. The condition of the old building seemed only to add to its prestige. Dancers from all over the country vied for the opportunity to take their places at the barre in this dismal, decaying old building.

On many days, I danced from early morning until late at night. By the time I returned home, my legs would ache so badly I dreaded the climb to my upstairs bedroom. I often awakened in the morning so sore I couldn't make myself walk downstairs, and so I sat on the steps and scooted down them on my bottom.

I continued competing in beauty pageants and signed with a theatrical agent and a modeling agent. Like most "hopefuls," I auditioned regularly, clutching my portfolio, praying each time that I would be the next discovery.

I loved my college speech and drama classes—everything associated with the theater excited me. I felt alive when I was performing. And, hiding behind the characters I portrayed, I could disassociate myself from Millicent Collinsworth, the girl whose childhood and adolescence had been more a battleground than a playground.

I met "Keith" in acting class. He was good-looking in a pretty-boy sort of way, and he dazzled me with his carefree, worldly manner. He possessed an aura of danger that both fascinated and frightened me. He came from a fine family—his credentials impressed even Mama—but he had an undercurrent of rebellion that contradicted the display of propriety he showed when he visited the old manor house. I sensed in him a capacity for meanness, but he could also be very affectionate and attentive. I was captivated and a little awed by the fact that he wanted to go out with me.

I fell in love with Keith's parents. The day he introduced me as his girlfriend, they accepted me as part of the family. Their arms were open to me, and, gratefully, I fell into them. Perhaps much of the attraction I felt toward Keith stemmed from my feelings for his parents.

Keith didn't view his family as kindly as I did. He criticized them incessantly, mocking their lifestyle and values. And after meeting Mama, he turned his critical eye on her as well. In time, I came to understand that Keith was critical and disparaging of all systems of authority.

When Keith started his tirades against my mother, terrible confusion raged inside me. No one had ever dared criticize Mama— except Daddy, and then only when he was in an unreasonable manic state. Listening to Keith, I felt overwhelmed by ambivalence. Part of me wanted to defend my mother against his assaults, but another part of me wanted to agree with him. At times, I allowed myself to echo his words—that she was too controlling of me, that she was domineering. When I said these things aloud, the sense of release I felt was both liberating and a little frightening. Tentatively, for the first time, I dared to admit the anger I felt toward my family. And I found in Keith a sympathetic, even encouraging, advocate for my frustration and fury.

Keith embodied every cliché associated with college students in the 1960s. A talented musician, he played with a blue-grass band and introduced me to coffeehouses, folk singing, and hootenannies. Together, we saw Gordon Lightfoot, Carol King, Bob Seger, and Peter, Paul, and Mary at the Troubadour. I applauded proudly when Keith's band played at the Whiskey A-Go-Go in Hollywood and at The Ice House in Pasadena.

Rebellious and unhappy, Keith spoke loudly against the war and in favor of drugs. He bragged about "dropping LSD" and called it an "uplifting spiritual experience."

I allowed him to introduce me to marijuana. The first time I smoked it, I coughed convulsively and hyperventilated, but in time, I learned how to smoke it.

Keith's defiance of all things "establishment" disturbed my strong sense of tradition, but in true Collinsworth fashion, I denied all the evidence of impending disaster. I desperately craved the attention of this arrogant young man; I willingly enslaved myself to his wishes. I felt special when he drove up to the Diamond Horseshoe and picked me up in his little red sports car. I liked hearing the other girls at the theater talk about how attractive he was. I liked being able to date and go places with someone besides my mother. I liked the element of danger evoked by his rebel stance. I liked it, and at the same time, I feared it.

We had been dating only a short time when Keith asked me to marry him. I agreed, just as I agreed to everything Keith asked of me. He represented independence, and I desperately wanted to be independent of Mama and the horrors of the old manor house. Afraid of appearing naive and childish to him—he was very worldly and sophisticated—I agreed with whatever he said and acquiesced to him in every matter until I lost myself in the pursuit of his approval.

Mama saw the signs of danger before I did. She tried to warn me, but I wanted nothing of her advice. I was defensive and secretive—smoking pot on weekdays with friends, and then going home for the weekend to her rigid rules. We had no basis for communication.

I resented Mama's criticism of Keith. I wanted to believe he was right for me. His jealous rages were an evidence of his love for me, I thought. His obsessive need to have me with him at all times further proved how much he needed me. Keith resented Mama's power over me. He said he wanted me to "grow up," to be free of my mother's influence over me, to be able to think and act for myself. I imagined he wanted what was best for me. I never foresaw the destruction ahead.

When I completed junior college, I quit my job at the Jerry Singer Studios, enrolled at California State University in Los Angeles, and moved into an apartment nearby. My major in recreational therapy offered me exciting classes in addition to requiring me to serve an internship with a parks and recreation department.

I was thrilled when I was accepted as a recreation leader for the Los Angeles County Parks and Recreation Department. I was assigned to the performing arts division, where I would teach dance and drama. It was a job made to order for me, and in a short time my classes grew to a record enrollment of three hundred students. The county parks department had never before had one recreation leader attract so many students.

My success was exhilarating. I loved hearing congratulations and accepting praise from every sector of the county. I was nineteen years old and already making a name for myself in my chosen field. When parents of my students asked me to coach their children privately, I began accepting students. My basement studio in the old manor house became "The Collinsworth School of Performing Arts," and I, its proud owner and director.

I loved my college classes and my new career goals and opportunities. Keith, however, was not finding life as exhilarating and satisfying as I was. He grew dissatisfied with school and decided to drop out to accept a job as producer of a late-night talk show. Our relationship began to deteriorate.

Keith despised everything I did that excluded him. He demanded that I give up everything and become his wife. He hated my acting in summer stock and stage reviews. He pressured me to quit showroom modeling, even though the pay was good. And he nagged me to drop out of the university and to quit my classes at the American School of Dance. It seemed that everything I loved, he loathed. The arguments we had left me feeling miserable and confused.

"Mitty, you are becoming an emotional hostage to that boy," Mama told me over and over again when I went home for the required weekend visits. I didn't want to listen. My visits home became farther and farther apart.

It wasn't only Mama who saw Keith's manipulative ways. My friends tried to convince me that he was insecure and unstable, but I ignored all their warnings. Then, one night, during an argument, Keith slapped me. A few days later, we argued again and he grew so angry that he grabbed me by the throat and tried to choke me. I was terrified, and later, he was remorseful. I forgave him and tried to convince myself that I was probably as much to blame for his violence as he. But somewhere, tugging at my consciousness, was the knowledge that he had wanted to hurt me.

Something was terribly wrong. Keith had always said he hated violence. He had spent weekends marching in protest against the Vietnam War. He had loudly denounced the use of force in every sector of society, even going so far as to register as a "conscientious objector." But now, his words and his actions were in conflict.

I couldn't help comparing Keith to my heroic brother, Laddie. In a graduate program by this time, Laddie carefully watched his student deferment, but I knew that if he were called, he would put on a uniform without hesitation. In Laddie there would be neither hypocrisy nor cowardice.

An awful turmoil churned inside me. I grew more and more uncomfortable with the idea of marriage to Keith, but I hadn't the emotional courage to break off the engagement. I didn't want to lose the loving relationship I enjoyed with his parents, whose friendship was very important to me, but I was very frightened of the man I was supposed to marry.

Over the next two years, the fights with Keith intensified. I remember feeling helpless to understand how someone who came from such a kind and loving home could be so brutal. And I remember wearing clothes that would cover the bruises he left on my arms and neck. But then the memories end, and there is nothing more.

Nothing. Until nearly four months later. And even those memories are fragmented, scattered in my psyche like torn remnants of old photographs bearing scenes too horrendous to view.

I remember finding myself in my mother's bathtub at the old manor house, with no memory of how I got there. Frothy white bubbles surrounded me and, with trembling fingers, I lifted them toward the light. As my hands raised up out of the water, I gasped at the sight of fresh, jagged, purple-red scars on my wrists. Suddenly, I felt enclosed by panic, captured in a nightmare and unable to awaken.

"Mama! Mama!" I screamed.

"What is it, Mitty,?" Mama asked, rushing into the bathroom, breathless from her dash up the stairs.

"What happened to me, Mama? What's wrong with my hands?" I sobbed.

Water and translucent bubbles dripped from my hands as I held them up toward her. Mama instantly erased the frown of concern from her face and replaced it with an expression devoid of all emotion. In a low voice, she answered, "You tried to commit suicide, Mitty. You cut them."

I stared aghast at the raised, purple slashes so dark against the pallor of my inner arm.

"I cut them... "

Those were my father's words, that day after the storm, when I was six years old... My father had tried to commit suicide.

Daddy's sick—he's crazy. But I'm not... Why would I have cut my own wrists?

I couldn't think... What had happened? I had no memory of slashing my wrists... no memory of being ill—or crazy. What had happened to me? I was frantic for information, but scared of what I might discover. Why could I not remember?

Mama gave me a few incomplete answers: I had had a nervous breakdown; I was no longer engaged to Keith.

For the next few months, I awoke often in the middle of the night with fragments of nightmares skittering through my mind. I saw images that seemed vague and distant, as if they belonged to someone else, and yet they hovered in my thoughts, teasing me with bits of frightening memories. I remembered a hospital— I could see its bare walls and long corridors. I remembered lying on a gurney amid a pool of blood. I saw myself walking into a bathroom followed by a nurse. I asked for a brush for my hair, and I wondered why she had to stand and watch me.

Another night, I awakened to the memory of a bizarre volleyball game played in a fenced yard. Other young people my age stood about me, waiting their turn to smack the ball across the net.

I glimpsed myself sitting in a circle with a group of other patients wearing casual clothes. I was trying to weave a belt out of leather thongs.

The memory of a tall man in a dark suit flitted around the edges of my vacant thoughts. He talked about hugging. "This is an exercise for your healing," he said. He stood in a room surrounded by young people with empty expressions. And then he was standing in front of me, pulling me against his chest. "Put your arms around me and hug me back," he commanded.

I remembered my arms hanging limply at my sides.

Many nights I was startled from a deep sleep by the sound of crashing glass. Splintering shards crackled all around me. I sat up in bed, drenched in sweat, and realized I had been dreaming about a figure running down a dim hallway toward a large window. And then I knew it was not a dream, but a memory. And I remembered a voice screaming, "Stop her! Stop her! She's running toward the window again!" And then, startled, I realized the figure hurtling toward the window was me.

Mama told me my memory had been destroyed by the thirty-six electric shock treatments administered to me in a private psychiatric hospital. The dim images of people and blurred corridors that floated in my brain came from a time and place of which I had no knowledge. I was dependent upon Mama for every piece of information about my condition—about my life! She assured me the doctors were certain that my memory loss was temporary—I would remember it all soon enough. But twenty-three years later, I still have no recollection of the events of that time, nor of many events that occurred throughout a period of four years.

When classes resumed for the next quarter, I was too ill to register. Mama insisted I remain with her in the old manor house. I knew she was right, and I was too weak to argue with her, but I wanted desperately to be able to return to college. I was surprised to learn that some of my professors had called to inquire about me while I'd been hospitalized, and their show of kindness and personal interest made me even more determined to get well enough to resume my life. I wanted to be able to move back into my tiny apartment. I wanted to dance and act and model again. But my physical and emotional condition was pitiful.

I swallowed twenty-four different prescription pills every day. I needed sleeping pills to get through the night and antidepressants to get through the day. The hospital had sent me home laden with bottles of tranquilizers and stimulants—highly addictive barbiturates—that were supposed to enable me to function in a near-normal state. Sluggish and disoriented, I stumbled through each hour, confused and lost, unable to control my thoughts, unable to decipher my life and recent events.

"Mitty, if you want to move back to your apartment and return to school, you're going to have to stop taking all this medication," Mama said one day as she watched me toss a handful of pills down my throat.

She was right. I knew that. The side effects of the noxious drugs I was taking were awful. My body was swollen and bloated, and large sores had erupted on my skin. I felt either edgy or disoriented all the time. Either I tossed out the bottles of pills, or I tossed out all my dreams for the future. I could never return to dancing and performing in the shape I was in. I could never function in the classroom while in this drug-induced stupor. Mama forged a plan for my recovery. "We'll eliminate two pills at a time," Mama said. "We'll go slow, but you'll be rid of these in time for the next quarter."

"All right, Mama," I answered, placing myself completely in her hands. Two days later, I lay in bed, drenched in sweat and nearly comatose.

Alarmed, Mama called a friend for advice. Together they pored over a reference book of prescription drugs to see if I was in any serious danger from what they thought were withdrawal symptoms. Whatever they read in the book put their minds at ease, and they continued their plan to "detox" me. A few days later, Mama called a neighborhood pharmacist and told him what she was doing. He was appalled at the list of drugs I had been given by the staff at the hospital.

"She should never have been placed on those pills," he said, his voice sounding angry over the phone. "She's much too young to be treated with such strong medication!"

"Is she in any danger if we take her off them, two at a time?" Mama asked, needing reassurance that she was not harming me. "You're doing just fine," he answered. "Go slow and do it right... She'll be okay."

Slowly, carefully, two pills at a time, Mama backed me off the two dozen pills that swam in my bloodstream. In a few weeks, the bloating went down and the sores on my skin healed; but when I returned to school for the next quarter, I was still suffering many agonizing symptoms of drug withdrawal.

I attended every class, regardless of how I felt, and often I sat there, twitching and wriggling, my clothes drenched with perspiration. Sometimes I trembled and jerked with painful spasms, and my insides burned like a well-stoked fire. Knife-like cramps doubled me over. Many times I looked up to see my professor's eyes on me, willing me to hang on for just one more day. Every one of them passed me, although I'm sure I didn't deserve better than a failing grade.

I had great difficulty concentrating. And the memory loss I suffered further complicated my return to the classroom. For years I had compensated for my poor eyesight by depending on a photographic memory. I had learned to read a passage once and then "photograph" it and store it in my memory so I didn't have to overwork my weak eyes to read it again. Now that vault full of information and memories was locked.

The confusion and mystery surrounding my relationship with Keith troubled me terribly. Mama insisted there was nothing more to tell me—it was over, and that was that. I couldn't press her for more answers; I couldn't talk to her at all. I finally persuaded my roommate, Joan, to tell me the whole story.

"You were pregnant with Keith's baby," she told me, her voice angry, as if she resented having to be the one to tell me the sordid details. "You got deathly sick in our apartment—I thought you were going to die. I called your mother to come and pick you up. Your brother took you to the hospital where you had emergency surgery."

She paused and sighed deeply before continuing. "Mitty, it was an ectopic pregnancy. The baby had been dead a long time."

I stared at Joan, too stunned to speak. Numbly, I shook my head. It couldn't be true... It couldn't be... I didn't remember any of it... Why would anyone make up such a horrible story?

"That can't be... " I whispered.

Joan's face crumpled. "Oh, Mitty!"

I wouldn't believe her. I would ask Joe—he would tell me the truth. He was one of my best friends at school—I could trust him to be honest with me. But when Joe confirmed the story, I still refused to believe it. I couldn't allow myself to believe it until I heard it from Keith's mother. I knew she would tell me what had really happened. Her heart broke as she repeated the story Joan had told.

The truth suddenly illuminated many of the dark places I had been trying to maneuver through since the day I had discovered myself sitting in Mama's upstairs bathtub. Suddenly, the pulsing anger I had sensed in Mama made sense. Of course! She was angry at me for my wickedness. I had committed the unpardonable sin. I had gotten pregnant out of wedlock. I had humiliated myself, my family, and the Collinsworth name.

All those lectures Mama had given me over the years about lost virtue and young lust gone amuck—she must have wondered if I had ever listened to her or ever cared about purity and honor. I had listened to her—I could recite every one of her lectures verbatim—but shame had engulfed me every time she had warned me about being careful, about being a "nice" girl.

"You must never let a boy go too far, Mitty," Mama had said.

How could I have told her that it was too late for me? That none of her warnings applied to me? I was already soiled and unworthy, I believed. I had already been dragged past the barriers of decency and into the forbidden region by the time I was ten years old. The taboo had already been crossed. Nothing I would ever do in my life would match the evil that had already touched me. But how does a child describe such heinous crimes? How does a child ever speak of the unspeakable?

"Do you know how many thousands of dollars I have had to spend on your hospitalization?" Mama had yelled one day shortly after she'd taken me home from the private hospital. "I will not spend another penny on psychiatrists!"

One crazy person was enough for this family.

"The therapist wants to blame me for your behavior," she told me another time. "He wants me to believe that the Southern Baptist upbringing I gave you is causing you to feel unnecessary guilt—as if that's the reason for your behavior or your state of mind."

Mama's figure vibrated with rage when she spoke to me. My problems were of my own making, she had determined. And I would have to deal with them, without incurring any more cost to this family. With my discharge from the hospital, all psychological care and counseling had ended. There would be no further therapy and no outpatient care.

It was all my fault. I had become the consummate Bad Girl. I had forfeited all the dignity so carefully cultivated on the pageant runway and behind the debate podium.

I hated what I had done to my family's fragile pride. And most of all, I hated myself.

Guilt became my personal signature.

In the weeks and months that followed, I began learning to cope with the large empty places in my memory. At times, I felt like an emotional amputee. Huge portions of my life had disappeared, leaving me no clue as to their whereabouts. Often I found myself in awkward and embarrassing situations.

Many times, friends and acquaintances engaged me in conversation and I had no idea whom I was speaking with. I could be at a party, or driving down the street, or simply sitting in a room alone when a fragment of thought would tease me with familiarity. When I reached out to grab it, it flew away, leaving me feeling empty and confused. My head throbbed as if with the phantom pains of dismemberment.

Of the many difficult aspects of my memory loss, the fact that it need not have occurred at all is the most frustrating to me. When Mama committed me to the private sanitarium after my suicide attempt, she instructed the staff that I was not to be given any electric shock treatments. She was enraged when, against her wishes, the hospital administered thirty-six of them.

I was twenty-one and legally an adult, the hospital argued. She had no jurisdiction over the treatment of an adult child. Nor did the rigid requirements that governed state-run facilities monitor the private sanitarium where I had been confined. While electric shock was a controversial choice of treatment, it was still widely used in private hospitals, earning them the title of "shock mills."

I'm sure I can't begin to calculate Mama's agony when she learned what had been done to me. She had seen the injury to my father: his burn scars, his memory loss, the destruction of millions of his brain cells in an attempt to shock him into some level of sanity. Now, looking back at that period of time with adult eyes, I believe the rage emanating from her was much more than simply anger toward me for my defiance of her strict behavior code. It was surely a more complex mixture of emotions: fury, yes; but also guilt, fear, and the natural grief any mother would suffer when she has been helpless to protect her child from harm. Did she begin to fear at this time that I, too, suffered from the disease that had control of my father's life? Did she wonder if this breakdown and suicide attempt were the beginning of my journey into dementia? Did my mother wonder if one day she would find her only daughter skulking about in the darkness of the basement, destroyed and possessed by the demon of mental illness?

One question summoned up her greatest terror: Had her child begun to manifest the symptoms of manic-depressive disease?

Mama's unspoken fear for both her children had stayed hidden in some dark place deep inside her for many years. She simply could not allow it into the light. The horror of it was too great to be considered. For her husband, there had been no medical help. Institutions had not healed him. Medications had offered no hope. She could not bear to consider the possibility that she might now have to live out the rest of her days helplessly watching her child make the same long, slow trek into insanity. And so she adjusted her well-worn armor and clothed herself in yet another layer of stubborn denial.

Mama refused to allow me to be "sick." Instead, she called my problems "misbehavior," and she comforted herself with the belief that she could "correct" me. Misbehavior could be punished. Irresponsible children could be disciplined. Mama knew all about discipline and control, and in this, she could find a handhold for hope. Using all the tools of a determined parent, she informed me of my sin, and instructed me on how and what to do to redeem myself. And in a very short time, the force of her will hoisted me back up onto the model's runway and onto the dance floor, where I embarked on a quest for lost honor.

I returned to auditions and casting calls, dressed in outfits she had carefully selected, looking like the beauty queen she had always wanted me to be. On the outside, I appeared to have healed completely. I looked the part of the ambitious, confident would-be starlet. My clothes were perfect, my poise flawless, my speech and manners impeccable. On the inside, however, the healing process had not even begun.

All the hurts of the past—beginning with Daddy's first hospitalization—boiled inside me. Mama's anger spawned a white-hot anger in me that lay potent and dangerous just beneath my well-groomed surface. All-out rebellion erupted.

Laddie took the first volley in my private war. I'd always been proud of his outstanding scholarship, but now his academic success infuriated me. When he traveled to Europe in 1969, the summer before he began his student teaching, I was glad to see him go. He had usurped my place as the "golden child" in Mama's eyes— he had not sullied the family's name with promiscuity. While he was abroad, he wrote to Mama faithfully, sending snapshots and gifts from beautiful, exotic places. He became Mama's comfort— the confidant I had once been. I became the prodigal.

I was no longer tentative in my expressions of anger toward Mama. I screamed at her, venting all the frustration and fury that had been building inside me for so long. Things I had been afraid to say came spewing out of my mouth.

"Why didn't you leave Daddy years ago?" I shrieked. "Look what you have done to us! How could you have made us live with him like this?"

"You made that decision with me, Mitty," Mama answered. "We all decided it was best to keep Daddy with us."

"We were wrong, all of us!" I screamed. "Look what he has done to us! We should have put him in an institution years ago!"

Through the years, Mama, Laddie, and I had called family counsels to discuss our options with Daddy. It always seemed that when one of the three of us was about to break down under the enormity of the situation and argue for institutionalizing him, the other two would band together to insist that we must care for him ourselves. A democratic system at work, we were able to manipulate the minority; and Mama's wedding vow, "in sickness and in health," was renewed. Daddy would stay at home with us. A loving decision, we had called it.

Looking back, in reality we had few options. Private insurance policies would have paid for a maximum of thirty or sixty days of hospitalization for psychiatric care, at the most. Mama's insurance through the teacher's union did not cover even that amount. We would never forget the horror of Daddy's stay in the state hospital in Arkansas—how could we ever again knowingly subject him to that kind of indignity and abuse?

How many times had Mama rehearsed the dangers of putting Daddy in a California mental institution? How many times had she pointed at the hobos on board the trains that ran through our orchard community and reminded us that Daddy could easily become one of those pathetic, hollow-eyed men, riding alone on a train destined for oblivion? With morbid curiosity, Laddie and I had stared as the railroad cars clacked by, with their sad-looking population on board. We could imagine the scenario—Mama had painted it for us often enough: their families had committed them to an institution, and seventy-two hours later the men had walked out, never to be heard from or seen again, victims of an inadequate mental health care system.

"Think about it, children," Mama had said as we glimpsed the gaunt, disheveled men sitting in empty boxcars, their legs dangling from the open doors as the train rattled past. "That could be your father. If we put him in the hospital, he could leave on his own. By the time the hospital could notify us, he could have disappeared."

A strange interplay of hope and fear and guilt would swirl inside me when Mama set the stage for Daddy's disappearance. I dared not say the words... I dared not even think them...

Still, I could not rid myself of the anger I felt toward my mother for staying married to Daddy and for making me live with all the awfulness of his disease. My resentment of Laddie swelled. The ambivalence of my feelings for Daddy confused me and terrified me—how could a child feel both love and hate for her own father? My guilt increased, along with my sense of self-loathing. A volcano of putrefied emotions bubbled inside me.

The comfort of food helped assuage my pain, but I was soon swallowing diet pills to keep my weight under control. I had kicked the habit of barbiturates, but I had replaced it with another, almost as deadly, addiction.

It was 1969. I had never been so miserable.

The world was in shambles, or so I thought. On the news, reports of the war in Vietnam blared. Body bags seemed to fill the television screen every night. I was terrified that someday my own brother would be sucked into the inferno of gunfire and that his body would be returned to us zipped into one of those black plastic shrouds. As angry as I was with him, I couldn't bear the thought of his death. When I learned that one of my childhood friends, Jimmy Cunningham, a classmate from the Collinsworth's Little Red School House, had been killed, the war seemed suddenly much closer than twelve thousand miles away.

Jimmy, with his white-blond hair and his teasing blue eyes, had never backed down from a fight in our back-yard playground.

"My daddy can spit farther than your daddy can!" Jimmy taunted Laddie.

"Naw, my daddy can spit farther than yours!"

"You're both wrong!" their buddy, Tommy Cooper, threw in. "My daddy can spit farther than anybody's daddy!"

Dust flew when the three of them launched their bodies into the air and landed in the soil of Mama's garden. They rolled and tussled and finally stood up laughing. While Mama scolded them and brushed the dirt off their clothes, they opened fire with the next barrage.

"My daddy has more hair in his nose than yours!" Jimmy hissed.

As soon as Mama disappeared into the schoolhouse, Laddie answered, "He does not! My daddy has the most nose hair!"

And Tommy jumped into the fray. "You're both wrong! My daddy's got more nose hair than anybody's daddy."

And the war for playground supremacy began again, ending again with laughter and dirty, smudged faces. Jimmy's last war didn't end so gently.

A terrible depression enveloped me. Just about the time I thought I might become a casualty of my own private war, salvation came to me in the form of a funeral.

My father's mother died. At a hundred and three years old, Grandmother Collinsworth's reign over Five Oaks ended. Her will designated my father as the principal heir of the old home place. No one expected him to take his place as the caretaker of the family property—it would be held in trust and his closest family members would live there—but it was expected that someone from his immediate family would represent him at the funeral. Since Laddie was abroad and Mama had to care for Daddy, I was the only choice.

I arrived at Five Oaks with my carefully constructed facade in place. Looking like the model and beauty queen everyone had expected Pauline and Minor Collinsworth to produce, no one suspected that I was a defiant and defeated young woman who, not long ago, had wished for a plot of her own, six feet under.

I stood in the small sanctuary of the little Methodist church in Griffithsville, Arkansas, with its white clapboard walls and its pointed steeple, and watched dented and dusty pickup trucks pull up into the red clay driveway. Men, sunburned and stocky, uncomfortable in their Sunday suits on this weekday afternoon, and women in flowered cotton dresses and white patent-leather shoes, flowed into the summer-warmed church to participate in the simple ceremony that would honor my grandmother's life. Watching their faces, seeing their kindly expressions, and feeling the strong grip of their calloused hands on mine, I felt swamped by emotions I had held at bay for a very long time. These were simple country folk, and they were my people, my family. Their strong faith in God and country was a pulsing presence in the tiny, hot building, and it pounded away at the barriers that surrounded my aching spirit.

I don't know when I had lost my faith in the things these people held so dear. They sang about an "amazing grace," and they hoisted the American flag on poles on their front porches and decorated their trucks for a parade through town on the Fourth of July, while I couldn't even remember the last time I had prayed; and I wondered if I could still recite the Pledge of Allegiance. Had I seen too many young friends arrive home from a jungle war in boxes draped with the Stars and Stripes? Had the loud, boisterous voices of campus radicals dulled my hearing so that I could no longer hear anything but vicious, angry judgments against my country?

I had seen purple scars on my wrists and learned about a dead baby in my womb. I had felt great emptiness and had discovered no source for refilling. I had committed a great sin, and had found no forgiveness.

Suddenly, standing there in that peaceful, almost holy place, I recalled the morning of my baptism many years before in Searcy's First Baptist Church.

I was seven years old. I clutched a small, white zippered Bible. My name was inscribed in gold on the cover. Laddie held a black one just like it. Together we sat in the first pew of the church, our hair still damp from our dunking in the church baptismal behind the choir loft. I could feel the fabric of my ruffled Easter dress soaking up the water from the wet French braids that hung down my back. On this solemn occasion, Laddie and I sat quiet and tense, a little overwhelmed at the significance of the spiritual moment we had just shared. Immersed into the death and burial of Christ, then "raised to walk in newness of life," as the preacher had solemnly intoned, we had committed ourselves to follow Jesus as faithful disciples.

I couldn't speak for Laddie, but I knew I had walked many miles since that occasion and had arrived at a place far distant from where I would have liked to be. And then it occurred to me that perhaps it was here, among these people in this beloved place, that I could begin my journey back. Maybe here, I could begin my acts of penance.

Moments after the preacher spoke his final "amen" in the steaming church, I climbed into a car for the slow, winding drive to Dogwood Cemetery. The grass, neatly mowed and trimmed around the granite headstones, was soft under my feet as I walked toward a mound of fresh dirt piled beside the hole that would hold my grandmother's casket. I had to fight to control my wildly spinning emotions.

Home! my heart whispered. This is home!

For the first time in a long time, I was glad to be alive. I delivered a carefully written eulogy, in a carefully cultivated manner—my speech and drama professors would have been proud. I extolled the value of family and traditions; I gave my father's name the dignity it had once deserved. And when it was over, I returned to the home place at Five Oaks to mingle with other relatives and friends who had come to see Grandmother laid to rest.

The old house with its green shutters looked proud, in spite of its cracking paint and overgrown gardens. Time had exacted a heavy toll from it, but the oak trees surrounding it stood as strong and powerful as ever. I walked outside and basked in the peace of old memories.

"Mitty," a voice called to me. I saw my Uncle Rufus coming toward me. For as long as I could remember, he had been known simply as "Judge." He had already changed from his uncomfortable Sunday suit to the familiar old denim overalls I remembered from my childhood. A canvas safari hat rested low on his forehead.

"You did right fine, girl," Judge said with a nod and a smile. "Your grandmother would be mighty proud."

His words warmed me. "Thank you, Judge. It's great to be here. I've missed this place." And I've missed you, I thought, but the words would have embarrassed him. I wanted to step closer to him and put my arms around him and lean against his solid strength, but that too would have embarrassed him. Instead, I smiled at him and said, "I hope I can come back more often."

"You know you're always welcome," he said, and unshed tears glistened in his eyes. He blinked quickly and patted my shoulder awkwardly. And then, lowering his voice, he said softly, "There's something I have to tell you, Mitty." He glanced about to see if anyone had followed us outside, if anyone stood near enough to overhear. "You're all grown up—you've become a woman now. I think it's time—I think you're old enough to hear this... "

Judge cleared his throat and his rheumy eyes peered off into the distance toward the graveyard where we had left my

grandmother. I waited, uncertain. He looked back at me and I
sensed his discomfort. A shudder traveled down my shoulders to
the balls of my feet. What could the secret be? I wondered. Was
there a bastard in the family? A criminal, perhaps? What
Collinsworth skeleton was Judge going to reveal to me, now that
I had "become a woman"?

"Mitty... " Judge's voice dropped to a raspy whisper.
"Mitty... " he tried again, but paused to look around quickly
before he continued.

"Mitty, there's a Yankee buried in the family plot."

He waited, searching my face, watching for my response to
this scandalous revelation. I just stood there for a silent moment,
wondering what to say. My chest ached as I tried to contain the
peals of laughter that begged to explode. Judge lifted his hat and
patted his damp forehead with a crisp, cotton handkerchief. "It's
true all right," he said, "but we don't talk much about it."

I schooled the muscles of my face into a mask of serenity.
Meeting his eyes, I nodded slightly, accepting with dignity the
weight of my family's shame.

Judge was still shaking his head when he walked back toward
the house and the table in the dining room that sagged under the
weight of casserole dishes and gelatin salads. I watched him until
the porch door swung shut behind him, and then I leaned against
the trunk of an immense oak tree and let the laughter spill out.
Then, spinning away from the tree, I ran into the dense forest,
swinging my arms wide, drawing to myself all the warm and
precious things that were contained here, in this my father's
home place.

Pride and tradition, courage and tenacity—all these things
flourished here at Five Oaks, as they had for more than a hundred
years. Nothing had been able to destroy the Collinsworth's will to
survive—not the war, not even the certainty of a lost cause. Not
malaria; nor Indian attacks. Not even the shameful presence of
overpowering enemies. In the face of every foe, the Collinsworths
had always stood tall and strong and unbending.

I wanted so badly to tap into the root of that courage. Standing
there among the great oaks, I felt small stirrings of rebirth. A tiny
pulse of hope pounded in me. It died a quick death as thoughts
of the old brick house on Center Street came to mind.

I've lost it... I've lost it...

Anger at Mama surged inside me like a fire doused with
gasoline.

She sold the old brick house...

How is it that one can so idealize a structure of brick and mortar that it becomes the symbol of all that is safe and sane? Like a faithful pilgrim, I had turned my face and my heart toward my childhood home as though it were my Mecca, the place where I would find my miracles. And Mama, like the proverbial infidel, had desecrated that holy place by signing its ownership over to other hands.

It was irrational and unreasonable, but the house on Center Street had anchored me, preventing me from spinning off into a universe empty of meaning and purpose. Its presence had been my umbilical cord, feeding security and comfort into a private world devoid of sanity and safety. Mama severed that cord when she sold the house the year of my high school graduation.

For four years my fury at Mama had burned white-hot. For another nineteen years it would continue to burn. At times it would flare brightly, as if suddenly refueled; at other times, it would be little more than a softly glowing coal, still hot and dangerous to touch. For more than twenty-three years I would refuse to acknowledge my father's part in the loss of my beloved childhood home. I would block out all memory of his promiscuous life and his mishandling of our family's finances. I would believe Mama had been the one to arbitrarily dispose of the old brick house on Center Street.

All those years, Mama would be the target of my anger, absorbing it silently instead of deflecting it toward my father, whose illness had left him with no defense with which to protect himself.

I returned to California after Grandmother's funeral and immediately went in search of Daddy. I found him in his old room upstairs, sitting in his chair, rocking silently. His eyes, as always, were vacant and staring.

"Daddy, it's planting time at Five Oaks... I just came home from the farm... I saw Judge, and all the others... " I watched his face for some sign of understanding. His eyes never flickered. He rocked and his chair creaked and I groped in my brain for words that might unlock his psyche and allow entrance to memories of his old home place.

I had lost my anchor, my beloved home place, but Daddy had just received the deed to his—Five Oaks. It could never be taken from him, as mine had been taken. I wanted to give him the assurance that the place he so loved was still there, in all its glorious, green beauty. The trees stood taller, the soil rich and dark with nutrients that had fed his soul in better days. I wanted him to see it all, through my eyes. I wanted to assure him that no one would ever do to him what I thought Mama had done to me.

I recited the stories of the Collinsworths of Five Oaks, when the land had been young and the people on it stout and daring, when men and women had sacrificed everything to hold onto what they believed was theirs and theirs alone.

Daddy never twitched an eyelid. He never turned his head. He simply rocked and stared.

Mama walked around me, as though giving wide berth to an enemy.

I made many pilgrimages back to Five Oaks to represent my father at family funerals. Opposing emotions confounded me on these travels. My anger at my mother did not abate, and yet something inside me still craved her approval and her forgiveness for my moral failure. I wanted to regain the honor of the Collinsworth name, and I thought I could do that by going back to Five Oaks for her, and for my father. I thought this was one way I could make up for the shame I had brought upon us all. I could fly to Arkansas, looking lovely and polished, and make pretty speeches at family funerals. I looked good enough on the surface to pretend, for Mama's sake, that Pauline and Minor Collinsworth had raised a good Southern daughter who understood the responsibilities of family.

In all the journeys back to Five Oaks, I stayed as far away from Center Street as I could. I spent my time instead at the homes of aunts and uncles and cousins, soaking up the stories of my ancestors, learning everything I could about my heritage as a Collinsworth. I often sat quietly on the porch at Five Oaks and tried to absorb all the gentle, country sounds to take back to California with me. With the concentration of a musician seeking a certain pitch, I listened to the tune of the wind in the oaks and dogwoods. I memorized the reticent, rural ways of my uncles as they stuffed their wads of tobacco into their cheeks. I grinned when they spit a brown stream off the side of Grandmother's porch, ever careful not to soil the green fretwork of the railing.

I walked the fields and waded through the lazy stream that flowed near the main house. I sifted the soil through my fingers and plucked branches of dogwood to take back to Daddy. And always, when I returned to Charter Oak, I ran to him with another prize from his old home. But he never acknowledged my gifts. He never acknowledged my presence.

"Why didn't you divorce him?" I shrieked at Mama in a fit of frustrated rage after yet another hour with him as he rocked silently while I regaled him with stories of his family and the old plantation. "Why in Heaven's name did you stay with him?"

It was an old argument, but it had not lost its bite.

"Why didn't you save yourself, not to mention your children? Were your wedding vows more important than Laddie and me?" Mama had no answers. She turned her back to me and walked into the kitchen. I followed her, screaming, "Didn't our happiness have any importance? I hate you! I hate him!"

I ran upstairs to my old room and threw myself across the bed and sobbed. It wasn't true—at least part of it wasn't. I didn't really hate my father. At that moment I believed I really did hate Mama, but it was myself I hated most of all.

I failed you, Daddy... I was bad, and I couldn't help you...

My charm and beauty had not been enough to heal him. In the end, my sweet, childish songs had not possessed the power to tame his disease.

I had been powerless to keep the promise I had made on the driveway of the Arkansas mental institution.

Worst of all, I had been unable to prevent myself from loving him.

That was Mama's fault, as was everything. If she had left him, I would never have known him. I would never have experienced the excruciating pain of loving him.

At that moment, I made the decision to stop loving altogether.

I made the trips to Five Oaks when it was required of me, but I no longer carried back stories to Daddy. I closed myself off from every gesture of affection. I spent weekends at my apartment, instead of going to the villa to see Mama. I went to the old manor house only to teach my dance students in the basement studio. I abdicated my position as the dutiful daughter and left Laddie with the chore of loving our parents.

Laddie became the man of the hour. He visited Mama daily, bringing her little gifts and cards and words of encouragement. He searched for things—anything—that might bring a focus to Daddy's vacant eyes. He had brought Daddy an expensive collection of hand-carved pipes from Europe and now he made it his personal quest to fill them with every blend of tobacco he could find. Daddy never lit even one of the pipes. It was the pocket calculator Laddie gave him that brought a light of recognition to Daddy's eyes.

Mama watched as Laddie placed the calculator in Daddy's hands.

"Honey, don't continue to spend your money on Daddy," she said. "He's not aware of anything you bring home."

"I know, Mama, but I have to try."

Laddie crouched down next to Daddy's rocking chair and patiently, as if talking to a child, he explained the calculator to Daddy. Daddy sat perfectly still, as if he saw nothing and heard nothing. Laddie stood up, sighed deeply, and left the room with Mama. He returned a few minutes later to find Daddy working problems and calculating formulas.

Brilliance still lived in Daddy's tormented mind. His accuracy as an accountant had once been second to none. A member of an association of CPAs that evaluates accountants' accuracy on a regular basis, Daddy had received a perfect rating every time. His work was flawless. Now old and gray and vacant, he sat with Laddie's little pocket calculator and tabulated numbers over and over and over again. He was unaware of the passing of time. Day and night, his fingers tapped at the keys on his new obsession. Numbers penetrated the wall of his insanity, where his family had been unable to make even a dent.

Laddie's breakthrough contact with Daddy further solidified his position as the "golden child." He could do no wrong. My resentment of him grew larger every day. When he began making trips to Five Oaks, he returned not with twigs from the trees, but with a box of slides. He had pictures of every angle of the house at Five Oaks and every field and every bend of Dogwood Creek. He set up a slide projector and a screen in Daddy's upstairs room— Daddy had taken to migrating from the dark basement up to the light, and then back to the darkness again. Hour after hour, slides skipped across the screen in front of Daddy, showing him the house with the green shutters, the huge oak trees that shaded the porch, the fields lush with sprouting soybeans and rice. Daddy sat and rocked, his eyes never registering the view in front of him, his hands—when not busy with the pocket calculator— gripping the rails on his rocking chair.

Chapter 8

I met "Mitch" my senior year of college. I would never have
even considered dating him—he had a dark sullenness about
him—but a passing comment from Mama drove me toward him
like vertigo might drive one to leap off a twelve-story building.

It was springtime, and my basement studio at the old manor
house was filled with sets I had designed for my students' dance
recital. I recruited some of the campus "jocks" and their friends to
help me load and transport the equipment and the stage props to
the recital location. Mitch joined the volunteers. Mama noticed
him among the others—something about him set him apart from
the rest of the football giants who traipsed through the house
that day.

"Who was that dark, powerful-looking young man with the
thick eyebrows?" she asked later, after the gang left the house.

I didn't have to think long before I knew who she was talking
about. "His name is Mitch," I told her.

"I didn't like him," Mama answered. "He's so dark and coarse-
looking—he scared me."

I made a date with Mitch that week.

Mitch was only another in the long chain of young men I
dated because I knew Mama would not approve. Deliberately,
and with great glee, I brought home every kind of young man
whose background or manners I knew would offend my mother.
My plan of revenge was simple: use the men in my life to hurt
Mama, just as she had hurt me.

Rebellious and filled with rancid anger, I would have done
anything to cause pain to my mother during that time. I would
have used anything, anyone—and Mitch was a convenient and
willing tool. His arrogance was an affront to Mama's aristocratic
Southern ways. He offended her ideas of genteel propriety. And
worst of all, his size intimidated her.

Mama liked people who recognized her strength, who respected
her for her own unique brand of power. Mitch, with his lineman's

physique and his disregard for all things holy and right, possessed an irreverence that both irritated and frightened Mama a little.

At first Mitch scared me, too, but I didn't let Mama know this. I had felt a sinister power emanating from him that day he came to the manor house to help move sets. Danger radiated from him as he stood in the dining room watching me. The dark brows knitted across his eyes sent a message of silent anger. His size overpowered the dimensions of the room, with its intricately carved antique furniture. He looked as if only a small annoyance would be enough to incite him to violence. With one powerful motion he could have crushed Mama's delicate, valuable pieces.

Mitch had already acquired a reputation for savagery. Rumors swirled about him—rumors I later confirmed. As a youth, he had killed a man in a gang fight. The only child of very powerful parents, Mitch had been sentenced to ROTC at a Big Ten university instead of to prison. His family had pressed their influence on the case, and the authorities had agreed to seal the police records.

Violence continued to follow him. In a forbidden escapade with his parents' car, Mitch drove off into a dense fog one night and crashed the car, nearly killing himself. His throat was slit when he flew through the window, and he was left with multiple injuries and a long, jagged scar that ran from below his ear down his neck and throat. The injuries from the accident released him from his military commitment, and he began focusing all his energy and strength on his football career. Sometime during those turbulent years, he had been married and quickly divorced.

In the beginning, it was Mama's aversion to Mitch that made him seem very exciting to me, in spite of the ugly scar on his neck. But as I grew to know him, I saw him as quite appealing. He was older than I, and his dark looks gave him a mysterious allure. Of French-Basque ancestry, he had black, curly hair and skin that tanned to a golden brown. His black moustache gave him a Burt Reynolds look that was really quite charming. His roguish good looks could obliterate the danger signals that flashed from him.

Mitch's father had been an all-American athlete, an Olympic decathlete whose name is found in the Helm's Hall of Fame. His goal for his son had always been professional sports. An adopted child, Mitch had lain in his father's arms when he was eight days old, and his father had wept at the size of his new son's feet. "They're so small—will he ever be able to play sports?" he had mourned. Mitch lived every day of his life driven to convince his father that he could indeed play sports, and play them very well.

When I met Mitch, he had just received the title "All-American." He had left his Big Ten university and signed as a free agent with the Houston Oilers. His size and manner served as mighty intimidation factors on the gridiron. At six feet five inches and 245 pounds, he was a formidable foe wherever he decided to pick a fight. The question of his shoe size was never a concern after his infancy.

Mitch and I had dated only a short time before I learned that there was a gentle, caring side to this giant of a man whose looks Mama considered coarse. Romance flowed in his veins, and he often brought me flowers, candy, and champagne.

This man is strong, I thought. He's not weak like my father... He will never be sick like Daddy...

He made me feel small and fragile and cared for. I believed he would protect me and keep me safe.

I agreed to marry Mitch for all the wrong reasons. At twenty-four, I was terribly young and childlike. I interpreted Mitch's protective manner as love, and while I could not honestly say I returned his love, I did feel a strong attraction toward him. The fact that he was not exactly what Mama would have chosen for me also played a large part in my decision to become his wife.

I was still nursing anger toward Mama. Defiance was still a daily pursuit. But as Mama considered the idea of my marriage to Mitch, she began to concede that perhaps it wasn't a terrible thing.

"It's simply a matter of the right breeding," Mama had always said about marriage. And Mitch, while not exactly what Mama would have chosen for me, did have the family connections. He came from power and prestige, and in Mama's eyes, this gave him a good "pedigree." He was well-educated; and, although not exactly refined, he was good-looking in a rugged kind of way. And he was a football hero.

Like Mama, I had found myself an athlete from a wealthy, prestigious family. Only I would fare better than Mama in my choice, I believed. Mitch was strong and healthy and protective. He would not become sick, like Daddy. He would always be there for me. He would take care of me. All these factors weighed heavily in my decision to marry Mitch, but near the top of the list, I liked the idea that Mama would really have preferred someone else for a son-in-law.

Of course, Mama, always proper, always the great lady, acquiesced to our plans with a measure of grace. She poured all her creative genius into planning the grandest, most lavish wedding she could afford.

Throughout the months of our courtship, Mitch and I spoke seldom of love. Neither of us really understood the workings of a marriage. Growing up in the shadow of Daddy's illness, I had seen nothing of a normal, healthy relationship between a husband and a wife. I anticipated my role with no idea at all of what Mitch expected from me. And I had no idea what to expect from him.

Our marriage was doomed before it even began.

We seldom talked about important things—we liked none of the same things. Mitch liked football and I liked ballet. He loved sports on television; I loved the symphony. He was a football hero; I was a beauty queen. The only things we shared in common were our trophies. Mitch, like me, had grown up with an obsessive need to please his father. Athletics had been his venue. Winning was everything.

On December 18, 1971, we said our wedding vows. The ceremony was held in the chapel at Webb Preparatory School, a prestigious private school set on a bluff overlooking great craggy cliffs. A Gothic-like, stone structure, the chapel was the perfect setting for the regal storybook wedding my mother had always dreamed of giving me. It was like a scene out of *Camelot*. My bridesmaids wore vibrant, red velvet, fur-trimmed dresses and bonnets. The men in the wedding party wore Edwardian suits.

As I dressed for my wedding in my cream-colored velvet gown, I couldn't quiet the thoughts that troubled me.

This is a mistake... This is a terrible mistake...

I turned in front of the full-length mirror in my room. The velvet, fur-trimmed train on my dress spilled out behind me and swirled about my legs like a pool of rich cream.

It's all so beautiful, I thought, but it's all so wrong!

It's too late... There's nothing I can do.

I walked to the doorway of my father's room. He sat in his rocking chair, silently absorbed in some faraway scene only his eyes could see. I walked toward him, the creaking of his chair a macabre accompaniment to the swishing of my long, velvet dress.

"Daddy, this is my wedding day."

No answer. No movement.

"I just wanted you to know, Daddy, I'm getting married today, and... and... I love you, Daddy."

It was Laddie whose arm I gripped in the doorway of the

chapel that day. It was Laddie's voice I heard, whispering above the organ music, "Don't be nervous, Mitty. You look beautiful... "

A cold wind swept over me as I stood there in the entrance of the stone church, seeing Mitch's dark figure at the end of the aisle. I looked up at Laddie, silently begging him to hear and understand the words I couldn't speak just then.

I love you, Laddie... Please understand.

It had been so long since we had said civil words to each other. His to me had been laced with criticism, mine to him, poisoned with resentment. Yet, in those final moments before he walked me down the aisle to give me away, all our conflicts seemed to simply dissolve.

"Don't worry," Laddie said softly, leaning his head down close to mine so only I could hear, "I'm here to make sure everything goes just like it's supposed to. Everything is going to be fine."

Once again, he was my heroic big brother, making promises I wanted to believe. Once again he was a little boy wearing a Confederate uniform, wielding the weapons of a soldier in defense of a lost cause. Wearing the doomed gray of a Rebel, he had believed then, mistakenly, that he was the victor. Proud and courageous in his ignorance, he had blithely enjoyed his childish fantasies, pretending he had won when in fact he had lost.

Was this another of our lives' lost causes—this wedding of mine? Would we spend all our lives dressed in Rebel gray, clothed in the costumes of the defeated, claiming victory, while history would record our feeble gestures as failures?

Perhaps, for Laddie, everything *would* be fine. Perhaps someday he would be able to don the victor's garb. His chances were better than mine, it seemed. He dated lovely, proper girls whom Mama adored. He had worked hard at his studies and had become an outstanding teacher. He had put aside his hatred of our father and replaced it with gentle understanding and gestures of kindness. Laddie was the loving, caring, obedient son. But what would become of me—the rebel who seemed bent on destruction?

The organ chords sounded loudly and I stepped forward, clutching Laddie's arm, walking in time with him, moving inevitably toward the fate that awaited me as Mitch's wife.

After the ceremony, I stood on the stairs at the old manor house and looked about me. Mama had transformed the downstairs into an exact replica of a Currier and Ives setting for my wedding reception. Candles and garland and Victorian touches lit every corner of every room of the house. All the beauty and magic she had performed on the old brick house on Center Street had come to rest here, in this villa among the orange groves. For Mama, it was a moment of triumph. She had created an unforgettable scene of Christmas charm for my wedding day. I gripped my bouquet and smiled at the crowd of friends gathered beneath me, awaiting the traditional toss. Suddenly, I sensed the presence of a child behind me. I turned to look, but no one was there.

Shivering, I knew she was there—I could *feel* her there— although no eyes could see her. A little girl with French braids and thick eyeglasses pressed against me, tugging at me, her plaintive voice reaching only my ears.

"You promised, Mitty, you promised... I heard you, that day at the hospital, when they dragged Daddy away, you promised you'd make him better."

I shut my eyes tightly against the memory.

I can't think about this now... I can't think about this now...

Pasting a smile on my face, I tossed my bouquet into the air and turned around quickly to run to my room. With shaking hands, I took off my wedding dress.

I can't think about it...

I kept telling myself that, but the image of the little girl followed me about my room, nagging me and scolding me as I changed my clothes and combed my hair. She walked with me to Daddy's room and stood nearby, accusing me, as I leaned down to kiss his cool forehead.

"Goodbye, Daddy," I whispered.

Mitch and I drove away from the villa amid shouts of good luck and best wishes. Mama stood in the doorway, looking weary but patrician, and lovelier than I had seen her look in a very long time. Laddie stood behind her and his eyes bid me a somber goodbye. On the porch nearby stood a little girl in pigtails and glasses whose expression spoke eloquently of betrayal.

Our marriage began to disintegrate within hours of our spoken vows. On our wedding night, I dressed carefully in a soft, filmy peignoir and stepped out in front of my husband, trembling with trepidation.

"Do you love me, Mitch?" I asked, my hands nervously gripping the satin fabric of my gown.

Mitch's black-brown eyes locked with mine for only a second, and then he looked away quickly.

as a baby (above), and (inset) as a senior in high school, class of 1965.
dit: Millicent Collinsworth Collection

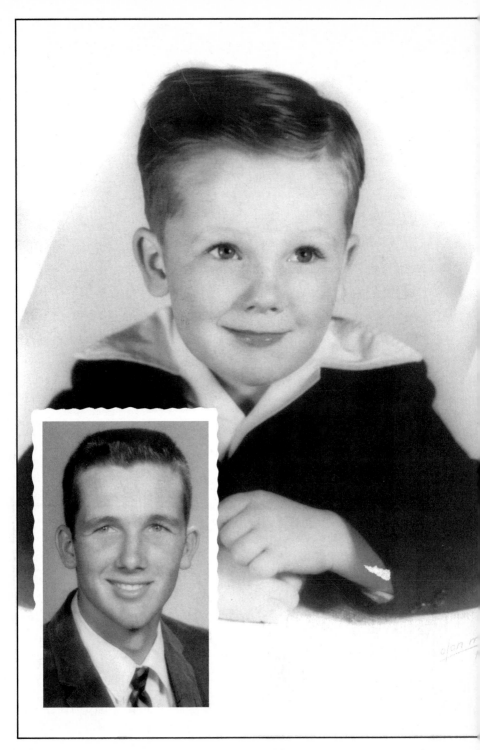

Brother, Laddie, four years old, 1949. (Inset) Laddie's graduation picture, 1963.
Credit: Millicent Collinsworth Collection

at age 16, as a dancer at the Diamond Horseshoe Theater, and (inset) at age 10, 1957.
lit: Millicent Collinsworth Collection

A modeling picture of me, circa 1966, and (inset) as a college freshman, in the same year. *Credit: Millicent Collinsworth Collection*

o modeling photos of me, both circa 1968. *Credit: Millicent Collinsworth Collection*

Standing with Laddie before my wedding to Mitch, December, 1971. (Inset) Laddie a▪
me as children, ages 6 and 8. *Credit: Millicent Collinsworth Collection*

th these photos show my progression with bulimia nervosa during the late ’70s and early 1980s. Note the telltale circles under the eyes (above) and the ulting emaciation (inset). *Credit: Millicent Collinsworth Collection*

Gary and me on our wedding day, and (inset) on stage in a production of "Wait Until Dar
Credit: Millicent Collinsworth Collection

ore at his "Hero Dog" awards ceremony, May, 1988. (Inset) Eeyore as a Seeing Eye
ppy in Morristown, New Jersey. *Credit: Millicent Collinsworth Collection*

My grandfather, grandmother, and uncles. Daddy is the baby in the center. (Below) Searcy High football team of 1924. Photo still hangs in Stotts Drugstore. Daddy is in the center row, second from left. (Inset) Daddy, in 1935. *Credit: Millicent Collinsworth Collection*

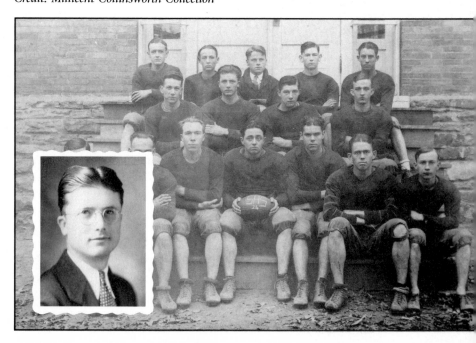

Wedding photos of Daddy
and Mama, 1937.
*Credit: Millicent Collinsworth
Collection*

Only photograph of Old John, who stands behind Great-uncle Minor, and my grandmother. *Credit: Millicent Collinsworth Collection*

ove) The drugstore soda fountain in Tuckerman, Arkansas, where Mama ate her
ch as a young bride. (Below) The Rialto Theater in Searcy, Arkansas, where Laddie
I spent our Saturday afternoons. *Credit: Millicent Collinsworth Collection*

(Above) Dogwood creek, a meandering stream that borders Five Oaks in Griffithville, Arkansas. (Below) The original sign from the Collinsworth's Little Red School House, Searcy, Arkansas. *Credit: Millicent Collinsworth Collection*

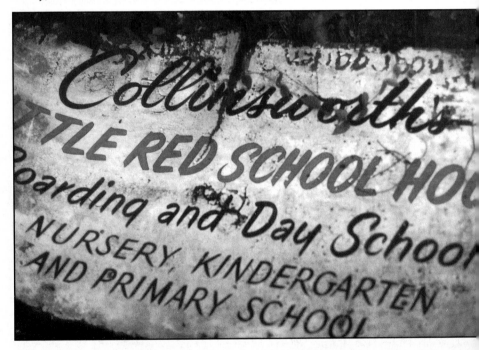

(Above) The old brick house on Center Street, in Searcy, Arkansas where Laddie and I spent our early, idyllic years. (Below) The old Manor House, in Charter Oaks, California.

Two different views of the Collinsworth family homestead, Five Oaks, in Griffithville, Arkansas. *Credit: Millicent Collinsworth Collection*

No... something's terribly wrong...

"Mitch?"

He sat on the edge of the bed, leaning forward with his elbows resting on his knees. His huge hands clenched and unclenched as he sat there, troubled and uncertain.

I could feel hot tears spill onto my cheeks.

"Mitch, please, I have to know... "

"No," he answered, in a voice that was gruff with misery.

"Then why did you marry me?" I whispered.

He shook his head, as if he wasn't sure how to answer me. His huge shoulders shrugged. "I couldn't stand to let anyone else have you."

I felt as though a cannonball had just burned through my chest. It was my wedding day. I wanted to hear my husband declare his undying love for me. But there was no such declaration. Nor could I have said the words to him.

What have we done? I thought, looking at my husband.

I stood there, shaking, wondering how I could stand so calmly while such pain was ripping through my insides.

So began our wedding bliss.

Our marriage contract, for my part, might have read like a contract for a hit man. "I, Mitty, take you Mitch, as a weapon for the purpose of wreaking revenge on my mother for every fault and injury I hold against her."

For his part, Mitch might have said, "I, Mitch, take you, Mitty, to place among all my other trophies, to show off and lend me prestige, until your beauty begins to tarnish, or until challenged by another, more impressive trophy."

Neither one of us had any idea of the workings of a healthy marriage relationship. Neither of us had the tools to build a loving family. Our marriage mocked the idea of emotional intimacy and mutual support. The sweet gestures of romance I had enjoyed from Mitch before the wedding, ended almost as soon as the vows were uttered. We lived like strangers in our small apartment near the university.

I spent very little time trying to analyze our estrangement. Reason and logic had little place in my life. I lived according to emotions—emotions sadly skewed by the bizarre lifestyle of a household dominated by the presence of mental illness. While not a contagious disease, my father's illness had been a toxic contaminant in my fragile, developing young adulthood. In many ways, I was as sick as my ailing father.

Mitch's career with the Oilers could have been measured in hours. His knees, already damaged from playing college ball, put him on the injured list almost immediately, and, in a matter of weeks, he was sent home. Angry and disappointed, he enrolled in graduate studies at California State and threw his energy into strengthening himself for another try at the pros. He spent every spare hour working out in the gym and pursuing contacts that would get him into a training camp for another tryout. He left home early every morning and returned late at night, often after I had already gone to bed.

I spent many hours in my new studio not far from our apartment—I had so many dance students now that I had outgrown the basement studio. I accepted dancing and choreography jobs and invested a great deal of time trying to look the way Mitch wanted me to look.

Before our marriage, I had taken his comments about my hair and clothing style as little more than suggestions, and I had made changes, hoping to please him. After the wedding, Mitch's comments became harsh criticisms, and there were no more suggestions, only demands. He disliked the style Mama had taught me—classic, understated elegance. He insisted I wear clothes that were showy, almost gauche. To keep peace, I acquiesced to him in everything, letting him pick my dresses and dictate my hairstyle. And I let him convince me that I needed to lose a few pounds, so that the outfits he chose would look even better on me.

Anxious to please him, I dieted constantly, as I had been doing for years, and kept a prescription of diet pills handy. Faced with the pressure of his unrelenting criticism and his insistence on having a wife with a perfect figure, I began to binge and then to quickly purge myself by taking laxatives and diuretics, or by vomiting.

My marriage was not turning out to be the haven of safety I had believed it would be, but the Collinsworth in me would not allow me to admit failure. I would not give up and go home to Mama. I would make this marriage work, no matter what it took. I was determined not to give Mama another reason to be ashamed of me.

The first time Mitch hit me, I was stunned. I had sensed the violence in him, but I had never expected it to be directed toward me. But one day, while we were driving down the freeway, something I said irritated him, and he slapped me. His ring split my lip and my head snapped back with the force of his swing. I was terrified at the power of his anger, but even more terrified that such rage could be invoked by nothing more than a simple statement.

Mitch pulled off the freeway at the first exit he came to.

"I'm sorry, Baby, I'm so sorry... I'm so sorry," he said as he stroked my head and pressed a handkerchief to my bleeding lip. "You okay, Baby? Please say you're okay!"

I couldn't speak. I felt dead inside.

"It will never happen again, I swear it, Pookie... Tell me you forgive me! Please, Baby, I'm so sorry!"

I listened to his remorse, and I forgave him. But from that day forward, I was very frightened of my husband.

The next time he hit me, he broke my nose.

It seemed I was destined for an odyssey of abuse. It had begun with Mr. Simpson when I was ten years old. His assaults on my innocence had hurled me into a caravan of horror that seemed unstoppable. His vile acts had convinced me that I was vile, too. I believed on some level that I deserved all the horrible things that happened to me because I had been a party to the filthy actions of a cruel, perverted old man. And yet, some part of me possessed great pride—a Collinsworth deserved better than this! But I didn't know how to get out of harm's way.

Mitch's propensity for violence continued, unabated. Small comments, little irritations, would trigger uncontrolled outbursts of anger that would end with profuse apologies and the application of an ice pack to some part of my body. Time after time, I accepted his apologies, acknowledging that somehow I had caused his anger and was in part responsible for the pummeling I received. And I believed that somehow we would learn to live together without violence.

I believed that, because I knew another side to Mitch. I had seen his kindness before, and at times I saw in him great humor. I had seen him control his strength and replace it with restraint and gentleness. It would happen when we visited the old manor house. Mama, wearing her "Bumblebee" sweatshirt and a whistle tied around her neck, would say, "Put a headlock on me, Mitch," as she stepped toward him. He would grab her around the neck and in the next instant Mama would pin him to the living-room floor.

Mama would stand up quickly, square her shoulders, and toss her long braid back over her shoulder before offering Mitch a hand up.

"Very good, Mrs. C," Mitch would tell her, grinning.

"The Bumblebees have a tournament next week," she'd say to him as she walked into the kitchen to pour herself a cup of tea. "I think we're good for a first-place trophy in this one."

Then, cradling a china cup in her hands and sipping delicately, Mama would once again become the Southern matriarch, all dignity and propriety and gentility clad in an oversized sweatshirt and a whistle on a string. And I would wonder if I had imagined it, or if I had really just seen her toss my giant of a husband to the floor.

In the rough barrio neighborhood where Mama taught, none of the teachers, male or female, wanted to linger after school hours with athletic teams. On the edge of East Los Angeles, the area was already infiltrated by gangs and drug use. Safety was a major concern for the teachers and administrators, as well as for the children. But Mama seemed not to care. The students needed a sports program, so she had volunteered to coach. She was soon staying late every day, shouting commands and encouragement to sweaty fifth- and sixth-grade boys learning to wrestle in a hot, dingy gymnasium. Day after day, she took on the biggest, most aggressive, most dangerous adolescents, and many times, she pinned them easily.

Mitch would let her practice her moves and various holds on him. Then, armed with confidence after felling such a giant as he, Mama would take her skills to the barrio school. She led the Bassett Bumblebees to several championships, in cross-country as well as wrestling.

With Mitch's powerful physique, he could have crushed Mama easily. But time after time, he sheathed his strength and let her throw him down, as if she were David and he the doomed Goliath. At those times, I glimpsed tenderness in an otherwise angry, imposing man, and I thought perhaps we could once again learn to deal kindly with each other. And when he extended that tenderness toward my silent, staring, catatonic father, there was no doubt in my mind that there was truly something to love in my fierce, frightening husband.

"I'll go with you to visit your folks, but only if I can watch the football game," Mitch would sometimes say when I asked him to go with me for a weekend visit to the old manor house.

"Mitch, the television set is in Daddy's room," I would remind him.

"That's okay," he answered. "Just leave me alone and let me watch the game."

And so, on many weekends, we would drive to the old manor house and Mitch would climb the stairs to Daddy's room. He was too big for Mama's delicate, antique furniture, so he would sit on the floor next to Daddy's rocking chair and watch sports on television while Mama and I visited downstairs.

I could hear Mitch's voice rise in response to the action on the screen, and sometimes he would swear and bang the floor in frustration over an intercepted pass or a fumble on the play. I would often creep upstairs and stand in the doorway of Daddy's room, listening and watching the strange interplay between the giant football player seated on the floor and the frail, tortured old man who rocked back and forth endlessly.

"The quarterback steps back into the pocket... He's got the hand-off! He's looking for a receiver, and there he is down field!" Mitch's voice mimicked Howard Cosell's as he gave Daddy a play-by-play report of everything that was happening on the color screen.

"What do you think, Mr. C?" he'd ask Daddy. "Think they can score on this next play?"

He would respond to his own question, as if Daddy, with the astuteness of a former football hero, had come up with the answer himself.

"You're right, Mr. C. I don't think they can do it either. The line's too weak—the defense is going to mow 'em down."

Knowing there is no statute of limitations when it comes to greatness, Mitch, in his own unique way, paid homage to my father. He brought him a little gift of respect with every visit. He made us remember something long forgotten: that this man in the rocking chair had once been a shining star.

"Mitch, I want to thank you for being so gracious to Mr. Collinsworth," Mama said to him one day after he had spent an afternoon playing "color commentator" for a Sunday-afternoon game in Daddy's room.

"I don't think of him the way he is now, Mrs. C," Mitch answered. "I think of him the way he used to be."

The way he used to be... My daddy, the football hero, was suddenly a young man again, sprinting down field to score the winning touchdown amid the screams of the hometown crowd. Tall, muscular, and aristocratic, he carried his youthful strength with the dignity of a star.

I thought in surprise, What an immense leap of faith! My sickly, insane father transformed into a jersey-clad football hero or a track star, running and leaping with the fluid, agile motions of a born athlete—Mitch can see that!

Then why can't he see that we've got to do something to save our marriage? I wondered. Why is that so hard for him to see?

He was blind, yes, but so was I. Reasonable, rational solutions are seldom bred in unreasonable, irrational environments. I had married this man for all the wrong reasons. I was as responsible as he for the mess of our relationship. The only positive element in my favor was that I believed in our commitment, misguided though it might have been. And I didn't want to chalk up another failure.

In spite of my motives for marrying him, I really did want to make Mitch happy. I really wanted to find some common ground on which to base our marriage. If he wasn't willing or able to make an effort to involve himself in the things that interested me, I would try to cultivate an appreciation for his interests. I would have to make a place for myself in his world.

"Camping!" I exclaimed in response to Mitch one evening. "You want me to go camping with you?"

"There'll be other couples along. We'll be near a lake, do a little water-skiing—it'll be great. What do you say, Pookie?" Mitch had that funny, carefree look on his face, the one he wore when he was playing Howard Cosell in my father's room. It was the look that could make me forget his dark side. It could make me say yes to almost anything.

Camping. By a lake. Maybe it wouldn't be too bad... I envisioned a cabin in the woods, the sound of the lake lapping against the shore... It could be romantic. I dug out Mama's antique wicker picnic basket and loaded it with linen napkins, silverware, and crystal goblets. I packed a sexy peignoir and put on a happy face. If Mitch wanted to camp out, we'd camp out in style.

The campsite, a muddy bog near a small lake, held no cabin. The other couples roared when they saw my gear for the weekend.

"Mitch, I can't stay here!" I wailed. "Where will we sleep... No! You're kidding! I've never slept on the ground before!"

Mitch's friends had little patience with my whining. They all voted to leave me behind when they went out on the lake to water-ski. "Fix us some lunch, Pookie. We'll be back in a little while."

It would be my finest hour. I'd show them all how a Southern belle serves lunch, I thought.

Meticulously, I cut the crust off the bread and made lovely

little tuna salad sandwiches. I hauled in rocks and created intimate "conversation" circles, laying out my linen napkins and crystal and making "table settings" for everyone. When the gang came in off the lake, laughing and dripping wet, the sandwiches were limp and hot from hours under the sun, but they were all too hungry to care. In the early hours of the next morning, we all fled to the nearest hospital with food poisoning, and my camping career screeched to a halt.

Mitch only reluctantly believed me when I insisted that I hadn't deliberately tried to murder him and his friends. But it seemed that nothing I did could remove the barriers that stood in the way of our happiness. I wondered if having children would supply our marriage with the missing element. Would a child cement us together and bring some love to our relationship?

"I can't stand children," Mitch said, when I suggested we try to have a baby. "Pregnant women are ugly. I've never known a man who didn't cheat on his wife while she was pregnant."

I was appalled. Having a child would be a beautiful thing, I believed. I became consumed with the idea of having a baby. Maybe a new life inside me would make up for the tragedy of my earlier pregnancy. And perhaps a child, a son, would provide Mitch with new interest in our marriage. I tried to imagine him as a proud and loving father, coming home with bundles of toys and athletic equipment for a dark-haired, round-faced, little boy. But during our first year of marriage, when I told him I was pregnant, there were no expressions of tenderness.

Enraged by the news that a child was on the way, Mitch seemed determined to punish me. I couldn't convince him that a child would be good for us. When I talked about lessening my work schedule so that I could rest and enjoy the pregnancy, he was furious. So I continued to accept more dance students, increasing my hours at the studio, trying to placate him while hoping he would catch my excitement about the coming baby. A month later, I miscarried.

A second miscarriage occurred several months later. While I hadn't been trying to get pregnant, I'd been pleased and excited when I learned the news. The doctor had warned me that I was in the high-risk category, because of the previous ectopic pregnancy. I had tried to rest as much as possible and still keep up with Mitch's demands, but the pregnancy ended before it reached the first trimester. I was devastated. Mitch was relieved.

Mitch's second chance at the NFL came when the Denver

Broncos invited him to come and try out. When he didn't make
the cut, he came home maniacally angry. His knees had given
out on him again. The weight he needed to carry in order to play
his position at center was too much for his already injury-weakened
knees. But Mitch refused to give up on his dream. He would do
anything to make a place for himself on an NFL team. Anything...
anything at all.

Mitch traveled to Mexico to get his hands on Dianabol, a
substance used flagrantly by most of his friends. In a very short
time, his body resembled that of the "Incredible Hulk." He split
out the seams of his clothes, and when he sat on Mama's delicate
antique chairs, I thought they would collapse beneath him. We
had constantly to find ways to accommodate his immense size.

Mitch was no stranger to substance abuse. Since high school,
he had taken steroids to build his physique to mammoth size. He
had started popping amphetamines during college play—his
coaches wanted the team aggressive and mean, so they fed the
players "uppers" before each game. Steroids and drugs were just
another part of the sports world Mitch inhabited. He could not
be persuaded to stop taking them. Bleeding ulcers didn't stop
him; personality changes didn't stop him. His violent temper
outbursts became a daily occurrence. Even a simple conversation
could trigger his uncontrolled, irrational fury, and unleash his
powerful fists.

If our marriage had been the scene of anger and conflict before,
it was now like a war zone. Nothing about Mitch resembled the
man he had been during our courtship. Over the next several
months, living with him was much like navigating through a
minefield. I never knew when a misstep might ignite an explosion
that would destroy me.

This marriage is a mistake, I thought, day after day, admitting
only to myself that once again I had failed.

When I was with Mama, I pretended that all was well. I visited
her occasionally, talked about my work, about dancing, and about
my apartment. I accepted her sympathy for the miscarriages, but
I never disclosed to her the horrible state of my marriage. I could
never let her know what a terrible mistake I had made—again.
But, of course, Mama knew. She knew, but she never said anything
about it either. It was the Collinsworth way: Endure stoically.
Deny the pain. Ignore the evidence of disaster.

And the evidence was strewn all around me. Mitch was
unfaithful to me, almost from the very beginning.

There had been times when he was good to me—these just
made me feel more confused whenever I thought about them. It
hadn't been so long ago that he had showered me with flowers
and gifts. He had been strong and caring and protective. Once,
when we were courting, we had been caught in a sudden rainstorm.
Mitch had grabbed my hand and pulled me into a department
store to wait out the downpour. We had found ourselves in the
children's department, surrounded by tiny pink and blue articles
and huge stuffed toys. Mitch had laughed at the delicate baby
clothes, and his huge hands had picked up a pair of tiny baby
sneakers, size zero. He had dangled them from his fingers and
said, "Let's buy them. We'll save them for our first son. They'll be
his first football shoes."

Together, we had laughed and carried the package out of the
store to save for the day when we would have a son. But there
had been little laughter since our wedding. And the idea of a
child had lost its appeal, at least for Mitch. When I became
pregnant for the third time, my joy was tainted with fear.

I wanted this child very badly. I did everything I could to take
care of myself so that I would be able to carry it to term. I also
tried to please Mitch in every little thing. I did not want to risk
his violence. I didn't want the child I was carrying to be injured if
he should hurl his anger at me. I would do anything to ensure a
normal, healthy baby. I made no comments about the growing
evidence of his infidelities. I didn't dare confront him. I closed
my mouth and allowed Mitch to dictate to me in any way he
liked. I let him select my eye shadow, the color of my lipstick,
and my hairstyle, if it would keep peace.

One day, at a weak moment, I told Mama that Mitch wasn't
attracted to pregnant women. Almost immediately, she began
spending huge sums of money to dress me in designer clothes
that would hide my pregnancy and make me look attractive,
even glamorous, for my unreasonable, dangerous husband. And I
continued dancing and working out so that I did not gain a great
deal of weight in the early stages. By the fifth month of my
pregnancy, the baby was only a tiny bulge beneath my waistline.

Christmas, 1973, was only a few days away. Mitch had a football
conference in San Francisco and a plane to catch in a hurry. He
rushed about our apartment—nearly crushing the delicate
Christmas decorations I had carefully placed in every room—
trying to finish his last-minute packing. I walked over to the
Christmas tree that stood in the corner of our tiny living room

and turned on the antique train that circled its base.

"Run to McDonald's and get me an Egg McMuffin, will ya, Pookie?" Mitch asked, while he stuffed another pair of socks into his duffel bag.

"Sure," I answered. I pulled my hair back into a ponytail and made a quick face at myself in the mirror. I wasn't dressed to go out. I was wearing one of Mitch's old oversized football jerseys, but a trip to McDonald's didn't warrant a costume change. I grabbed my car keys and drove the two miles to the "golden arches."

Breakfast customers crowded the counter. I stepped into the shortest line and waited my turn. I couldn't help but notice the stares of a man in the next line. He placed his order and then looked back over his shoulder at me several times. It wasn't a friendly, open stare, and it made me uncomfortable, but moments later he was gone with his coffee and it was my turn to order. He was waiting for me when I reached my car.

"I think I know you," he said, looking at me intently.

"Oh?" I answered. I juggled Mitch's breakfast and my keys and hurried to open the car door. "I'm sorry, I can't place you."

"I'm sure I know you," he said again, standing closer than I liked.

"You must be wrong," I said, slamming the door and quickly starting the car. I glanced in my rearview mirror as I drove home. The man had disappeared into the parking lot with the rest of the morning crowd.

"Breakfast!" I called out as I entered the apartment. Mitch took the bag from me and sat down to devour it before he left for the airport.

"There was the strangest guy at McDonald's," I said, as I poured myself a cup of coffee and sat down beside Mitch while he ate. "He seemed to think he knew me from somewhere. I think he was just a little crazy."

"He wasn't coming on to you, was he?" Mitch answered, grinning. "No man in his right mind would find a pregnant woman attractive—the guy probably was crazy!"

I pretended his comments were humorous, not hurtful. I said goodbye a few minutes later as he slammed the door behind him and headed for the airport. I changed my clothes and drove to a rehearsal at my studio.

It was late in the afternoon when I returned to the apartment, bringing some of my students home with me for a short break from our dance practice. The boys and girls made themselves at home. They drank sodas and fussed over our dog, a miniature whippet we had named Occi in honor of Occidental College, Mitch's father's alma mater. Shy and timid, Occi followed the kids through the apartment, watching with nervous eyes as they fingered all the Christmas decorations and amused themselves with the toy train that circled the tree.

"Something smells funny in here," one of the boys said to me as he moved about the small apartment with Occi at his heels.

I sniffed the air, noticing something unfamiliar and unpleasant, but at the time it seemed insignificant. A little while later, I drove the kids back to rehearsal. That night, I returned to the apartment alone.

Occi greeted me at the door with a nervous bark. She hung about my legs and trembled as I walked toward the Christmas tree in the corner.

"What's the matter, girl?"

I plugged in the flashing lights and turned on the toy train, smiling as the little engine jerked forward to begin its route around the tree. The only sound in the apartment was the click-clicking of tiny wheels on the track.

And then, the silence of terror drowned out all other noises.

Someone is in this apartment!

The presence of danger flooded the entire apartment. I turned around slowly, and there, in front of me, stood the man from McDonald's.

I knew he was going to hurt me. My only thought was for my unborn child.

"What do you want?" I tried to keep my voice steady. "Money? Is that what you want? You can have it... You can have anything! Just take it and get out!"

Occi hovered behind my legs. The man stepped toward me. In one hand, he held a straight-edged razor. The acrid smell of him assaulted my nostrils.

"I'm pregnant! Take anything you want, just don't hurt my baby!"

With his next step, I knew he could not be stopped by words. I screamed. He lunged toward me and together we slammed to the floor. The Christmas tree toppled over, sending ornaments spinning across the carpet. A table lamp crashed. Occi's high-pitched barking reverberated in my ears. The man's weight crushed me and he dragged his blade through my clothes, slicing my chest and my thighs. My throat ached with the need to scream louder, to summon help. I thrashed about beneath him, but I could not escape.

"Please... please! My baby... don't hurt my baby!"

Grotesque in its cruelty, the face above me suddenly melted into the face of Mr. Simpson. I saw him clutch at a little girl with pigtails and glasses. I saw him toss her over his shoulder, as if she was nothing more than a bag of rags. Suddenly, the fear vibrating inside me erupted into fury.

"No!" I screamed, rolling and tossing and pushing against the weight that pinned me down.

"No... this can't happen! I won't let this happen!"

I was no longer a ten-year-old child. I wasn't a helpless little girl anymore. I wouldn't let this happen to me! I couldn't let it happen.

My baby... my baby... I can't let him hurt my baby!

A surge of fire-hot rage fed me a strength more powerful than anything I had ever felt before. But it was not enough. Though I kicked and screamed and twisted and clawed, his was the greater force.

When he climbed off of me, I felt a wrenching spasm in my abdomen. A gush of blood poured out onto the floor around me, and I knew I was going into labor. I knew I had lost the fight for my baby's life.

The rapist left quickly. I heard the sounds of a door closing and then I heard nothing... nothing, until sometime later, when I opened my eyes and saw the lights still flashing on the toppled Christmas tree and heard the urgent chugging of the toy train as it tried to force its way through the forest of fallen tree branches that blocked its path. Its motor sounds grew to an insistent whine as the engine came to a dead stop, its wheels spinning just inches from where my head lay on the floor.

The phone was on an end table across the room, but it seemed like miles as I pulled and scooted myself toward it. Occi huddled nearby and whimpered while I called the police and a friend who lived in the neighborhood. Everyone arrived at once. The police burst in, paramedics lifted me onto a gurney, and neighbors crowded around the doorway.

"We heard a commotion, but it never occurred to us that someone was being hurt," my next-door neighbor told the police. "I heard the dog bark, but that didn't worry me any."

A couple from downstairs had heard the crashing of furniture, but they thought it was probably a domestic squabble. No reason to investigate, they had told themselves. And the attacker had left my apartment just as he had entered it, unseen.

Mitch could not be located in San Francisco for three days. There was no record of him at the hotel where he had told me he would be staying. When he finally returned home and received the news that I had lost our child—a son—his outrage stunned me.

Mitch acted as though the child had been his one reason for living. He played the grieving father and blamed me for the loss of the baby. Our tenuous marriage became even more fragile.

I closed the dance studio. We moved out of the apartment and rented a place near the beach in Playa del Rey, and Mitch took a coaching job nearby. The police investigation into the rape and assault yielded few clues, and as time passed, Mitch began to pressure me to stop pursuing it.

"Forget it. It's over. Let's move on... " he would say.

I tried. I really tried. By silent assent, we never spoke of the crime and we never spoke of our child. I grieved privately, mourning the son I had already named Tad Kelly.

Several months later, a similar crime took place in a nearby neighborhood. A young woman was attacked in her home. The rapist used a straight-edged razor to kill her boyfriend, who had tried to intervene. The police felt certain it was the same man who had assaulted me, but the case was never solved.

Mitch threw himself into his coaching job. I floundered. Suddenly, and for the first time, I was without a job of my own. I began spending time on the sidelines of the football field, watching Mitch, and coaching the cheerleaders in their gymnastics and choreography. I was trying, once again, to make a place for myself in my husband's world. I knew nothing about football, but there had to be something I could do that would please Mitch, something that would unlock the tender feelings I knew existed inside him.

Many hours each week I worked with the cheerleaders, teaching them jumps and routines. I watched Mitch working with his players out on the field. I admired his knowledge of his profession, and I hoped that he would notice that I was close by, that he would make a move toward me, that somehow we could close the ever-widening chasm between us. But I could not reach him. He seemed oblivious to my presence until one evening, during a game, when I instructed the cheerleaders to begin chanting, "Block that kick, block that kick!"

Mitch was crouched down on the sidelines, staring intently at the line of players on the field. As soon as the cheer hit his ears, he stood up, spun around and grabbed a megaphone.

"Dammit, Pookie, it's *our* ball!" he shouted up into the stands.

I cringed and tried to shrink out of sight. The crowd in the bleachers bellowed with laughter.

All I could think was, I'll never understand this game...

In reality, I understood very little about anything during that period after the attack on me and the death of my child. I was lost. I was empty. And my husband, lost in his own private despair, was too far away to be reached.

If Mitch had found me unappealing during my pregnancy, he now found me abhorrent. His hands never touched me. We seldom spoke and he seldom came home. Whatever feelings he had had for me in the past had now completely dissolved. He offered no tenderness, no solace. And I, filled with pulsing grief, had no idea what to offer for his healing.

In the months after the assault, Mitch began leaving blatant signs of his infidelity, as though he wanted me to find out. I didn't know what response he wanted from me, but I had little emotion left inside to fuel any kind of outrage. Only when I learned that he was sleeping with a woman I considered to be my friend did I summon enough rational response to decide to end the marriage.

Deep inside, I had known for a long time that Mitch and I weren't going to make it. Finally admitting it to myself, these many months later, I felt a sense of release. The hard part would be telling Mama.

I drove out to the old manor house, feeling nervous. The lovely front lawn, perfectly manicured, lay behind wrought-iron gates. I walked up to the front door, across the wide porch, and caught the scent of the roses around the fence. The villa had never looked more beautiful. Stepping inside, I felt myself smiling at the sight of Mama's delicate antique pieces in the living room— how hard Mama had worked to be able to buy them. It had taken a long time, but she had managed to turn this manor house set among orange groves into an almost exact replica of the old brick house on Center Street. She had made this crumbling, abused old structure a gracious home, worthy of the name Collinsworth on the mailbox out front.

I found Mama in the kitchen, polishing an old silver bowl. I waited while she buffed and rubbed, and when she carried it back into the dining room to replace it on the sideboard, I said, "Let's go shopping, Mama."

She picked up her handbag and followed me out of the house.

"I'm not married anymore, Mama," I said, my eyes staring straight ahead at the road as I drove through town. "Mitch and I decided to divorce."

Mama laughed a low, guttural chuckle. It was almost a moan. She said nothing.

For hours that day, we shopped and laughed and talked about nothing of any consequence. We had coffee and discussed fashions and designers and the symphony schedule. We tried on clothes and fingered fabrics and peered at window displays; and finally, late in the afternoon, we returned, exhausted, to Mama's house.

"I'll call soon, Mama," I said, hugging her goodbye.

"Mitty, wait a moment."

Mama reached for her purse and then pressed something into my hands. I looked down at a check made out to me for four hundred dollars.

"You're going to have to be prettier now than you've ever been before," she said, her head held high, her eyes defiant.

I straightened my shoulders and tried to look proud. She would be looking for a sign of weakness, of resignation, and I would not let her see it. I would play her game. I would pretend that all was well, that beauty and presence would be enough to see me through this, but inside I was praying, Oh God, she can't see it—this has nothing to do with being pretty... I've lost my child and my marriage, and Mama wants me to buy a new dress and have my hair styled and my nails manicured!

I looked down at the check in my hands and then back at Mama. Her red-and-gray-streaked hair lay on top of her head in a perfect braid. Her gray eyes sparkled with spirit. Her whole body was tense with readiness for the fight ahead. All her life she had prepared me for this day. She had groomed me for the hour when I would be completely on my own, when my beauty and my poise and manners would give me that vital edge in the race for survival.

I stood before her now, college degree in hand, polished by Cotillion and an expensive finishing school, experienced on the pageant runway, and newly divorced. And in her mind, it would be my beauty and presence that would make the difference in my fight to survive.

Both lovely and tragic, Mama appeared to me that day as an enigma. A part of her believed that the value of a woman could be measured by a mirror and bathroom scale. Another part of her knew that her beauty had been of no use in the battle against my father's illness. It was her education and practical skills that had kept this family from becoming destitute all these years.

And yet, I wondered, what good were skills and knowledge if she had possessed no pride, no determination to fight on against the huge odds stacked against us?

There we stood in the doorway of the old manor house: me, with my life in tattered remnants, and Mama, with her feet planted deeply in the South of the nineteenth century. I wanted to shout, "It's over! I failed! I give up!" But Mama's stubborn stance warned me eloquently, Not yet, Mitty! Not yet! Not while you still have enough strength left to square your shoulders, apply fresh lipstick, and walk back out into the fray.

I tucked the check into my purse. If Mama wanted me to buy a new dress, I would buy it and consider it not a frivolous thing, but one more piece of armor in the uniform of a soldier. I was going out into the world alone, to fight for a place. I would need every possible advantage.

I walked quickly upstairs to see Daddy. I stood in the doorway of his room, listening to the creaking of his rocking chair. I knelt beside him.

"Daddy, how are you today?"

His eyes peered into nowhere.

"I'm going home now, Daddy, but I wanted to come see you first. I love you, Daddy."

His hands lay on the rails of his chair, limp and still.

"Well, I'll come back soon. You take care."

I drove to my apartment in Playa del Rey, thinking about the four-hundred-dollar check in my purse. I would buy a new suit— not a flashy one, like the ones Mitch had picked out for me, but one that suited my taste. Its understated elegance and fine fabric would lend me a sense of self, a sense of the woman I had once aspired to be. A woman of pride and self-confidence.

A few weeks later, I wore a lovely, classic suit into the offices of the city of Torrance and applied for a position as a recreational program specialist. I was hired to develop the city's recreational programs for all age groups, from preschool through senior citizens.

It was a dream job. I should have paid the city to let me do it. Every day I worked at the things I loved the most, using the abilities I had honed since childhood. All the private music, drama, dance, and gymnastics lessons Mama had provided me over the years now equipped me to teach with expertise. The work was not only fun, it was very satisfying. For the first time in a very long time, I found myself laughing and smiling effortlessly. I found myself at peace in the evening, often after working twelve or fourteen hours.

Every day, I worked with people—wonderful people of all age groups. But I loved the children best. Their uninhibited affection was like balm to my sore spirit after the loss of my own child. I soaked up all their sweet words and treasured their sweaty, sticky hugs. Their childish gestures of friendship filled the vacancy inside me, and I threw all my love and energy back at them.

It seemed everything I had ever learned in my life could be used in some way in the recreational program. I had long dreamed of starting a children's theater, and the idea delighted the Torrance city officials. Soon, I was directing and choreographing children's productions. As word of the exciting things happening in Torrance began to filter out into neighboring communities, nearby cities called to inquire about our program. I began consulting with surrounding cities to help them develop similar programs. I began to think that maybe my life, which had seemed like such a waste a short time earlier, wasn't a complete loss to humanity after all.

Maybe I had been able to achieve something. Maybe I wasn't an embarrassment to the Collinsworth name. I began to believe that maybe Mama could find a reason to be proud of me now, in spite of my earlier failures. And I began to notice that my pain did not pulse so strongly inside me anymore.

The scars on my wrists were now a pale pink. The rapist's razor slashes crisscrossing my chest and legs had begun to heal, leaving only pale red markings that appeared to fade a little more every day.

It seemed my injuries were healing.

The chaos of my life had quieted.

Chapter 9

"Miss Collinsworth! Miss Collinsworth! Watch me!"

A leotard-clad child jumped into the air and tossed herself over in a backward flip on the mat. She landed awkwardly and then grinned as she pulled herself up tall and straight and squared her narrow shoulders.

"That was beautiful!" I called to her, walking through a dozen or more children who clambered about my legs, begging for my attention.

If I closed my eyes, I could pretend I was in the back yard of the house on Center Street and the children were the students of the Collinsworth's Little Red School House. The recreation center in Torrance became the back-yard playground, and I became my mother.

A master teacher, Mama's style flowed through me when I worked with the children. All the magical lessons she had taught replayed in my mind, and I modeled my teaching technique after hers. People had always told me I looked like my mother, but now the similarities were even more striking. Tall like Mama, I had hair that was also dark auburn, but without the gray that streaked hers. My eye color was my father's, but everything else was Mama's. The irony of it was not lost on me. For so many years I had resented this woman. Now it seemed I had become her.

My classes at the recreation center grew until I was teaching five hundred students each week. Hundreds more filled waiting lists. I was the teacher every parent wanted for their child. Or rather, Mama was. My title read "Recreation Program Specialist," and my degree in recreational therapy qualified me for the job. But it was my training in the back-yard playground that really equipped me to work well with the children.

I had been with the city of Torrance for about a year when the school district requested aid for its special-education department. Inadequate funding and insufficient staff had mainstreamed the community's "special" children, putting them into social and physical situations they could not handle. I was assigned the task of designing a pilot physical education program for these disabled students.

The program had to fit the diversified needs of students who had suffered brain injuries, and physical and sexual abuse, and children with multiple learning disorders and severe cognitive and motor deficiencies. There were deaf, blind, and wheelchair-bound students as well. The program would be implemented in the city's sixteen schools, elementary through high school, and in the beginning, I would be the only teacher.

The challenge was huge. Every day I found myself facing children of all sizes. Only the size of their problems was uniform: extra large. All the children carried pain, emotional as well as physical. Autism, attention deficit-hyperactivity disorder (ADHD), obsessive-compulsive behavior—I saw it all in the first few days. And within a couple of weeks, I felt overwhelmed by the volume of needs represented by each of my students. I knew I was inadequate to meet them all working alone. I needed help.

I needed an assistant, someone energetic and creative, who enjoyed children and cared about them. It had to be someone who would support me in discipline. This became painfully clear after a few confrontations with angry teenagers who were twice my size and weight. I needed someone strong, and yet not so strong that the timid children of abuse would be afraid. It would have to be someone very special.

"Zachariah" was that special person. Zach, with his curly black hair and Hawaiian print shirts and brightly colored shorts, had already endeared himself to children and adults alike in the city's recreation program. At six feet eight inches tall, he towered over everyone he met, and yet he exuded an uncommon gentleness. Powerfully built and as handsome as an Adonis with a mustache, he was the ultimate California surfer—all muscles and suntan and ready humor. Everybody loved him.

Zach was the perfect person to assist me in the special-education program. I knew him from classes we had taught together at the recreation center and from working together in the children's theater. He was completing studies in recreational therapy; he was an outstanding athlete and an accomplished musician; and he loved kids. His teaching and coaching experience had been limited to mainstream children, but I was sure he could learn to work with those labeled "special." I had no doubts we could work together well.

It was 1975. Women in leadership positions, supervising men in lower-paying positions, were becoming less of an oddity. But to Zach, assisting me, taking instruction from me, and receiving less pay than me were new experiences. He respected me as a professional, but I sensed that, on a personal level, he resented his inferior position.

He's too good to let it get in the way, I thought. He's a pro... We can work it out. We both have the children's best interests in mind. We can solve any problems that arise.

In the beginning, Zach accepted my leadership with grace, following at times reluctantly, but with good humor.

With his lively laughter and his breathtaking good looks, Zach provided the classroom, the gymnasium, and the children's theater with a constant flow of comic relief. I, the technician and taskmaster, offered a much needed sense of order and control in which the children could feel safe to venture into new experiences. Together, Zach and I were the perfect partnership.

One bright southern California day, Zach and I herded a group of our students up a hill and turned them loose with kites. Soon the hillside was swarming with brightly clad children of various sizes, and multicolored kites dotted the sky. I looked around for Zach. He was usually easy to spot because of his size, but I couldn't find him among the scores of running, giggling children. The sound of his booming laughter came from a distance. I hurried toward it and found him lying on his back in the grass. Children were climbing on him tugging on his hands, which held the strings of a kite soaring high overhead. The children's voices, noisy with their gaiety, echoed across the hill. Like Gulliver in Lilliput, Zach lay pinned to the ground, tangled in kite strings, a laughing, roaring prisoner of happy children.

For Zach, life was a carnival full of delights, and almost against my will, I was drawn into his celebration. Uninvited emotions stirred inside me. With Zach, there was no savagery, no horror, no anger. Life had not beaten him down and made him bitter. When I was with him, I could forget all things ugly and violent.

Magic crackled between Zach and me. When we entered a room together, heads turned, drawn by his immense size and beauty. I felt great pride, probably not unlike the pride Mitch had felt in me, his beauty queen. But at the time, I didn't consider Zach a trophy to be won. A challenge, yes, but not a trophy. I was again my mother's daughter. I was again knee-deep in denial.

Rumors circulated about Zach, but not frightening ones like

murder and divorce. The gossip surrounding Zach focused on the fact that no woman had ever been able to capture him. He had loved many times, but he had never been tamed. I thought, He's never been in love with a Collinsworth.

I took him home to meet Mama.

When we drove up to the front of the old manor house, Zach exclaimed, "Wow!"

He stood for a moment next to the gate and shook his head in wonder. "It's like the twilight zone! We get out of the car in the twentieth century, and when we open this gate, it's like we've stepped back into the 1860s!"

I grinned and laced my fingers through his as we walked toward the wide porch. Mama opened the front door and stepped outside to greet us. Zach, dropping my hand, made three long strides and landed on the porch in front of her. There, without pause, he grabbed her and pulled her into a huge hug and then swung her about him as he did the children on the park playground. Mama's prim, pinned-up braid broke loose and spun behind her, and her feet flew up off the ground. She gasped and then made a little sound like a high-pitched squeal, and when her feet were back on the ground, her face glowed bright pink.

"Well, well, Mitty," she said, while her hands pinned her hair back into place, "I take it this is your friend, Zach."

Zach graced her with his incomparable smile, and Mama giggled.

I stared at her. Mama, blushing and giggling like a schoolgirl?

But that was Zach's style. He could charm everyone, even a proper Southern lady who considered giggling very undignified behavior.

In Zach's company, Mama would forget her rigid rules of propriety. Her natural reserve unbent just a little when he visited the villa. She, who habitually held herself aloof from strangers, would allow herself to be hugged by this huge, handsome man with the curly black hair. She would learn to care for him—I believe she adored him—but his orthodox Jewish background would always stand in the way of her complete acceptance of him. She wished he came from a nice Southern Baptist family.

Zach's family heritage, with its traditions and holidays and loud boisterous gatherings, was another of the many things I was beginning to love about him. I was willing to accept everything about this beautiful giant of a man. I realized, with each day that passed, that nothing I had ever felt compared with the intensity of my feelings for him.

Being in love with Zach was like being the heroine in a torrid romance novel. My memories, the good ones, sparkle with vivid, red-gold sunsets and wild, laughter-filled chases on the beach; with weekend getaways to Acapulco and Palm Springs; and with quiet mornings tangled in satin sheets. But, as in every love story, there existed a danger. For us, that danger was the very thing that had brought us together: our professional relationship.

Zach had been uncomfortable with his position as the subordinate from the beginning, but I had believed we could handle the tension and work through it because we loved each other. I had no idea that his jealousy would grow to include everything I did as a teacher and as a performer. He grew angry when I found a well-paid job singing blues in an upscale nightclub in the area. He ridiculed my freelance work as a dancer and choreographer for the nearby colleges and community productions. In Zach's eyes, my successes and performing opportunities diminished him.

Zach had told me often that he was attracted to strong, capable women, but his growing criticism of me contradicted his words. Suddenly my looks, my work, my career goals were subject to his critical analysis. Intoxicated by the passionate, physical aspect of our relationship, I allowed him to scrutinize everything I did, and I tried to make adjustments. I didn't understand at the time that he was attempting to mold me into a woman who would not threaten his own ideas of success. I didn't see the flashing signs warning me of trouble ahead.

Once again, I found myself trying to measure up to someone else's idea of beauty and perfection.

I joined Zach in his fitness regimen. We both lived near the beach, and so we jogged together, worked out together, and ate most meals together.

"How many miles did you run today, Babe?" he asked one evening as we settled in our patio chairs to watch the sunset.

"About three," I answered, feeling proud.

"I'll bet you could run three more," he said. "And it wouldn't hurt, especially after that meal you just ate."

"I'll try tomorrow," I replied, determined to run six miles if that would make Zach proud of me.

I got up and left the patio quietly. I closed the bathroom door behind me and gagged myself until I vomited the high-calorie dinner I had just consumed. Tomorrow I would take another diet pill and a diuretic.

The cycle had begun again. Bingeing and purging, running and exercising, taking diet pills and laxatives. Whatever it took to be slim and attractive for Zach, I would do it. If I could still breathe after three hundred sit-ups, he would urge me to try three hundred more. If I was still standing after an aerobic workout, I would push myself to continue through another series of exercises. I drove myself mercilessly to meet or exceed his expectations of me. I wanted nothing more than to please him.

Every day I ground myself into bits and pieces and then tried to rebuild myself, molecule by molecule, into the woman that Zach would love unreservedly. And every day I worked with the children in the special-education program, trying to help them see themselves as unique, valuable, and worthy. I poured love and encouragement into them to give them hope, to try to save them from self-destruction, but I never saw what I was doing to myself. I never suspected that my own emotional and physical condition was at least as fragile as that of the disturbed and disabled children I taught every day. I never imagined I was as desperately in need of help as they.

The pilot program for Torrance's sixteen schools succeeded far beyond anything the city had expected. My special education students and my performing arts students combined totaled more than 1500 students a week. I worked every morning with students who were considered unreachable and unteachable. Every afternoon I returned to the recreation center for the regular community classes. These seemed tame and almost uninteresting after the challenge of the troubled youngsters.

I developed a system for working with those children no one else wanted to bother with. Recalling the days on the back-yard playground at the Collinsworth's Little Red School House, I relied on behavior modification and positive conduct conditioning. Remembering Mama's three cardinal rules for teaching, I never made a promise that I didn't keep, I never delivered an ultimatum that I didn't fulfill, and I never allowed myself to be seduced by the need to be liked or loved by a student.

In the classroom, where structure and reason had to prevail, I had no problem seeing that respect was the weightier substance, the more valuable entity in a relationship. But where Zach was concerned, I was blind. Reason and logic melted down in the presence of our lovemaking. I was gladly seduced by my need for his love.

It didn't matter that I was twenty-eight years old. I was still the child with the bifocals and the braids, pleading to be held and hugged and assured that everything was going to be all right. I clung to Zach, unknowingly begging him to be everything my father had never been. Like a small child, I often climbed into his lap, rested my head against his chest, nestling close to draw warmth and security from him as if he were the only source in the universe. When he wrapped his arms around me, all the empty places in my life filled up and overflowed.

I loved Zach with every part of me, nothing withheld. We romped and played with the raucous abandonment of children.

"Come on, Mitty, up on my shoulders," he said, grinning down at me, as we walked across the beach one day.

"You're kidding."

"No, come on."

Zach knelt down in the sand, and I climbed up on his shoulders. When he stood up, with his great height I felt like a little girl who had just found the highest and best place on the planet. I was suddenly Daddy's little girl, giggling and swaying and squealing with mock terror.

"Look out! I'm falling... Zach!"

"Hang on!" Zach shouted, running down into the waves. Diving, he thrust us both under the foam, and I catapulted off his shoulders headfirst into the ocean. Coughing and laughing, we surfaced and swam together toward the beach.

"You're a knockout, Mitty," he told me as I tossed my hair back from my face and wrapped myself in a towel.

"So are you," I answered.

He grinned. His black eyes sparkled.

"I love you so much, Zach."

"Well, now," he said, wiping droplets of water off his face, "you know I love you, too."

I would do anything to keep those words on his lips. I would do anything to safeguard his love for me.

Many times, I would remind myself of those moments on the beach, the intimate moments of loving. They reassured me. Whenever I felt the niggling fears, I would make myself recall the carefree times, the fun. Our laughter could always dissolve the tensions of an earlier conflict, and the heat of passion could quickly cauterize any wounds inflicted when we argued. I could endure the difficulties in our relationship as long as I did not have to give up the ecstasy.

Had my mother and father known such ecstasy as this, I

wondered after each visit to the old manor house, when I saw my father so pathetic, so unlovely, and so ill? Their relationship had always been such a mystery to me. Was it the memory of this kind of passion, the memory of better times, no matter how long ago, that bound Mama to Daddy through all these long years of his illness? Nothing had been able to drive her away. Nothing had induced her to abandon him. Even now, when his condition was ever-changing, she remained devoted to him.

"Pauline, you must go to the store and buy Pop-Tarts," Daddy said one day, meeting Mama at the back door when she returned from work.

"Pop-Tarts, Minor? Whatever for?" Mama asked, dropping her books on the table and staring at Daddy. When had he heard of Pop-Tarts?

She heard the blare of the television from his upstairs room. An advertiser's catchy jingle played loudly. Daddy looked toward the stairs, and Mama understood. His recent fixation with the television had introduced him to scores of products that, in his dementia, he was certain he had to have. He handed her a grocery list and followed her from room to room, nagging and scolding her until she agreed to go to the store.

When she came home with the packages, he was as excited as a child. It was the beginning of what became a daily habit. She humored him most of the time, bringing him whatever she found on his list. But when he asked for liquor, she refused to buy it. So she was at a loss to know where the six-packs of beer and the bottles of wine were coming from. Later, she discovered that Daddy had coerced the gardener into buying them for him.

For more than ten years, Daddy had not left the perimeter of the yard, but during the spring of 1976, he began venturing outside, timidly, and for only a few moments at a time. Talking to him as though he were a little boy, Mama would urge him to go a little further every day until he cautiously crossed the porch and walked to the driveway. A few days later, he climbed into the front seat of the car, and by the end of that week, he let Mama drive him around the block.

Little by little, Mama lengthened their afternoon drives until Daddy was content to ride until dusk. He would roll down the window and peer out in wonderment. Land that had been spliced by orchards and narrow country roads was now carved by four-lane highways and dotted with small tract homes. The scent of smudge pots and orange blossoms had been replaced by the smell of exhaust. The engine noises of heavy earth-moving equipment had long since drowned the Latin songs of migrant workers. The villa, with its high walls and iron gates and wide gracious porch, looked out of place, an incongruous relic in an urban neighborhood dominated by sameness and adorned by graffiti.

Daddy took it all in, shaking his head in disbelief. When they drove past a little tavern on the edge of town that advertised Mexican food, Daddy fidgeted, turned in his seat, and bellowed, "Stop! Stop here!"

"Here, Minor? This is a honky-tonk, for goodness sake!" Mama answered.

Daddy demanded that they go in. Mama, drawing a deep breath, maneuvered the car past the dozen or more motorcycles and pickup trucks parked out front. She gripped Daddy's thin arm and helped him out of the station wagon and into the cafe. In the dim light, she could see dirty, long-haired ruffians shooting pool across the room. Rowdy men in old work clothes sat at the bar swigging beer. Gathering all her dignity about her, Mama held onto Daddy and led him to the closest table. She seated him gently and then reached for her own chair.

"Let me, ma'am," a hoarse voice spoke from behind her. A large, hairy, dirty hand pulled out her chair and held it until she was seated.

"Thank you, sir," Mama drawled in soft Southern tones, giving him a regal smile that sent him backing away with a broad grin on his face.

Mama and Daddy became regulars at the little honky-tonk cafe where country-western music blared on the jukebox and stale smoke thickened the air. They would enter quietly, and yet all heads would turn to see them. Greeted as royalty and ushered to their usual table, Mama would stand patiently while a smelly, often inebriated, man slipped from his bar stool and came over to pull out her chair for her. She and Daddy would eat tamales and tacos and refried beans, and then they would drive back to the old manor house where Mama would make herself a cup of tea.

For months, Mama and Daddy enjoyed their strange dinner dates at the tavern on the edge of town, he on one side of the table, she on the other. I wondered if, when shrouded in the dimness of the smoky tavern, Mama could see Daddy as he had once been: an aristocratic man whose love for her had kept him waiting for eight long years to make her his bride. I wondered if the shadows hid his gray hair and his tortured eyes, so that she could see him as the vital, athletic young man with whom she had fallen in love.

Whenever I thought of Mama sitting across from Daddy in a cafe filled with bikers and construction workers, I would remember the story she used to tell me about the first time she saw Daddy's face, the day she had looked into the well.

"It was the May Day celebration in Sidon. Every year, on the first day of spring, all the young women in the area would go outside in the early morning and wash their faces with the dew," she said. "Then they would take a mirror to the old well and hold it at an angle toward the water below. Custom said that the face of true love would appear in the well."

I felt shivers all over when Mama first told me the story.

"I was just about your size one May Day when I decided that I wasn't going to be left out of the custom just because I was still a little girl. I got up early in the morning with my sister and washed my face in the dew. I ran with her to the well, and she lifted me up so I could hold my mirror and look down into the water."

Mama paused.

"What happened? Did you see Daddy's face?"

She smiled. "I saw the water in the well become very still. And then on the smooth surface I saw a field surrounded by a split-rail fence. Dust clumps flew up from the ground, and I saw a dog running—it looked like it was running toward me."

I gasped.

"The silhouette of a man sat on the fence. He had a rifle draped across his lap, and he was shouting commands to the running dog. The dog quartered the field, stopping and turning exactly as the man commanded."

"Mama, that's just what Daddy's dogs do when he takes them hunting!" I exclaimed.

"Yes, it is, isn't it, Mitty?" she nodded. "But when I was your age I hadn't ever seen anything like that before. On our farm in Sidon there weren't any championship hunting dogs. And I'd never seen a man in a hunting suit either, but there in the well, reflected in the mirror, I saw a man wearing a suit exactly like the one your father wore when he hunted with the dogs after we were married."

"It was really Daddy?" I whispered.

"Yes, it was your father's face in profile."

Perhaps it was the silhouette of a man on a split-rail fence that Mama saw when she looked across the table at Daddy while they dined on Mexican food. She never stopped believing that he was her true love. She never doubted that it was her destiny to love and care for him.

As abruptly as their dinner dates had begun, they ended. Daddy's behavior, which had been both harmless and poignant, began to waffle between childlike tantrums and very adult anger. His hands, which had done little more than grip the rails of his rocking chair for so many years, turned into fists that threatened Mama. She was afraid to take him out in the car.

Daddy was dangerous now, and Mama was weary.

"I'm not sure I can care for him much longer," she told Laddie during the summer of 1976. "He's still strong enough to hurt me. He wouldn't mean to, but he doesn't know what he's doing. I don't think I can do this alone any longer."

"What can I do to help, Mama?" I asked her when I called home.

"There's nothing anyone can do, Mitty."

Resignation dulled her voice. I wished I could make it easier for her, for all of us. But as always, we had no tools, no resources. We would simply endure. We were Collinsworths.

Daddy's condition continued to deteriorate throughout the following months. In typical Collinsworth style, I threw myself into my work, forcing myself to forget the pain that resided at the old manor house. I was trying to stay busy enough to ignore the problems that persisted in my relationship with Zach as well. I focused all my energy into being the best I could be, for him, and for the children of the city of Torrance.

Teachers, parents, school administrators, and city officials often dropped by the school to observe the pilot program in action. I knew when they were unobtrusively observing. I trained myself not to be influenced by their eyes. I carried out my plan and forced myself to be just as tough and unrelenting with the children as I would have been without an audience. Zach, supportive and innovative on the job, held up his part, and together we stunned the watching officials and parents. They wholeheartedly endorsed both our plan and our method of executing it.

The program thrived. Neighboring communities sent representatives over to watch us in action and to ask for advice. I began consulting with other recreation directors, lending suggestions and advice on how our program could be adapted for their communities. Both Zach and I reveled in the success of our work. We had achieved something worthwhile, and we knew it.

Tiny miracles marked the way for us. A small child who had entered the classroom bearing the obvious emotional markings of abuse—defiance, aggression, anger—now came in with an eager face lit with laughter. The older kids who had used to slink into the room with flinty hatred in their eyes now rushed in, looking for a new challenge, expecting another victory. Nothing had been easy, but we were winning against these children's despair.

Together, Zach and I turned our kids into swim teams, soccer teams, baseball players, and track stars. We taught them to turn their anger and pain into fuel for excellence. We gave them an arena, a safe environment, for acting out the frustrations they could not articulate with words. And I watched silently, unable to speak of my own deep scars, while coaching these children in ways to rid themselves of theirs.

For many months, I tried to pretend that the conflict between Zach and me didn't exist. I tried to ignore it, but it was, in fact, escalating. His control over my appearance created a terrible tension inside me. I wanted to be everything he wanted me to be, but some things just wouldn't work for me. I didn't have the skin type to court the deep, dark tan he liked to see on a woman. To please Zach, I needed to be thinner still. I needed to wear less makeup, look more "natural." I needed to adopt a style very different from my own.

Every relationship has its difficulties, I thought. Ours are no worse than those of others. Everyone has to concede something… We can do it. What we have is so great. We'll make adjustments for the sake of our love. I'll do whatever it takes.

As the competition between us increased, generated by Zach's jealousy over my professional stature, so did my unease. No matter how hard I tried to equalize our relationship in the workplace, I failed. Zach loathed the fact that my career was ahead of his. I was three years older than he; I had invested that much more time in my career, but he didn't want to see it that way. He was consumed with the need to move out in front. He didn't want to play catch-up with me, or perhaps he feared he couldn't. He wanted me to simply move aside and let him have the lead.

"I'm sick of taking orders from you, Mitty."

Zach's voice came at me hard and low, like a well-swung club. I dropped my eyes.

"Please, Zach." I looked around me at the other diners sitting nearby at small tables in the quiet restaurant. "Can we talk about this at home? Let's just enjoy our dinner."

"It's not going to go away, Mitty," he said, his voice getting louder. Why does he do this? I wondered, hating the embarrassed looks on the faces of the people beside us at the closest table. This was not the first time Zach had chosen a public place to express his anger.

"Why do we have to discuss this here, now? I thought we were going to enjoy a pleasant dinner." I was pleading now.

"What kind of man do you think I am?" Zach asked, leaning toward me, his eyes flashing fury. A waiter hovered over our water goblets, pouring icy water from a sweating silver pitcher. Zach ignored him.

"You shout commands at me all day long, and I'm supposed to jump! Do you know what a turn-off that is?"

"Zach, that's not fair," I said, whispering. "How can you say that?"

"Do you know how I feel, having to take orders from a woman? Do you like making me feel like a weakling?"

My eyes burned and I blinked hard.

"I'm tired of jumping every time you speak! No job is worth this! Oh no... no tears, Mitty—tears aren't going to work!"

I sniffed and tried to control myself.

"Stop right now!"

Shuddering, I reached into my purse for a handkerchief.

Zach shook his head and looked away from me. Making a sound of disgust, he said, "I can't stay with a woman like this! You aren't even feminine, ordering a man around all the time... Oh, Mitty, this isn't working."

"We can make it work, Zach. Please, can't we talk about this later?"

Later, the conversation ended without really ending. There was no resolution. I wanted to make Zach happy. I really thought I could! I wanted to understand him, to make it easy for him to do his job alongside me—we were really a great teaching team! But the city of Torrance had put me in charge of the program. I was responsible—I'd been hired to be the leader. Why couldn't he just accept that fact? Why did my being a woman have to be a factor?

Zach's frustration erupted again a few days later, in the classroom. He gripped my arm and pulled me toward the back of the room.

"How long am I going to have to listen to you telling me what to do? Are you trying to make me feel inferior?"

"Zach, you're deliberately misunderstanding me. You know I consider you my partner. It's not a question of superiority. I've never treated you as an underling. We're equals, you know I believe that."

"It's not that simple, Mitty. The truth is, you're in charge and I'm your lackey."

"No, Zach. It's not like that at all! We're good together—we're great together! Inside the classroom and outside it. I love you, Zach. Don't do this to us, please." I pulled my arm out of his grip. "Come on, we've got to get back to the children."

Zach heaved a big sigh, shook his head and rejoined the children. From across the room, I watched him moving in and out among the children, his flowered Hawaiian shirt a vivid splash of color.

Why? I wondered. Why is he doing this?

I remembered recent incidents when I had asked Zach for advice in the classroom. I had sought his ideas for the program. Often, I looked to him for creative ways to help the children we worked with. I truly considered him my partner.

I'm doing something wrong, but I don't know what it is, I thought. I can't lose him. I have to find a way to fix this. We have to work it out.

But I could feel it falling apart. The anger, the resentment built up each day, and by evening, Zach fired it at me with the precision of a sharpshooter. When he added infidelity to the volley of charges against me, I was devastated.

"Zach, how can you even think that I might be cheating on you?" I asked, stunned. "You know I love you."

"No, I don't know anymore, Mitty."

Day by day, our relationship deteriorated until anger and tumult were the only adjectives to describe it. I was losing him, I knew. I had to do something to try to hold him. I made the decision to quit my job. I would get out of the way, let Zach have the position of prominence in the recreation program. He was more important to me than anything else. I would step aside and let Zach have the lead.

I thought perhaps we would both benefit from some time away from each other, too. We were together all the time—at the school, the recreation center, and at home. Being apart during the workday would be good for us. My professional skills had been the original source of contention between us. Perhaps, I reasoned, with that eliminated, the other rough places could be more easily smoothed out. I was willing to give our romance every chance to heal and grow stronger. And so I wrote a letter of resignation to the city of Torrance, effective in a few weeks' time.

Over the next month, I grappled with my decision, but I convinced myself it was the right one. My freelance work as a singer and choreographer would be adequate until I found a new position. But as my decision to leave the field of recreational therapy solidified, I thought perhaps it was time to end my career as a performer and choreographer as well. It was time for a fresh start. I wanted a whole new beginning, one that would not offer any potential for competition between Zach and me.

It was October 1976. I would spend only a couple more weeks in the classroom with Zach before I would walk away from my career. I was feeling sad and apprehensive about the decision when I turned to leave my apartment on the morning of the twenty-ninth. I heard the telephone ring just before I closed the door behind me.

"Mitty, Daddy had a heart attack this morning," Mama said. Her voice was calm, but I could feel the undercurrent of urgency traveling through the telephone lines.

"He collapsed on the living-room floor just as I was about to leave for school. The paramedics have just left. They're taking him to San Dimas Hospital."

Numbness crept over me.

"Do you want me to come, Mama?"

"No, honey," she answered. "Go on to work. I won't know how bad it is until I get to the hospital. You can call there in a little while and I can tell you how he is."

"I'll call, Mama," I answered, and then I hung up the phone.

What should I do? I wondered. She needs me... No, she said go on to work... It'll be okay. Daddy will be...

Before I could finish the thought, I knew with a bizarre kind of certainty that my daddy was going to die that day. I drove to school anyway, unwilling to acknowledge what I knew in my heart.

I joined Zach in the classroom with a score of kindergarten children who had come to school expecting a Halloween party. These were the children whose case histories read like horror stories. Most of them, no more than five years old, had endured divorce, abuse, foster care, and incest. They rarely smiled, seldom spoke, and often sat in wet and soiled clothes because they couldn't control their own bodily functions. But slowly, over tedious weeks, we had seen tiny flickering lights of hope begin to burn in their eyes. We had witnessed small miracles. And today, with their hopes set on a party with games and costumes, I could not deliver them another disappointment. The show must go on.

The party occurred as scheduled, with cupcakes and laughter and gooey hugs. From time to time, I escaped the noisy classroom and hurried to the pay phone down the hall to call Mama and ask about Daddy. Early in the afternoon, I heard the words I had been expecting all day.

"Come quickly, Mitty," Mama whispered. "He's slipped into a coma. Be careful, but hurry. Get here in time to say goodbye."

"I've got to leave, Zach," I said, hurrying back to the classroom to grab my purse. He gave me a quick kiss, and a cluster of miniature witches and gypsies and goblins hugged his legs while he waved to me. I drove as fast as I could down the California freeways, thinking all the while, Don't go, Daddy, please... not yet, Daddy. Not just yet... I want to hear you say you love me, Daddy. Don't go until you say "I love you, Mitty."

Cars sped by me; the radio blared with traffic reports. I heard and saw it all, but while the miles sped past, I fantasized, seeing myself in Daddy's hospital room. I imagined him rising up from his bed, reaching out his arms to me, and saying in a strong voice, "I love you, Mitty."

I pressed down harder on the accelerator and thanked God that no red lights flashed in my rearview mirror. An hour later I parked at the hospital and burst through the double doors that guarded Daddy's room in intensive care.

The room was empty. Linens lay neatly folded on the end of the bed. A young nurse walked in behind me.

"Miss Collinsworth? I'm sorry... You're too late."

No! No!

"Your father died a few minutes ago. Your mother and brother were with him."

He couldn't have died... He wouldn't cheat me—not again... not like this...

The nurse's soft voice droned on, telling me where I could find Mama and Laddie. Her hand touched my shoulder with a gesture of condolence, but I felt only the icy cold grip of loss.

This can't be... it just can't be... I thought.

"Miss Collinsworth, I'm so sorry."

I stood there, silent and unmoving.

"Miss Collinsworth?"

Again the nurse's hand touched me, and I felt myself stiffen.

"It's all right. I'm fine." I heard my voice, but I couldn't understand where those words had come from. I wasn't all right. I would never be all right again, ever. My father was dead. He had gone without saying he loved me. He had gone without saying goodbye. Nothing would ever be all right for me.

I drove to Charter Oak, dry-eyed. I pulled into the driveway and saw Laddie raking leaves in the front yard. He greeted me with a nod, and I said, "Hello, Laddie."

His eyes were red and puffy from crying, but he said nothing more than a passing hello.

Inside the old manor house, I found Mama in an upstairs bedroom with a dust cloth in her hands. Her face, red and haggard, showed grief, but her words were matter-of-fact and void of emotion.

"It was his heart."

"I know, Mama."

"He didn't suffer at the end."

"I'm glad, Mama."

I took the rag out of Mama's hands and began dusting every piece of furniture in sight. Mama gathered laundry, as if it were an urgent chore, and Laddie raked every inch of the front yard. All afternoon until dusk, the three of us worked in silence, looking for solace in the doing of some inconsequential task. In the manner of the Collinsworths, we hid our sorrow in the shroud of stoicism. Only when I stepped into Daddy's room and saw his empty rocking chair did I allow myself to come out of hiding.

Daddy's slippers rested on the floor next to his chair, as if awaiting his feet. His cane stood against the wall, and I carefully hung it over the doorknob. His keys lay on his antique desk next to his pipes, which scented the room with the aroma of his tobacco. I picked up his gray Fedora and stroked its fine, felt brim before hanging it on the coat tree in the corner.

This room had been Daddy's cell, our home his asylum. And yet, at that moment, it looked like the room of any cultured, distinguished gentleman, with its paintings and fine antique furniture. Daddy had once been a man who appreciated such things, but it had become harder and harder to remember him that way. I turned and walked downstairs. I found Mama standing near the doorway to the living room.

"Is there anything else I can do?" I asked, thinking she looked weary and suddenly very old.

"Not tonight, sweetheart. Go home and get some rest."

"I'll be back in the morning."

Laddie walked toward me from the kitchen, stopping a few feet in front of me.

"Good night, Mitty," he said, folding his arms across his chest.

"Good night, Laddie," I answered.

Mama leaned toward me slightly as I moved to her. Tentatively, we reached for each other. I kissed her cheek and then quickly stepped back. Our eyes never met. None of us could allow ourselves to reveal the flagrantly naked grief we were feeling. We could neither expose it nor express it. And so, with hidden faces, we each turned away.

I drove home almost without seeing. My mind was filled with images of my father. I saw him as he had been on the good days, when he had taken me with him to Grandmother's house at Five Oaks. When I had stood on the porch and awaited his call to join him among the dogwood trees. I tried to remember the sound of his voice when he spoke of the legend of the dogwood.

Your miracle never came, Daddy... My throat ached. I couldn't swallow. Springtime never came for you...

Tears blurred my eyes and the image of my youthful father changed into that of the gaunt and tortured man who had sat in his creaking rocking chair in the upstairs bedroom of the old manor house; the crazed and pathetic man who had slid across the dining-room floor, chasing phantom touchdown passes while I marched to "Pomp and Circumstance." I saw him as he had been on the morning of my wedding, his eyes vacant and staring. I had been close enough to touch him, but his illness had pulled him far away, to a place too distant to be reached by a daughter's hand. He had been too far away to hear me beg him, "Grope for sanity, Daddy, just long enough to stand beside me at my wedding and give me away."

A whole montage passed before my eyes that day as I drove home. In the final view, as if in reprise, I saw Daddy sitting in a swing in the yard of the mental institution, his arms outstretched to me, trying to pick me up but unable to. And it struck me that this had been the theme of my life: always reaching, never touching. Even in death, we had been unable to meet.

Dry-eyed, I drove through the darkness toward my apartment

an hour away. Tears would not come, but pain throbbed hard in my chest, making my whole body feel ill.

For so many years, Mama, Laddie, and I had prepared ourselves for Daddy's death. All my life I had been waiting for my father to die.

Relief tickled at my consciousness.

He's finally gone, I thought. His agony is over.

My words sounded unselfish, forgiving. But they rang false in my own ears. "The waiting is over... "

"He's been dead to me for years... " I argued.

And then a child's voice, "You promised you would make him better... You were supposed to be the one who would be the healer... "

I glanced in my rearview mirror, half expecting to see the face of a child with thick, bifocal glasses and French braids. But I saw only the darkness swallowing up the road behind me. Darkness seemed to swallow everything around me.

Mama planned a simple memorial service for Daddy. At the old North Church at Forest Lawn, his Masonic brothers conducted a short ceremony. The church was nearly empty, except for Laddie, Mama, and me, and a handful of teachers Mama knew from school. Zach's absence was no surprise. Ever since his own father's death several years ago, Zach had had an aversion to funerals and anything associated with death. I had assured him I needed his presence in the classroom with our special students more than I needed him at the funeral.

Mama sobbed softly while organ sounds echoed in the small chapel. When the service was over, she stood up stiffly, lifted her chin, and dabbed at her eyes with a lace hanky. Laddie and I followed her outside to a waiting car.

A few days later, I found her standing in the yard of the villa watering her rose bushes.

"How are you today, Mama?"

"Oh, Mitty, dear, I dreamed of your daddy last night." Mama's voice was husky and she seemed to be far away, as if she were talking not to me but to Daddy.

"I dreamed we were beautiful and in love," she said.

I stood there listening to her, feeling as if I had intruded on an intimate moment between two lovers. Her face had an almost ethereal look about it. The haggard look was gone, and in its place was a softness that I hadn't seen in many years. Daddy's death had not only released him from the bondage of mental illness, it had released Mama too.

"Daddy craved ice cream. Did you know that, Mitty?"

"Yes, Mama."

"His favorite was Cherry Vanilla. He loved it."

"I know, Mama."

"I bought it for him by the gallon. At the end, it was about the only thing he was interested in eating."

"I remember, Mama."

Mama stooped down to pat the earth around the base of a rosebush. The soil was freshly turned, as if the bush had been planted only yesterday. A few small buds graced the ends of its branches. I reached down to remove the tag which still dangled from one stem. "Cherry Vanilla" the tag read. With a quick snip of her gardening scissors, Mama cut a bud.

"I'll take this up to Daddy's niche at Forest Lawn," she said. And she turned away and walked into the house briskly.

It was over. Death had freed both my mother and my father from the agony of his illness, or so I believed as I watched my mother's softened countenance. But had my father's death really freed me? Would my life now change because my father, in his heartbreaking state of dementia, was no longer a physical presence in the old manor house? Would I not always remain bound, in some way, by the fetters of my father's mental illness? By the horrors of so many years lived in a house that was little more than an insane asylum?

I returned to my apartment by the ocean and to Zach's arms, more determined than ever to hold on to him. The problems in our relationship were not insoluble. We could make it work. I would do whatever it took to keep Zach with me and to keep him believing I was worthy of his love.

One day soon after Daddy's death, I sat on the beach watching Zach play volleyball. A friend of mine, Don LaPane, casually mentioned that a nationally known restaurant chain was advertising for a public relations director. Don was an entertainer and my number-one fan. He and I had performed together on stage and in nightclubs for the preceding few years.

"You'd be perfect for the job, Mitty," he told me. "The company is looking for someone attractive and articulate. You'd be willing to travel, wouldn't you?"

Travel? I'd love to travel, I thought. It would be good for both

Zach and me if I were gone sometimes.

"The salary is outrageous and the perks are unbelievable! I'd apply for the job myself if I were qualified," Don chuckled.

Laughing, I said, "It sounds great. I'll think about it."

"You'd be a fool not to interview."

Zach agreed.

"It sounds great, Mitty," he said that evening when I told him about the opportunity. His eyes scanned me, and he smiled. "You're exactly right for the job. I think you should go for it."

"Are you sure, Zach? Absolutely sure? Because I'll only interview if you promise me a change will make things right between us."

"I'm sure, Babe," he said, pulling me close and hugging me tightly. "I'm sure."

After the first interview, I was hired as public relations director for the El Torito–La Fiesta Restaurant Division of W. R. Grace & Company, an international conglomerate. Overnight, I left the world of dirty gym socks and noisy, sweaty children. I traded my leotards and teacher's ledger for a leather attaché case.

Instead of dealing with the PTA and city officials, I conferred with CEOs and stockholders. The company limousine took me across town to meetings in the company boardroom. Often, I crisscrossed the country in a corporate jet.

From the first day, I loved the idea of being a lady executive. I had a generous expense account, a clothing allowance, and a company car. "Presence" was a valuable commodity in the highly visible position I now held, and I was encouraged to look good at all times, at all costs. The cost was considerable, but the company picked up the tab.

Mama couldn't have been more elated. She had taken great pride in my position with the city of Torrance, but she had always wanted something more for me—something more glamorous, more prestigious. Something that would utilize all the gifts and talents she had worked so hard to develop in me. Now, employed by W. R. Grace & Co., I had the opportunity to use all those gifts. The style and "presence" Mama had instilled in me was now an integral part of my success. I now occupied a position of honor— at least in her eyes. It was the prize she had always hoped I would win.

It's too late, it's too late... Those words haunted me at all times. I rushed through airports, expensively dressed and perfectly coifed, headed for meetings with powerful executives, but I couldn't escape the sound of my own guilt.

You promised... you would achieve honor, restore the family pride and heal your father...

The honor had arrived, and on its heels some measure of family pride had been restored. A Collinsworth was once more on top. But the ascent had been made too slowly. Daddy had not lived long enough to see me make the climb. I had not been able to pull him up with me. I had not been able to save him.

Unreasonable...

Irrational.

I knew that. I know it even better now, but then, I was still gripped in my own kind of mania. Every scene in my life played out against the backdrop of the Arkansas state hospital. Every step I took I measured against the length of that gravel driveway. My father's struggling figure and the white-coated attendants who restrained him overshadowed even the sunniest days of my life. My vow to heal him would come close to destroying me.

Zach greeted my success and my new career image with a less than warm welcome. This baffled me. I had left a job I loved in order to salvage our relationship, but it didn't seem to be working. Zach's voice and his actions continued to carry a distinct undercurrent of insecurity. I didn't know how to respond to him when he announced that he too had decided to leave his job with the city of Torrance.

"I'm going to take a year's sabbatical, Mitty," he told me one evening while we walked together on the beach.

"Zach, why? I don't understand."

"I'm getting a lot of pressure to take over the family business." He stopped walking and turned to look down into my face. I was struck again by how gorgeous he was. I smiled at him.

"But that's nothing new, Zach," I answered, linking my arm through his and pulling him along beside me. "They've always second-guessed you, ever since you turned your back on the import/export business—ever since you chose to do what would make you happy instead of what would make you rich."

"I know, Mitty," Zach replied. He pulled his arm out of mine and, crouching down, he stared out at the darkening ocean. The churning water matched the tumult I sensed in him.

"I'm the only son, the only male left in the family."

His voice sounded dead.

"Now that my father and my uncles are gone, my mother and everyone else expects me to take over."

I would never understand Zach's family. I wanted to shout,

"This is the twentieth century! Women can run businesses, be executives, even govern countries, for Pete's sake! Zach isn't the only one who could take over the family business!" But in their orthodox thinking, such matters were considered the responsibility of the men, and Zach was the only man left.

In many ways, Zach's family was much like mine. Both were governed by individuals whose ideas were locked in another era. I knew that much of his consternation over my "strengths" and my career success arose out of a system of belief that did not easily accept women in visible positions of leadership. I understood how confused he felt at times when, against his will, he admired my accomplishments and my drive to succeed. He admired my skills, yet at the same time he was in conflict with them.

"I've given this a lot of thought, and I'm going to run the business, on a trial basis, for one year. I owe my family at least that much."

I had no answer for him. He looked up at me, shrugged, and then stood. His great height towered over me.

"If I don't like it, I'll come back to the kids," he smiled. "I have to give it a try, Mitty, for my family's sake."

I wouldn't talk him out of it. I would only hope it was the right decision. For him. For both of us.

And so both Zach and I found ourselves hurrying through airports to make connecting flights, trying to schedule our trips so we could be in the same city at the same time. In many ways, it was quite romantic. We found each other in New York City over a weekend. Sometimes we met in San Francisco; at other times, in Seattle, or Denver, or Dallas. Together, hidden away in elegant hotels in distant cities, our relationship took on new excitement. The passion and ardor we had experienced before sprang to life again. Our problems seemed to recede. We began to talk about marriage, about having children, about growing old together.

My success, very separate from his, no longer posed such a serious threat to him. And as he discovered that he was very good at running his family's business, his own confidence surged. We were no longer competitors. We were free to be lovers.

For the first time in my life, I believed I was moving in the direction of complete fulfillment. It was in sight, almost within reach. At times I felt delirious. The shadow of my father's struggling figure began to fade, lost in the sunshine and heat of the love

Zach and I shared. Contentment moved closer by the minute. I could almost touch it.

I moved into an expensive apartment in Manhattan Beach and filled it with antiques and beautiful pieces of art. I invested in lovely pieces of jewelry and lavished gifts on my family and friends. Little by little, I moved farther and farther away from the pathetic, bespectacled child in braids, leaving her somewhere among a stash of memories I no longer cared to recall. And I introduced myself as "Millicent" now. Only my family and Zach would be allowed to use the childish nickname, "Mitty."

Immersed in the lifestyle of a sophisticate, I left myself only small allotments of time to spend with my mother at the old manor house, deliberately distancing myself from anything that would be a tie to painful memories. But when she called one day, summoning me for a visit, I promptly drove out to Charter Oak.

I arrived at the old manor house, and Mama, looking younger than I'd seen her look in a long time, met me on the front porch.

"Come in, come in," she said. Excitement radiated from her.

"How are you, Mama?" I asked, shrugging out of my jacket and sitting down on a chair in the living room.

Mama continued to stand. "I have a surprise for you."

She turned to leave the room and I rose to follow her.

"No," she said. "Stay there. I'll be right back."

Mama returned to the living room carrying a huge box.

"For me? What is it, Mama?"

"Open it," she said, smiling at me.

I lifted the lid and gasped when I pulled back the layer of tissue. Inside lay a full-length, black mink coat. For several moments, I couldn't speak.

"You'll be traveling in cold weather, Mitty," Mama said. "I want you to look beautiful and be warm at the same time."

"Mama... "

"Shush, now... Just put it on."

I pulled up the collar of the coat and buried my face in it. It was the most splendid piece of clothing I had ever seen. Only Mama could have picked out such a perfect garment. I didn't know what to say or do.

"How did you...?"

"It fits well, doesn't it?" Mama interrupted me.

"It's perfect, Mama. I love it."

"Well, then. That's that."

Neither Mama nor I was accustomed to effusive shows of

emotion. In silence, I took off the coat and laid it beside me, stroking it occasionally while Mama and I drank tea. I spoke my thanks later when I got up to leave, but it sounded so inadequate, so small next to so grand a gesture. I would never know what Mama had denied herself in order to afford this gift for me.

"Wait, there's one more thing," Mama said, just before I went out the door.

She pressed a small box into my hands. "This is the most important part of all. I know you're running late—open it when you get home."

Later that night, while sitting on my bed, I opened the box and found it filled with a dozen pairs of little white gloves. I fell back against the pillows and burst into laughter.

"A lady just isn't a lady without her gloves." How many times had Mama told me that?

In white gloves and a mink coat, she has outfitted me to conquer the world! I thought. She now believes there is nothing I cannot achieve.

I picked up the phone and called home. In my most reverent tone, I said, "Thank you, Mama. I'll never leave home without my gloves in hand."

Mama still lived in the South of the nineteenth century. Never mind that California was her place of residence and had been for more than twenty years, she had never moved an inch from her Southern way of life. It wasn't a matter of geography or distance, nor even style or custom. For Mama it was more a blood type. To try to alter her would be to destroy her.

The more Mama stayed the same, the more I struggled to change. The more she clung to the old ways of her ancestors, the more I tried to let go. The past held sad remembrances and scenes of betrayal. Why not set myself free of all those painful memories? I was determined to look forward, to the future. A future with Zach. A future filled with the promise of contentment.

I became obsessive about severing all ties with the past. I became consumed with the idea of selling Five Oaks.

I'm never going back there, I told myself. I've severed myself from the house on Center Street—we ought to do the same thing with the old home place, I reasoned. What is the point in keeping it?

I thought about the dilapidated old house with its green shutters hanging crookedly. I imagined the sleepy little creek meandering under the oak trees alongside the fields. With a sniff of disgust, I thought, These are not the trappings of a jet-setting sophisticate! These are not the images I want to carry with me for the rest of my life!

I wanted to erase from memory all the visions of that pigtailed child who had clung so tenaciously to the past. I wanted no more of her accusations of betrayal and failure. I wanted to rid myself of her presence, once and for all. I determined to find a realtor who would be willing to list Five Oaks. But first, I'd have to convince Mama and Laddie that we should sell.

"It is deteriorating fast," I said, trying to keep my voice calm as I spoke to Mama. "Daddy's family are all too aged to care for the property. Something has to be done with it. I think we should consider selling it."

Mama listened silently. Her hands were steady as she cradled her china tea cup.

"I have a friend in real estate who thinks we could sell to foreign investors, Mama. I'm going to call Laddie and see if he will meet with the agent."

Mama and Laddie arrived at the realtor's office and greeted me icily when I rushed in late. I shrugged off my mink coat, tugged at the fingers of my kid gloves, and flashed a huge smile all around.

"Did you tell them about the investors who are interested in the property?" I asked my friend, the agent.

"Yes, Millicent."

"And did you point out that the real estate market is booming right now? This is the ideal time to sell and reinvest for top dollar, Laddie. We can't afford to hang onto the property for nostalgic reasons, Mama. It's too valuable, and now is the time to buy out here. I think we should do it—now, today. So. What do you say? Mama?"

Mama's gray eyes pierced me. I had to look away.

"Laddie?"

He, too, stabbed me with his eyes.

"This isn't about money, Mitty," Mama said.

The realtor looked across his desk, first at Mama, then at me, then at Laddie.

"I don't want to sell, Mitty," Laddie spoke quietly.

"The property is not for sale," Mama said.

I stared at them both. I should have expected this, I thought. The realtor, suddenly uncomfortable, started to speak.

"Don't bother," I said, holding up my hand. "It won't do any good." I gave Mama and Laddie a chilled little smile. To the realtor I said, "Thanks for your time." I stood up and, shaking my head, I marched out, sweeping the floor of the office with my mink coat.

This is nothing but stupid sentimentality, I thought as I strode toward my car. How long must we rob ourselves in order to honor the past? What past? I, for one, am not looking back again. There is nothing there... nothing there...

Nostalgic fools, that's what they are, I thought. They probably still believe in the dogwood legend... in second chances... Well, not me. I'm not a little girl who believes in miracles anymore.

Even as I thought the words, I knew I was wrong, but I continued to argue with myself.

The old brick house on Center Street is gone. Daddy is gone. What can be gained by keeping Five Oaks?

Mama and Laddie, at that same moment, were trying to imagine all that would be lost to us if we gave up our ancestral home to foreign investors. The cost, in their estimation, would be incalculable.

I returned to my lovely apartment by the ocean and flung myself into Zach's arms.

"They won't sell," I told him, still angry and fuming.

"It doesn't matter, Baby," Zach said, speaking softly against my hair. "Nothing matters except us, you know that."

I closed my eyes and let myself soak up the smell and feel of this man I loved with all my being. Against the darkness of my eyelids I saw the face of a little girl, her features pinched and terrified as she watched rough hands drag her father down a gravel driveway. Would she never leave me in peace, I wondered, this child who had made such an irresponsible vow to a demented man?

I hugged Zach tightly. Someday I would be rid of that miserable child. Someday I would be rid of all reminders of that other life, where promises made could never be kept.

Someday I would find a way to break free.

Zach's arms calmed me. He was the one person in the universe who was able to soothe my frenzied emotions.

They don't understand, I thought. Mama and Laddie don't know that I have to let go of everything that reminds me... If I'm ever going to be happy, I have to let go...

Oh Mama, Laddie—I'm not trying to hurt you. Please believe that! I just need to escape the memories. It hurts too much to remember. It hurts too much to hold on...

Every day I made a deliberate decision to let go of another piece of the child who had stood on the porch at Five Oaks. I made myself dismiss her presence whenever she tried to approach me. I refused to let myself remember the promise of miracles, the legend of second chances. More and more, I distanced myself from the little girl who had reached out for an armful of dogwood blossoms. I tried to pretend she had never existed.

It was easy to forget about the homely little girl of my past when I was swathed in furs, splashed in expensive perfume, and gliding through crowded airports. I spent three weeks out of each month visiting every major city in the United States to introduce the chain of restaurants my company owned. I found myself on television talk shows, sharing air time with our master chef, presenting elaborate cooking demonstrations, and chatting with celebrity guests. I planned and scheduled groundbreakings, ribbon cuttings, and grand openings. I designed corporate exhibits for my employers and represented them at stockholders' meetings. I was assigned the task of planning and hosting gala, black-tie events for powerful charity organizations. And, though I was able to escape the haunting presence of the little girl I used to be, I was unable to escape the presence of my mother.

Once again, I became Pauline Price Collinsworth—the woman of exquisite taste and bearing whose presence commanded attention and respect in any setting; the woman who could transform a simple, ordinary room into an incomparable scene of beauty. I would never forget the old brick house on Center Street when Mama had prepared for a family holiday or a club luncheon or a school "open house." For decades, she had demonstrated for me the art of gracious entertaining, and now those skills were a part of my job description. Once again, my college degree was helpful, but the things I had learned from Mama equipped me to move in the circles of the elite.

With the ease of an accomplished actress, I stepped into the role of a socialite, making friends with the wealthy and the prominent in nearly every city in the country. I became one of the "beautiful" people.

When I walked into a room full of dignitaries, my arm linked in Zach's, I could feel the rush of approval that blew our way from friends and strangers alike. I basked in it, knowing people considered us the "golden couple."

The world was very nearly perfect. But not quite.

Every day I had to confront the bathroom scale.

My business was food. I worked for a restaurant chain.

Everywhere I went, some tantalizing flavor or aroma awaited me. Business associates took me to lunch and dinner. Television appearances required that I cook, discuss recipes, and then eat what I'd helped prepare. And, of course, the camera added its proverbial ten pounds. Eating was a twelve- or fourteen-hour-a-day preoccupation for me. The other ten or twelve hours in each day I spent trying to rid myself of the calories I had consumed. Once again, the terrible cycle spun out of control.

Three times each week, I swallowed a bottle of one hundred laxatives. Another two days each week I increased my dosage of Lasix, a diuretic, from twenty milligrams to one hundred. In every restaurant, I found the shortest route to the restroom so I could quickly vomit whatever I had just eaten. When at home I allowed myself to eat whatever made me feel good. Then, when the good feelings turned to guilt, I hung over the toilet bowl and eliminated the cause of my misery.

The first time I collapsed and awakened in the emergency room, I couldn't believe it had happened.

"I've had a bad case of the flu," I lied when the ER nurse quizzed me.

"You're seriously dehydrated, miss," the doctor told me after probing and examining me. "I want you to force liquids and rest. See your personal physician if you don't feel better in a couple of days."

I promised I would, and left the hospital.

The second time I collapsed, I told the same story. I had to. I had no label for my bizarre behavior. "Bulimia" was not part of medical jargon in the late 1970s. I never imagined I suffered from a disorder that could cause serious injury, possibly even death. For me, my behavior was necessary. I had to remain slender, not only for Zach, but to keep my job. The pressure to look good, to be slim almost to the point of being skinny, had increased a thousandfold.

It never occurred to me that others might be indulging in the same disgusting little ritual that found me sweating and weak on the bathroom floor after every meal. Who would have suspected such a thing? Surely, it was not something I would admit to. Certainly I would never have disclosed my secret to a stranger in an emergency room.

On June 9, 1979, I awakened early and dressed for work with special care, checking and re-checking my appearance in the mirror. This was not to be just another day spent in a boardroom or in an airport or on a television talk show. This was an event I had planned for months—a tribute to Beverly Sills. In honor of the International Year of the Child, the March Of Dimes had selected Ms. Sills as the "Mother of the Year." On this day, my company would host a gala brunch to honor the famous opera diva.

Everything had to be perfect. It was my job to see that it was. For weeks I had overseen the plans and the creation of a Victorian garden scene on a grassy knoll near our Irvine restaurant. Formal gardens and trellises smothered with flowers transformed the hillside into a lavish scene. In the middle of it all stood a gazebo festooned with dozens of brightly colored international flags. Life-size posters of Beverly Sills in all her major operatic roles stood among the formal gardens.

I wandered through the crowd of waiters dressed in white morning suits and hostesses wearing forest green Victorian gowns and straw hats with streaming ribbons. Nervous fingers checked the floral centerpieces on each white-draped table; busboys hovered over trays of crystal stemware and bottles of champagne; March of Dimes volunteers scurried about, making final adjustments to the seating arrangements. I made one last check on the hors d'oeuvres arranged on the sterling platters and then began mingling among the arriving crowd of international dignitaries, politicians, city officials, corporate executives, and entertainment figures. Standing a head taller than everyone, and looking like a golden god, Zach strode toward me, and the day began to sparkle.

Arm in arm, Zach and I wandered through a magical kingdom peopled by beautiful ladies and gentlemen dressed in expensive haute couture fashions and morning suits. I smiled and accepted the congratulations offered to me all day long. Comments of appreciation, praise, and adulation kept me smiling and floating.

"No one could have done it better."

"Everything is perfect, just exquisite, Millicent."

"How did you ever think of a Victorian theme?"

Ah, Mama, thank you, thank you...

Hours later, the celebration ended, but the sense of exhilaration lasted long into the night for me.

Two days later, on June 11, 1979, I answered the phone at my office and heard the frantic voice of the restaurant manager on the other end.

"The owner of the gazebo is furious! He's jumping down my throat!" he shouted.

"What's wrong?"

"The volunteers who cleaned up after the brunch didn't take down the flags."

"They were supposed to strike the entire set," I answered. "I don't understand."

"Well, the flags are still flying above his gazebo, and he wants them down pronto!"

"I'll get a crew over there right away. Don't worry. I'll personally see that it's done today."

After a couple of terse phone calls, I drove to Irvine to make good on my promise. I would make sure the huge flags that irritated the gazebo owner came down today.

It was noon when I arrived at the site. A handful of workers carrying posters passed me as I walked across the grass toward the gazebo.

Shoot, I thought, as my high heels sank down into the soft, damp earth. I'm not dressed for a construction site. I wish I'd worn something else... I must look like Lady Bountiful wearing a green silk sheath to speak with a construction crew...

Oh, well, it can't be helped, I thought. Shaking my head and smiling to myself, I walked carefully toward the gazebo and the one lone worker on a ladder who was trying to gather in the fluttering folds of a huge flag.

The sun was directly overhead. I squinted up into the glare to watch the man above me struggle with his chore. From his perch twenty-five feet above, he leaned forward, and then a rustling sound—was it a trick of the sunlight, or did his ladder appear to sway out from the gazebo?

He's falling! I thought. He's going to fall!

Rushing forward with awkward steps, I lifted my feet high, pulling against the soft, cloying earth that sucked on my spike heels. I tried to hurry, but the mud dragged my motions into slow gear. I threw myself against the tottering ladder. Just as my hands reached its base, I looked up into the sunlight and, blinking against the brightness, I saw the workman careening backwards toward the ground. As he plummeted, his hammer slipped from his hands and traveled toward my upturned face.

Move! Move! my brain screamed.

My feet stuck in the boggy earth. My eyes froze on the spinning shape of the hammer. A crunching sound echoed in my ears, and a curtain of blackness engulfed me.

Chapter 10

Across a vast darkness, a voice traveled toward me, calling my name. I reached toward it, pushing against heavy eyelids, finding only a tiny slit of light. The blurred face of a young intern peered down at me. Pounding pain reverberated in my head and face, and I thought I was going to vomit.

Blood covered everything—my dress, my arms, my chest. It ran like a river into my nostrils, my ears, my hair. I could feel it pouring down my throat, nearly gagging me.

"Miss Collinsworth, can you hear me?"

I couldn't nod. I couldn't speak. I tried to focus on the face above me, but the swelling tissue around my eyes cut my view down to a narrow sliver.

"Miss Collinsworth, your nose is shattered in several places. You have a hairline fracture under your left cheekbone and a concussion."

The gurney I lay on was saturated with my blood. Men and women in white uniforms and surgical greens moved around me, moving me, touching me, lifting me. Finally a plastic surgeon stood above me, his perusal of my face lit by a bright lamp that hurt my eyes.

"I'm going to stitch the cut in your lip, Miss Collinsworth," he said. "It's a zigzag slit from under your left nostril to the top of your upper lip and down to the bottom right side. You'll need to see a dentist about the chipped and broken teeth."

I tried to follow his words. My face is cut... It hurts... Oh God, it hurts.

"There is too much swelling right now to do anything more than sew you up. When the swelling has gone down, we can talk about reconstructive surgery. For now, I'm more concerned about infection. That hammer was filthy."

His voice droned on, giving orders to nurses, narrating his actions as his hands worked on my face. Finally, the stitching was done.

"I'm going to send you home with some powerful antibiotics. Take them! Do you understand?"

I peered up at him blankly.

"We'll schedule the plastic surgery for two weeks from now, if the swelling has gone down. Meanwhile, take your medication and stay in bed."

René, an acquaintance from work, picked me up at the hospital and drove me home. She tried to hide a shudder when she first looked at my face.

"You're going to be all right, Millicent," she said as she gripped my elbow and helped me into my apartment.

It was a stroke of good fortune that René had moved in to share my apartment only a few days before the accident. She had needed a place to stay while she sorted out some roommate problems. We both worked for the restaurant chain and both of us traveled most of the time. Because Zach would be in Europe on business for the next two months, a temporary roommate was no inconvenience. As it turned out, René was a godsend.

"I'll take a couple of days off, just until you're feeling a little better," she promised.

Three days passed. I lay in total darkness, my eyes swollen shut. When, on the fourth day, I was able to open them, I saw two of everything. Double vision, however, seemed the least of my problems when I glimpsed my ragged, purple face in the bathroom mirror. The tissue and cartilage that had once been my nose lay smashed, a piece of excess flesh shoved flat against my right cheek. Bruised and torn tissue around my mouth and eyes made me unrecognizable. My features, misshapen and distorted by stitches and swelling, looked hideous.

No... no... no!

I reached up to touch my face and then my hands drew back as if scalded. I put my fingertips up against the cool glass of the mirror instead, and traced the reflection of the puckered, stitched line that ran down from my torn nostril and across my lips. Almost against my will, I stood and studied my appearance. If not for the throbbing pain I was feeling, I would not have believed that I was looking at my own image.

Thank God Zach is out of the country, I thought. I can't let him see me like this.

Two months... he'll be gone for two months. That has to be long enough. I'll be well by the time he finishes his business in Europe... I have to be well by then.

I called Mama that day. I had to tell her what had happened, but I didn't want her to see me like this. I couldn't let her know how bad it was. I tried to minimize the seriousness of it.

"I've had an accident, Mama," I said, speaking softly into the phone.

"Mitty, are you all right?" I could hear concern in Mama's controlled voice.

"I'm okay... No, you don't need to come. My friend René is with me. I'll need surgery in a couple of weeks, but it's not really anything too serious," I lied. "I'll be fine, but I just thought I should tell you."

Within a few days after the accident, infection set in. The two weeks' wait for my reconstructive surgery stretched to four weeks. The doctor ordered me to stay in bed, hoping this would prevent the spread of the infection. I spent every waking moment fighting a growing sense of panic. I was terrified that the doctors would not be able to repair my face, terrified that I would go through life damaged and scarred. I imagined people looking at me and turning away, sickened. Mostly, I imagined Zach turning away from me.

Please, God, let me get well. Let me get well.

As the days of waiting passed, despair wrapped itself around me. Would the doctor never set a date for the surgery? Would the company I worked for fire me because I was no longer beautiful enough to represent them? Would Zach come home and find me unlovely and unlovable?

And accompanying these haunting thoughts were the constant sight and smell of blood.

Everywhere I looked I saw blood. It coated every surface and soaked into every garment. The stench of it filled my nostrils. Against doctor's orders, I climbed out of bed and into the shower. Several times each day I stood under a stream of hot water and lathered myself, trying to scrub away the awful odor of blood.

"Can't you smell it, René?" I asked, my voice near hysteria. "This whole apartment reeks of it!"

René, looking confused, answered, "I haven't noticed anything, Millicent. You must be imagining it."

"I'm not imagining it. The smell of blood is so strong in here it makes me sick! I can't believe you don't smell it!" I could feel panic pulsing in my veins.

If she couldn't smell it, then she probably couldn't see it either... Oh, God! I'm losing it... I'm seeing blood everywhere! It was on my clothes, on my hands, on the face reflected in the bathroom mirror. Blood covered everything I looked at.

I'm the only one who sees it, I thought. And I'm the only one who can smell it.

Terror dragged the air out of my lungs, leaving me gasping.

Get a grip, I commanded myself. Breathing deeply and slowly, I tried to steady myself, saying over and over again, "It's going to be okay... It's going to be okay." I closed my eyes against the sight of darkening pools of blood, but I couldn't stop breathing. I couldn't escape the stench of blood.

Toward the end of August, the doctor agreed to operate on my face. I went home with my face swathed in bandages.

My recovery, on sick leave, lasted about six weeks. The surgery, which had used cartilage from my forehead and my ears to create a bridge and rebuild my nose, appeared to be successful when the bandages were removed. The bruises inflicted during surgery had faded, and the swelling that had distorted my features was gone. My torn lip was repaired and, while I looked not exactly as I had before, I was at least presentable. Except for the continued double vision and the odor of blood that still burned in my nostrils, I thought I was ready to return to work.

It was October 1979. I stood in the bedroom of my apartment, dressing for my first day back on the job. I studied the assortment of beautiful dresses in my closet and reached for a linen coat dress. Before my hand touched it I drew back in horror. Blood! On my hands... on everything I touched!

No... this can't be... I shrank back from the doorway of the closet and leaned against a wall, shivering and panting for air.

It's a delusion, a hallucination... It has to be... I'm becoming my father! I'm insane, just like he was! Oh, please God, no! This can't be happening!

My mind raced backward at high speed, taking me to the driveway of the Arkansas state hospital. My father's fear entered me, and I imagined it was I, not he, that white-clad figures dragged across the gravel toward the doorway of the building where steel bars striped the windows.

I can't let that happen to me...

The vow made to protect my father now became a secret pledge to myself. I had to ensure my own safety. I could never let anyone know about my delusions. I could never expose myself to the danger of a mental institution. I would hold myself together at all costs. I would will myself to sustain a measure of sanity.

Drawing a deep breath, I dressed and returned to my job, determined to maintain at least the facade of health and normalcy.

If co-workers observed anything strange in my behavior at first, they said nothing. I believed I was compensating rather well for a woman who saw two of everything and who saw and smelled blood at all times. I was playing a part: the part of a sane and sensible woman. But behind the facade I was constantly nauseous and terrified. I could neither eat nor sleep. When my weight dropped drastically and I began to look skeletal, the people at the office noticed and expressed their concern.

The only concern I wanted was Zach's. Still abroad, he had extended his trip, and our only contact was by phone. I missed him desperately. He had sent me generous gifts and messages of love and encouragement throughout the ordeal, but now I was desperate to be with him. Every day I prayed that he would be able to come home soon. And every day I prayed that I would be well by the time he arrived. That I would not lose my sanity altogether.

I did everything I could to grab hold of things reasonable and sane. When it occurred to me that my vision problems might be causing the nausea that I felt, I was almost lightheaded with relief. The reasonable thing to do would be to see an ophthalmologist. Of course! I would do the reasonable thing. It was what any sane person would do!

I dialed the number of a well-recommended ophthalmologist and made an appointment. Then carefully, and with great forethought, I entered his office a few days later, my speech rehearsed, ready for delivery.

"I think I might need reading glasses."

In the course of the examination, the doctor, quite young and personable, discerned that I was seeing double.

"Have you always been troubled with double vision?" he asked.

"Oh, yes," I lied.

The doctor's troubled expression made me uncomfortable. I glanced down at my hands in my lap. Did he know I was lying to him? How could he help me if I didn't tell him the truth? But I found I could not tell this gentle young doctor all my defects. I could not open myself to him, even if it meant he could not give me his best care.

All my life had been lived in the shadow of secrets. I had invested years in perfecting the art of hiding my hurts. Layers of emotional scar tissue covered the wounds I had incurred growing up in a household turned asylum. Why would I now purposely parade my injuries before anyone—even those injuries so recently sustained?

The habits of the psyche are hard to break. And so the only information I offered to this intense young doctor was that my eyes had not worked together with fusion since childhood. I told him this because, since my injury, my eyes had begun to "roll" again. He tried every kind of lens, trying to fit me in glasses that would force my eyes to work together, trying to stop them from wandering in toward my nose, and trying to correct the double vision. But nothing worked. After several weeks, the doctor finally admitted defeat.

"Miss Collinsworth, we are not having any success. I think I could operate and correct the rolling so that your eyes would look normal, but you won't have fusion."

No stranger to the pursuit of beauty, I prepared myself to accept the trauma of surgery once again.

The night before the operation, I gaped at myself in the mirror. My reflection appeared bloodied and bloated. Nearly gagging with disgust, I reached into a cabinet for a bottle of diuretics and a package of laxatives. The following morning, I presented myself to the surgeon with forbidden substances swimming in my bloodstream.

The surgery went well, but afterward, when my electrolyte count dropped to a dangerously low level, I was suddenly in serious trouble. My eyes were bandaged, so I couldn't see anything, but I heard nurses scurrying about me and anxious conversations in muffled tones. In a little while, I fell asleep, assured that the crisis had passed.

In the morning, the ophthalmologist entered my room and sat down on the foot of my bed.

"Millicent, we need to talk," he said. "You are dangerously dehydrated. You could easily have suffered a heart attack on the operating table. Do you realize that?"

I said nothing.

"Your roommate tells me you abuse both laxatives and diuretics and that you constantly make yourself vomit. Is that true?"

"No," I whispered, clenching my fists and turning my face toward the wall. "I don't abuse anything. I don't know what René is talking about."

The doctor left the room silently.

I lay in my bed and cursed René for her betrayal. How could

she have told anyone my personal business, my personal habits? I had done her a favor, letting her move into my apartment. Didn't she know anything about loyalty and privacy? I was enraged and, at the same time, embarrassed. My disgusting little habit was no longer secret.

René had thought she was helping me, but she had crossed the line. She had delved into matters of privacy. Collinsworths did not allow such things. I would never forgive her for this.

Within a few hours after the bandages were removed from my eyes, I knew the surgery had been a failure. The doctor's look of disappointment told me the bad news: my eyes now rolled outward, independently of each other. I was devastated.

"This isn't what either of us wanted, Millicent," my kind doctor said. "I'm very sorry. As soon as you've fully recovered, I want to send you to a specialist at Jules Stein Eye Institute at UCLA," he said. "I'll assist him, but I want the specialist to operate the next time."

I went home from the hospital feeling sick and depressed. Less than three days later, I returned to the hospital with a serious eye infection. For two weeks, I lay in darkness, my eyes medicated and bandaged. An IV of antibiotics poured into me. Depression dug an even deeper hole into my spirit.

When the infection appeared to be healed, I returned to work once again, weak and disoriented, my rolling eyes a source of embarrassment to me. But several public relations campaigns were pending. Grand openings had been scheduled throughout the nation. I had important matters to attend to. I could not afford to miss any more work. But oh, how difficult it was to concentrate and perform when I was dizzy and nauseous at all times.

"I can give you some temporary relief, Millicent," my doctor told me when I went to him for a follow-up examination. "If you wear an eye patch over one eye, it will help you maintain your equilibrium and it might curb your nausea as well."

I would have laughed at the irony if it hadn't been so embarrassing. The pirate's patch had returned. It had been difficult to wear it as a child; it would be excruciating to wear it as an adult. The corporate moguls I worked with were appalled at my appearance when I entered the office with the black patch pulled down over one eye.

"It is only temporary," I said, trying to be flippant about it. I tried to give myself a sort of jaunty style to accompany the mystique of the black patch. When I had to make a television

appearance wearing it, I made light of it and smiled with a forced
show of confidence. But on the inside I was crumbling into pieces.
I waited impatiently for Zach's return from Europe. He was the
one person who could comfort me when my fears grabbed hold
of me.

Zach finally returned with the decision that we needed to give
each other "space"—just while I recuperated from my injuries
and the surgeries. He came to see me twice and phoned me often,
assuring me that he loved me. But he told me several times,
"Being around sick people gives me the creeps."

Our phone conversations were filled with laughter and promises
and reminders of the dreams we shared. I told myself often that
many people get queasy around illness. Zach loved me, I knew he
did. As soon as I was well again, things between us would return
to the way they had been. But as time passed, I grew less and less
certain of that.

I was losing it all—everything the Collinsworths stood for,
everything I had promised to gain, for Daddy's sake. I had garnered
it all—too late for him, yes, but not too late for me. I had left
behind the sorrows of the little girl in glasses and pigtails. I had
carved out a niche for myself among the prominent and the
powerful. I had achieved the beauty that had eluded me in
childhood. And, for a time, I had felt safe in the love of a handsome
man. But I had no sense of safety anymore. I had no confidence
in my success.

I had no choice but to try to maintain some semblance of
normalcy, even though I felt as if my life were falling apart. I
continued to do my job, wearing the eye patch, and I made
frequent flights to distant cities, as I had always done, to oversee
the opening of new restaurants. And every day was a bloody
ordeal for me. The stench of blood still resided in my nostrils,
and often, without warning, I looked down at myself and imagined
blood soaking into my clothing. Catching myself before I could
gasp or scream, I schooled myself to close my eyes and gather my
wits about me. I forced myself to pretend I wasn't crazy.

I don't know how I continued to function. Deep within me
the fear of my own insanity was an intense, throbbing terror. I
felt abandoned by Zach, but I would not acknowledge that his
love for me had changed. I pretended all would be well because I
had not the emotional stamina to cope with the thought of
losing him. The world I lived in screamed at me with horrifying
possibilities and sickening realities. But every day I worked and

traveled. And, on cue, I stepped into place in front of television cameras and exchanged witticisms with talk-show hosts and sampled tasty recipes in front of millions of viewers nationwide.

As the Collinsworths had always done, I adjusted my mask and wrapped myself in a cloak of denial. Every day I stepped closer to the edge of the precipice, teasing fate. I played my game just inches from the ledge that was crumbling beneath me. I would plunge headlong into the abyss one day. It would not be an altogether unexpected tragedy, I thought. Until then, I would continue to pretend.

I was traveling for my company when I first had a serious nosebleed. Startled by the amount of blood, I didn't know whether to be frightened or relieved that it was in fact real blood. This was no delusion; it was a massive hemorrhage which left me weak and feeling ill. When I returned home, I made an appointment with the plastic surgeon who had repaired my nose. He cauterized and packed my nasal passages.

Over the following weeks, the hemorrhages occurred frequently and without warning. I was making a presentation in the boardroom of the company one day when blood began to spurt from my nose. Men and women in expensive business suits stared appalled as I thrust my head back and hurried out of the room. Again, the doctor packed and cauterized my nasal passages.

A few days later, I began to notice that I was losing time during the day. At first, minutes would elapse and I would have no memory of what I had done. Then hours would pass, and I would have no knowledge of where I had been or what I had been doing. Soon, entire days were wiped out. I became convinced that I had truly lost my mind. I had become my father's daughter. It was over for me. The descent into madness had begun.

My fragile facade finally crumbled one morning when I was driving down the freeway toward work. I was gripping the steering wheel, lost in thought, when blood spurted from my nose and spattered the windshield. With every pulse, blood spewed out, making my hands slick on the wheel. Frantically, I tried to maneuver my car toward an outside lane while reaching for something to staunch the flow.

Somehow I reached the side of the freeway and collapsed against the steering wheel while the blood continued to pour from my nose.

I remember awakening on a gurney in a hospital emergency room and seeing a strange face close to mine. The hospital was one I'd never been in before, and the staff was unfamiliar to me. A team of doctors examined me, each tilting my face, probing and peering at me. Finally one of them, an ear, nose, and throat specialist, spoke.

"On the outside, your reconstructive surgery looks absolutely perfect, Miss Collinsworth," he said. "But inside, your nasal cavity looks like a war zone. You have a massive infection that is very dangerous. It could even be deadly."

I learned that my Beverly Hills plastic surgeon had left a large jagged bone spur inside my nasal cavity that had burrowed through and punctured the septum. The team of doctors at this hospital was enraged.

"This job is so botched you will have to have the entire reconstructive job done over again."

I heard the words. They were spoken by the plastic surgeon who was a member of the team that had just examined me. I couldn't react to them. I could only lie there with my eyes closed against the view of blood everywhere.

"Of course, we cannot attempt this repair until the infection is healed. In the meantime, you should consider yourself a very lucky young lady that you got into the hospital when you did, Miss Collinsworth."

Lucky? I had neither the heart nor the energy for laughter, but it was suddenly very funny to hear myself described as "lucky." How could anything have been further from the truth?

"Miss Collinsworth, would you please explain why you're wearing the eye patch," the doctors asked me. They all stood around the bed in the emergency room, watching me, as if waiting to hear the next chapter in this pathetic tale of human destruction. Wearily, I told them about my eye problems. They immediately called my ophthalmologist. He was added to the team of doctors readied to oversee my treatment and my recovery.

I left the hospital a few days later, feeling almost hopeful. At least I was willing to believe that I was going to get the kind of care I needed in order to get well. But when a phone call informed me that the team of doctors would include a psychiatrist, I was first shaken, then outraged.

"A psychiatrist!" I shouted. "Do you believe this? They think I need a psychiatrist!"

I sat in a comfy chair in my Manhattan Beach apartment, overlooking the coast. The vivid red of the sunset spilled into the room, casting a pink hue on the walls and the furniture. René sat nearby on a sofa, watching me with a look of caution. Another friend, Marshall Goldberg, stood in the archway near the kitchen, sipping a glass of wine. I saw him glance quickly at René and then back at me.

"Maybe it's not such a bad idea, Mitty." Marshall spoke with forced nonchalance.

"It's a lousy idea!" I hissed. "I don't need a shrink! What I need is a decent plastic surgeon who won't butcher me!"

Marshall walked toward me, his footsteps muffled in the deep carpet. He crouched down next to my chair, his face close, his dark eyes level with mine.

"Mitty, do you realize your entire body trembles most of the time?"

I stared at him and then looked quickly away.

"Don't you think it's time you let your guard down with someone?"

My brittle emotions teetered as Marshall's gentleness blew over me. I had to grip them quickly to keep them from crashing and shattering into a thousand pieces. I ducked behind the elaborate facade of perfection I had depended upon for so many years, and the Collinsworth heritage of denial stood firm. Glaring at this slender young man whose face held such concern for me, I said, "There is nothing wrong with me!"

My hands clenched and unclenched in my lap. My lips trembled as I spoke. Fragile emotions vibrated inside me, tossing me into confusion.

Marshall smiled at me and squeezed my hands. "Mitty, think about it, will you? Just think about it."

When he opened the door to leave my apartment, it was as though a cold wind swept out all sense of order and safety. I shivered and pulled my arms up tightly against my chest.

Next to Zach and my brother Laddie, I loved Marshall better than any other man I knew. A Phi Beta Kappa from Harvard, he had come west to attend Stanford Law School. After graduating, he had joined a law firm in Pennsylvania, but in time, his dreams of becoming a screenwriter had drawn him back to California. Bringing his soft-spoken, ivy-league manner with him, he, like thousands of other hopefuls in the film world, studied his craft and waited for his break. We had met at a party one night and had become almost instant friends and confidants. How desperately I needed his friendship now!

The Collinsworth pride and my intense need for privacy had

prevented me from forming many close friendships. And besides, Zach had always been enough for me—I hadn't seen any need for other relationships. But Marshall was special. I could talk to him about anything. He listened when I needed to tell someone how baffled I was by Zach's recent behavior.

Zach's only contact with me was by phone. That was our only link these days. He assured me he loved me. We would have a future together, as soon as our lives became more stable, he promised. My injury, his travel—everything was against us. Things grew even more complicated when he decided to quit the family business and go back to school for a graduate degree. He decided he belonged in the field of education—he wanted a career as a school administrator. All these things interfered with our being together, he said. In time it would all work out. He loved me, he said. Silently, I begged for it to be true. But it was Marshall, not Zach, who drove me to a private sanitarium a few days after that conversation in my apartment. It was Marshall, with his courtly manners and his kindly sincerity, whose voice assured me that everything would be all right.

The new team of doctors who had taken over my care had concluded that I was too fragile, emotionally and physically, to endure the series of surgeries that lay ahead for me. They told me I had an eating disorder and they wanted me under the daily care of psychiatrists who would monitor my diet and enforce rest while involving me in therapy sessions. All this was for the purpose of strengthening me for surgery, they said. I had no intention of cooperating with their scheme, but I had no energy for fighting; and, I realized, if I wanted the surgery, I would have to at least appear to be accepting therapy.

No one on the team of doctors knew of my father's manic-depressive illness. I would have died before I told them. I couldn't allow them even a glimpse into the Collinsworth's secret. If they knew, perhaps they would deduce that my father's illness was now mine. Perhaps they would certify me as crazy. I couldn't take that chance.

When I was introduced to my psychiatrist, Dr. Sandler, I shook hands with him and presented him with a haughty display of Collinsworth pride. He smiled at me with a look that accepted my unspoken challenge. I thought he might be a worthy opponent. Tall and athletic-looking, Dr. Sandler had dark eyes that conveyed the message that he could see many things that I, his patient, could not yet see. I stiffened under his perusal and determined to keep the curtain drawn about me at all costs.

"I won't wear a hospital gown," I told him. The specter of vacant-eyed mental patients in drab, dingy gowns made me feel ill. I would not allow myself to become one of them.

"You can bring your own clothes," Dr. Sandler said, assuring me my comfort was the only thing that was important to him. "If it will make you feel more at home, bring anything you like."

Marshall helped me pack my designer suits, high-heeled shoes, and expensive perfume. I seethed the entire time.

I'll play their silly games, I said to myself, my hands shaking as I stuffed silk lingerie into my suitcase. All I need is to get my nose and my eyes fixed—I don't need their therapy sessions.

I reached into the closet for a pair of wool slacks and a matching sweater.

I'll sit through their sessions, but I won't share anything personal... They'll just have to accept that. I'm not one of their crazies who needs a shrink! I'm not going to dress like one and I'm certainly not going to open my psyche up for them to dig into it.

My expensive silk blouse was drenched with perspiration by the time I had finished packing.

Throughout the drive to the private hospital, I fought the urge to jump out of the car and run away. When Marshall drove up to the entrance, I could not control my shaking.

A wire fence surrounded the wide lawn in front of the granite and brick building.

This is all a nightmare...

Coils of wire spun across the top of the fence at the south end of the lawn and toward the back of the building.

This is not my life, it's my father's life...

Steel bars encased the windows on the side walls of the building.

I'm not the one who needs to be in a mental hospital... This can't be happening!

I squeezed my eyes shut and heard a child's husky voice, You should have kept your promise... You should have kept your promise...

"Mitty? You okay?"

I glanced at Marshall. He was staring at me as if I had suddenly changed colors.

"Of course. Let's get this over with."

My high heels clicked loudly on the concrete path as I walked up to the large front doors. Marshall carried my suitcase and walked beside me. I forced myself to look only at the potted plants that stood in the tiled entryway. I would not look down the hallways for a view of patients standing about. I'd seen all that before, and I did not want to see it again. I would not look at the empty, tortured faces, the trembling hands, the bruised arms. I looked only at the smiling attendant at the counter who handed me papers to sign.

Marshall put his arms around me. "I'll be back in a few days," he said.

I nodded and pulled away from his touch. My face split into a huge artificial smile.

"Well, I'll see you then."

"Call me if you need to talk," he said, hesitant to walk away from me.

"I'm supposed to talk with the therapist, remember? I'll be all talked out, Marshall. You'll have to do all the talking," I answered, chuckling at my private joke. He smiled at me and touched my cheek before he walked out the door.

I wore a couture suit by Yves St. Laurent to the first therapy session. Dr. Sandler welcomed me and motioned toward an empty folding chair. I sat down and crossed my legs at the ankle, exactly as any well-bred young woman would do. Lifting my chin and straightening my shoulders, I adopted a lofty manner that I hoped would alert this group of crazy people that I did not really belong among them. I would do nothing to cooperate with this charade. I sat in silence, pretending I was somewhere else, enduring until I could escape to the solace of my private room.

Three days later, I learned that the surgeries planned for my eyes and my face would have to be postponed indefinitely.

"What are you talking about?" I shrieked when the hospital representative told me the news.

"Miss Collinsworth, your injury was caused on the job. There is litigation pending. Several insurance companies are involved. None of them wants to take responsibility for paying your doctors' fees and the hospital bills until the courts determine liability."

"But I must have both surgeries immediately!" I said.

"That can be arranged if you can pay both surgeons and the hospitals in full before the operations. You can collect from the insurance companies later. Otherwise, this will have to be put off until a settlement is reached in the courts."

It was a common dilemma. The doctors didn't want to perform surgery and then wait years for a court to order an insurance company to pay them. Neither the eye surgeon at the Jules Stein Eye Institute nor the plastic surgeon was willing to treat me unless I could assure them of payment at the time of treatment. The hospitals involved would not admit me without an insurance company's assurance of payment, or payment from my own pocket in advance.

I was stunned. And terrified. I called Marshall. With his legal background, he would be able to tell me if this was true.

"With an injury sustained on the job, this happens, Mitty," he told me. "Private insurance companies often want to wait until the matter is settled in court."

I felt ill when I hung up the phone. Where was I going to come up with the thousands of dollars necessary to pay for two different operations? I made a generous salary, but I had spent it generously too. I had some savings, but not nearly enough for the kind of medical bills I was facing.

I could not return to my career wearing an eye patch indefinitely. And I could not continue having massive nosebleeds. The surgery was not optional—I had to have it; but how was I going to be able to afford it?

With shaking hands, I picked up the phone and dialed Mama. She listened in silence while I told her my situation.

"Mitty," she answered in a tentative voice, "I know you're upset, and I'm sorry. But the surgeries will just have to wait. That kind of money would deplete my entire savings and I would have to take out a second mortgage on the house."

My breath stuck in my throat.

Mama's voice dropped to a whisper. "Mitty, I can't do that again... Can you understand? I've already lost one house by taking out a second mortgage. I can't risk it again. If I lost this house it would kill me."

She couldn't risk the house. Not for me. Not for anyone.

I suddenly felt very ill.

You don't understand, Mama, I wanted to say. But it was too late for explanations. I had chosen to minimize my injuries when the accident happened. I had done everything I could to spare her the awful details of my condition. She had not seen me in months. We spoke only on the phone. She didn't know that my eyes rolled away from my nose as they had when I was a child, that a black eye patch covered one eye so that I could stand upright without losing my balance.

I had not told her about the hemorrhages or the botched

surgery that had caused such a dangerous infection. She only knew I needed some corrective surgery and, in her mind, it was optional. She saw no urgency. And for that, she would not put at risk the beloved villa she had re-created in the image of the old brick house on Center Street.

I hung up the phone and sagged against the chair. What was I going to do? The surgery could not be postponed indefinitely. I had to have it before I could return to work.

Why hadn't I told Mama everything in the beginning? I chided myself. If I had, would she still have put the villa ahead of me?

Anger smoldered in me. I paced the small square footage of my hospital room, raging at myself for not telling Mama everything as it had occurred: the seriousness of the original accident, the multiple eye infections, the butchered job performed by the first plastic surgeon—all of it.

But how could I tell her? I argued. Daddy's illness put her through so much... I couldn't make her live with that kind of worry again. What would it do to her to find out about my eating disorder and all the complications?

I felt ashamed too. I had not been strong enough or capable enough to tend to my own problems. I had had to depend on someone else. That someone else was Mama, and how I hated having to ask her for help. How I hated hearing her turn me down!

Maybe she really does love the old manor house more than she loves me... I should have told her that I smell blood all the time, that I see it everywhere... No, that would have done her in... She couldn't take that. It would be my father all over again. She'd be convinced I'm crazy too.

I refused to cry. I forced myself to gather my wits about me, not to panic, not to give up.

Think, Mitty. There has to be a way. There has to be some way to work this thing out...

I was brooding in my private room, looking out the picture window but not really seeing the view of green lawn and trees, when a knock sounded at the door and a familiar voice interrupted the silence.

"Hello, Mitty."

Zach was leaning in the doorway, grinning at me. I tried to smile at him, but suddenly self-conscious, my hand went up quickly to finger the black patch over my eye.

"How are you, Babe?" he asked, walking in and letting the door close behind him.

"I'm okay. You?"

"Great."

He stood near the door, not crossing the small distance between us. His hands plowed through his thick, shaggy hair.

"I can't stay long, Mitty," he said. "I just wanted to see how you're feeling."

"Better. Much better now that you're here," I answered. I took one step toward him, smiling at the sight of the familiar bright print shirt he wore.

"You look terrific, Zach. It's so good to see you."

"It's good to see you too."

He continued to stand near the door. His eyes shifted to a place on a far wall.

"I have to talk to you... I know you're not expecting this, but, well... "

"What is it, Zach?"

"It just happened, Mitty... I've met someone, a girl. You'd like her. She's cute as a button, just like you used to be. I'm in love with her, Mitty. I know—it surprised me too! But I'm really madly in love with her."

The words tumbled out of his mouth so quickly I could hardly follow them at first. And then the meaning exploded inside me.

He's in love with someone else... It's over... I'm ugly and alone...

"She's waiting for me in the lobby... I have to go... "

He said more words, but I stopped listening. He left the room quickly and the door closed behind him.

I had no thought, no plan, only grief-powered adrenaline, when I grabbed the wooden chair next to the bed. With a wail that tore my throat, I thrust the chair through the large, plate-glass window in my room and lunged toward the shattered glass. While shouts echoed around me, I grabbed a jagged shard and sliced both my wrists. Blood puddled near my feet, but it wasn't enough. I dragged the glass across my throat, making my final, desperate gesture of self-loathing complete.

Screams split the air around me, filling the room, and then a slowly descending silence swallowed me—the silence of a country scene, bordered by a narrow, lazy stream, and lush, green, neatly plowed fields. Daddy's voice called to me from the bank of Dogwood Creek.

"Mitty! Come look!" he said. "The dogwoods are in bloom!"

A little girl in pigtails ran across my view, hurrying toward the

tall man who stood beneath the trees. A dogwood branch covered
with white blossoms lay in his arms.

"Millicent... "

A strange voice interrupted my reverie.

"Can you hear me, Millicent?"

Drugs and dreams churned about in my brain. I didn't want to
open my eyes and leave the scene on the bank of the creek, but
the stern voice commanded me.

"Open your eyes, Millicent."

I felt my shoulders clamped in a powerful grip. Shaking me
roughly, Dr. Sandler barked at me, "I said, open your eyes!"

Intense brown eyes bored down into my face.

"Remember me, Millicent?"

I closed my eyes. He shook me again.

"I don't intend to let you die, Millicent. Do you understand
me?"

His face was so close to me I could feel his breath. The anger
in his voice confused me.

"Why do you insist on treating life like a TV game show? You
don't win the washer-dryer combination, so you just give up!" he
shouted. "Don't you have any pride?"

My tongue wouldn't work any better than my brain. I could
form no words to rebut his furious tirade. He jabbed a long,
skinny finger in my face and bellowed, "The world is in need of
strong women, not beauty queens!"

Dr. Sandler strode out of the room, leaving me in the hands of
nurses in a tiny, cell-like room in the intensive care unit of the
psychiatric hospital. Half a dozen tubes and wires attached me to
a blinking, beeping apparatus and a respirator. A plastic bag of
blood hung above my head, replenishing what I had lost. I was
alive, but the only emotion I could identify was disappointment.

Throughout the next few hours, Dr. Sandler tried to locate
Mama and Laddie. He summoned them to the hospital for a
conference as soon as possible. Three days later, he led them
down the halls of the hospital, through the open wards and then
beyond, into the netherworld of the mentally ill. Behind two sets
of locked doors, he escorted them down a corridor lined with
doors that opened into small, windowless rooms that contained
"high-risk" patients.

"These patients are considered a risk to themselves, or to
others," he told Laddie and Mama, gesturing toward the locked
doors with small slit windows in them. He didn't know they had

toured the halls of other psychiatric wards in the past. He didn't know they had spent most of their lives evaluating risks, removing weapons.

Inside my room, Mama and Laddie gathered around my bed and listened to the doctor explain to them how precarious my condition was at that moment as a result of my suicide attempt and deliberate starvation. He watched as the family dynamics of the Collinsworths played themselves out once again against the backdrop of a mental hospital. He didn't know he was seeing an encore performance.

"How could you do this?" Laddie shouted at me. "How could you do this to Mama and me, especially after all Daddy put us through?"

I turned my face toward the wall.

Mama sat in stony silence, letting Laddie do all the raging. His tall, thin form leaned over my bed and his face was white with fury. His hands were clenched into tight fists, and his voice broke as tears gathered in his throat.

"Don't you know we love you, Mitty? Isn't that enough to live for? Don't you know Mama and I both love you? And we need you, Mitty. Can't you understand that?"

His trembling sent vibrations through my bed, but I steeled myself to feel nothing. To show nothing.

Dr. Sandler watched me from his front-row seat, puffing quietly on a pipe. I saw him put his hand up and signal Laddie that the session was over. Mama stood up and my eyes followed her to the foot of my bed. She gripped the metal railing near my feet. Her voice was quiet when she spoke.

"Mitty, life is not fair."

I closed my eyes and willed her to go away.

"Mitty, this behavior is both weak and cowardly. It is not befitting a Collinsworth," she said.

I wanted to cover my ears but tubes and needles pinned my arms to my sides.

"You are my daughter, and I love you deeply, but I will not stand idly by and watch you wallow in self-pity. When you decide to accept whatever challenges life is now going to present you, and meet those challenges with dignity and grace, I will be there to support you."

Dignity! How much dignity can a woman have when she is scarred and ugly?

"I will help you in any way I can. I will walk with you every mile. But as long as you insist on lying in this hospital bed, feeling sorry for yourself, you are going to have to lie here all alone."

It doesn't matter... Nothing matters any more...

"I will not be a partner to your self-destruction."

Mama's speech was over. She walked out of the room without a backward glance.

I watched the door close behind her and wished again that I was dead.

Only years later did I comprehend the magnitude of Mama's actions that day when she stood at the foot of my bed. I think of it today—the letting go, the relinquishing—and a flood of memories rushes in. I remember her voice, when I was a small child, spinning tales of family heroes, telling me about my great-great-great-grandfather, Benjamin Franklin Collinsworth; of how he had stood in his field, his gnarled hands gripping the plow, his eyes blurred with tears, as he watched his three sons march off to fight for the Confederacy. He was too old to go himself— his chest ached with the pain of it; this would have to be his sons' war. He couldn't fight it for them, nor could he protect them. One by one, they said goodbye and entered the fray. One by one, they fought the enemy.

Every day the old man stood in his fields and watched the horizon, praying for his sons' safe return. When word came to him of his first son's death in battle, he hitched his aging mule to his wagon and drove through enemy lines to the battlefield to gather his son's body. Driving back through a barrage of fire, he returned to the farm and buried his son on his own land. Soon after, he learned of his second son's death, and again, with his broken-down mule, he journeyed across blood-soaked battlefields to search for the body he would take home for burial. When the third son lay wounded in a Confederate hospital, the old man, now nearly destitute from the years of war, once again took to the war-ravaged roads. On a makeshift pallet in the back of his wagon, he carried his one remaining son back to the family farm. War's violence had stolen what little he had, but his land remained, and while life pulsed in him, he vowed he would always bring his children home.

"He released his children to the fight," Mama had said. "But he would never be reconciled to their loss. And he swore he would always bring them home, alive or dead."

That day, Mama relinquished me to the fight. She knew she

could not do battle for me. She knew I would live or die alone. It would be my choice. She steeled herself to let me go into the war zone, praying I would survive. Every day she watched for me from a distance; only that one time did she brave enemy territory and venture into the dreaded halls of the psychiatric hospital. If my private war had been over then—if I had won, or even if I had died—she would have taken me home. But I had not yet begun to fight.

The battle lay ahead for me, and so Mama offered me the best she had, the weapons wielded by generations of Collinsworths. Dignity. Grace. Pride. She placed each one in my hand, challenging me to rise up and face the enemy and defeat it. She could only wait now to see if I would choose to fight. It would be my decision. She would wait at home, watching with anxious eyes, to see if I would live through this horror. In the end, she would welcome me home, or bury me. In the end, I would choose my own fate.

The letting go was not without its price. Mama's heart broke. Literally. When next I saw her a few months later, she had aged as though she had borne a century of suffering. Weakened by both sorrow and disease, her heart never recovered from the injury dealt it on the day she left me alone to face my private war. It was a wound that would never heal.

During the next three weeks, I stubbornly refused to eat or drink. My weight dropped to eighty pounds. A naso-gastric (NG) tube was inserted in my nose. A constantly dripping IV hung overhead, feeding me nutrition I didn't want. I wanted only to die. And Dr. Sandler knew it. He ordered me tied to the bed in five-point restraints, including a straitjacket, so sure was he that I would try to kill myself at the first available opportunity.

During those days of misery and self-hatred, I found perverse pleasure in being able to maneuver myself out of the straitjacket. After so many years of dancing and acrobatics, I was quite limber, and agile enough to contort my body into positions that could release me from the hospital's restraints. I could yank out the IV tubes and the NG tube and the catheter and lie in my bed awaiting death. Only in this did I find a kind of twisted satisfaction. Dr. Sandler and the nursing staff found it exasperating.

"Don't leave her alone for even a second!" Dr. Sandler shouted after the third time he found me lying in my bed, disconnected from the tubes that were sustaining my life. "I want her watched twenty-four hours a day! I'm ordering private-duty nurses around the clock!"

He watched me for a sign that his words had broken through to me.

"Look at me, Millicent."

His voice gentled and I allowed myself to meet his eyes.

"I told you once that I wasn't going to let you die. I meant exactly that. You can fight me all you like, but rest assured, Millicent, I am not going to let you die."

Thus began a vigil in my tiny cubicle in the back hallway of the intensive care unit of the psychiatric hospital. True to his word, Dr. Sandler placed a nurse in my room at all times to be sure I would not harm myself. Every bodily function was monitored, every move of my eyes noted while I lay there wishing for death.

For three long weeks, I prayed to die. And Dr. Sandler waited. Each day, he peeked in on me through the slit in the door, believing I was gaining strength from the IV feedings; expecting me to improve under the constant supervision of the private-duty nurses. He was enraged when he entered the room at the end of the third week and examined me himself, only to find me in worse condition than before.

My weight had continued to drop. Bedsores had erupted on my back and my hips, and my arms and legs were swollen and bruised from the tightened straps on the restraints. With a look of absolute horror on his face, Dr. Sandler swore and loosened the bindings. He bent over me, and in a gentle voice he said, "It's all right, Millicent. Everything is going to be all right."

He left my room, and I heard his voice in the hallway as he loudly dismissed the nurses whose care for me had been less than healing.

Everything's going to be all right, he'd promised me. How could that be true? How could anything ever be all right for me again? My only wish was for oblivion. The silent, dark envelope of death was the only thing that could isolate me from this cloying sense of despair. Or so I believed.

Dr. Sandler believed differently.

Othello entered my hospital room the next day. Well over six feet tall, she was an enormous black woman of indiscernible age whose massive presence filled my tiny, windowless cell. Every day she came to me, staying with me for hours, bathing me and dressing me in clean, frilly nightgowns. Every day she carried me to a rocking chair in the corner, and with my skinny, long-legged body draped across her lap, she rocked back and forth, back and forth. Her breath bathing my forehead, she crooned sweet, silly songs to me, or whispered about the heat of the day's sunshine, or the feel of the snapping wind.

Wrapped in Othello's arms, I felt the warm pulse of life and did not recoil from it. For those moments, I let myself travel back to my childhood, back to the warm kitchen in the old brick house on Center Street. As though once again in the presence of Corinne and Ruby Jean, I listened to the words of bittersweet spirituals and recalled hours flavored with innocence. Enfolded in safety, I slept and drifted into dreams of music and childish games and loud, belly-deep laughter. When I awoke, the dreams fled.

"I'm gonna brush your hair now, Mitty," Othello told me every morning. And she lifted my hair up off my neck and brushed it until my scalp burned.

"Let's put on something clean and fresh," she would say, after she had bathed me in lavender-scented water.

I never answered her. I never spoke to anyone.

Every morning promptly at eight, Dr. Sandler arrived in my room. I overheard him talk to Othello; I heard the word "catatonic."

I knew its meaning. I'd lived with it, with all its horrendous manifestations, in the manor house turned asylum. And now its definition applied to me. But I could not summon the energy or strength to defy it. I could not redefine myself now. It had all been preordained anyway, hadn't it? I was destined to become my father. Fate had damned me from the beginning. Born condemned, I would die in my madness, as my father had. There was no other way for me.

Days slipped past, unseen, unnoticed. Tubes fed me. Othello rocked me and sang to me and bathed me. She dressed me in flannel gowns trimmed with ruffles and lace and stacked dolls and stuffed animals all around me, as though I were a child who could be enticed by toys to reenter the world of the living. I ignored it all. There was no reason to come back. No reason to grasp at life. It held nothing for me beyond the terror of insanity.

I had little conscious thought, except to wish for death, to wait for it and expect it. Still, Othello came to me every day. Others must have entered my room, if only to spell Othello, but I was aware of only this one presence. At times, I fancied she was Aunt Sarey come back to life to rescue me, much as she had saved the children of Five Oaks when malaria orphaned them. Was this large, gentle woman the twentieth-century embodiment of Aunt Sarey, sent to nurse another of the children of Five Oaks? So all-encompassing was the strength of her spirit, she could have overpowered the limits of time and space. She had no style or manner that defined her or bound her. Wearing only a shapeless black dress that hung like a tent on her huge frame, she could have stepped into my life from any niche in the past. Her ageless face showed the markings of suffering well borne, and when she laughed, her whole body swung with the rhythm of her laughter.

Like a guardian angel, Othello set up camp around me, refusing to let death snatch me away. Wooing me toward life, she seemed to absorb my horrors into her own massive body, and when she rocked me in her arms, I slept, safe from the nightmares that haunted my waking hours. I may have refused all sustenance for my physical strength, but my soul drank deeply from Othello's spring.

Every day Othello read to me the get-well greetings sent by friends and acquaintances around the country. She arranged and rearranged bouquets of flowers that arrived often, setting them on a table near my bed, hoping I would catch their sweet scent and notice their beauty. Every day I continued to stare blankly, fulfilling the unspoken prophecy of my madness, living out the legacy of my father.

Each day was like the one before. I uttered no sound and acknowledged no living presence. I lay and awaited death.

At times I thought of Zach, and the pain of losing his love. I remembered my damaged face, my lost beauty. I remembered all the miserable failures of my life, all the unfulfilled promises. All the awful sins of my life. All the horrors of insanity that awaited me. And I remembered why death seemed preferable to life.

Then one day, three months after I entered the private sanitarium, Othello entered my room, unknowingly bringing with her a message of pardon that would open the gates of my private hell.

"Mornin' darlin'," she said, pushing open the door to my tiny cell, her arms filled with a stack of laundry. She had begun taking my nightgowns home and washing them herself, bringing them back to me sweet-smelling and soft. Her voice cheery, she plopped the pile of laundry on a chair and came to the side of my bed. With plump hands, she fluffed the pillows around my head and retied the ribbon at the neck of my nightgown. "You know it's nearly Easter?" she said. "My Lord, time's a flyin'. Well, how you feelin' today, sweetie?"

Othello's words meant nothing to me. She chatted on, her voice little more than noise. I shut my eyes and turned my head away from her.

"Here's a card from your Mama, Mitty. Here, I'll just open it for you."

Othello sank down on the edge of my bed and she ripped open the envelope.

"Well, what's this?" she said, as something small and white slipped from the envelope and fluttered down, landing on the bed near my hand.

"What's she say now?" Her husky voice read the words written on the card:

"Dearest Mitty,
Spring has come, as it always does,
and you should be here to see it."

With gentle fingers, Othello gripped my chin and turned my face toward her. "Now lookit this here," she said, picking up the small, pressed flower that had fallen out of the card and floated onto my bed. "What kind of flower is this?"

Dogwood.

Recognition stung my eyes.

It's a dogwood...

Small, blood-tipped blossoms, sometimes white, sometimes pink...

Innumerable horrors crowded the space of my psyche, but nothing could obliterate the long-held memory of the dogwood.

The promise of miracles...

The legend returned to me now—the sacred mantra of the Collinsworths. Somehow, in spite of the loud cacophonous voices of delusion and despair, the sweet sound of hope began to hum softly in my brain.

Second chances!

Second chances!

At first, I had to strain to hear the chorus above the other sounds. Then, as if a full symphony carried the theme, the music thundered.

New beginnings!

New beginnings!

I closed my eyes and saw a tall, handsome man with blue-green eyes standing along the bank of a lazy creek. He called to me, holding a dogwood branch toward me as I ran toward him.

"Never forget the promise of new beginnings, Mitty," he said softly.

A tall, red-haired woman with gray and brown-flecked eyes smiled down at a bespectacled child who looked up at her with awe. Her hands gentle as they plaited the child's hair, her voice firm and resolute, she said, "You must never forget that spring will come."

Beloved voices entered where no other forces could penetrate. Springtime. Easter.

A slow melting began, a stream of tears the first sign of the long-awaited thaw.

"She's cryin'! Oh, my Lord! Dr. Sandler, come in here!" Othello hauled her massive body off my bed and scrambled toward the door. "Get Dr. Sandler! She's cryin'... She's cryin'!"

Chapter 11

For more than a hundred years, the Collinsworths had held onto the legend of the dogwood, seeing the small, delicate blossom as a sprig of hope. As I made my sudden reentry into the land of the living, I saw the pink and white flowers, not as pastel splashes of color against an emerald forest, but as symbols emblazoned on a banner, gripped in the hands of a warrior. The mantra of hope became a war cry as I determined to fight for my life.

It would be years before I would slay enough of my enemies to feel safe, and years before I would be able to reclaim even a portion of all that had been torn away from me, but the call to battle had been sounded. And Dr. Sandler joined me at the front to direct the strategy in this very personal and desperate war. His first order commanded me to make a short foray out into the demilitarized zone: I was to spend an hour each day in the communal day room with other patients in the hospital. The thought terrified me.

"You can't be serious," I said, gaping through blurred vision at his intense face.

"Oh, but I am, Millicent. You can't continue to hide away in here, coddled and cared for like a spoiled child."

Horror etched itself on my brain. I lifted a hand to my face and fingered the black patch over my eye. A thin, transparent tube trailed from my wrist and another protruded from my nose. A urine bag hung from my waist.

"Look at me!" I held up my hands, gesturing at my pitiful appearance. "I can't face anyone looking like this! I will not be humiliated!"

"Your personal vanity is immaterial, Millicent," Dr. Sandler answered. "Starting right now, you will spend time with the other patients in the day room."

I can't do it, I thought. I can't do it...

"Can't I wait until all the tubes and bags are removed?" I asked.

"We aren't waiting any longer."

"Dr. Sandler, please. I'll talk about anything you want to talk about—anything! But please," I argued, almost begging, "can't we do it in this room? I can't be seen like this!"

"Your appearance does not matter, Millicent. I told you once before, this world needs strong women, not beauty queens." His voice was firm and stern. "You will spend one hour each day in the day room, whether you like it or not."

He marched out of my cell, signaling Othello to follow him. I sat alone amid pillows and stuffed toys and bowls of flowers. Perhaps Othello's cosseting had spoiled me, I thought, but how peaceful it was to pretend I was a little girl once more. How comfortable it was to burrow down into the safe haven Othello had created for me, where danger seemed only a distant illusion.

I was pondering how I could persuade Dr. Sandler to recant his orders when an attendant pushing a wheelchair entered my room. Picking me up as though I were no heavier than a rag doll, he placed me in the wheelchair and began fastening straps across my body. I writhed and twisted, trying to evade the bindings, and shrieked, "No! No! I won't go!"

Othello lumbered back into the room and leaned close to me, whispering to soothe me, but suddenly she was the enemy. I kicked at her with my small strength and fought against the straps, but I was powerless. The wheelchair rolled down the corridor, propelling me past one locked door, and then another. Moments later, I sat in the day room where a cloud of stale, gray smoke hung like a storm warning.

Hunched down in my chair, my chin resting against my chest, I peered cautiously about the tile-floored room to which I had been sentenced for the next hour. Their forms blurred through the vision of my one eye, I could make out men and women wandering about the large room. Some of them looked like ordinary people who had discovered themselves mistakenly routed for a bizarre holiday. Some patients sat very still, their bodies' only motion the rise and fall of their chests as they sucked on dying cigarettes; others rocked to a silent rhythm, their eyes staring out the window at mythical scenes on the back lawn. Others, intrigued by the diversion of a new presence, came toward me, staring at me and touching my hair, pointing at the leather straps that held me upright in the wheelchair. Babbling incoherently, they blew their rancid breath on me and leaned against me in soiled and rumpled clothing.

Seething, I kept my head down, trying to hide the ugly black patch I wore. How dare he! I thought. How dare he subject a Collinsworth to such humiliation?

With a desperate lunge, I reached into the arsenal Mama had built for me and summoned my first weapon. Pride fitted itself to my hands quite naturally and I gripped it tightly, feeling a surge of power enter me.

I am not one of them, a voice thundered in my brain. I am not crazy, not like these people! Not like my father!

I was determined to leave the scene of this madness. I couldn't expect Othello's help—she would never disobey Dr. Sandler's orders. If I was going to retreat from this first battle, I would have to rely on myself. I concocted what I thought was an ingenious escape plan.

I could see Othello's massive, dark shape across the room, so I knew she would not be able to reach me quickly. If I acted now, she could not stop me. Rocking in my wheelchair, I shifted my weight and pushed my body forward toward the edge of the seat. The restraints around my chest and abdomen held fast, but the movement was enough to tilt the chair slightly off balance. Othello's dark form remained at a distance, I noted, and hoped she was distracted by the hum of other patients. I pushed forward again and thrust my weight against the leather straps. The force was enough to send the chair teetering over, throwing me face-first onto the floor.

With a loud crash, the IV unit attached to me hit the floor. The urine bag I wore split open when I fell, and yellow liquid spread across the tile. Patients screamed and attendants scurried into the room, corralling the hysterical horde out of the way of the mess.

I lay face down on the floor, trapped by the weight of the chair. Othello's voice shouted for help and, moments later, the chair was righted and I was wheeled back down the hallway to my sanctuary in intensive care. I smiled smugly and congratulated myself while Othello, fussing over me like a hen over her chick, washed my hands and face. I had won the first skirmish, I thought, as she pulled my soiled nightgown off of me. I had outwitted Dr. Sandler.

The thrill of victory was short-lived. The remaining battles went to the stubborn doctor. He dismissed my behavior in the day room as childish and unimportant and restated his orders firmly. Ignoring my protests, he sent an attendant with a wheelchair to my room every day for the journey through the corridor to the day room. Cringing, I heard the clack of keys as doors closed behind me, locking me away from my safe cubicle and forcing me out into the unknown. I gripped the handles of my wheelchair and breathed deeply, waiting for panic to make its metamorphosis into anger. My head bowed and my heart pounding with fury, I arrived in the day room where I sat and fumed for the requisite hour.

For days, I endured the hour pouting and indignant, refusing to lift my head, refusing to speak or acknowledge the presence of other patients. After about a week of sulking, I gave in to curiosity and began studying the inhabitants of this purgatory. With ever-worsening eyesight, I peered at the people around me and discovered, not with any surprise, that madness reigned in the day room.

The "germ lady," her nose and mouth concealed by a surgical mask, cowered by herself in a far corner. Fearing the demise of the human species by germ warfare, she refused to take off her mask, lifting it with careful fingers only to spoon in food at mealtimes.

A young man with a flowing mane of hair believed he was Jesus Christ. After speaking with me one day, he became convinced I was Mary Magdalene.

An attractive figure in fashionable clothes captured my attention and made me yearn for an appointment with a hairdresser and a manicurist. When we introduced ourselves, I discovered "she" was a family man in full drag. Believing he was possessed by his wife's spirit, every day he dressed himself in women's clothing and a bouffant, brunette wig. His hand gestures, flashing bright fuchsia polish on long, tapered nails, were the final feminine flourish. We became instant friends, exchanging beauty tips like coeds in a freshman dormitory.

It mattered little to me which sex hid behind the feminine facade of silks and chiffons and bright nail polish. For all of us who inhabited the day room, life was a perilous game of hide and seek, and this place had become our "King's X." Costumed and coiffed, masked and deluded, we all existed in a kind of limbo, not quite captured, not quite free. And each of us covered ourselves with whatever gave us comfort. Who was I to judge the costume of another player in this mad game?

I mingled with all the lost souls of the day room, feeling separate from them, but strangely akin to them. We each faced our own enemies. We each faced our own terrors.

Over the next few weeks in the sanitarium, I regained physical strength slowly, finally ridding myself of the tubes and catheter, but the effect of the many drugs prescribed for me was devastating. I was either ravenously hungry or vomiting from severe nausea caused by double vision and the constant smell of blood. Other drugs caused my body to bloat as though it were about to explode.

My vision, which was becoming more and more cloudy, interfered with my equilibrium and my eye-hand coordination. Once I was strong enough to get out of the wheelchair, I had to learn to walk again. Off-balance and swaggering, I moved through the hallways of the sanitarium like a drunk just in from a long binge. Simple chores like fastening a button defeated me. But every day I awakened with the sure knowledge that my decision to live had been the right one.

Daily therapy sessions gave routine to my life. Every morning I attended a group session with other patients, and listened without speaking as they described their various phobias and traumas. I sat with them, but I remained outside the circle, aloof and distant from them. Later each day, in private sessions with Dr. Sandler, I played a different game. Exuding all the characteristics of the Southern aristocrat, I held him at bay while entertaining him with charming stories of my childhood in the old brick house on Center Street, filling the hour with anecdotes about a genteel Southern family and a lovely, ancestral home named Five Oaks.

Every day Dr. Sandler smoked his pipe and faced me, pencil and pad in hand, and listened to me play the part of the perfect hostess, as though I could ring a bell and order mint juleps for us to sip while we chatted.

"Millicent," he said one day, interrupting me mid-sentence, "no more amusing stories and sweet childhood reminiscences. Look around you! This isn't a tea party. You're in a mental hospital!"

I glared at him.

"The time for cute stories is past. We've got work to do, and it is going to start now. If you want to get out of here, you're going to have to stop playing 'lady of the manor.' You're a patient in a mental ward, Millicent."

I know, I know, I thought, but I can never tell him the things he wants to hear.

I could not betray Mama by discussing private family matters; the Collinsworth pride could not be damaged; nor could I risk disclosing my own very real horrors. And so I gave him only snippets from the fabric of my life, choosing to leave out many parts of the whole, afraid to let him see the entire tapestry for fear he would discard it as hopelessly beyond repair.

Dr. Sandler was not fooled. He knew I wasn't ready to reveal all my ills, so he forged a plan to focus on what he saw as the two major issues at stake in my life: first, the possibility that I was going blind; and second, my all-consuming need for perfection, which he believed had played a major role in my suicide attempt.

"I want to involve your family in your therapy, Millicent," he announced to me one day.

"They won't come," I answered, appalled at the idea of the Collinsworths sitting in an office discussing their separate and collective woes.

"When you leave this hospital, there is a strong possibility that you will be blind," he continued. "You're going to need a strong support structure on the outside if you are going to survive. Your family will be the basis for that support. We must start building on that now, while you're here."

My unspoken fear roared into a shout. My head injury, combined with the subsequent eye infections, had so damaged my eyes that some degree of blindness seemed inevitable. How quickly my blindness would occur, no one knew. But the darkness was traveling quickly and my doctors had no doubt it would overtake the light. I had to begin learning to live in the shadows. And Dr. Sandler believed my family should be nearby to help me make that adjustment.

As expected, Mama refused Dr. Sandler's request to participate in the family counseling sessions. Her disdain for psychiatric medicine was legendary in our household. Laddie, however, agreed to come, and the news both surprised and upset me.

"My brother and I have been estranged for a long time," I told Dr. Sandler. "I don't want him in my therapy sessions."

"That's not your decision," he answered.

I stared at him angrily.

Remembering the scoldings Laddie and I had been giving each other for more than ten years, I could not imagine sitting in the same room with him, listening to him judge me and condemn me. I was certain he had never forgiven me for the destructive and irresponsible behavior that had been a way of life for me since I was eighteen. And I could never forgive him for being upright and noble.

"Laddie wants to come," Dr. Sandler said.

Of course he wants to come, I thought. He's the perfect one, the golden child. He always does what's right, even if it hurts. What must he think of me now? I wondered. He must hate me for what I've done...

What would I say to him? How would I face him? My last contact with Laddie had been that day when he stood at the foot of my bed in the sanitarium. He had railed against me, furious at me for following in our father's footsteps; for dragging our family back into the haunted halls of the mentally ill. Would he pound me with his anger again?

The next day when Laddie entered my room, he greeted me with a terse nod. He sat stiffly in the chair next to mine, and I waited for him to fire his first volley at me.

"I'd like you to tell me why you came here today, Laddie," Dr. Sandler said, his pipe dangling from the side of his mouth.

"I want to help my sister," Laddie answered in a flat voice.

"Why?" Dr. Sandler asked.

"Because I love her and I'd like to see her well."

My eyes burned. I gripped the arms of my chair and rocked gently back and forth, my head angled so that I could look at my brother with my one good eye. His slender body was rigid, his lean face hidden behind a reddish-brown beard. When he turned toward me, his face close to mine, I sensed the silent message emanating from him. My brother had come, not to destroy me, but to try and save me. Wearing the look of a determined soldier, he had entered my room armed and intent upon rescuing me. He was once again cast into the role of my hero, but this time he had left behind the gray uniform of the defeated. A tender place in my heart throbbed, but I was afraid to touch it.

Twice each week, Laddie entered the psychiatric hospital and seated himself next to me and across from Dr. Sandler. After several sessions which had yielded few helpful insights, Laddie, in a matter-of-fact voice, stated, "Dr. Sandler, I think you should know our father suffered from manic-depressive disease with psychosis."

For several long moments, Dr. Sandler said nothing. He just looked at us, from one to the other, and then he shook his head. "How long did you intend to withhold such a vital piece of information from me?" he asked.

With that revelation, Dr. Sandler concluded that I had inherited my father's disease. Convinced and comfortable with a niche into which I could be fitted, he prescribed the appropriate medications for treating manic-depressive illness.

"Our therapy sessions will continue," he assured me. "But we will begin medicating you for a chemical disorder. I want to focus on several emotional issues—we've got a lot of work ahead for us, Millicent, but I believe this is a monumental breakthrough. I think we've just discovered the missing piece."

Per Dr. Sandler's orders, I ingested large quantities of drugs for more than a month, taking lithium, the prescribed wonder drug for many manic-depressive patients. However, the doctor did not see the expected results. Every drug produced a toxic reaction. No medications triggered any kind of positive mental or emotional change; they only further aggravated my already bloated and swollen condition. After six weeks, Dr. Sandler ordered all medications stopped and backpedaled to reassess his diagnosis of manic-depressive disorder.

"I think we have to conclude, Millicent, that you have inherited a tendency toward depression, but you are not suffering from manic-depressive disease," he told me.

I closed my eyes and let his words wash over me like a cleansing stream.

I'm not like my father! I'm not like my father!

"I believe you are suffering a major clinical depression, but unlike your father's illness, it has occurred in response to trauma."

Yes! Yes! It is different!

I remembered the years with Daddy when, without cause, he would suddenly determine that life was not worth living. Hiding away in his basement asylum, he would pass months without venturing up into the light of day. No tragedy triggered his sudden depression. It simply occurred, without cause.

Once Dr. Sandler learned the secret my family had so carefully guarded, he seemed intent upon digging up all the other secrets I had protected for so many years. With every therapy session I found it more and more difficult to keep him at a safe distance. He refused to accept my witty answers, which were not answers at all. Probing for the reasons for my self-destructive behavior and my intense need for perfection, he refused to give up, even when I changed tactics and became sullen and uncooperative. When that didn't deter him, I played the part of Walter Cronkite and recounted childhood incidents with the dispassionate, detached manner of a network anchor.

"You've just said your father never told you he loved you, Millicent," Dr. Sandler said, leaning toward me as I sat in his office one day. "That is an extraordinarily painful admission, and yet you smiled the entire time you said it."

I continued to smile.

"Don't you see how inappropriate this behavior is?"

I shrugged.

When I smiled during the telling of our family's journey to the state mental hospital to have Daddy committed, Dr. Sandler removed his pipe and shook his head.

"You have just recounted what I believe was one of the most devastating events of your life, yet you have shown no emotion," he said, sounding stupefied.

Like a gracious Southern hostess, I inclined my head toward the doctor and smiled. My hands folded and resting in my lap, my legs crossed at the ankle, I waited patiently for Dr. Sandler to dismiss me.

"Millicent, listen to me. You have detached yourself from all feelings because of the pain. In psychiatric terms this is called splintering. Severe trauma or great emotional loss can cause the mind to protect itself by shutting out the feelings associated with the pain."

He wasn't going to dismiss me.

"Sometimes the mind can shut out all memory of the pain. I believe you learned to do this at an early age, and that is the reason you are incapable of responding appropriately."

The doctor's words grated like the scratch of fingernails on a chalkboard. I didn't want to listen to this. I could feel my face stiffening as I pinned my smile in place.

"I want to help you relearn how to summon the appropriate emotions at the appropriate times, Millicent," Dr. Sandler said. "Sadness and tragedy are part of life. Expressing grief and anger is healthy. And," he added, "so is crying."

"I don't like to cry," I said, still smiling.

"Why?"

"It's a sign of weakness."

"What do you feel when you cry?"

"Nothing," I answered. "I feel nothing, because I rarely let it happen. It's a shameful thing to do."

"Why is it shameful?" he asked.

"I don't know... I just know that when I cry I feel weak and full of shame." I remembered the few times when I had allowed myself to weep. "I don't let myself cry very often. I do everything within my power to prevent it."

Dr. Sandler pounced. "Aren't you really saying that you are afraid to cry?"

The smile faded.

"Millicent, isn't that what you're saying?"

Silence hung in the room.

"Millicent, answer me."

My hands shook. My voice trembled as I whispered, "All right... yes... I've always been afraid that if I started to cry over all the hurtful things I would never be able to stop. Do you think it's possible to drown in your own tears?"

Day after day, Dr. Sandler pressed me to talk to him about my life. Cautiously circling the most horrendous of my childhood memories, I allowed myself to speak of my father's illness and the hopelessness of it; I spoke of the sadness I had felt at losing my childhood home; I spoke of my career as a child performer, and of the relationships that I had had, speaking only briefly of Keith, Mitch, and Zach. Finally, one day, I told him about the child I had lost during the fifth month of pregnancy. Dry-eyed and with stoic calmness, I spoke of the baby I had loved even before his birth, but I could not speak of the attack and the rape that preceded his death.

"Were you allowed to grieve over the loss of your baby, Millicent?" he asked.

"No," I answered. "Mitch wouldn't let me talk about it."

"How did that make you feel?"

"I didn't feel anything!" I snapped, suddenly irritated. "Nothing! Mitch acted like it was my fault. He was the angry one!"

"Was it your fault, Millicent?"

This was dangerous territory.

"I don't want to talk about this anymore." I stood up to leave the room.

"What's wrong?" Dr. Sandler asked. "Am I making you feel angry?"

"Civilized people don't get angry," I answered.

"If you're not angry, why are you gripping the back of that chair until your knuckles are white?"

I scowled at him and began pacing the room.

"Why are you frowning at me like that? Admit it, Millicent, you're furious, and you'd like to bite my head off right now."

He was right. But civilized people didn't bite off the heads of yuppie psychiatrists who wore Gucci loafers and smoked pipes.

Every private session with Dr. Sandler was the same. Mercilessly, he battered me with the truth and pulled me toward reality.

"Did you have a name for the baby?" he asked one day.

"Yes," I replied, surprised by the question. "I had named him Tad Kelly."

"Had you started planning a nursery?"

"I had a few things, but Mitch hated everything to do with babies and pregnancy. He didn't want me spending a lot of money on a nursery."

"What happened when you lost the baby?"

My heart felt as if it would explode as I recalled the days after the attack. I had recuperated at Mama's house during the three days when Mitch couldn't be located. Choosing my words carefully, I told about going back to the apartment, finding that all the baby things had been removed, learning Mitch had burned them. All of them. All except one pair of tiny shoes—the pair we had bought together on that rainy afternoon before our marriage. Those I had kept in a secret place in my closet. Those had escaped Mitch's destruction.

"How did you feel when you came home and found it all gone?" Dr. Sandler probed.

Shuddering, I whispered, "Empty. Just empty."

"Would you have made a good mother?" he asked.

I could no longer contain the tears. They spilled down my cheeks and choked my throat.

"I'd have made a wonderful mother," I sobbed.

The hurt of it all tumbled over me, bruising me and pummeling me until I ached all over. My voice broke as the words poured out. "I kept a journal during all the months of my pregnancy. I used to talk to my son and describe the world to him... Those little shoes... I brought them with me to the hospital, Dr. Sandler. I couldn't leave them. They're in my suitcase."

Dr. Sandler was silent for a long time. When he finally spoke, his voice was soft, almost tender.

"Millicent, you will someday be able to grieve, and you'll be able to let the little shoes go." Pausing, he stood and reached across the desk to hand me a tissue. "You're not crazy, or manic-depressive. I think we've established that beyond question. You don't need medication. Your cure lies in communication, in learning to express your grief—feeling it, and then letting it go."

But would the pain ever let go of me?

"You'll be able to move on one day, Millicent."

I didn't think I would ever be able to move away from the sadness that seemed to have overwhelmed me at that moment.

"You're already progressing, Millicent. Can you sense it? You've felt the pain, and it didn't kill you. You're still here, alive. This is the beginning of your healing. Now you have to allow yourself to feel the anger. This is the only way you're going to grow strong."

"I can't ever get angry about the loss of my son," I answered, muffling my words behind trembling hands.

"Why not?"

"Because... " I could feel the pressure building inside me. "Because... " Sobs tore out of my throat.

"Millicent, tell me."

"It was my fault!" I shrieked. "I killed my baby!"

The story of the rape spewed forth, bringing with it all the horror to be relived in the telling.

"I had to fight, Dr. Sandler! I had to protect my baby! I couldn't let that man hurt my baby like I had been hurt... "

"Had you been hurt before, Millicent?"

"Yes!" I screamed. "Yes! I was hurt before!"

Like a volcano that had been storing its lava for centuries, the story of Mr. Simpson erupted. Suddenly the room was filled with the searing tale of a child's molestation and rape, ending with the death of my tiny son, Tad Kelly.

My whole body rocked with the force of the grief that hit me as I told the awful story. Great heaving sobs shook me.

"I shouldn't have fought... if I had just taken it... if I hadn't tried to fight, my baby might not have died. It's my fault... It's my fault my baby died... "

Dr. Sandler's words reached me over the sound of my crying. "Millicent, don't you realize that had you not fought, you would probably be dead now? You did what you had to do. The guilt does not lie with you."

His words did not instantly absolve me. I continued to cry until my chest heaved with dry sobs. Finally, the sobs became soft whimpers, and I knew I had no tears left. Dr. Sandler laid aside his pipe and walked over to stand near my chair. His hand touched my shoulder and he spoke softly, "I'll take the little shoes now, Millicent. Tad Kelly is gone."

My whole body throbbed as I left the doctor's office that day, but I sensed a quietness in my heart. My tears had not drowned me, as I had feared. Mingling with the pain was a kind of serenity that was new to me. I approached the next day's therapy session with less trepidation than before.

"Millicent," Dr. Sandler said, pressing pungent tobacco down into the well of his pipe, "you must accept the fact that you are emotionally locked in time and space. You are thirty-two years old, but your emotional growth stopped at age ten, when you suffered sexual abuse."

With the aroma of smoke circling our heads and the sound of tree branches tapping the window outside his office, Dr. Sandler explained to me that every choice I had made, since the time I was traumatized by sexual abuse, had been affected by that act.

"Many of the decisions you've made have been unwise, especially in regard to men, Millicent. Can you see that?" he asked.

I thought about Keith, and Mitch, and finally Zach.

"The emotional abandonment you felt from your father began to manifest itself in the splintering of your emotional psyche that we talked about in earlier sessions. When you invented the imaginary friend, Bad Girl, at age seven, you were already learning to detach yourself from emotional pain.

"Millicent, you should consider yourself extremely lucky," Dr. Sandler said. "You were strong enough to hang on to your sanity. Most often, when children start splintering at such an early age, they manifest multiple personality disorder. But somehow, in spite of your father's abandonment and Mr. Simpson's assaults, you were able to hang on."

As the sessions with Dr. Sandler continued to probe the abuse by Mr. Simpson, I wondered again and again if the pain was worth it. Did I really believe I would find health on the other side of this agony?

"Let's talk about what it's like to be ten years old, Millicent," Dr. Sandler began one day. "Let's talk about what it's like to be raped by your landlord and to be small and helpless and unable to protect yourself."

Images long ago buried were now putrid with age, but they had not decayed. Rancid, smoldering with filth, they lay exactly as I had left them, and the sight and smell of them made me suddenly ill.

"I can't do this, Dr. Sandler," I pleaded. "Please don't make me do this."

"Tell me how you wore your hair, Millicent."

Confused and momentarily distracted from the picture of horror he was asking me to draw for him, I answered, "I wore long French braids."

"And did you have the patch?" he asked.

"Yes."

"Were you tall and slender or short and chubby?"

"Oh, no, not chubby. I was slender, nearly five feet tall by the time I was ten," I answered. I recalled how Mama had always told me how slender and beautiful I was. "Breeding always tells," she used to say.

"I wore little girl dresses with Peter Pan collars and white socks with Mary Jane shoes," I remembered, and suddenly I choked on the incongruity of the memory.

"And after Mr. Simpson began to abuse you, what was it like?"

My breath froze in my throat. I didn't want to answer. I wanted to flee to my room or to the day room, anywhere!

"Talk to me, Millicent. What was it like?"

Slowly, my voice barely audible, I began to speak, at first, haltingly. And then the words began to tumble out as I answered every question. Seeing every detail of every event, feeling again the hurt and the humiliation and the terror, I described what it was like to be the victim of a cruel, amoral old man who delighted in the desecration of innocence and the destruction of a childhood.

"I didn't want to get up in the morning," I whispered. "I didn't want to go to school."

"Why, Millicent?"

I swallowed. "I couldn't sit down comfortably... The desk seat hurt me... Sometimes it hurt too bad to sit still... "

"And when that happened?"

"My teacher scolded me for fidgeting... She was always angry at me, as though I was deliberately trying to disrupt her class." Mumbling, I went on, "I didn't know what it was then, but now I know. I had a chronic vaginal infection throughout that entire year. Sometimes I saw blood on my panties. It terrified me."

"Didn't your mother ever notice anything?"

"Oh, no!" The terror I had felt as a small child suddenly engulfed me again. I shivered at the thought of Mama discovering the awful secret of Mr. Simpson. "I was afraid she would think it was my fault, that she would be angry with me."

In an uncommon flash of insight, I suddenly saw myself as a frightened little girl in pigtails, innocently dragged into a scene of horror but afraid to ask for help, afraid she might be implicated in the crime. I could almost see the foolishness of it. Almost, but not quite.

"How did you keep your secret from your mother, Millicent?"

"I hid my soiled panties in my school bag and took them to class with me, tucked underneath my books and my pencil box. During class, I asked to be excused, and I took my bag and went into the girl's bathroom and rinsed out my underwear. Then I stuck them back in the bag and took them home and put them in the laundry hamper."

"What else do you remember, Millicent?"

My head bowed, my shoulders sagging, I said, "I remember my jaws always ached."

"Why, Millicent?"

"I can't tell you," I whispered.

"There is nothing you can say that I haven't heard before," Dr. Sandler answered in his mild tone.

My face burning, my whole body trembling, I told him, "He forced his penis into my mouth."

Gagging, sobbing, I buried my face in my hands and wept until I was ill.

Dr. Sandler sat quietly and allowed me to empty myself of all my tears. Finally, I slumped against my chair and heard his voice coming toward me, calmly, quietly, and with conviction.

"Millicent, I want you to listen to me very carefully. What happened to you was not your fault. Do you understand me?"

I could not lift my face and look across the desk at the doctor, so great was my shame.

"The child is not guilty for the adult's crime. And it *is* a crime, Millicent. A crime that is committed against one out of every three girls and one out of every four boys under the age of eighteen. Did you know that, Millicent?"

I didn't know.

"And the most common form of child molestation is oral copulation. Did you know that, Millicent?"

I knew none of the facts, only the horrendous, soul-severing consequences.

"Millicent, no child is ever guilty or responsible for an adult's perversion. You were only a child, a little girl. You were not bad. You should not feel guilt or shame. You should be feeling overwhelming rage."

Rage. I was too empty, too weary to feel such a powerful emotion. Or so I thought. But as Dr. Sandler continued, I began to feel a mild stirring inside me.

"What did you feel when you heard your father's chair creaking down the hall while Mr. Simpson raped you?" he asked.

"I didn't feel anything. Daddy was sick. He couldn't do anything to help."

"That's right, Millicent. He was sick. But how did that make you feel?"

The stirring grew turbulent.

"I said I felt nothing!" I shouted. "Why are you doing this to me?"

"It is not possible for a little girl to feel nothing when she is being raped," Dr. Sandler answered in a mild tone.

"All right! I felt angry! I felt angry! Are you satisfied now?"

"Tell me why you were angry."

My voice was shrill now with fury. "Because I was a child, and my Daddy was supposed to take care of me! But he never took care of me... I always had to take care of him!"

My clothes were wet with perspiration. My hands trembled as I pushed my hair away from my face.

"Did you ever try to tell your mother what was happening?"

I recalled the incident in the car, when Mama had asked me if Mr. Simpson was trying to touch me.

"I didn't know how to make her understand," I said, again depleted after the sudden rush of rage. There had been times when I had tried, but how does a child put such horror into words? And once reduced to words, how does one summon them into the mouth, so great is their poison?

No, Daddy had not heard. And Mama had not understood. And I had remained mute and afraid. For decades I had buried the anger and loneliness I felt, and now, suddenly, in this room, it became a visceral presence. Its weight was more than I could bear.

"Sometimes it was as though she forgot to be a parent. It was as though she was blind and deaf to all the signals I tried to send."

My shoulders sagging, my head aching, I stood up and moved toward the door. Dr. Sandler stopped me.

"Millicent, you must understand that you are not alone."

Not alone.

"Most children who are being sexually abused by a friend of the family are incapable of expressing clearly what is happening to them. Parents misunderstand what the child tries to say, and so the abuse continues. This is not uncommon."

The words "not alone" continued to echo as I stood there at the door of his office, my hand on the doorknob.

Other children had suffered what I had suffered. I felt a strange mixture of relief and horror, as though I had just been informed that I was only one of hell's many inhabitants. I had joined a huge company of tormented children, and I wondered if any of us would ever be able to escape the demons that haunted our present world.

"Millicent, listen to me. You have every right to feel angry at being unprotected," Dr. Sandler said. "Your cries for help went unheard, and you have legitimate cause for anger. But I want you to hear this too: You must also realize that you are no longer ten years old. You are thirty-two. You are an adult, and you are not helpless. By speaking now, by telling what happened to you, you have renounced the wickedness of an old man and given voice to the thousands upon thousands of children who remain silent victims of sexual abuse."

A strange energy overtook me at that moment. I felt as though I had found some new strength, as though the disclosure of my own past horrors had been a sort of war cry uttered for the great army of children who, as adults, were mute with the shame of our shared horrors.

"Molestation victims are not unlike the survivors of the holocaust, Millicent. They must speak of it, because speaking offers a kind of cleansing, a kind of validation."

Listening to Dr. Sandler, I grabbed hold of one word: survivor.

I had survived, yes, but I had become a victim of my own holocaust. I had not turned predator, as do many molestation survivors, wreaking violence on others; but I had turned violent toward myself. In my anger, I had sought to destroy myself.

"Millicent, only forgiveness will heal your rage and release you from the need to harm yourself. Forgive yourself—you are innocent! And when you accept the reality that your mother did the best she was capable of at the time, you will be able to let go of the rage you feel toward her. That is an adult response, Millicent, and you must begin to respond to your life as an adult."

I wanted to. Oh, how badly I wanted to become the assured adult Dr. Sandler wanted me to be—whole, and at peace.

"Your mother's actions were neither malicious nor negligent, Millicent. They were uninformed and perhaps insensitive, but they were typical of the actions of most adults in the fifties. Few parents of that decade had any realm of reference for dealing with such atrocities as child molestation. Our society had no systems in place to help us recognize the evidence of secret crimes carried out against our children. Your mother was not deliberately cruel, Millicent. She was simply ignorant of how to navigate through uncharted social issues."

I wanted to believe him, I wanted to listen. I returned to my chair across from his desk and he continued.

"Millicent, life is a choice. You can choose to spend the rest of your life simmering with rage over the inadequacy of your mother's and father's parenting skills, or we can discuss it rationally," he said. "We'll work together, acknowledging the reality of the situation, and we can try to grasp some measure of understanding."

Sitting there that day, drenched in perspiration, I understood the choice that was being offered me: I could choose to continue in self-hatred; I could choose to remain angry and estranged from healthy relationships; I could allow the actions of Mr. Simpson to rob me of more than my childhood and young adulthood—I could allow him to continue to victimize me and to claim the remainder of my life as his spoils. Or I could become the victor.

The choice was simple. Without trumpet fanfare, I announced the defeat of my enemy. I declared myself a conqueror. And I vowed to do whatever was necessary to establish inner peace and give contentment a chance to reign.

In the sessions that followed, I discovered that I was stronger than I had believed. I wanted to be whole. I wanted to claim the rest of my life for myself. I wanted to recapture hope, and so, with new enthusiasm, I cooperated with Dr. Sandler and listened intently when he approached the subject of eating disorders.

"Your family dynamics were a fertile breeding ground for an eating disorder, Millicent," he said.

"My body shape and size were the subject of family discussions even before I entered puberty," I told him. "For years, Mama, Daddy, and Laddie had praised and admired me if I was thin; if I gained weight, they were critical."

"Well, Millicent, you're the ideal candidate for anorexia or bulimia," he said, reading me a page out of one of his medical books. "Young, white, professional woman from upper-middle class; perfectionist tendencies; insecure." He shut the book and looked at me. "Like most of your fellow patients, you appear on the surface to have total control of your life, but in reality, you have little or no control over *any* aspect of your life."

I could easily see how eating had become a power fest for me.

"Millicent, as a victim of child molestation, you are an even more likely candidate for an eating disorder," Dr. Sandler went on.

My eating disorder had begun the year I turned ten. As happens to nearly all victims of sexual abuse, I was locked into the emotional age at which the assaults began.

"Eating became your obsession," Dr. Sandler explained. "But again, I want you to understand that you're not alone, Millicent. One out of every ten women suffers from an eating disorder; and of that number, eighty percent are the victims of child sexual abuse. All of them, like you, use food as a combat weapon after being sexually molested."

Not alone. Again, I found myself a part of the community of the injured. Again, I felt that mixture of relief and horror. Others shared my ignominy.

Anxious to understand, I listened as Dr. Sandler described the different forms of eating disorders.

"Some young women eat to the point of obesity. They cover themselves with weight in an effort to hide their injured forms behind one more layer of self-loathing. They are hoping to hide any shape that would draw attention to their sexuality.

"Others, those diagnosed with anorexia-nervosa, starve themselves, often to the point that their menstrual cycles cease. They are resisting growing up so they won't have to function as adult women."

I could see the logic behind each behavior, but neither of them described my eating habits. I was neither obese nor starved to the point of emaciation. Dr. Sandler saw my puzzled look.

"You, however, are seldom overweight by more than five or ten pounds, are you?" he asked.

"No, never. My weight seldom fluctuated as much as a dress size," I said.

"Your condition, Millicent, has only recently been named bulimia-nervosa. Bulimia means appetite of an ox."

I shuddered, thinking of the huge portions of food I had consumed. An ox could have made a hearty meal from any of my "snacks."

"Bulimia is the most difficult of the forms of eating disorders to identify because it is not obvious," he went on, tapping his pipe on the edge of his desk. His casual manner gave no hint of the life-and-death issue he was addressing with me. "In most cases, the patient's weight doesn't fluctuate. You never gained or lost large amounts of weight before you came into the hospital, did you?"

I shook my head.

"Most bulimia sufferers maintain what they think is an ideal weight. They look the same most of the time, but what they have to do to themselves in order to maintain that weight while consuming thousands of calories, is the thing that eventually kills them."

I thought of the hundreds of laxatives I had taken in a single day. I recalled how the sound of Carter's Little Liver Pills rattling in the tin could trigger my gag reflex.

Day after day, while Dr. Sandler's pipe smoke circled his head, I listened to him and answered him and, at times, grew impatient with the process that he promised would yield healing. At times furious, I stood and roamed about the room, railing and screaming, talking non-stop and often cursing. Sometimes I sat silently in the rocking chair and listened to his voice assure me that I was moving ever closer to health and strength. Sometimes I simply cried.

It seemed all my problems were intertwined. And often, the therapy sessions revolved around my feelings for my mother. In an unguarded moment, I admitted to treason: to feeling suffocated and controlled by the sheer force of her love. I admitted that all my life she had been an intimidating presence who easily manipulated me, rendering me full of anger and confusion.

"You know how some animals eat their young?" I asked one day as we sat together in his office.

I sensed him smiling.

"I think Mama's love devoured Laddie and me. She ate us, both of us, spiritually and emotionally."

"Go on."

"Well, I think I became my mother's alter ego. I lived out all her goals, but formed none of my own."

"That's possible."

Exploring as I went, I traveled further into this strange territory. Cautious, uncertain, I continued, "From the time I was very young, about the time Daddy was wrenched out of my arms and dragged into the state hospital, I believed I was the only vessel that could carry joy for my mother."

"That's a solemn responsibility for anyone, even an adult. How much more so for a child."

"But can you see how that would happen?" I asked.

"It's a very reasonable conclusion, Millicent, and I think it explains a lot about your need to be perfect, to do the right thing, to succeed and perform."

"Yes," I answered, thinking about all those years I tried to heal my daddy and make Mama proud and happy.

"Do you fear your mother?" Dr. Sandler asked.

Fear her? Yes, I feared her. I feared disappointing her, not pleasing her. I had spent the first portion of my life in terror of committing the one sin that I knew a Collinsworth could never forgive: weakness. And throughout the remaining years, I had punished myself for having committed that very sin. Was not attempted suicide the ultimate manifestation of weakness?

The family therapy sessions, when Laddie was present, followed a less volatile path than did my private sessions with Dr. Sandler. During the biweekly hour with my brother, helping us to build bridges of communication and comfort was the doctor's goal. He pulled us toward each other, leading us to the place of trust we had inhabited as children. One day, at the close of such a session with Laddie present, Dr. Sandler ended the hour by saying, "Laddie, I get the very strong feeling that you would like to hug your sister and tell her that you love her."

I gasped. Laddie and I hadn't touched each other with tenderness in over ten years.

Laddie stood up and faced me. I waited, wondering if his commitment to my healing included this very intimate, unnerving act. When his arms circled me, I stiffened. He pulled back quickly, his arms dropping to his sides. I looked away as he left the room.

Dr. Sandler celebrated a small victory that day. He had brought Laddie and me together. We had reached a new plateau in the climb out of our deep valley. He was pleased with us, with himself.

Outside of the sanitarium, another uphill climb progressed slowly. My friend Marshall played the part of an advocate, working on my behalf to urge the insurance companies and the lawyers to reach a reasonable compromise with the hospital and the doctors so that my surgeries could be scheduled. Finally agreeing to payment on lien, the doctors agreed to operate and the hospital agreed to admit me as a patient.

Every day, more and more light faded from my vision, leaving me in a world of shadows and vague double images. Dr. Sandler's prophecy that I would lose my sight haunted me, but I never stopped hoping that, with surgery, all would be made right.

An ophthalmologist at the Jules Stein Eye Institute at UCLA operated on my eyes, but two days later he informed me that the surgery had been unsuccessful. A third operation yielded the same results. I returned to the sanitarium to convalesce and await news of the next step in my treatment.

"Millicent, there is no next step."

I don't want to hear this...

"You are now legally blind."

The surgeon's words hit me like a physical blow. I stifled a sob and forced myself to listen as he continued his explanations.

"Millicent, your low vision should qualify you for the visually handicapped program at UCLA," the surgeon said, "and we could help retrain you as a legally blind individual."

A blind individual... The words ricocheted off the drab walls of the doctor's small office, traveling a frantic path without order or logic. I couldn't tame them. They were like wild things that defied all the laws of reason and good sense.

"... I say *should* qualify you, but, well, we have a problem... You see, Millicent, in order to admit you to the program for the blind, I have to state an official diagnosis, a reason for your blindness. I have to tell you, I don't honestly know what's wrong with your eyes."

I didn't know if I should feel greater fear at that confession or if I should take comfort from it. If the specialists didn't know what was making me blind, perhaps it was not a permanent or irreversible condition. Perhaps I would regain my sight. Perhaps something could still be done. But while the dark was steadily falling, how was I to cope with life in a world designed for the sighted?

Only two things were clear to me at that time: one, I was blind by all legal standards; and, two, I did not qualify for any programs that would teach me how to live as a blind person because the doctors treating me did not know conclusively what was causing my blindness.

Life became a dark pool swirling with confusion, fear, and frustration. After numerous examinations, one group of doctors reported that my blindness was the result of the multiple childhood surgeries, and the accident with the hammer had only exacerbated the condition of my already traumatized eyes. Others believed that the severe infections after the accident had caused me to lose my sight. On one point, however, they all agreed: my brain should have been capable of shutting out the double image after a certain period of time, but for some unknown reason, was unable to accomplish that task.

Midway through a fourth eye operation, the surgeons concluded that the procedure was too dangerous because of the amount of scar tissue. All hope for a surgical cure to my blindness was finally abandoned.

It was now early summer, 1980. Almost a year had passed since the accident, four months since the break with Zach and my suicide attempt. I had gained some physical and emotional strength and was no longer a danger to myself, but the psyche does not repair itself quickly nor easily. Dr. Sandler was not yet ready to release me from the hospital. During the remainder of my stay, he would spend some time in therapy every day focusing on my impending blindness.

Some of the doctors consulted about my eyes believed it was possible I was suffering from hysterical blindness. If that were true, perhaps therapy could heal me. If it weren't true, then therapy would have to help me adapt to my darkened world. In either case, there was much to be said about my eyesight.

"Millicent," Dr. Sandler told me one day, "it is possible that a life riddled with tragedy, as yours has been, can reach a stage where the psyche unconsciously attempts to shut out the world and all its accompanying pain. We have to acknowledge that you could be shrouding yourself in a cloak of darkness."

Was it possible? Could I be causing myself to lose my sight? Did I subconsciously want to be shut off from the light, to hide away in the darkness?

Foolishness! It had to be! Since childhood I had been terrified of the darkness! Why would I now, consciously or unconsciously, toss myself into it?

I listened to Dr. Sandler, but I rejected his theories.

"Perhaps you are shutting out physical sight in the hope that what you cannot see cannot hurt you... " He spoke without conviction, rambling on in psychobabble.

The ophthalmologists at the Jules Stein Eye Institute continued to study my case, looking for answers to my mysterious blindness. In addition to the loss of my sight, severe nausea assaulted me whenever I took off the eye patch and tried to function using both eyes. I constantly took medication for motion sickness.

No easy answers presented themselves.

After all the hours of therapy with Dr. Sandler, I still withheld one secret from him: the fact that I continued to smell and see blood. Visual and olfactory hallucination, the condition is called. But then I could give it no name, and so I hid it, fearing all the progress we had made in my therapy would be wiped out by my admission of this one obvious symptom of insanity.

During my hours in the day room, I came to understand that the company I kept was indeed distinguished. A subculture of crazies brought their antics to the day room, of course; but also present were a number of doctors, lawyers, high-powered executives, professors, and nurses who shared my guarded world in the private sanitarium. Some had abused alcohol and drugs. Others suffered severe depression. Some had given up on living after the trauma of a divorce or the death of a child. All of us shared a common grief: we mourned the loss of hope. Some of us found comfort in each other.

Dr. Chen became one of my best friends. A small, middle-aged Oriental man, he was a brilliant neurosurgeon who had finally admitted he was an alcoholic. He came to the sanitarium to "dry out." A friendly, compassionate man, I found myself comfortable with him. One day, desperate to tell someone my secret terror, I told him that I smelled and saw blood all the time.

Dr. Chen listened to me describe the accident with the hammer. Then his questions flew at me with the precision of a world-class archer.

"Did the hammer knock you unconscious? How long were you unconscious—minutes, hours, days? Did you feel an increased sense of thirst after the blow? Did your bladder evacuate spontaneously when you were injured?"

Some questions I couldn't answer. I simply couldn't remember all the events surrounding the accident. But even my lack of memory was significant to Dr. Chen.

"I wish I had my bag with me," he said, his voice impatient, frustrated. "I could give you a preliminary examination, even here."

Something is wrong with me, I thought, feeling exhilarated and a little scared at the same time. Something that the other doctors haven't found yet!

Still afraid to say anything to Dr. Sandler, I waited—for what, I'm not sure. But somehow, I would find a way to be examined by a neurosurgeon who would be able to tell me my hallucinations were not a symptom of insanity. A way presented itself the following week.

Alice, a gentle, overworked, scatterbrained nurse who carried all the hospital keys with her, laid her key chain on a counter near the day room and walked away. The boy who believed he was Jesus picked it up and brought it to me.

"I don't believe this!" I gasped. Every key to every medicine cabinet and every examining room dangled from the chain in my hands.

"Dr. Chen," I whispered, "look! Come on, let's find an empty examining room!"

Dr. Chen glanced around the day room.

"Do you see Othello?" I asked him, unable to see much more than dark shapes.

"She's in the nurse's station, chatting with some of the staff," he answered.

"Good, let's go."

Othello was still my private-duty nurse, and she often followed me to the day room, but Dr. Sandler was weaning her away from me a little more every day. I thought Dr. Chen and I could escape for a short while before she noticed I was absent.

Like mischievous children, Dr. Chen and I scurried down the hall and sneaked into an empty room. Dr. Chen helped himself to medical instruments he found in cabinets and drawers. For the next twenty minutes, he examined me, peering into my eyes, asking questions softly, lest anyone hear and discover us.

"You obviously need a more sophisticated and comprehensive exam than I can give you here," Dr. Chen told me as he quietly shut a cabinet door. "But it is my belief that you are not even remotely going crazy, nor is your deteriorating eyesight due to hysteria."

Relief poured into me, bringing with it both excitement and uncertainty.

"You have suffered a severe head injury that, for the most part, has gone untreated. You exhibit the classic symptoms of a person with a brain injury. Your olfactory and visual hallucinations, the double image that manifested itself immediately after the initial blow, your lack of coordination, and your short-term memory loss—these are all highly indicative of a brain injury."

His hand resting on my shoulder, Dr. Chen continued, "You need to be placed in the care of a neuropsychiatrist, not simply a psychiatrist."

I was unfamiliar with the medical title.

"Neuropsychiatry is a new field dealing with the emotional challenges that are presented to an individual with severe brain trauma," he went on. "The brain is like a computer, and certain injuries can make it malfunction. I suspect that your brain can no longer communicate sight to your eyes. It is the brain, Millicent, not the eyes, that makes you see."

For me, Dr. Chen's diagnosis was like a pardon, releasing me from the sentence of insanity. To Dr. Sandler, however, it was an impertinence.

"Dr. Chen is a patient here, Millicent!" he raged upon learning of our clandestine medical appointment. "He is a recovering alcoholic! He is not competent to examine or diagnose your ills!"

"He's in for four weeks, Dr. Sandler," I countered, trying not to scream in frustration. "'Detox' does not mean demented! He's neither crazy nor incompetent."

"In here, he has no credentials!"

"I don't care what you say, the man is a respected, highly regarded neurosurgeon. His skill and knowledge didn't suddenly evaporate simply because he's had a change of address for a month!"

I was furious. Dr. Sandler was offended. And Dr. Chen's professional opinion was dismissed as the raving of an inpatient of a mental hospital. I determined to make an appointment with a neuropsychiatrist as soon as I was out of the hospital. Dr. Chen said he would be glad to recommend one for me when we were both on the "outside."

Dr. Sandler returned to the premise that my problems, both physical and emotional, were rooted in hysteria due to sexual abuse and childhood trauma. When my speech grew thick and sluggish, it was labeled an emotional response. My swaggering, off-balance gait he linked to the trauma factor. I was drenched in perspiration after the struggle to pick up a fork and handle a brush, having to concentrate to the point of exhaustion for every small task with a utensil, but Dr. Sandler insisted this was further evidence of my being severely disturbed.

With every passing day, I seemed to lose more memory. Excruciating headaches and mild seizures, accompanied by what migraine sufferers call an "aura," became commonplace, almost daily, occurrences. Neurological symptoms mounted, but still Dr. Sandler relegated everything to stress and trauma. When I finally disclosed to him that I smelled and saw blood, he again blamed my childhood.

"It is all stress-related," he said. "The blood merely symbolizes the self-hatred you feel."

I saw no point in arguing. Instead, I determined to seek the help of a neuropsychiatrist as soon as I was released from the hospital. And I spent hours each day trying to prepare myself for the day I would go home.

Life outside the hospital would be grueling for me. I was incapable of performing many small tasks associated with the routine of daily living. Buttons, buckles on shoes, hair brushes— every day I faced these items as though they were grizzlies to be wrestled to the death. And every day, I handled the notes and cards of encouragement sent by friends, fingering them and pressing them to my face, hoping to absorb from them courage and strength for fighting each new day's battles.

Some of my friends became my personal cheerleaders. Don, the entertainer who was my dear friend, came to see me nearly every day. Patricia, whom I had known from my job with the city of Torrance, came several times each week to join Don and assist with my physical therapy. I listened to them shout as I staggered down the hallways, "Stand up straight, don't lean! That's it! You're staggering, stand up!"

Patricia's husband, Jack, left his real estate business every day to sit with me during visiting hours as I struggled to color with the large crayons he and the others had brought me. With coloring books stacked beside me, I painstakingly worked my way through the pictures, straining to decipher the lines on the pages and the colors of the crayons, all the while listening to the gentle, childlike instruction, "Color inside the lines, Mitty."

Laddie's visits continued. In addition to the time with Dr. Sandler, he spent hours each week teaching me to handle money and make change with coins. I had once handled million-dollar accounts, but now I couldn't remember that three quarters, two dimes, and a nickel equal one dollar.

My friend Marshall also came to visit me regularly, bringing me stories of his latest screenwriting adventures. He updated me on my insurance and legal matters and reminded me with every visit, "You can do it, Mitty, we all know you can. Don't give up. Just keep on trying."

Every day I heard the words of encouragement. Every day I knew I had to keep trying to reclaim my life, with or without my sight.

Mama still refused to visit me in the hospital. Unable to cross the threshold of the sanitarium, she phoned me and sent me letters and gifts with Laddie.

One morning Dr. Sandler announced, "Today your eye patch is coming off, Millicent."

I trembled and began to protest, knowing that as soon as it

was removed, severe nausea would strike me.

"The world is not built for the blind, Millicent," he interrupted. "If you're ever going to leave the hospital and function like a normal person, you're going to have to start looking like one."

Dr. Sandler placed his waste can next to my chair and spread newspapers around it.

"Take off the patch," he ordered. "If you feel ill, use the waste can on your right."

I paused, and then, with shaking fingers, I removed the patch. As soon as my eyes tried to focus together, I felt ill. Groping for the waste can, I vomited while Dr. Sandler sat quietly puffing on his pipe.

The next day, Dr. Sandler repeated his command. I removed the patch and waited only a minute before the nausea attacked again. The next day, five minutes passed before I grew sick. Day after day, the ritual continued until I could sit for an hour without feeling nauseous. Dr. Sandler and I were both pleased.

During the next phase of my recovery, I left intensive care and moved into a room in the open ward, saying goodbye to Othello. I was now expected to take care of myself.

The chores that had been so difficult for me in earlier weeks were growing a little easier every day. I could now brush my hair and dress myself. I could take off the eye patch for no more than an hour, but I was able to stand up straight when I walked, and even though legally blind, I knew my way through the hallways and could maneuver without help. Soon I would be able to leave the sanitarium. I was growing more and more ready to leave every day.

At the end of the summer of 1980, I packed my suitcase and walked down the hallway of the hospital for the last time. Four eye surgeries had done nothing to correct my vision problems nor to prevent the onslaught of blindness. Three dental surgeries had given me back my beauty-queen smile. Three separate operations had rebuilt my face, making me look almost perfect, but much of my face was numb, and I couldn't draw breath through my nose. Still haunted by short-term memory loss, I had great trouble with cognitive reasoning as well. The excruciating headaches that occurred in bright light continued, forcing me to wear very dark glasses as well as the patch. Doctors could give me no specific time when my eyesight would be completely lost, but they warned me to expect total blindness.

The prospect of life outside the hospital should have terrified me, but as the front doors opened and I stepped into the morning fog of that California summer, I felt only anticipation. I was alive! I had endured the pain and survived, as Dr. Sandler had said I would. My eyesight may have been fading, but I believed I had a fresh view of the world, and from this plateau it was not so daunting as it had been before.

I felt overwhelming gratitude toward Dr. Sandler. He had given me another chance at life. He had introduced me to the truth about myself, about my family, and my relationships. With his help, I had found a new appreciation for this woman named Millicent Collinsworth, and I wanted to give her a chance to experience a life of joy, unfettered by guilt and the exhausting, futile pursuit of perfection.

It would not be easy, I knew, to break free of my old habits and ways of thinking. I could not instantly dismiss myself as Mama's vessel of joy. It would take more than the few short months of therapy with Dr. Sandler to remove all the old ghosts and the memory of their fearful hauntings, but a change had taken place. He had helped me plot a new course for myself. I had made a strong beginning, I thought, and I was no longer on a path leading to self-destruction.

Groping for a handrail as I stumbled on the wide stairs at the hospital's entrance, I thought, How strange! While I have been steadily losing my physical sight, I have been gaining insight.

In the presence of encroaching darkness, I had discovered light.

Chapter 12

The landscape of the world changes abruptly for one whose eyesight is reduced to blurred images and varying shades of gray. Where once sturdy markers had stood, ready indicators of shape and size and distance, now only vague shadows teased and shifted. I stepped into this new world cautiously, uncertain of where to place my foot, uncertain of how to plan my journey.

Inside the sanitarium I had memorized the length of hallways, the sounds of voices, and the distance across each room. I could navigate with some degree of confidence. Outside, however, I had to measure every move. Decisions that had once belonged to me alone suddenly became the property of others as rapidly diminishing eyesight swallowed my independence.

"I don't like this, Mitty," Patricia said as she helped me unpack my suitcase and return my clothes to the closet of my Manhattan Beach apartment. "With René moving back to Colorado, you're going to be alone here. I don't think you're ready for that yet."

She was right, I knew, but what were my options? I could move home with Mama, but I didn't think that was a good idea—not at this time, when I was trying very hard to learn to know myself as a person separate from the powerful woman whose dreams had dominated me for so many years. And I wanted to return to work as soon as possible, so it was important that I stay in the city.

"Why don't you move in with Jack and me?" Patricia suggested.

"You're sweet, Patricia, but I can't crowd you and Jack."

"Nonsense! We want you to live with us!"

Patricia and Jack's two-bedroom cottage on the beach was quaint and charming, but it was very tiny. Between them, they used every square inch of space. I couldn't imagine where they would put me.

"We'll fix up the gardening shed!" Patricia exclaimed. "It's about the size of a small bedroom. We'll finish out the walls, carpet the floor—it's perfect. You can use the kitchen and bathroom inside the cottage. Come on, Mitty, it will be fun. Jack and I want you to come."

Accepting no arguments, Jack and Patricia helped me arrange storage for my furniture and, in a few weeks, I was ensconced in the small room built next to their garage. I had no plumbing or heating and no means of cooking, but I had the privacy I craved after six months in the sanitarium.

Within a short time, Jack and Patricia and I settled into a comfortable routine. Each morning, I waited until they left for work before going inside the cottage to shower and eat breakfast. In the evening, we sometimes shared dinner and visited a little while before I retired to the garden shed alone.

Loneliness assaulted me at night, when cool, damp air penetrated the poorly insulated walls of the tiny shed. While breathing the pungent odor of peat moss mingled with the scent of the ocean, I yearned for my eyesight, to be able to read with ease, to pick up a novel or thumb through a magazine during the long evening hours. Instead, I sat on my bed in the darkness, with my knees tucked under my chin, hugging myself for comfort. Listening to the sounds of field mice scurrying across the floor, I imagined they considered my presence in the garden shed an intrusion and wondered how long it would be before Jack and Patricia felt the same.

"I won't feel sorry for myself," I said many times each day, renewing my vow to learn to take care of myself in spite of my rapidly fading eyesight.

My first day back at work was both exhilarating and terrifying. How glad I was to be back in the office, surrounded by creative people, challenged by projects and plans that needed fresh ideas! But short-term memory loss threw my workday into havoc. The skills I had been so proud of suddenly deserted me.

I could not remember names; I could not see features on faces unless I was nose-to-nose with the person. My vision extended to a distance of about three feet, and everything contained in that space was blurred and shadowy. In order to read or write anything, I had to place my face almost on top of the paper, angling my head so that my one good eye could study it. And of course, the eye patch was always in place. I could take it off for no more than an hour before reeling with nausea.

My work had always required travel, and suddenly I was unable to drive. Public transportation terrified me. How would I know where to catch the bus? Which bus to get on and where to get off?

Working no longer challenged me; it defeated me.

After several frustrating weeks, I wrote a letter of resignation to W.R. Grace and the El Torito Restaurants.

"Don't worry, Mitty," Patricia reassured me. "Something will work out, I know it will."

I wanted to believe her, but I felt so helpless.

I discovered that my greatest enemy, now that I had left the hospital and had gained some degree of emotional healing, was my eating disorder. Within days of leaving the sanitarium, I had returned to my habit of bingeing and purging. I bought laxatives and diuretics and continued the practice that made me feel in control and, at the same time, miserable and ashamed.

When discouragement attacked, my first thought was food. Food comforted me; it covered the humiliation I felt over my inadequacies; it made me feel satisfied, in spite of the other sources of dissatisfaction surrounding me. Some days I felt as though I spent every hour fighting the temptation to binge. Some days I gave up before even beginning to fight. And then, feeling wretched, I purged, as I had done for so many years.

"Bulimia is like alcoholism, Millicent," Dr. Sandler told me when I confided to him that I was again bingeing and purging. "You will never be completely healed. You will be a recovering bulimic all your life. Every day will be a new beginning, just as it is for a recovering alcoholic."

Family sessions with Laddie ended when I left the hospital, but I continued to meet with Dr. Sandler three times each week. Gradually the appointments would taper down to twice, then finally once each week. He listened to me, sometimes shaking his head when I talked about my obsession for food.

"You've substituted one form of abuse for another, Millicent," he told me. "I'm not worried about you slashing your wrists anymore, but I thought you understood this: bulimia is another way you can kill yourself."

Shame, humiliation, embarrassment all poured through me during those sessions. But none of those feelings was stronger than the comfort food provided me.

"All your other battles will pale in comparison to bulimia," Dr. Sandler said. "But let's not lose sight of the gains you *have* made, Millicent."

In spite of the daily combat with bulimia, Dr. Sandler believed I was faring well in the battle to reclaim my life. I depended on the sessions with him and on the constant encouragement of my friends. These were my life-support systems. But sometimes, in spite of the strides I'd made in therapy, and in spite of the kindness of my friends, I grieved for all that I had lost.

One afternoon, while riding up the coast highway toward Santa Barbara with my friend Don, I allowed myself a moment of self-pity.

"I'll never be able to dance again, Don."

"What?" Don exclaimed.

I felt the car swerve suddenly off the road and stop.

"What's happening, Don?"

He turned in the seat and his face was close to mine. "What do you mean, you'll never dance again?" he asked.

"How do you expect a blind woman to dance?"

"Just like this," he answered. With a swift motion, he turned up the radio, grabbed my hands and, pulling me out of the car, led me toward a grassy meadow beside the road.

"Don, what are you doing?"

"Put your hand on my shoulder, Mitty, and stop whining."

With the radio blaring a favorite country song and cars whizzing by on the highway, Don led me in a fancy Texas two-step. His brown hair covered with a cowboy hat and his tall, lean form dressed in crisp jeans, he twirled me around the open field. Our laughter echoed around us as the last notes of the song faded.

It was always that way with Don. The love we shared for one another was like that between a brother and a sister. He was always there for me, and never more so than when I planned my last event for El Torito restaurants before my resignation became effective.

It was to be an extravagant Christmas party for the employees. I selected a waterfront site on a lovely marina and hurled myself into the planning of what would be my career's swan song. Working harder than I'd ever had to work before, I presented my plan for the gala and then nearly fainted when a corporate officer suggested I perform for the event.

My professional performance background was well known in the company, but only a handful of people knew how seriously I had been injured. Even fewer were aware that this was to be my last gala event for the company before I resigned. Before I could squelch the idea, the news spread throughout the company that I would be reprising a nightclub act for the Christmas party.

Panicked, I called Don.

"What am I going to do? I can't perform!" I screamed into the phone. "I can hardly function! You've seen me, Don! I can't remember my own checking account number... Patricia has taken over all my money matters! Sometimes I forget my phone number!"

"Calm down, Mitty." Don's voice tried to soothe me.

"How can I possibly remember dance steps and lyrics? I can't see three feet in front of me, and I can't stand up straight unless I'm wearing the patch. I can't perform, Don, you know I can't. I have to tell them I can't do it anymore."

"We'll do it together, Mitty. It will be like old times. Just you and me. We used to make a great team, remember? I'll lead and you'll follow."

Could we do it? I wondered. Could we really pull it off?

"We'll sing duets, and if you forget the words, I'll cover for you. We can arrange the choreography so that you're never more than an arm's length from me... "

I could hear the confidence in Don's voice. He was sure we could do it. He *wanted* to do it—with me, for me.

We'd had such fun together dancing and singing for other affairs in years past. Was it possible we could really do it again? Don had always been the ultimate partner, the best dancer I'd ever worked with. Remembering those good times and the feel of the music coursing through me when I danced, I began to catch a little of his excitement.

Rehearsals began almost immediately. I memorized the size and shape of the stage and the placement of microphones and trailing wires. Don took charge of the choreography, insisting that we use much of our old material, including numerous difficult steps and lifts.

"It's too dangerous," I argued. "It's hard enough to get the timing right when your partner can see you clearly. I can barely make out your outline, Don, and I can't see your hands. What if I miss? We could both be hurt."

"Just shut up and try it," Don answered. "Come on, Mitty, you used to be able to do this stuff with your eyes closed. Just pretend that's what you're doing now. I've never dropped you before, have I? Now just run toward me and jump. I'll be there."

I measured the distance of the stage in my mind. I listened to his voice and, stepping back a pace, drew a deep breath and ran toward him. As I leapt into the air, I felt Don's hands grip my waist and lift me high above his head. The music surged in a crescendo and my heart pounded with the exhilaration of the dance.

Yes, yes! I wanted to shout.

As my feet returned to the floor, Don grabbed me in a tight hug, swung me around, and shouted, "We did it, Mitty! See there? We did it!"

The night of the celebration I felt like Cinderella at the ball. The clock was ticking on this magical world Don had helped me create; when it was over, I would have to return to the reality of my impending blindness, my memory loss, and the end of my career. But for this one evening, with Don's help, I would be the dancer-entertainer I had once been. I would be beautiful and talented and capable, if only for these few hours.

Dressed in a white silk gown and a white eye patch that sparkled with sequins, I joined Don on the stage and positioned myself behind the microphone. This final performance had to be perfect. When the show was over, I would exit with pride, leaving the audience with the memory of a beautiful, vivacious woman. I would make my final bows as a victor, not as a victim.

Don and I danced and sang with greater energy and excitement than ever before. I threw myself into the air with total trust, never doubting that his arms would be there to catch me. At the close of the show, the audience rewarded us with a standing ovation. Few people present that night knew that they had been watching a blind woman perform.

The magic dissolved after that lovely night on the marina. I awakened the next day, and every day for the next year and a half, with a sense of emptiness and uncertainty. The search for a job I could perform became a demeaning, humiliating experience. Day after day, Patricia drove me to interviews, only to drive me back to the cottage again, where I wrestled with feelings of defeat and rejection.

Dr. Sandler insisted I keep on trying, even though every prospective employer found good reason to tell me I wasn't suited for the job. I didn't have the necessary skills, or I was overqualified, or my memory loss made me a miserable candidate during the interview. On several occasions, the stress of the interview threw my mind into shutdown. I couldn't remember the simplest facts, such as my phone number, my educational background, my work experience. Potential employers accused me of lying or attempting to hide my past.

Hide it? I thought. I can't even remember it!

"It will get better, Mitty," Patricia kept telling me. "Don't worry. You'll find something, something good, I know you will. Don't give up."

Dr. Sandler reminded me, "You were the golden girl once, Millicent. You can be that again, but you'll be different this time. Don't give up."

Don't give up. I had to keep saying those words to myself after every disappointing and humiliating rejection.

Those words were not enough after one especially miserable appointment with a potential employer. Because I was terribly nervous, I became quite confused during the interview, forgetting simple things and feeling very agitated. The woman interviewing me grew impatient and, in a curt voice, asked, "How many months in a year?"

Flustered, I gaped at her in silence.

"You do know how many months there are in a year, don't you?" she repeated.

My mind struggled to find the right answer.

"Miss Collinsworth, I am a busy woman. I can't believe you would waste my time. We are looking for bright young professionals in this company. It is obvious you don't fit that category."

And so I floundered about, trying to find a place for myself in the work force, trying to figure out how I could earn enough money to live on my own again.

I wanted desperately to be able to afford my own apartment, but even more, I wanted to be able to pay for the services of a neuropsychiatrist. The sight and scent of blood still troubled me, but I couldn't afford to consult with a doctor who was not already a part of the team the insurance companies had engaged. Each day, I deliberately ignored both the visual and olfactory hallucinations, trying to pretend I was unaffected by them.

I refused to ask Mama for help. We spoke on the phone often, and I knew she would have welcomed me back into my room at the villa, but I could not put myself under her rule. I was trying hard to establish my own identity, separate from Mama's, and I wasn't ready to risk being swallowed by her. Thanks to Dr. Sandler, I was learning how to set boundaries with Mama and enforce them, even if a battle ensued. But the battles were few. I learned that when Mama relinquished me to the sanitarium to fight for my life, she accepted the reality that if and when I returned to her, I would return a different person. She still struggled to make peace with the changes in me, I knew; but in most situations, she accepted my altered behavior and my new responses to her in typical Collinsworth fashion: with grace and dignity.

Every day I had to summon every shred of that Collinsworth dignity when I lifted the phone to make appointments for job interviews. Every day I disciplined myself to face rejection with grace. And every day, I prayed I would find a job that would enable me to be self-sufficient again.

The medical and legal matters concerning my injury remained in a quagmire. I had filed a personal injury suit, but the case could not be brought to trial until a definitive diagnosis and the extent of my disability was determined. However, since my head injury had occurred during working hours, the corporation's workers' compensation insurance carrier continued to send me to their own doctors who insisted there was nothing wrong with me—that I should be able to return to the workplace immediately.

Both my personal injury and workers' compensation lawyers told me there was little that could be done until my personal doctors released me. Of course, I couldn't be released because my condition continued to deteriorate. No one could say when the dilemma would be resolved. And in the interim, I remained ineligible for financial and medical help from government agencies that existed solely for the purpose of serving the needs of the legally blind individual.

More than a year had passed since the eye surgeon at Jules Stein had told me that my eyesight qualified me for their Visually Handicapped Program, and my vision had deteriorated steadily since then. But still no doors opened to me. I was denied entrance to job retraining programs for the visually impaired. I had no option but to teach myself to function without sight. With or without the help of government programs or insurance settlements, I had to get on with my life.

Friends helped me simplify my hairstyle and organize my wardrobe. I practiced applying make-up and arranged my personal-care items so that I could take care of my grooming needs without mistakes. I readied myself to go out into the world as though I were a sighted individual.

I had pretended and performed, as if the world were a stage, for most of my life. I would do so again. If I couldn't get the equipment and training I needed to function as a blind person, I would just have to function as if I could see. I saw no other options.

Dr. Sandler supported me in this plan.

"It seems a little contradictory," he said, "after you have worked so hard to stop living in a state of denial. But in this instance, if you can't be treated as a blind person and retrained as one, perhaps you will fare better if you act as though you can see."

Act as though you can see.

My first bus ride across the city was both terrifying and exciting. Wearing dark glasses over my patch, I blended in with the other passengers. No one would have suspected that I was blind. Feeling my way down the aisle, I sat down in the first empty seat my hands located. As the sound of the air brakes wheezed, I asked people near me where we had stopped. Gauging the distance between stops, I estimated my location and planned where to get off. For one entire day, I navigated the city, returning home hours later, exhausted but feeling triumphant. After several excursions alone, I told Patricia I was ready to go to job interviews alone.

I became a sort of "sensory detective." By walking close to the walls of buildings, I could keep a tactile record of where I was and how far I had to go. I learned to identify my location by sounds and smells. The faint scent of salsa with peppers and cilantro told me I was on the corner near a popular Mexican restaurant. Across the street was a real estate office. Two doors down I could hear the sounds of a print shop. And back across the street the bus wheezed to a stop in front of a law office.

Armed with a new awareness of my surroundings and a determination to survive, I continued to search for employment. Patricia and Jack continued to help me, letting me live rent-free, encouraging me, and refusing to let me give up hope that I would once again find a satisfying, fulfilling career.

Finally, in 1982, my workers' compensation attorney negotiated a retraining program for me as part of my eventual settlement.

"It's a godsend!" I told Patricia. "Finally! You and Jack may get rid of me yet!"

"Mitty, you know you can stay with us as long as it takes," she answered.

I knew that was true, but how desperately I wanted to get on with my life, to regain my independence, have an apartment again, to contribute something to the world besides frustrated, embarrassing interviews.

I met with the counselors at the retraining center.

"Frankly, Miss Collinsworth," they told me, "we don't quite

know what to do with you. You see, we've never had to retrain an executive before. We're not sure exactly what we can do."

I sat in shocked silence.

"Most of our caseload is made up of factory workers, people injured on the job. Most often, these are people who have lost a limb. These we can retrain for another factory job. Occasionally, we have retrained office personnel, but we've never tried to retrain someone on the executive level. And we've never retrained someone who is visually handicapped."

I left the office with weak promises ringing in my ears.

Soon after that disappointment, I learned about an opportunity with a personal management agency in Beverly Hills. The owner was looking for someone who could develop public relations campaigns for his celebrity client list.

The idea of working on the other side of the entertainment industry intrigued me. I believed I could do the job, if I didn't have to work under great stress. I had enjoyed a successful run as a public relations executive. Perhaps I could do it again. I wanted a chance to try.

"Karl Hoffman," the owner of the agency, scanned my portfolio and my resume before firing questions at me.

"Have you ever worked on this side of the music industry?" he asked.

"No," I answered.

"Have you ever dealt with the temperamental egos of superstars?"

"No, sir."

"Have you ever dealt with record companies, disc jockeys, radio stations?"

Again, I answered no.

"Do you have any idea how to chart a hit?"

My heart was sinking fast. My every answer revealed to this man that I knew nothing about his business or the job for which I was interviewing. With my last "no," Karl said, "Well, don't worry. Not many people have any experience in this field." I could hear a smile in his voice. "I like you, Miss Collinsworth. I'm impressed with your portfolio, and I think you'll learn fast. And by the way, I like your patch. It looks sexy."

I reached up to finger the black patch over my eye. In other interviews, I had sensed that my pirate's patch was an offense, perhaps a reason to reject me. This man, however, was not offended. He offered me the job.

I called the counselors who were still trying to find a position for me. Surprised and relieved that I had found an executive position, they contacted the workers' compensation board and arranged a meeting with Karl to outline my benefits and the details of my retraining.

The workers' compensation board would pay Karl's agency a monthly allotment for one year to retrain me. They would also pay for any costs incurred in relocating me to an apartment near my new job. In addition, they would pay all my living expenses for the next year. At the end of the year, it was expected that I would be offered a salaried position within the agency.

Karl agreed to train me as a publicist for the entertainment industry under the supervision of the workers' compensation board. A few days later, I left the gardening shed, with its scent of peat moss and its tiny night visitors, and moved into an apartment on Spaulding Drive in Beverly Hills.

The first night in my own home was perfect bliss. My apartment, part of an old, renovated Spanish hacienda, enfolded me. I whirled about the living room, savoring the freedom that, at times, had seemed like an impossible dream. I touched each piece of furniture, resisting the urge to hug the lovely old antiques that had been locked away for more than a year. Good feelings warmed me, convincing me that, with or without my eyesight, life could be good again. I was sure of it.

For the next twelve months, I learned all I could about the entertainment business, in spite of Karl. A cocky, temperamental man, he was a caricature of the typical high-powered personal manager to the stars. Wearing gaudy gold jewelry and flashing large amounts of money, he welcomed sports legends, recording stars, actors, and other celebrities into his office. His quintessential claim to fame was that he had been a personal friend of Elvis Presley. Cocaine would be his ultimate undoing.

Karl made no effort to teach me anything about his business, but I learned how to serve his clients by listening to them, taking note of their interests and their needs. I learned to give each of them the special attention they required. In a short time, I established a strong rapport with many of his clients and accepted invitations to accompany them on personal appearances and concert tours.

Once again, I entered the world of the beautiful people, traveling in chauffeur-driven limousines, attending black-tie affairs, and standing backstage at the Hollywood Bowl and the Greek Theater during concerts. Traveling to Hawaii, New York, and Nashville on behalf of Karl's clients, I learned the inside secrets of the entertainment business.

Most of the people I spent time with had no idea that I was legally blind. My patch alluded to my eye problems, but only one or two knew that I was blind. Those who did know helped me maintain the illusion that I was sighted. If a meeting or a party was scheduled at a concert hall, sound stage, or recording studio at eight, my friends drove me there at six and took me through the facility, pointing out the stairs, the doorways, the restrooms. Sometimes we made our scouting expeditions on the day before an event. I memorized every inch of space and, when clients and guests arrived, I mingled among them with ease.

If I had to attend an out-of-town affair, I stayed close to friends who gave me constant clues throughout each event, sometimes gripping my elbow to lead me toward people I couldn't see across the room. Without standing out as a person with a handicap, I worked and traveled and enjoyed a social life much like that I had enjoyed before the accident.

I also continued to struggle with bulimia.

When stressed or tired or frustrated with Karl's mercurial temperament, I assuaged my pain with food. And then, because I didn't dare gain too much weight, I purged immediately. While I was consuming thousands upon thousands of calories, my weight fluctuated very little, staying near the 125-pound mark that looked good on my five-foot-eight-inch frame. But other indications of my eating disorder began to be visible. My face was often puffy from ingesting the large amounts of laxatives and other purgatives; deep, dark circles lay beneath my eyes; and the whites of my eyes were red-lined because of blood vessels that had burst from the repeated purgings and forced vomiting. My gums were tender and often bled, and my neck grew thick from swollen, enlarged glands.

My sessions with Dr. Sandler, now only once a week, were devoted almost entirely to my compulsive eating habits.

"Millicent, do you know what you're doing to yourself? This can kill you, you know that. We've established that you don't have any reason to harm yourself. Why do you feel the need to continue with this?"

All the ready answers I'd spouted a year ago in the hospital deserted me. I only knew that food was my obsession, and the cycle of bingeing and purging was now threatening to tear apart the fragile cloak of self-esteem that I had only recently begun to weave about myself.

As my year with Karl Hoffman neared an end, I worried about my future with his agency. I had watched him grow irrational and paranoid over the last few months. He had fired or driven away most of his employees. His finances had dwindled and many of his clients had deserted him. What would become of me when my tenure was over?

One of Karl's friends, a beautiful woman named Felicia, answered that question for me in the final weeks before my training period was due to expire.

"You'll come to work with me," Felicia stated. "I'm developing a company that will design promotional campaigns for corporations. I plan to produce business videos and executive seminars. With your background and experience, you'd be the perfect partner."

"Felicia, that sounds wonderful!" I said.

"It *will* be wonderful. With your creative ideas and my contacts, we're practically guaranteed success."

Felicia's contacts were legendary. When she was younger, she had been a top model with the Eileen Ford Agency in New York, and her face had graced the cover of every major fashion magazine. She had married into an "old money" family in Florida's Palm Beach, only to find that her blue-collar background didn't fit in with the Palm Beach society register. When she divorced her first husband, she migrated to California and remarried. Husband number two didn't mind that she kept her first husband's surname—to her, it was a symbol of prestige and wealth, a moniker recognized and revered by the financial community worldwide. It was a daily reminder that she had been able to flee the ordinary life of the middle class and establish herself among the truly rich and refined. And it often served as a natural entree into social events that might have been closed to her otherwise.

In spite of her somewhat snobbish manner, I liked Felicia from the first moment Karl introduced us. She responded to me with an almost conspiratorial manner, aligning herself with me in my frustration when Karl's behavior grew especially nasty. After only a few conversations, I knew that Felicia and I understood each other. I sensed in her the same powerful need for dignity that pulsed in me. We both valued pride and a good name. As we grew better acquainted, we discovered we shared similar passions: we both loved music and dance; we adored the symphony. We spoke the language of the arts.

It was an exhilarating friendship. I could think of no one I would rather work with. And the idea of being partners—I could hardly believe my good fortune! To be working at all was a miracle, but to be able to have a company of my own, with someone like Felicia—would that not be the final proof that I had been able to reclaim my life?

"We will be great together, Felicia," I said.

"Then you'll do it?" she asked, gripping my hands and laughing.

"Of course I'll do it. I can hardly wait for my year here to end so that we can get started," I said, laughing with her.

"You'll be behind the scenes, of course, since you're not exactly 'front-of-the-house' material," she said, and then added quickly, "you don't mind, do you, Millicent?"

I touched the black pirate's patch and smiled at her. Coming from anyone else, those words would have stung, but from Felicia, I could forgive them.

"No, I don't mind," I answered. "I just wish we could start today."

"I know," she said, cooing, "but I'll be putting things together while you finish with Karl. We'll have our own company soon. Oh, Millicent, I'm so happy!"

I worked with new energy during my remaining weeks with Karl. I ignored his petulance and his free-flowing criticism. His erratic, sometimes abusive behavior was due to his cocaine habit, I knew, and I felt relief every day when I thought about the opportunity that awaited me when I could finally leave his agency. I had a place to go. I had a future to anticipate. How could life be so good?

A few days later, on February 19, 1983, I learned how much better life could be.

I was peering at contracts on my desk, my face nearly touching the papers, when the phone rang. Mama's voice was urgent with the news that Laddie's wife, Jean, who was expecting their first child, had gone into labor.

"Laddie took her to the hospital a little while ago, Mitty," she said.

"Today? Oh, Mama! Is everything all right?"

"Everything's fine, but if you're going to be here for the birth, you'd better hurry!"

My hands shook as I stuffed papers into a file cabinet and locked my desk.

"I'm leaving, Karl!" I shouted as I ran out the door.

"Where are you going?" he bellowed.

"I'm going to become an aunt!"

The bus ride to Covina was interminable. I felt restless, impatient, and more than a little concerned. I thought about my family—my brother—and I wondered what kind of a father he would be. I remembered him as the little boy he'd once been, so gallant and chivalrous, the beloved playmate of my childhood. How the years had changed him—first, into a silent, tortured youth, then into an angry, intense man of volatile temper. How much of Daddy's abuse had marked him? Did he know anything at all about being a father?

Laddie's wife, Jean, had come into our family the year after Daddy's death. A quiet, refined woman of British descent, her beauty and sweetness had gentled Laddie. A brilliant woman, she shared Laddie's passion for literature and learning. She epitomized good breeding, and for that Mama had immediately accepted her. In a short time, she had learned to love her for other qualities, as I had. But could Jean, with her noble heritage and her innate kindness, make up for whatever damage Daddy's illness had wrought in Laddie? Had her upbringing better equipped her to parent a child than Laddie's?

The decision to have a child had not been made lightly. Now that the moment was imminent, I wondered how Laddie would respond to this new life. I wondered if the sins of the father would be visited upon the child, and the grandchild. Would this baby suffer at the hands of a father who had known so little of his own father's love? Would Laddie know how to be tender and gentle? And Mama? Could she love this child without consuming it? And what of myself? Would our injured family be able to nurture this child as it deserved to be nurtured?

A few hours later, we welcomed Bryan Bayne Collinsworth into our family. I put my face down close to his and, with my nose nearly touching his, I studied his tiny features. My fingers measured the length of his toes and the size of his hands. His sweet baby scent filled my breath and I forgot that the universe contained anything but beauty and bliss.

This is joy, I thought. Pure, uncomplicated joy.

With Bryan's birth, it was as though the Collinsworths were being offered a second chance at happiness. With our shared love for Bryan, we came together, learning again what it meant to be a family. Mama revived the old ritual of twilight time as each evening Jean and Laddie bathed Bryan and drove the short distance from their home to the old manor house. Seated in a wicker swing on the wide veranda, Mama rocked her grandchild and told him fairy tales and poems and the stories of past generations of Collinsworths. Before he fell asleep, Bryan cuddled in his daddy's arms and together they sat on the steps of the old villa and searched the sky for the first evening star.

I traveled to Covina nearly every weekend to share in this revival of family traditions. Laddie and Jean made room for me at their house, and I slept on a cot in Bryan's room. Each night I fell asleep listening to his soft breathing. In the early evenings, I rode with them to the villa and joined Mama on the porch swing. Listening to her voice recite the stories and songs that I had loved as a child, I felt myself transported back in time to the gentle days at the old brick house on Center Street. I heard Laddie's voice, low and melodic, as he taught Bryan the poem we used to say together at twilight time:

I see the moon,
The moon sees me.
God bless the moon,
God bless me.

Every trip to visit Bryan was like a dose of healing tonic. The arrival of this small child seemed to have sparked sweet memories into life. Memories of good times and the strength of family. I thought about the drive to Five Oaks, Laddie and I in the back seat, peering out the car window, anxious for the first glimpse of the white house with its green shutters and the sight of our grandmother on the front porch, waiting for us.

I remembered my father's admonition to honor the past in order to pursue the future.

I wish you could see us now, Daddy, I thought many times as I placed my cheek against Bryan's and traced his sweet features with my fingers. With the birth of this baby, it seemed our family's pain had begun to subside. We had each laid aside our singular hurts and together we had bonded in the celebration of a new life, a new generation. By silent assent, we had agreed to honor the past in order to provide a future for this child, and in that very act, we would secure a future for ourselves as well.

Chapter 13

In the winter of 1984, I ended my year in the entertainment management business, just as Karl's agency folded. As I had expected, he had driven away nearly every client with his irrational, erratic behavior, and he had sniffed away his profits, corroding his nasal passages with hundreds of thousands of dollars worth of cocaine. I walked out of his office and directly into Felicia's waiting fold.

"We'll be great together, Millicent," she said, squeezing my hands. Pressing her face close to mine, but without quite touching, she kissed the air near my cheek.

"Here's the way I see our partnership working: You've got the knowledge and the education, and I've got the contacts. And, of course, don't forget the 'look,'" Felicia said, laughing and leaning back against plump sofa cushions in the living room of her lovely Brentwood home. "I've definitely got the 'look.'"

Felicia did indeed have the "look." Now over forty, she had not lost her cover girl glamour. A small woman, only five-feet-four-inches tall, she had eventually yielded the fashion runway to the Ford Agency's super models, but her beauty had not diminished. Luxurious black hair framed her oval face and dark, almond-shaped eyes. Her Chinese-Portuguese-Irish ancestry gave her beauty an exotic, alluring quality. Her career, as well as her short time among Palm Beach's elite, had taught her impeccable style and good taste. I had no doubt she could move among the most celebrated citizens of the country, making deals and proposing the campaigns I would create. I had no doubt she could use her assets to push open doors that would make our company successful.

Felicia possessed every prop needed to present herself to the corporate community as a public relations magnate. Wearing only haute couture fashions and expensive, understated jewelry, she drove a Jaguar and lived in a luxury neighborhood. She exuded poise, opulence, and what Mama would have described as "presence." But hiding behind Felicia's glittering facade lurked a shrinking bank account.

In the years since Felicia's divorce from her wealthy first husband, her lifestyle had outdistanced her income. No longer able to earn obscene amounts of money as a model, she had moved from one moneymaking scheme to another, always hoping to hit the jackpot, trying to stay ahead of creditors. She discovered me at Karl's agency just before bankruptcy would have been her next viable option. She believed that my skills would be the key to her financial comeback.

"We're partners," she said, gripping my hand and giving it a firm shake. I grinned, feeling almost giddy with excitement. "We'll build the best promotions and public relations company in the country. We'll have the most impressive clientele ever assembled."

I thought of the scores of successful public relations projects I had created during my years with W.R. Grace & Company. I knew I could do it again, with or without my eyesight. The brain devises ideas and concepts, I reminded myself. I would be the brain, Felicia would be my eyes. Together we would build a powerful business.

"In the beginning, of course, neither one of us will take a salary—at least, not until we establish a substantial client list," Felicia said. "But that won't be long, I'm sure."

No salary? My savings account had dwindled to nearly nothing over the last four and a half years since my accident. Only the income from my job and the help from the retraining program had kept me from becoming penniless. How would I survive without a salary?

"As soon as the money starts coming in the front door, we'll split everything fifty-fifty," Felicia added, sensing my unease.

"Don't you think we should have something in writing?" I asked.

Leaning close to me and flashing a huge smile, Felicia said, "I don't believe in written contracts, Millicent. I believe in friendship, don't you?"

Before I could answer, she rushed on, "Now, I'll be the up-front person who delivers the ideas to the clients. You'll be behind the scenes, developing the promotions and the public relations campaigns. Only my name will appear on the company letterhead, but we both know that we are partners. Agreed?"

Drawing a deep breath, I smiled and answered, "Agreed."

We can make this work, I thought, reassuring myself. We will be drawing an income in no time, I'm sure.

I shoved aside niggling doubts. I was confident of my abilities; I was certain we could build a strong, successful company. The question was: How soon? How soon would the profits begin rolling in?

Perhaps I would have been less accepting of Felicia's terms if I had believed I had other options, but I'd already learned how few opportunities exist for the blind executive. I was willing to take a chance; I was willing to sacrifice for a while, just until the business got going. In the end, when Felicia and I were the owners of a successful public relations company, the sacrifices would seem small, and the lean days would be quickly forgotten. Or so I believed.

Every day I rode a bus across town and met Felicia at her home in Brentwood. There, with her watching my every move, I studied and designed promotional ideas for potential clients and tutored Felicia in marketing and the presentation of corporate promotions. Like a sponge, she soaked up every word and every concept. When she rushed out the door, portfolio in hand, to make the presentations I had designed, I forced myself not to be jealous.

She's right, I thought. I don't look like a creative, successful person anymore.

My months with Karl had allowed me to spend time with many celebrities who had appreciated my work. And for a while, basking in their acceptance, I had felt some of my old confidence return. But standing next to Felicia, with her alluring, flawless style and her dainty size, I was painfully aware of my fallen status.

My patch was a constant reminder of lost beauty. I could see only blurred and shadowy images. I had few clothes suitable for wearing into an executive boardroom, and I had no money for buying a new wardrobe. I was draining my already nearly empty savings account to pay rent and utilities and buy food and bus fare. I was grateful that the clothes I did have were of good fabric and classic styles. But they had had to last longer than I had expected and were beginning to look worn. I felt like "Poor Old Jonathan Bing" who had sent his regrets to the king because he had no suitable clothes to wear to tea.

Week after week, Felicia flung herself out the door of her house and into the corporate community, taking with her the promotional ideas I had created, assuring me that, in time, the business would show a profit, promising me that a salary would be coming soon. And week after week, I continued to work harder than I'd ever worked to come up with the ideas and campaigns that would finally establish our company and produce a generous profit. And I continued to believe.

I believed in my abilities to create winning ideas. I believed in the need for our company. And I believed in Felicia.

Always effervescent, vibrant, and beautiful, Felicia oozed success and accomplishment. I wanted so badly for us to make it, that for months I made myself accept the other, less appealing aspects of her glittering personality.

I didn't need to be a Rhodes scholar to figure out that Felicia was using me and claiming all my ideas as her own brainchildren. When she took the business plans and the promotional ideas to clients, she never mentioned the partner she had at home, stashed away behind closed doors.

I suspected that Felicia was leaving me out of the presentations shortly after we began our partnership, but in the beginning I was willing to forgive her anything. She had noticed me at Karl's agency; she had invited me into her glittering, glamorous world. She had recognized my skills and, as only Felicia could, she had wooed me into friendship. She had given me a chance to make a comeback. For that, I was willing to overlook her sins. At first, I felt proud that I could offer an in-depth education to this already accomplished, cultured woman. She wanted to know everything, and she praised me constantly. And I accepted it shamelessly.

"I can't believe you know so much, Millicent," she would say, gushing over an idea I showed her. "This is brilliant! The client is going to love it!"

Then she would rush out of the house, shouting over her shoulder, "Today I'm going to bring home a huge check!"

She would return and find me with my face buried in data and art designs. She'd pull me away from the drudgery and pour us tea from a delicate Limoges tea set. She'd tell me about the people she had seen and the way she had handled the presentation, and she'd praise my work, ask me how I had gotten so smart, and promise to pay us both soon and generously.

Sometimes we talked about our families. I told her about the old brick house on Center Street; I shared anecdotes about the Collinsworths of Five Oaks; I talked about the family dignity and pride that had been a staple of the Collinsworths for generations. Felicia disclosed the pain she had felt when her first husband's family had rejected her. They had dubbed her "Willi's shopgirl" because she worked for a living and came from a blue-collar family. She confided how their barbs had hurt, how they had celebrated when she finally left the family. But hers was the final revenge, she declared, for she had taken their old and revered name with her when she left Florida and planted it among California's *nouveau riche* and famous.

Together we had exchanged stories and giggled like schoolgirls, and I had come to rely on her companionship because I had begun to isolate myself from all other associations, including the friends who had been so important to me after my accident. This isolation was imperative. Bulimia nervosa is a disease that forces isolation.

I binged almost daily, and so I had to purge daily. I spent each evening trying to rid myself of the many thousands of calories I had consumed. I turned down evening invitations from Don and Patricia and Jack because, after swallowing more than a hundred laxatives, I had to stay home and wait for the medications to begin their awful chore. Only on weekends, when I traveled to the villa to visit Mama and my new nephew did I leave my medications at home, but even there, my body was so accustomed to purging that simply leaning over a toilet bowl caused me to gag.

I was once more out of control. The financial uncertainty of my situation was making me a nervous wreck. I was budgeting the final dollars of my bank account, trying to figure out how much longer I could survive without a paycheck, and in my misery, I turned more and more to the comfort of food. I feared every meal would be my last.

Dr. Sandler could see the evidences of my constant bingeing and purging: dark circles under bloodshot eyes, the puffy face and swollen neck. All these were telltale signs of classic bulimia nervosa.

"Millicent, if you don't get control of this, I'm going to have to hospitalize you again," he said during one session. "You and I both know your insurance coverage for a private hospital has run out. That means you'll have to go into the county hospital. That's your only option. You can stop this if you want to. It's your choice."

I sat in the chair in Dr. Sandler's office and felt terror grab hold of me. My hands trembled and my head ached from the lights in the room. I reached into my purse for my dark glasses.

"Dr. Sandler," I said, "I can't. I just can't... "

"Yes, you can," he said sternly. "Look, just try to stop purging.

If you binge, well, don't worry about it. It's okay. But don't allow yourself to purge. That's all I'm asking from you right now. All right? Will you try?"

"I'll try," I whispered.

"Millicent, this will kill you. Do you understand?"

I nodded, mute and miserable.

"If I put you in the hospital it is only to prevent your death."

I coughed from the smoke of Dr. Sandler's pipe and stood up to leave.

"You won't have to put me in the hospital, Dr. Sandler."

Returning to my apartment, I made up my mind about two things: one, I would stop purging, at least as much as I could; and two, I would do whatever I could to hang on a little longer and give our company a chance to produce an income.

I remember standing in my apartment that evening, surrounded by the exquisite antiques I had collected during my affluent years with W.R. Grace & Company, and realizing what I had to do. Picking up the phone, I called an antique dealer and arranged to sell some of my most expensive pieces.

One by one, I emptied my apartment of furniture and used the money to pay rent and utilities and to buy food. I sold paintings, pieces of jewelry, even clothing, in order to hang on until my work with Felicia could pay me. After all my valuable, one-of-a-kind pieces were gone, I sold my refrigerator and bought a small ice chest. I sold my bed and slept on the floor on a comforter. And finally, I sold my car, letting go of the last reminder of the days before I lost my sight.

Rattling around in my empty apartment, it occurred to me that I was the only partner in this company who was making drastic sacrifices to stay afloat. Felicia, for all her complaints about the proximity of her creditors, continued to drive her Jaguar and wear her beautiful clothes. Her furnishings continued to stand in their usual places, and her hands continued to glitter with expensive jewels. I, however, had begun to resemble a rather chubby Cinderella *sans* fairy godmother.

I was true to my word to Dr. Sandler. I quit purging, but I couldn't quit bingeing. I gorged myself, using every coin that could be spared from my meager budget to buy food. My weight ballooned to over 170 pounds, and my wardrobe, which had been sparse to begin with, became a pathetic collection of clothes from resale shops and discount stores as I outgrew the more expensive, if somewhat worn, classic styles of a much smaller size. Felicia's disgust for me became apparent.

"I'd take you with me on this call, Millicent," she said one day as I handed her a proposal for a client, "but look at yourself! I can't take you anywhere looking like that."

Standing next to Felicia's petite and exquisitely clad figure, I felt like a shabby amazon. I skulked back to my desk and buried myself in the next project, relieved to hear the door slam behind Felicia.

"You're eating because you're angry, Millicent," Dr. Sandler said during a session one day. My weight gain had become a much discussed subject each week. "In the same way you stuff your feelings, you're stuffing yourself with food."

"I'm not angry," I answered.

"Then you should be. Felicia is using you. Are you telling me you don't resent that?"

"Of course not. We're partners."

"Millicent, what are you getting out of this partnership?"

It was a fair question and one I had asked myself many times. I always answered it with one word: friendship. But the friendship did seem to be growing more and more one-sided. I was giving (and giving up) everything I had, and I was gaining nothing in return.

"Felicia gives me money when there is money to be given," I said, smiling at Dr. Sandler, as if all was well in the world.

"It is not money given, Millicent. It is money earned," he answered. "And it is not nearly enough for the work you have done. You deserve much more. And you may not be angry about the inequity of this relationship, but I certainly am. Instead of stuffing food, why don't you just let yourself get good and angry?"

Again, Dr. Sandler was suggesting that I was unable to express healthy and appropriate emotional responses. Week after week, he pushed me, baiting me until I could finally say the words: "All right! I'm angry at Felicia! But what can I do?" I asked, pacing the floor of the doctor's office, almost overcome with the intensity of my rage. "I've invested all these months with her! The client list has grown... I know there is money in the company. If I leave now, I'll lose even more... "

"Why don't you just tell Felicia that you are angry? Tell her you want to be paid. Don't let her dole out little bits of money to you. Demand your due."

He was right. It was time for me to stand up to Felicia.

The next day I asked to be paid for my work.

"Soon, Millicent, soon," Felicia promised. "I can give you two hundred dollars for now, but with the phone bills and our overhead—paying the printers and the artists—it all adds up so fast. Millicent, there just isn't any money left over."

I swallowed down the anger that was rising inside me and returned to my desk. Later that night I went home and devoured everything edible in my apartment.

I thought often about Mama during those months of extreme poverty. Once again our lives had taken parallel paths. I remembered the lovely antique pieces disappearing from the old brick house on Center Street when Mama was trying to pay the costs of Daddy's care in the private sanitariums. I remembered when ten cents for the city plunge might as well have been ten thousand dollars, so scarce were our funds. I remembered Mama wearing old, out-of-style dresses because she could no longer afford to buy new ones; and I remembered the hand-me-downs, the too-large shoes, and the empty pantry. And I wondered what events would intervene before I would be hungry and homeless.

I approached Felicia the next day, telling her I couldn't continue to work without a salary.

"It won't be much longer, darling," she answered. "You know, Millicent, I admire you so much. You are doing a wonderful job, and you know so much about everything."

Felicia was gushing again. I shook my head. Walking across deep, plush carpet, I returned to my desk in her den. She followed me.

"Millicent, you really are the brains of this company. I love the things you say. Sometimes, when I'm at a party, I use your lines and pretend they're mine. You don't mind, do you, darling?"

"Of course not," I murmured, while anger simmered at a low temperature inside me.

She walked out and I heard her pick up the phone in the next room. I couldn't help listening to her conversation. It was like listening to myself! She was using my expressions, my phrases! I heard my tone of voice and my unique speech patterns used as she spoke with a client, presenting some ideas I had offered for his campaign, and then she told him how lovingly and how hard she had worked to create the campaign she would be showing him next week.

It wasn't long after that first eavesdropping incident that I heard Felicia recounting a funny story I had told her about my family. Felicia adapted the story as if it were her own, and I listened to her insert her name where mine had been in the original version. Appalled, I wondered what I should do. Should I confront her? Should I keep silent and wait?

A decision had to be made. Should I continue to endure this poverty? Or should I exit now? If I left, where would I go and what would I do?

The Collinsworths were not strangers to difficult choices. I thought often of my mother and the hard decisions life had forced her to make. Visiting her at the villa on weekends, enjoying the company of my family, I realized, perhaps for the first time in my life, how her strength had shaped me.

Mama talked easily when her grandson Bryan was in her presence. She relaxed and reminisced, laughing with a gaiety that I hadn't heard since we left the old brick house on Center Street. She whispered sweet stories and sang songs in her rich, contralto voice, and although I was considered legally blind, I thought I saw my mother with new eyes.

Unless I was very close to her I could not discern the furrows that lined her face. I strained to see the color of her hair, but I remembered my childish fascination with its shiny red glints, and so I visualized her as she had been in her prime. Sitting next to her on the wicker porch swing, I smelled the scent of rose water that clung to her clothes and I wished I could tell her how I felt about her, how I had begun to change toward her. But the feelings were too new, too fragile.

Only with Dr. Sandler could I trace the path of my heart. In each weekly session, he had pushed me to talk about Mama. Delving into secret thoughts, he had urged me to reveal my true feelings about Daddy's presence in our household. He had pushed me, making me speak of the conflicting feelings—love, anger, hatred, fear—that resided inside me.

"I know you believe it was a selfish decision on your mother's part to keep your father at home all those years, Millicent," he said one day, "but I think it was more than an emotional issue."

"She chose her husband over her children, Dr. Sandler."

"Maybe she believed that was the only reasonable decision available to her," he answered. "Look, Millicent, based on what I know of the mental health system in California during the twenty years your father lived with you here, I'm convinced your mother did what she had to do."

"I don't believe that," I said.

"Just look at her options," he challenged me. "Then you tell me what you think your mother should have done."

And so for several therapy sessions, Dr. Sandler led me on an exploration of the mental health care system in California. I learned that when my family arrived in 1956, the state operated a mental hygiene department that often placed the retarded and the mentally ill, whether dangerous or benign, together in the same facilities. Severely overcrowded, the hospitals were sadly understaffed, which often resulted in a ratio of thirty to fifty patients per staff person, and it was not uncommon to find patients caring for each other. The asylums were thus often in the uncertain hands of the inmates.

Patients often had to wait five days before being examined by a doctor, and the exam was seldom more than a five-minute procedure, grossly insufficient for diagnosing or treating a complex mental disorder like manic depression. It was a pitiful offering for both the mentally ill and their desperate families. Mama had been wise to fear for Daddy's safety in such an environment, I thought.

"Social reform in the 1960s emphasized the return of the chronic patient back into society, Millicent," Dr. Sandler told me.

That meant that by the mid– to late–1960s, when Daddy had sunk into a deep and irreversible depression, most mental patients were being moved out of custodial care and into foster homes and outpatient care centers.

"The system would probably have discouraged, or flatly denied, your mother if she had tried to have your father committed at that time," he said.

"Ironically, as your father aged and his condition deteriorated, your mother would have found it even more difficult to commit him to an institution," Dr. Sandler continued. "The state had discovered that many people were using mental hospitals as dumping grounds for the elderly. The death rate for these people was staggering—in one study, four out of five died in the first year of their stay. The state wanted to put an end to this, and I'm sure your mother would not have willingly condemned your father to such a pathetic death."

No, that was something Mama would never have done.

"Millicent, in California, a patient hospitalized against his will forfeited his right to vote and to own property and possess a driver's license. In your father's case, he would have been prohibited from ever practicing his career as an accountant as well."

"Mama would never have done anything that would have

robbed Daddy of his dignity or his basic civil rights!" I exclaimed.

"Perhaps she would have considered that a nominal loss if hospitalization had offered something more than meager care," Dr. Sandler suggested, "if she had really believed he could be cured. But that would have set up an ironic 'Catch 22,' Millicent. Your father might have come out of the hospital cured but unable to pursue his career or resume the kind of life he had always enjoyed."

Laddie and I had had no idea of the awful dilemma Mama had faced. We had felt sad when we saw the hobos on the trains, when Mama had said, "That could be your father... " We had not wanted to think of him alone and confused and hungry, traveling across the countryside in tattered clothing. We had never imagined, however, that other complex issues were at stake in the matter. I had never understood the agony of Mama's decision.

"Millicent, your mother could have divorced your father on the grounds of mental illness and turned him out onto the streets. But that was something she would never do. She could have put him in the hospital, where his safety would have been in jeopardy and his chances of recovery were zero. Or she could keep him at home where he could be cared for by three people. She chose to keep him at home. If the choice had been yours to make, what would you have done?"

Sitting there in Dr. Sandler's office, I recalled the stories Mama used to tell me about her childhood. She had learned as a little girl that life was not always easy. As a small child, with a bag of cotton slung across her back, she had learned to adjust to her load. Throughout her adult life, she had done the same. Silently she had carried her burden, expecting Laddie and me to follow behind, carrying our own load, just as she did.

Her decisions regarding Daddy had been desperate, impossible decisions which created irresolvable dilemmas—decisions no one should ever be asked to make. After all the years of agony and stoic resolve, she deserved a time of respite. I wanted to give her that.

I wanted to stop blaming her and begin understanding her. For Mama, there had been no "happily ever after." She had not found a smooth road to travel, and so she had taken the only route available. She had walked a steep and rugged path. Alone. For that, I pitied her with the kind of pity that shares the agony of desperation. And I realized that not only did I love her fiercely, I admired her as well.

Everything about Mama spoke of courage, strength, and

audacity. She'd never sought an escape. She'd never run from the difficult choices.

Nor would I.

When the city shut off the gas in my apartment, I wrapped myself in an extra layer of clothes to stay warm at night. I awakened in the morning stiff and cold, and renewed my determination to stay with Felicia until I could get out of this company at least a portion of what I had already invested.

I will not give up and go running home for help, I told myself a dozen times each day. I will not go home to Mama...

And then, before I could call it back, another thought raced forward: And neither will I allow myself to be anything less than the woman my mother is.

Thanks to Dr. Sandler, the metamorphosis was nearing completion: Mama had traveled through my life, her form changing from teacher to nemesis, and now finally to heroine. I could look at her and not feel angry with her or inferior to her. I could take pride in the courage she displayed. And I could point to her indomitable spirit as a source of inspiration.

Again, I committed myself to the success of the company Felicia and I shared. No matter the sacrifice, I would not consider giving up.

When Felicia made the decision to move our company office out of her home and into a suite of offices in a building in Bel Air, I knew the time had come to exert myself. As I walked through the new office, my heels clicking loudly on parquet floors, I caught up with Felicia.

"Felicia, I think it's time we had a serious talk."

"Oh, darling, I'm in a hurry to catch a plane," she answered over her shoulder while she loaded materials into a briefcase.

"Felicia, I am not Bob Cratchett," I said, standing near her desk with my hand on the stack of papers she was trying to stuff into an envelope. "I will not continue to hide away in the back while you peddle my ideas and take credit for them. I am the creative partner in this business and I insist you take me with you on the presentations and give me a more visible part in the company."

"Oh... well, uh... of course, Millicent," she said, stunned by my unexpected outburst. Then her polished poise returned. "Yes, you're right."

"And, I must have a salary."

"All right," she answered, smiling her glimmering smile and

waving a bejeweled hand as she rushed toward the door. "We'll talk about it, just as soon as I get back from New York."

She hurried out of the office and sped away to the airport, leaving me standing there surrounded by a cloud of expensive perfume.

Felicia was always flying to some distant city to meet with a client and show off my promotional ideas. And I was always left behind, tucked away in my small office, hidden from view because I was overweight and poorly dressed. But no more, I vowed. I was determined to go with her.

Mentally apologizing to Dr. Sandler, I began purging again—only to take off the ugly weight I had gained, I told myself. I did not want Felicia to be able to find any reason for leaving me behind on future business appointments. I would do whatever I had to in order to be slender and attractive again. I was determined to be "front-of-the-house" material from that day forward.

Once again, my eating habits spiralled out of control. I was again consuming hundreds of laxatives and diuretics and swallowing ipecac; I would do almost anything that would enable me to eat what I wanted and then regurgitate it quickly so that my weight could return to its normal 125 pounds.

By the fall of 1985, I was again slender, but very, very miserable and frustrated. My workers' compensation and personal injury cases were still tied up in litigation, although both my lawyers assured me that both matters would be settled within the next year. My eyesight continued to deteriorate, and I could see only silhouettes and very blurred shadows. My headaches, accompanied by seizures, had intensified and occurred with almost weekly regularity. It seemed that no relief was available for either my physical or my legal woes.

In Dr. Sandler's office, I tried to sort through each problem and gain some level of understanding. I was completely unprepared one day when he announced that he was dismissing me as his patient.

Stunned, I blurted, "I don't understand! What has happened?"

"I have been treating you for nearly six years without payment," he answered. "I can't do it any longer."

"Dr. Sandler, you spoke to my lawyers just the other day," I said. "They both assured you that my case would be settled within a year and that you would be paid in full!"

"I know," he answered. "I know I promised to stay with you until the end, but I have a family and financial responsibilities. Millicent, I am no longer comfortable with this arrangement."

Speechless, I leaned back against my chair, feeling as though he had just struck me a physical blow.

"I'm sorry, Millicent. I know this is hard for you to understand... "

I didn't listen to the rest of his words. I stood up and walked out of his office.

He's abandoning me. He promised to take me all the way through this... It's not over yet, not until the case has been tried in court...

I can't believe he's just leaving me like this...

There was light at the end of the tunnel, the lawyers had said so only last week. The settlement would be coming; all the doctors would be paid in full for their services. Why was he deserting me now, when we were coming so close to the final battlefield, the courtroom? How would I make it through the stress of a trial alone? I would have to relive the accident with all its trauma and face the relentless assaults of trial lawyers who hoped I could be bullied. And now I would have to do it without his support.

I was devastated. And terribly alone.

I wasn't expecting this... I can't believe he is going back on his word, after all the trust I placed in him...

I couldn't make sense of it, but neither could I change it. One more cause for fear, I thought; but then, because Dr. Sandler had done his job well, I realized this was also one more opportunity for courage.

I'll be all right, I told myself. I'll get through this without Dr. Sandler. I'll take care of myself, and I'll be just fine.

I returned to the offices I shared with Felicia and found her breezing in, just back from a trip to Palm Beach.

"I was marvelous, Millicent! Just marvelous! You should have seen me," she said. "If I'd been on Broadway I'd have gotten rave reviews! I had to say the ideas in the presentation were mine, but you don't mind, do you, darling? I really was a smash. Oh, say you understand, won't you?"

"I'm tired of understanding, Felicia," I answered.

"You don't mean that, Millicent," she gushed. "Oh, all right, I know they're your ideas, and I promise next time I'll give you all the credit." She hurried past me into her office. Spinning gracefully, she said, "Now, let's see what we can do about this World Trade Center promotion. You remember Kenneth, don't you? His company in New York is going to work with us to plan that affair. It will be our biggest project ever."

"Felicia, stop. Listen to me. I *do* mean it," I said. "I'm going with you on the next trip. I don't care where it is, I'm going. And I will accompany you on the next presentation and take credit for the work I've done. Is that clear?"

Felicia was silent, stunned, and more than a little perturbed. But she was also smart. She couldn't risk losing me—she had to accept my terms, or at least placate me. A few days later, I flew with her to New York to meet with Kenneth.

Kenneth's posh office on Park Avenue wasn't the place I would have chosen for my "coming out," but I wasn't going to back down now. I summoned all the Collinsworth pride I could muster and walked into the conference room to meet this man who, until today, I had spoken with only by phone. I discovered him to be just as pompous and artificial and condescending in person as he was long-distance. But I was determined to take my rightful place in this company, and that meant confronting this man and claiming credit for my creative contributions.

I had meticulously studied and designed a theme for the celebration of the tenth anniversary of the observation deck at the World Trade Center. I was adamant with Felicia, insisting that I be the one to present my ideas for the affair. And I planned to accept the credit I was due for this campaign. Kenneth stood and interrupted me midway through the presentation.

"May I see you in my office, Felicia?" he said in a tight voice.

Outside the conference room, I heard their angry exchange.

"Who is this person?" Kenneth bellowed. "Why is she here? How dare she come in here and take over this meeting! You'd think she was a full partner or something!"

Felicia's words were muffled, but I knew what was being said. And I was suddenly sure of what she had been saying to our clients for more than two years. She had pretended I was her private secretary and personal assistant. She had never told Kenneth, or anyone else, that I was the creative person behind every campaign she presented. She had never told anyone that we were partners.

Kenneth was outraged to learn that the partnership he had formed with Felicia included a third person. Stomping back into the conference room, he stood in front of me and perused me from head to toe.

"If I have to present her to our clients as a partner," he said, sniffing with disgust, "at least dress her up. And can't you do something about that patch? It is so distasteful."

"How dare you talk about me in such a despicable fashion!" I said, in a quiet voice controlled only by the power of pride too long suppressed. "When you two were hoping you'd find someone of class and prestige to marry you and give you a leg up into society, my family had already been there for generations!" My hands were shaking and my mouth dry, but I wasn't yet finished with these pretenders. "You two are always so concerned with pedigree and credentials. If we're comparing, you two are plow horses and I'm a thoroughbred."

They stood there: Kenneth, who had married wealth and dreamed of his own eventual grandeur, and Felicia, who had ridiculed me while at the same time mimicking me, cloning my mannerisms and my style of conversation.

Ignoring their blustering and stammering, I continued, "You should know, Kenneth, that I am the brains of this company. I created every campaign Felicia has sold. I tutored her in marketing as well as in the methods of presentation. I have taught her everything she knows about the business of public relations. I demand that you show me the respect I am due."

Drawing a huge breath, I added, "And furthermore, Kenneth, if you do not like the way I am dressed, then I suggest you write me a check immediately for my third of the fee the clients have paid for this project, and I'll gladly dress in a manner more suited to an executive."

Kenneth and Felicia sat down and listened in silence while I completed my presentation. Kenneth could find nothing to criticize in the campaign I proposed, and before leaving the office, we made plans to meet with the clients and present our promotional ideas later that evening.

"But not until we've gone shopping for clothes for you," Felicia said, grabbing my arm and hailing a taxi.

"I haven't any money to spend until you pay me, Felicia," I said, climbing into the cab beside her.

"Never mind," she answered. "I've got plastic."

Felicia pulled out her credit card and told the cab driver to take us to Bloomingdale's. Later, outfitted with a designer ensemble and a raincoat, we made a stop at a salon. When I had been primped and coiffed and manicured, Felicia declared me acceptable company. I was ready to meet our New York clients.

Throughout the remainder of the trip, I kept my distance from Felicia and Kenneth. We maintained a professional courtesy during the meetings and the presentation, but my relationship with Felicia had lost any small spark of warmth it might once have had. The

clients' enthusiasm for my ideas warmed me, however, as did the
large check Kenneth wrote to me for my one-third of the fee for
our professional services. When we left New York, it was with the
understanding that we would return before Thanksgiving and
stay throughout the holidays to oversee all the arrangements for
this gala event.

Mama planned a Thanksgiving feast early that year so I could
be with the family before I had to leave for New York. On a
Sunday afternoon in November, we all gathered around Mama's
antique dining-room table and ate turkey off the family china
and silver.

Bryan, now a toddler, charmed us all with his latest words and
his busy antics. After dinner, I picked him up and snuggled with
him, straining to make out his blurred features, memorizing the
shape of his nose, his ears. Unless my face was nearly touching
his, I could not see the brown of his eyes. His smile was fuzzy and
at times obscured by a thin veil of gray, but throughout the day I
pressed my face close to his, trying to memorize every detail of
his appearance.

I was losing the race against darkness. Soon, I would not be
able to see my nephew's face. Nor Laddie's and Jean's. Nor Mama's.

I wanted to hold their faces in my hands and study them. But
Collinsworths are not comfortable with such intimate gestures,
nor was I comfortable declaring to them that I believed I was
seeing them all for the last time. So, unobtrusively, I tried to sit
close to them and store the picture of their faces in my heart.

Mama, always tall and stately, had grown frail, and when I
stood next to her, she seemed small and fragile. Her skin, once
like fine porcelain, was now deeply lined and weathered, but her
patrician features remained beautiful. Her hair was the same; her
thick braid wound about her head, glistening like a silver and
auburn crown. As regal and proud as she had ever been, her
presence reigned over the dining room in the villa as though it
were Windsor Castle and she the queen of England.

I memorized Laddie's features as if studying a portrait in a
gallery. I settled on the arm of his chair and watched him while
he held his son. While he was unaware of my scrutiny, I peered
down into his face, examining the shape of his eyes, the curve of
his jaw, the color of his thick, auburn beard, the flash of his teeth
when he smiled his rare smile.

Jean, radiant with happiness, shone like a light in my shadowy
vision. From that day forward, I would always imagine her as

youthful, her fair skin flawless, her eyes blue, her expression of joy almost ethereal. What happiness she has brought into this family, I thought.

Before I left the villa that day, I climbed the stairs to Daddy's old room. His cane, still hanging on the doorknob, clanked against the door when I pushed it open. His Fedora hung in its familiar place on the hat tree just inside the room. I walked over to his desk and squinted at the items that had not been moved in nearly ten years. His pipes sat in their holder, just as he had left them, and the faint scent of tobacco hung in the room. His keys lay next to his pipes. Touching each item tenderly, my fingers left a trail in the dust that lay undisturbed on his desk.

Clutching the afghan folded neatly next to his favorite chair, I sat down and rocked, listening to the familiar creaking that had been the constant, if macabre, accompaniment to my childhood. The sound was too painful, too filled with memories. I stood up and walked across the room to study the picture which hung on the opposite wall.

Standing with my nose almost touching his portrait, I peered at the man who was my father.

"Daddy, I haven't forgotten my promise to you," I whispered. "So much has happened since you first told me the legend of the dogwood... so much. You were right, Daddy—we do find strength in our pain and indignity. But sometimes it's so hard... "

My throat ached with the effort to hold back tears.

"Daddy, I still want to make you proud of me... But I know now that I could never have made you well, even though I wanted to so badly. Nothing I could have ever done would have healed you, but I can heal myself. I have to do that, Daddy. I have to stand tall for myself. This time, the promise I'm making is for me."

Kissing my fingertips, I placed them against the canvas portrait.

"I'll never forget I'm a Collinsworth, Daddy. That is the promise I'll make you today. I'll never forget the courage of my ancestors, I promise."

I flew to New York with Felicia the next day. For a few hours each day, as we navigated through the traffic and the noise and excitement of the city, we seemed able to forget that we were estranged. We worked on the details for the event at the World Trade Center during the day and attended parties and shows in the evening. I remember playing with the toys in F.A.O. Schwarz and pressing my nose against the windows of Macy's and

Bloomingdale's to try to see the sparkling holiday decorations that lit up the displays. We rode through Central Park in hansom cabs and ate roasted chestnuts. While ice skaters sped by, we sipped hot chocolate and watched the lights on the tree in Rockefeller Center sparkle to life.

I must remember all this, I thought. I'll never be able to see it again.

Engrossed in every sight, however dim and blurred, I vowed to memorize every color my eyes could see and every shape I could discern.

Plans for the celebration of the tenth anniversary of the observation deck at the World Trade Center were progressing well. After nearly a month in New York City, we had only a few more days to finalize the arrangements for what we hoped would be remembered as one of the most spectacular extravaganzas ever held in the city's twin towers. I was standing on the observation deck at the top of the building, amid crowds of tourists, discussing with Felicia the last, deft touches we would make for the affair, when Kenneth paged her and asked her to join him in the lobby on the ground floor.

"If I'm not back in fifteen minutes, meet me downstairs," Felicia said as she hurried toward the elevators.

"All right," I answered, turning back to face the windows that offered a view of the city. The distant panorama was little more than gray shadows and blurred images to me.

My head was throbbing, as it did nearly every day, but that day, the intensity of the pain seemed worse than ever. As I pushed through the crowd to leave the deck, a sudden explosion of fireworks erupted behind my eyes and I grabbed my head and sagged against a wall. With my eyes shut tightly and my hands cradling my pounding head, I waited for the pain to subside.

It's never been this bad, I thought, clenching my teeth and fighting the rise of nausea.

I've got to get downstairs... have Felicia take me back to the hotel...

My head felt as if it were about to explode. Huddling against the wall, my fingers pressing against my temple, I tried to calm myself.

Take a deep breath now, Mitty, I told myself. Just take it easy... you're going to be all right. Just head for the elevators...

Stepping away from the wall, I straightened my shoulders and opened my eyes. Total darkness greeted me.

No gray shadows moved. No blurred shapes teased. Masses of people stood milling about the room, but I could see none of them, no fuzzy figures, no vague images. Nothing. As though an immense blanket had been thrown over the building, the room lay swathed in total darkness.

No! No... Oh, God! I can't see... I can't see anything!

Disoriented and confused, I spun about, trying to gather my wits and determine the direction of the elevators.

I've got to get to the ground floor, was my only thought. I've got to get out of here...

Captured by a horde of tourists making their way toward the nearest exit, I moved with them and found myself swept into an elevator. I strained to hear over the commotion of the crowd, listening for a clue that would tell me what floor I was on as the elevator stopped and started.

Hysteria rose in me and I tried to swallow it down.

I can do this, I told myself. I can get to the lobby... Felicia will find me there. It's okay, I can do this.

As the doors opened, I tried to move forward but the crowds pushed me back. Crushed against the wall of the elevator, I felt panic pounding inside me. All the preparation I had made in anticipation of this day dissolved. It didn't matter that I had memorized portions of this building, that I had navigated alone in the shadows for nearly six years, that I had been told to expect total blindness. The sudden fall of darkness obliterated all sense of order. I could only ride the elevator up and down, up and down, until I was finally pushed out on the ground floor and caught in the crosscurrent of hundreds of thousands of commuters dashing for the subways.

Masses of people shoved past me and I stumbled, reaching out blindly for something to grab hold of. Clutching an arm, I murmured, "Please, can you... " But the arm wrenched away from my grasp and I felt myself thrust into a swirling vortex of humanity traveling at terrifying speed. Panic energized me, and I thrust myself against the wall of bodies and pushed until, sobbing, I felt myself collide with the cold solid surface of a wall. Collapsing, I fell to the floor and buried my head in my arms.

In the lobby, Felicia paced and fumed and looked at her watch, wondering why I hadn't joined her. It was after five o'clock. We had another appointment to keep. Felicia was angered that I had delayed her. Half an hour later, her anger turned to concern. She summoned the building security to search for me.

Huddled against a wall, exhausted and terrified, I waited for what seemed like hours for someone to find me. Finally, after the chaotic flood of rush-hour commuters had subsided, I felt a hand on my shoulder and heard a voice ask my name. A security guard took me to the lobby where Felicia waited.

The remaining days in New York City were a nightmare. I clung to Felicia, hating to have to lean on her, but terrified of stepping into oncoming danger. The gala at the World Trade Center surpassed all our expectations, but I was unable to share Felicia's and Kenneth's elation.

I returned to Los Angeles, glad to be on familiar terrain, but uncertain, fearful of what awaited me now that I was completely blind.

Thrust into darkness, I found myself less prepared than I had expected to be. The shadows and faint light of the past six years had been markers, if inadequate and sometimes confusing ones, but now I had none. No mileposts, no visual handholds, blurry or otherwise, for maneuvering through my world. And I felt unsettled, often afraid, much like a child who has discovered that, when the lights are turned off in her cozy room and the night is allowed its reign, her familiar toys and furnishings suddenly become unfamiliar, ferocious. The friendly becomes unfriendly.

So it was for me. The familiar things, like curbs and trees and doorways and human bodies, became my enemies. I stumbled and floundered and, at times, cursed, angry at the loss of light and the threat of danger from such common, otherwise benign objects. And I wondered what the rest of my life would be like.

I stayed close to the places that had already become habit for me. I was able to ride the bus to the office, meet with Felicia, and work on promotional campaigns, but I seldom traveled beyond the routes that I had already memorized, staying close to the boundaries that offered me some sense of security.

In the spring of 1986, my personal injury case came to trial. Throughout the seven years since the accident, my attorney, Janet Gullixson, had relentlessly fought for me, without payment, battling the legal system and the insurance companies. My lawsuit was considered risky because the injury had taken place during work hours, and many lawyers felt that it fell under the jurisdiction of a workers' compensation lawsuit. But Janet had not given up on her belief that this was indeed a personal injury case. She believed I deserved more than the fixed sum that a workers' compensation settlement would have given me. She was committed to seeing the case through to the end. And now, finally, a jury would hear my case.

"I believe in you, Millicent," Janet told me as we talked about the trial a few days before we entered the courtroom. "You have been grievously injured, and I will fight this to the bitter end. I don't know if we can win, the odds are against us. But you deserve a second chance at life," she said. "I'm going to give this everything I've got."

The pretrial costs would amount to twelve thousand dollars. I didn't have the money, of course, and I wouldn't have it until after the case was settled, and then only if it were settled in my favor. It was one more bitter irony: I couldn't go to court until I had the money, and I wouldn't have the money until after I went to court.

"Don't worry about it, Millicent," Janet told me. "I'll pay the pretrial costs."

"I can't ask you to do that, Janet," I answered.

"I want to," she said.

"You've done so much already... "

Janet touched my shoulder.

"I'll pay you back as soon as the trial is over," I said quickly. "You'll get the twelve thousand plus the percentage of the final settlement that is due you," I promised.

"I don't want the twelve thousand," she answered. "My percentage of the final settlement will be sufficient. Let's just consider the pretrial costs as my investment in you. It's my personal endorsement of you and your chance for a new beginning."

I had no words to express my thanks.

In the days before the trial, my workers' compensation lawyer negotiated with W.R. Grace & Company's insurance carrier and convinced them to pay all my doctor bills in full if I dropped my workers' compensation case against the company. The lawyers for the insurance company were convinced I had no case, and so, confident of their own standing, they agreed. Consequently, they waived the right to recoup their expenses from any settlement a jury might award me. If I won my case, every dollar of the settlement, after legal expenses had been deducted, would come to me.

The personal injury trial lasted seven days. At the end of the week, the jury voted unanimously in my favor. Cheers erupted in the courtroom when the foreman of the jury read the verdict.

"We did it! We did it!" Janet threw her arms around me and hugged me while I sat too stunned to move. The crowd in the courtroom continued to shout congratulations.

"It's over, Millicent!" Janet exclaimed, having to yell over the noisy celebration of spectators in the gallery. "The medical bills will be paid by the insurance company and every cent of the settlement is yours!"

It really is over, I thought. I'm going to get on with my life!

"You should see it, Millicent," Janet's voice was hoarse with emotion. "The judge's face is fairly beaming and the bailiff held up her fingers to make a 'V' for victory!"

I stood up and gripped the edge of the table, feeling weak with relief. Then, from beside me, the deep gravelly voice of an old man addressed me.

"Bless you, chile."

I reached toward the voice, and large, rough, calloused hands gripped mine.

"Your heavenly Father is watching over you, just as He watches over the sparrows."

I recognized the voice of the jury foreman who had read the verdict, but its deep timbre echoed with a familiar resonance from another place, another time. He gave my hands a gentle squeeze before dropping them, and then he walked away, leaving me standing there with the sense that I had just set foot in a sacred dimension.

"Janet," I called out.

"I'm here, Millicent," she answered from a few feet in front of me.

"Did you see the man who just spoke to me? What did he look like?"

"Like he'd just stepped out of the last century," she answered, snapping her briefcase shut. "Why, Millicent?"

"Just describe him for me!" I insisted.

"All right," she said, sounding a little surprised. "He's a very old, black gentleman—a giant of a man, with huge, broad shoulders, and he looks very strong and powerful. He's quite distinguished looking, with a great white head of hair."

Oh, Lord, I thought. Oh, my Lord.

"What was he wearing?" I was trembling now.

"A black suit," she said, gripping my elbow and steering me out of the courtroom. "The same one he wore into the jury box every day. And every day he sat there with this black hat in his hands. He wouldn't put it down."

Janet led me through the broad hallways of the justice building and out into the teeming crowds that lined the streets of downtown Los Angeles; but in my mind, I was many miles away from this scene of urban commotion. I was a child, standing in the doorway of the old brick house on Center Street, and next to me was an old black man in a black suit. His black hat in hand, Old John had just made the trek across a forbidden zone to comfort an ailing family all others had declared unclean.

I hugged the memory of that awful day when one black man's actions had brought solace to a sad and broken white family.

Other memories came quickly. I was at Five Oaks, skipping through grass as tall as I, my hand gripped tightly in Old John's work-roughened hands. I heard his voice, sounding like the music of a bass when the bow sweeps across the strings. I watched him smile and nod his head to the rhythm of a silent symphony of grace.

And in that moment, immersed in darkness, I thought I heard the first faint strains of my own symphony. I thought I discerned the theme of grace.

Chapter 14

Grace did indeed seem to become the theme of my life in the early months that followed the conclusion of my personal injury case.

I had a measure of financial security, thanks to the settlement the jury had awarded me, and so I moved to an apartment closer to the office I shared with Felicia. Westwood Village, near the campus of the University of California at Los Angeles, was easily accessible on foot and it was close to public transit. Located on the borders of Brentwood, Bel Air, and Beverly Hills, it was a simple community to memorize, and I was soon negotiating through it without difficulty.

I loved my tiny apartment. I enjoyed the challenge of finding creative ways to make it convenient and comfortable for a blind tenant. In spite of the fact that I no longer had my sight, my life was quite rich. And one of the reasons was my friendship with a woman named Geneva Andrews.

Ironically, Felicia had introduced me to Geneva. A manicurist working in the salon Felicia frequented, Geneva was an enigma. Witty and intelligent, she flashed a winsome, indomitable spirit. I felt an immediate kinship with her when I heard the Southern twang in her speech. And when I noted that Felicia treated her much as she treated me, I knew Geneva and I were destined to become great friends.

"Can you imagine," Felicia gushed, "a manicurist with a masters degree! Only in California!"

Slender and tall, with long, blond hair, Geneva was a brilliant woman. Cute and spirited, she had a kind of spunk that I envied. The daughter of a Texas preacher, she had chosen a career in the mental health profession. She had moved to Kentucky to become a counselor in a clinic tucked away in the foothills of the Appalachian Mountains and had served on the Lieutenant Governor's panel on domestic violence. A severe case of career burnout and a bad marriage had driven her to seek solace in sunny California. She learned the trade of a manicurist and accepted a job in an exclusive salon where, instead of counseling troubled mountain folk who seldom ventured out of the hollers, she spent her days bent over the dimpled hands of socialites.

Geneva listened to her clients as they talked about their divorces, their affairs, and their plastic surgeries. She listened, she sympathized, and, because she couldn't help herself, she also counseled them. "Problems are the same everywhere," she said often.

To me, she offered unconditional friendship.

After a day spent poring over promotional ideas and making presentations and listening to Felicia's superficial prattle, I felt Geneva's presence to be an oasis. Many evenings after work we shared dinner and sipped white wine at an outdoor cafe in Brentwood or Bel Air or Westwood Village.

Nothing I said shocked or disturbed Geneva. Her years as a counselor had exposed her to every kind of mental condition, every kind of terror and perversion. She had seen and heard it all. With Geneva, I could be myself. I didn't try to hide my imperfections. Now that I was completely blind, I no longer needed to wear the eye patch, but Geneva had first met me when I couldn't be without it, and she hadn't been offended or embarrassed by it. From our first meeting, she had accepted me without censure.

Our Southern heritage offered us a common meeting ground. Reminiscing about the gentle cadence of life in the South, we exchanged small-town stories from Texas and Arkansas and Kentucky. We remembered the sweet, simple times enjoyed in distant places. Sometimes, as we shared with each other humorous childhood episodes, we pretended that the past held nothing but good times. We both knew it was a game of pretend, but on those occasions, the journey home was untroubled.

Like me, Geneva also had her share of ghosts. Her past was littered with the trauma of disasters and horrors that she too had had to exorcise. Our common history, as well as the fact that we were both lonely souls, provided a strong bond for friendship. She, with her fiancé Ernie, far away in Princeton, New Jersey, appreciated the companionship of a friend; and I, searching for a place in my recently darkened world, loved her for her good-natured, unconditional acceptance of me.

Unlike Felicia, Geneva easily accepted my blindness, never making a derogatory comment, never deriding me for my handicap. Her friendship was like a healing salve after nearly three years of Felicia's scorching ridicule.

Talking with Geneva was as natural as breathing. Telling her the secrets I had never shared with anyone but Dr. Sandler became easy. When I told her about my ongoing battle with bulimia, it wasn't the professional concern of a counselor I heard in her voice—it was the sound of a worried friend.

"I know it's hard, Mitty," she said, "but bulimia can be controlled."

I didn't think I could ever overcome it. This area of my life defeated me. In spite of six years of therapy, it remained unresolved, unmanageable. Each day was a struggle of immense proportions. I craved food, and then I loathed myself when I indulged. And I continued to purge almost daily.

My feelings about Felicia were growing more and more antagonistic. She resented my presence in the company; she resented the money I demanded for my work. And I dreaded going into the office and enduring her company. The problem was growing, but I didn't know how to resolve it without dissolving our partnership. And I wasn't yet ready to walk out of the company I had worked so hard to build.

And so the feelings continued to ferment. And the battle with food continued to rage. Would I ever find the catalyst that would provoke lasting change? Would I ever find the strength to win over this life-threatening disorder?

"Let's see a movie tonight," Geneva suggested one evening when we met for dinner after work.

Laughing, I said, "I'm blind, Geneva. Have you forgotten?"

"It'll be great fun, Mitty! We'll sit on the back row and I'll tell you everything that's happening on the screen. Come on. What do you say?"

"What will the people around us say when you talk all the way through the movie?" I answered, imagining an usher asking us to leave the theater.

"No one will say anything. I'll whisper. Let's do it! Come on, Mitty!"

She was irrepressible. I couldn't say no. Sitting in the back row of the theater munching popcorn, we giggled and whispered throughout the movie. Geneva described the scenery, the actors' clothing—everything that I could not see. It was the beginning of what was to become a favorite outing. Together, we "saw" nearly every one of Hollywood's offerings.

Geneva was a reluctant accomplice in my game to pretend to the world that I was sighted. I wasn't ashamed of being blind—I just didn't want my blindness to be the focal point of my personality. I wanted to be able to move through life without the constant attention that is heaped on the handicapped. Geneva understood this, and so she agreed to aid me, but with certain stipulations.

"I'll play your game, Mitty," she told me as we walked down the street together one day. I held her arm and let her voice help me navigate past light poles, across streets, and up and down curbs. "But sooner or later you have to acknowledge that you are a blind woman," she said. "That is who you are now, Mitty. And it's okay. It's okay to be blind."

Images of stumbling, groping caricatures wielding white canes flooded my imagination.

"I don't like being viewed as impaired and dependent," I answered, hesitating and tightening my grip on her arm as a truck lumbered by, its muffler coughing loudly.

"Keep going," Geneva instructed me as we stepped off the curb and into the street. "Come on, there's a restaurant up ahead."

"It's important for you to acknowledge who you are," Geneva said, as we walked. "Steps straight ahead, two up, now turn right, okay... " I followed her verbal cues and we entered a restaurant. The maitre d' pulled out my chair and handed me a menu, as if I could read it and order the "special of the day."

"Mitty, you've got to face your blindness," Geneva said, leaning across the table toward me. "Stop pretending."

"I just don't like being perceived as 'needy,'" I said, thanking the waiter as he poured water into my glass. My fingers inched across the table to find the goblet.

"It's further to the left," Geneva instructed me. "Mitty, can't you see how ludicrous this is? You don't want to be perceived as 'needy,' but you need me to help you locate your water glass!" She made a sound of exasperation. "I can't always be with you like this, Mitty. You have to learn some skills that will make you independent."

"What are you suggesting?" I asked, patting the table, trying to locate my napkin and silverware.

"Don't you think it's time you enrolled in the Braille Institute?"

"Oh, no," I protested. "I'm not going to be a blind lady with a white cane. No thanks. I can do this with or without you."

"Mitty, that's crazy," she said, almost angrily, and then I heard

humor in her voice when she added, "I think we both know how
you feel about being crazy."

I had to laugh.

"Look," she said, "you do pretty well on your own, but there
must be many things you could learn at the institute that would
make your life easier. Why are you so against it?"

"They'll make me learn to use a cane, Geneva! Can't you see
it? The poor lady on the street with her cane, tap-tapping at the
curb while onlookers stop to stare." I shook my head and sighed.
"That's not for me, Geneva. I just can't do it."

"Mitty, that's ridiculous," Geneva scolded.

And she continued to scold until I relented and agreed to
enroll in the Braille Institute in downtown Los Angeles.

"Are you happy now?" I asked, when I returned and showed
her my newest acquisition: a hinged white cane with a red tip.

In reality, I was pleased with everything I was learning at the
institute, and I was anxious to show off my improved capabilities.
While Geneva applauded, I demonstrated new cooking skills and
showed her the changes I had made in my apartment. I opened
my kitchen cabinets and closet doors to display a new, easy-to-
remember arrangement, and I bragged on my beginning efforts at
learning Braille.

Three times each week, a mobility instructor came to my
apartment to teach me how to walk with my cane, taking me
down sidewalks and across busy streets, and finally back to my
apartment. Sensory perception classes taught me to employ my
other senses to compensate for the loss of my sight. All in all, I
thought I was adapting very well to my new status as a blind
woman.

I was discovering that, in some ways, it was easier to be
completely blind than to be partially blind. For years, I had felt
like a victim of sensory warfare. My four remaining senses seemed
to be forever battling with the residual eyesight I did have—
almost as though they wished to kill off a weak and dying member,
to get it out of the way and get on with the job of compensating
for its absence. Now that the last remnant of eyesight was finally
gone, my body seemed to relax. My other senses gave a collective
sigh of relief and, as though on cue, they began to contribute a
vast array of sensory clues for me to decipher and act upon.

Geneva had urged me to accept my blindness. Now the
Collinsworth pride drove me to become the best blind person on
the planet. There would be no awkward stumbling, no groping. I

would not become a pathetic character bent over a white cane, leaning heavily on a sighted guide. I would stand up straight, walk forward confidently. I would continue the proud stance of a Collinsworth. This objective, however, would not be easily achieved.

Every day I went to the Westwood Veterans' Cemetery to practice walking with my cane. Without attracting the attention of curious spectators, I walked across acres of pathways, occasionally meeting a groundskeeper. Using the long driveways and the rows of white crosses to keep myself in line, I practiced walking straight, forcing myself to stand erect, chin high, shoulders back.

I practiced eye exercises every day, forcing my eyes to track sounds instead of rolling around without purpose. The exercises triggered excruciating headaches that battered my skull, but I was determined. I learned to listen and track voices, sending my eyes toward the sound so that I could appear to be looking at the people who engaged me in conversation.

Concentrating, I schooled myself to hold my head up and to keep it still, fighting the tendency to let it roll from side to side, as many blind people do. I trained myself to be conscious of how I stood so that I didn't rock aimlessly back and forth.

I would not become a cliché. More than anything, I wanted to fit into the sighted world as unobtrusively as possible. I did not want to be relegated to the category of the disabled, where I would be defined by the fact of my blindness. It was an inconvenience, nothing more. I would not be diminished by the loss of my sight.

Now that I could afford the expense, I sought out a neuropsychiatrist, as Dr. Chen had suggested. I was determined to learn, once and for all, whether hysteria or brain injury was the cause of my ailments. After a multitude of tests and examinations, Dr. Chen's diagnosis was confirmed: My blindness, the memory loss, the confusion, the physical coordination problems that occurred after the accident, the disorientation, the olfactory and visual hallucinations, even to some extent the depression—all of these were the result of a severe brain injury that occurred when the falling hammer had collided with my face in the summer of 1979. All the physical symptoms that had been blamed on my emotional state were in fact caused by the accident.

Finally, after seven long years, I felt cleansed from the specter of insanity.

In some ways, my blindness seemed the least of my disabilities. I would spend the rest of my life learning to live with the plague of short-term memory loss and occasions of confusion over simple tasks. I would have difficulty with cognitive reasoning during times of stress. But the good news was that now I could account for all these disturbing conditions. I would become impatient, but not unnerved, when suddenly I was unable to remember how to perform a routine task. I would no longer become terrified when, without warning, I couldn't remember if I had combed my hair or taken a bath. I would remember the accident and remind myself that, in addition to the obvious injury—my blindness—I had also suffered brain damage. I would challenge myself once more to live above my limitations.

The final showdown with Felicia occurred early in the summer of 1986. I stopped by the office one evening while out with a friend. The account books lay open on Felicia's desk, and I asked my companion to read them to me. Discovering huge amounts of money entered in the accounts, I learned that Felicia had been lying to me about our company's finances since the first days of our business relationship. In spite of high overhead expenses, we had begun to make a profit shortly after we started working together.

While I was selling my furniture and living in an apartment without heat, Felicia had been advancing herself "loans." Using the money in the company coffers, she had paid for household expenses, employed a maid, and made payments on a new BMW. She had financed entertainment, vacations, clothing, and travel.

I wasn't very surprised to learn that Felicia had lied to me, but I was shocked to learn how lavishly she had lived while I was near destitution. Shocked, and enraged. The following day I confronted her about her deception and ended the partnership that had never really been a partnership. I walked out of her office and never returned.

I was still hot from the argument when I stopped by Geneva's apartment and blurted out the story of Felicia's deceit. Furious, I paced the floor and raved about all the misery she had caused me.

"She exploited me! All those months when I lived like a pauper, believing there was no money, she was making payments on a $50,000 car!"

"The best thing you can do now is forget it, Mitty," Geneva answered. "You'll never recoup your losses unless you take her to court. Do you really want to go through all that?"

"But she robbed me!" I shouted.

"Get good and mad, Mitty. It's healthy," Geneva said calmly, handing me a glass of wine. "Scream and yell all you want to, and then get on with your life. Cut your losses and move on."

Geneva was right, I thought, gulping down the wine and handing her my glass for a refill. I had no stomach for another round of lawsuits. I had my settlement, my professional skills, and a resumé showing a successful career in public relations. In a few weeks, I would complete my training at the Braille Institute. I could start over again.

I could go forward without Felicia, but the fact that I would have to do it without Geneva was breaking my heart.

Geneva's marriage to Ernie was months away, but in a couple of weeks she would leave Los Angeles and go to Princeton to plan the wedding. I was happy for her. She was lucky enough to be in love with a wonderful man. But I felt very sorry for myself.

One rainy evening, a few days before Geneva was due to fly east, we went to a movie together. We left the theater in a downpour. Giggling like two schoolgirls, we looked up into the cloud-heavy sky and let the raindrops drench our faces.

"Singin' in the rain, just singin' in the rain... " Geneva began to sing softly.

"What a wonderful feelin'," I joined in, harmonizing, "I'm happy again... "

Tapping my white cane against the pavement, I spun into an impromptu rendition of Gene Kelly's classic dance number, swinging around lamp posts and stomping in the gutters, splashing us both with sheets of dirty water. Geneva watched, stunned, and then burst into laughter as my red-tipped white cane danced across the concrete in rhythm to the song.

"Oh, Mitty!" she said, grabbing me and hugging me. "I'm going to miss you so much."

The music died. Tears mingled with the raindrops coursing down my face.

"I'm going to miss you too, Geneva," I whispered.

"You'll come to Princeton for the wedding," she said. "Promise me."

"Of course I'll come. I wouldn't miss it."

A few days later, we said goodbye.

I assuaged my loneliness by focusing all my energies on learning to become the best blind person I could be. Increasing my classes at the Braille Institute, I rode a bus into the heart of Los Angeles several times each week. I navigated through the streets alone, pushing through the city's huge population, tapping my cane against curbs and sidewalks, making my way past scores of pornographic bookstores, panhandlers, prostitutes, and drug addicts. It seemed the city's most desperate and disreputable citizens congregated along the blocks from my stop to the Institute's front door.

One afternoon as I left class, I heard footsteps approaching me from behind, pounding loudly, as though chasing someone. My cane scanning the sidewalk in front of me, I walked faster to get out of the way of the oncoming commotion, but suddenly the commotion surrounded me. I collided with a large body that reeked of alcohol and sweat. Rough hands wrenched my cane out of my hands. Harsh laughter erupted all around me as I grabbed at the air, searching for my cane as my tormentors tossed it back and forth among themselves. I did not need my eyes to know that I stood in the center of a gang of youths. Their leader stepped up close to me and yanked my sunglasses off my face.

Paralyzed with fear, I stood silently, waiting, listening, hearing first a chuckle, then a click. In the next instant a blast of heat hit my face. The smell of lighter fluid filled my nostrils. Terrified, I shrank back from the cigarette lighter that burned just beneath my nose.

Snarling like a pack of wild dogs, the thugs pushed me from one to the other, groping at me and tearing my clothes.

"She's not blind!" one of them shouted. "I told you she couldn't be blind!"

The flame of the lighter flicked across my face again and another voice whispered, "You're faking it, aren't you? You're too good-lookin' to be blind."

"Leave me alone," I pleaded. "Please, just let me go!"

Trembling and crying uncontrollably, I pushed against the hands that gripped me. Unable to scream, I gasped for breath between sobs.

"Hey! What's going on over there?" a man's voice traveled over the ring of terror, startling my attackers. "Hey, you animals! Leave that girl alone!" he commanded. "Take your filthy hands off her!"

"Let's get outta here!" someone shouted, and the gang fled into a nearby alley. I heard my cane clatter onto the pavement.

Dropping down on my knees, I groped about the sidewalk, searching for my cane and for one shoe that had come off during the tussle. My fingers closed on the handle of my cane and, using it as a prop, I pulled myself upright and leaned against a wall while I waited for my breath to return. A few minutes later, wearing only one shoe, I limped toward the bus stop, clutching the torn pieces of my blouse together and trying to control shudders of terror.

Badly shaken, I huddled in my seat on the bus during the miserable ride back to Westwood Village. I kept remembering a comment made by Dr. Sandler years earlier. "The world is not built for the blind, Millicent," he had told me. For the first time, I fully understood his meaning.

I also realized that my white cane, while in many ways a helpful tool, was also a liability. Like a neon sign, it announced my vulnerability to all would-be assailants. It identified me as easy prey for the human predator.

I need protection, I thought.

That day, I decided to apply for a Seeing Eye dog.

In July 1986, I received notice that I had been accepted for the fall term at the Seeing Eye in Morristown, New Jersey. I would have to miss Geneva's wedding, but she understood. We would try to see each other sometime during my stay in New Jersey.

The rest of the summer passed quickly. I continued with my studies at the Braille Institute and underwent surgery to successfully relieve the seizures that had troubled me since the accident. On weekends, I traveled to Covina to visit my family.

Excitement at the old manor house was running high. Laddie's wife Jean was expecting twins. Mama, proud and filled with anticipation, seemed well; and Laddie was more content than I had ever known him to be. Bryan, at three and a half, was a delight to all of us, but for me he was a source of special joy.

Affectionate and gentle, Bryan was a brilliant child who had learned to read before the age of three. He seemed at times a very somber little boy, too much aware, too often troubled by adult matters. My blindness disturbed him deeply, and I often sensed his sadness. Many times, he sat in my lap and caressed my face, his childish gestures almost an act of mourning for my lost eyesight.

A few days before I was to leave for New Jersey, I traveled to the villa for a last visit. Bryan, listening to the grown-up conversation around him, understood where I was going and that I would be gone for a while. As though the impact of my blindness had suddenly struck him, he crawled up into my lap and placed his hands on my cheeks, exclaiming, "Oh, Aunt Mitty, how ever will you see the world now that your eyes are broken?"

Silence dropped into the room. I could not think of what to say. Moments passed. I heard Mama sigh and Laddie cough. Then, a faint memory stirred. I remembered sitting close to Mama in the swing at the old brick house on Center Street. I remembered the sweet ritual of twilight time, when Mama's voice became a symphony of all things grand and mysterious, when magic could be found in the pages of a child's story book. And I knew the answer to Bryan's question could be found there, where I had first begun to understand the meaning of wonder.

"Bryan," I said softly, "there once was a prince who tamed a fox. It was not an easy thing to do, you know, but the little prince was on a quest."

Bryan snuggled close to me, resting his head on my shoulder. "What kind of quest?" he asked.

"He was searching for the secret of what is truly important in life. Now the fox was very wise, Bryan. He was able to tell the little prince the secret."

"What was the secret, Aunt Mitty?"

"It was a very simple secret, really. This is what he told the prince: 'It is only with the heart that one can see rightly; what is essential is invisible to the eye.'" [1]

I could imagine Bryan's somber face brightening with comprehension. His little head nodded against my shoulder.

"That is my secret too, Bryan. Now that my eyes are broken, I shall see the world with my heart."

The story lodged itself in Bryan's heart. From that day forward, he introduced me to his friends by saying, "This is my Aunt Mitty. Her eyes are broken, so she sees the world with her heart."

On October 2, 1986, I arrived in Morristown, New Jersey. Quaint and picturesque, the community is proud that it has been home to the famous Seeing Eye institute since 1929. Its residents are accustomed to seeing blind people and their dogs walking the streets with their trainers, practicing the disciplines necessary to mold them into an efficient team.

Deliberately ignoring the rule that stipulated only two bags per student, I arrived for my month-long stay at the institute with eight suitcases. While I was still busy unpacking, a staff member offered to show me the laundry facilities. Surprised, I asked, "Why, whatever for?"

"You'll be here a month, Miss Collinsworth," the woman said. "Surely you'll need to do some laundry, won't you?"

"Oh, you don't understand," I answered in my best Southern belle whine, "I don't do laundry. I never learned to do it when I could see, and I certainly do not intend to learn to do it now. Don't you have a laundry service?"

"Miss Collinsworth," she responded, "in our entire sixty-year history, none of our students has ever used a laundry service."

"Then I will be the first," I answered.

"I suppose we could call one of the laundry services in the town," she said. "It will be expensive, but if you're willing to pay for it, I suppose the institute has no objections."

I'd been there less than an hour and already I had disturbed the system. I had created a domestic crisis. I asked for directions to the nearest telephone.

"Mama!" I whispered into the phone, "what should I do? They want me to do my own laundry. If I'm willing to pay the cost of a laundry service in the town, they said I could send it out."

"Sweetheart, don't be a fool," Mama answered. "Just pay for it."

And so I did.

My second day was less disruptive. A trainer led me into a room and presented me with a black, male labrador retriever. He was one year old, and his name was Eeyore.

"Call your dog, Miss Collinsworth," the trainer instructed me, placing me across the room and several feet away from the large dog that awaited my command.

"Eeyore, come!" I called.

Instantly, Eeyore bounded toward me. His warm tongue bathed my hands, and when I petted him, I felt his entire body sway with the forceful rhythm of his wagging tail. I dropped to my knees and pulled him into my arms. Laughing, I realized that, in a single moment of introduction, this beautiful black beast had robbed me of my heart with little more than a lick and a whimper.

The next four weeks were grueling. Under the stern eye of our trainer, Eeyore and I learned how to work together to navigate through streets, hallways, crowded rooms, and open fields. We traversed every kind of environment on the surface of the planet. At night I fell into bed, exhausted, with every muscle aching and my left hand blistered from the tug of Eeyore's harness.

Each night, I broke the rules of the institute and invited Eeyore up onto my bed to sleep beside me. I swore my roommate, Annie, to secrecy, and I fell asleep in the darkness with his warm body lying close to mine.

Annie was a willing accomplice to my misdeeds at the institute. Irreverent and fun-loving, Annie was the one lighthearted presence in an otherwise rigid, somewhat harsh environment. Besides not tattling on me for sleeping with Eeyore, she pretended not to notice my frequent visits to the bathroom after meals. She ignored the sounds of gagging behind the closed doors, and I was able to practice my ritual of vomiting after meals without any unwanted interference.

Annie had been diagnosed congenitally blind since birth, but her disease was progressive. She still had quite a bit of residual sight, and she became my color commentator at the Seeing Eye, whispering to me, telling me about everything she could see with her limited vision, vividly describing the wide, gracious hallways and the antique furnishings of the institute. She stood me in front of tapestries and paintings and told me their colors and designs. One day, she paused next to a piece of furniture and, giggling, she said, "Reach down and feel this, Millicent."

Placing my hands on the delicate legs of a mahogany table, she led my fingers over the wood.

"Can you feel it?" she asked.

As my fingers roved over the carved shape, I could feel tiny, sharp indentations—the tooth marks of generations of Seeing Eye puppies that had broken their training while sniffing through these halls.

Often, during the four weeks of my training, I awakened in the night, terrified that something had happened to Eeyore. I checked his breathing to make sure he was still alive. I had come so far to get him, and I had fallen in love with him instantly. My trainer had impressed on me the urgency of caring for my guide dog as carefully as if he were a human being.

"His well-being is completely dependent upon you," I'd been told.

I was terrified I would fail this gentle, intelligent animal and somehow, I would lose him. Already I could not imagine my life without him.

Before my month of training ended, Geneva and Ernie came from Princeton to visit me at the institute. Proudly, I introduced them to Eeyore, and together we toured the grounds of the Seeing Eye. Eeyore pulled on his harness, forcing me to walk at a brisk pace, and both Geneva and Ernie followed, almost jogging, panting as they tried to keep up with us.

The joy of life overwhelmed me that day.

I'm free! I thought, elated.

Eeyore, magnificent and strong, walked ahead of me, pulling me along, setting a course around obstacles that once would have tripped me and thrown me to the ground.

My friends ran behind me, trying to catch me!

Ah, life was good. Life was wonderful.

Halfway through my training, Mama called to tell me that I had two new nephews, Scott Price Collinsworth and Seth Mackenzie Collinsworth. I began counting the days until I could take Eeyore and go home to California.

My last challenge before leaving the Seeing Eye was to spend a day in New York City, navigating the streets and riding the subways with only Eeyore to guide me. A trainer would follow at a distance, I was told.

"You will not know where the trainer is," an instructor said, as I prepared for my odyssey into the city. "He will not interfere unless he sees that your physical safety is threatened. You will depend solely on your dog. If you get lost, it is for you and your dog to figure out how to get back to the institute. The trainer will not help you. He is there only to be sure your life is not in danger."

It was the ultimate test of trust between dog and master, the final exam before I could graduate and return to California to resume my life. I was both excited and a little apprehensive.

Eeyore and I made our excursion into the city on a cold, rainy November day. We were standing on a corner at a busy intersection in Manhattan, drenched and freezing, when a man's voice spoke next to me.

"Miss, have you ever thought about acting?"

I turned toward the voice, wondering if I had heard correctly.

"Your animal is magnificent, and you're quite attractive too," the man said. "Together, you make an extraordinary team. Did you know that the television and movie industries are hiring more and more disabled people these days? And you certainly do have the 'look.'"

The "look?" Thoughts of Felicia flitted through my mind, and I almost laughed.

Smiling, I stammered my thanks and, pocketing his business card, I turned my attention back to the task of navigating through the city with Eeyore. Several hours later, after only a few unplanned "detours," Eeyore and I arrived back in Morristown, New Jersey, feeling exhausted but triumphant. A few days later, we flew home to Los Angeles, successful graduates of the Seeing Eye.

Back home in California, I couldn't stop thinking about the business card in my coat pocket. I hadn't decided what my next career move should be since leaving Felicia, and I kept wondering if it was possible I could once again find a place in the field of performance. It had been a long time since I had been in front of an audience and a television camera, but I remembered the thrill of it. I made a few inquiries and located an acting class in neighboring Bel Air. A week later I enrolled in a workshop that trained disabled actors, pairing them with able-bodied actors who already worked within the industry.

The first day of class I was as nervous as a kindergartner. Grasping Eeyore's harness, I drew a deep breath and entered the classroom, uncertain of what I would find and how I would be accepted. Inside, about twenty adults milled about, talking and laughing, and within minutes I knew I had found a very special place.

After a few classes, the acting coach assigned me to work on a scene with an able-bodied actor named Gary Krantz. Gary's deep, resonant voice seemed to travel down to me from a lofty height, so I knew he was a very tall man. Gentle in manner, he seemed quite shy, and he spoke very little, except to rehearse his part with me. A few days later, however, he was very friendly when I ran into him at a neighborhood grocery store.

Eeyore and I had just entered the store to embark on our first team shopping expedition. An employee approached us near the doorway to offer us his help. "We'd like to do this by ourselves, if you don't mind," I told him. And then I promised, "If I break something, I'll gladly pay for it."

I didn't need to be able to see to know that the store personnel and all the customers were watching us as we made our way through the produce section, into the bakery, and on through each aisle, loading our grocery basket. I had memorized the layout of the store and had very little trouble locating the items I needed, and when I pulled my cart up to the cashier to check out, the entire store began applauding.

A beautiful male voice spoke from a place just above my head. "That was terrific."

Looking up, I smiled, hoping my eyes had located the face that belonged to the voice.

"I'm Gary Krantz. You may not remember me, but I'm in

your acting class. We've done a few scenes together."

"Of course I remember you," I said, thinking the cadence of his voice was lovely.

"I've always wanted to talk to you after class," he went on, "but I wasn't sure what to say."

Picking up my groceries, Gary walked out of the store with Eeyore and me. "May I walk you home?" he asked.

It was the first of many walks and the beginning of a quiet, easy friendship. Gary began coming to my apartment on Saturdays to help me hang pictures or repair light fixtures and tend to whatever else needed doing. On Sunday afternoons we rented a tandem bike and rode together in the park while Eeyore, on his leash, ran alongside us. On cold evenings, Gary read aloud to me while we snuggled in front of the fireplace. Before many months passed, our friendship grew into love.

I wasn't at all surprised. Gary's presence in my life was one more verse in the chorus of grace.

In recent months, I had begun to pray: "Dear Heavenly Father, please send a very special man into my life."

Whenever I prayed that prayer, I thought of my great-great-great-great-grandmother, Alice Thompson Collinsworth. Her story was a favorite of Mama's, and Mama's dramatic telling of it had made it a favorite of mine as well. Alice had been only a teenager when, in the winter of 1792, her family's log cabin was attacked by a party of Creek Indians. Before the Indians dragged her away, she watched them slaughter her parents and her sister.

A terrifying journey took her to a village along the banks of the Tallapoosa River, where she was forced to live as a slave among the Creek nation. Every day her captors beat her to ensure that she remain submissive and servile. Using thorny briar branches, they bloodied her back and her legs, reminding her that she was not only a captive and a slave, but a hated enemy.

Throughout her captivity, Alice's relatives in Tennessee tried to ransom her from the Indians, but every offer was rejected. Finally, after two years, an Irish trader bargained with the Creek and convinced them to trade her life for eight hundred pounds of deer skins. Their value: two hundred sixty-six dollars. Family legend says that the trader placed Alice on a white horse and took her across the wilderness to a fort on the site of what would later become the city of Nashville.

An adventurer named Edmund Collinsworth was among the curious crowd at the fort on the day Alice and the trapper arrived.

He was captivated by the beauty and courage of the young woman astride the white horse, and he fell instantly in love with her.

"He didn't see her scars," Mama said. "He saw the beauty of her courage, and everything else seemed unimportant. He loved her, and that was all that mattered."

"Dear Heavenly Father," I prayed, "I have made so many foolish decisions. I pray that this time you would choose the man who will be my husband. I pray that he might be someone like my great-great-great-great-grandfather, Edmund. A man who will fall in love with my courage. A man who will not see my scars."

And in December 1986, I met Gary. Soft-spoken, Chicago-born Gary had come to California to pursue his dream of acting, although there was nothing "Hollywood" about him. A graduate of Ohio State University, he had a degree in logistics, but his passion for acting had drawn him west. Forthright and solid, his approach to life was practical and very matter-of-fact, but along with his Midwestern mind-set, he possessed a romantic, loving nature.

I didn't hide anything from Gary. I told him all the grisly stories that littered my past. I told him about the horrors of my childhood and the later suicide attempts. I told him about my years in therapy and my ongoing struggle with bulimia. And Gary's response was, "I love you, Millicent."

Scars and all, Gary loved me. Not the woman I aspired to be, nor the woman I used to be, but the woman I had become and the woman I would emerge into as the years passed. He loved me exactly as I was.

It didn't take long for the power of unconditional love to begin to work its sweet healing inside me. For the first time in almost thirty years, my obsessive craving for food subsided a bit. My habits began to change. When stress attacked and I was tempted to relieve it by eating, I felt safe in choosing other sources of comfort.

Gary, slender and fit and very serious about physical health, encouraged me to exercise instead of eating. He taught me the benefits of sound nutrition as opposed to crash dieting. And he continually reminded me that I was lovable, that I was loved. The bingeing and purging didn't stop instantly, but for the first time, I began to believe that I could win the battle with bulimia.

With every act and every conversation, Gary affirmed me, convincing me that I was valuable, that I was worthwhile. I began to believe him; I began to see myself as someone of worth, and the anger that had suffused me for so many decades began to dissipate. And the damaging grip of bulimia nervosa seemed to be loosening its hold on me.

Five months after our meeting in the grocery store, Gary asked me to marry him.

"I don't want to live with you, Millicent," he said. "I don't want an affair. I want marriage and everything that goes with it."

I knew my prayer had been answered. We planned a New Year's Eve wedding.

Happier than I had ever been, I didn't think anything could mar my blissful state. I didn't think anything could destroy this contentment that was so new to me, but one morning, while I was walking home from the store, violence shattered my sense of well-being.

My arms were full of groceries when a hand shoved me from behind, slamming my face into a chain-link fence. I dropped the groceries and, while Eeyore barked fiercely, an urgent voice commanded, "Give me that!" The attacker jerked my purse strap off my shoulder and ran away, leaving Eeyore and me standing on the sidewalk, surrounded by smashed eggs, broken glass, and crushed fruit.

With shaking hands, I grasped Eeyore's harness and we made our way home. Gary rushed to my apartment as soon as I sobbed out my story over the phone. After his rage over the incident spent itself, he began to think rationally about precautions we could take to ensure my safety.

"Millicent, we've got to do something," he said. "You can't continue to be so vulnerable in public places. We will both become hostages to fear. Maybe it would be a good idea to move you into an apartment that's more secure."

A few days later, Gary helped me move into a high-rise apartment complex in the Hollywood hills where a security guard toured the premises twenty-four hours a day.

I felt safe in my new home, but I couldn't stop feeling like prey whenever I ventured outside. I dreaded leaving the apartment compound. I knew my handicap made me an easy target for violence, but I had believed that Eeyore's presence would be a deterrent. It was startling as well as terrifying to discover that, even with a large black dog as my companion, I was not safe from criminal attacks.

The air in Los Angeles was thick with smog on June 1, 1987, when Eeyore and I boarded a city bus in Westwood for the ride across town to the apartment in the Hollywood hills. The combination of heat, humidity, and standing room only made the bus feel like a furnace. I sat down in the first seat I came to and Eeyore lay down on the floor between my feet. At each stop, more people climbed on the already bulging bus, and finally, from the back of the bus, a man shouted, "I can't breathe! I can't breathe! Let me out of here!"

Panicked, the man pushed through the throng that stood in the aisle, forcing the crowd to let him pass. As he stepped near my seat, his fist struck out and collided with my face. My head snapped back and, with stunning force, the left side of my face and my ear slammed into a steel pole. Screams and curses erupted as other passengers, now in a panic, stepped on one another and collided with each other in a frenzied rush of pandemonium.

Eeyore! I thought, suddenly terrified for him. He was trapped beneath my seat, his leash and harness clamped under someone's foot, and the leash was strangling him. Frantic, I pushed against the bodies that crowded me and bent down to free him. A booted foot cracked against my jaw, and I fell to my knees on the floor.

The commotion grew even more chaotic as the bus continued to speed down Sunset Boulevard. Sobbing, I yanked on Eeyore's harness with all my strength. When it came loose in my hands, I stood up, pressing against the crowd, forcing my way into the aisle. When the bus finally stopped and the door opened, I thrust my body toward it, feeling Eeyore against my legs, and together we staggered down the steps and onto the street.

Trembling with both anger and terror, I knelt down beside Eeyore and ran my hands over his body to make sure he was not badly hurt. His whimpers quieted and, when I stood up, he began limping down the sidewalk, pulling me behind him.

My face wet with what I thought were tears, I followed Eeyore's slow pace, uncertain of exactly where he was taking me. We had escaped from the heated furor on the bus, but I had no idea where we had been when we got off. I had no idea what cross streets were near. I had no idea whether we were headed toward home or whether we were moving farther and farther off course with every step.

For what seemed like hours, Eeyore pulled me along. My face continued to feel wet, and then to my horror, I realized my clothing was soaked as well. Blood was dripping from my mouth and my nose, and the entire front of my blouse was drenched with it, but still we walked down Sunset Boulevard, a limping guide dog and his bloodied master.

I could hear the noise of pedestrians all around me as Eeyore and I made our way down the street. In the delirium of fear, I couldn't ask for help, I couldn't ask for directions. I could only grasp Eeyore's harness and hang on as, haltingly, he drew me along behind him. Fifteen blocks later, I recognized the sloping terrain. I knew we were close to home. Eeyore pulled me up a steep hill and, with bloodied hands, I fumbled with my key and finally opened the apartment door. I reached the phone and dialed Gary's phone number before collapsing on the floor.

Neighbors passing my apartment noticed bloodstains on my door. Panicking, they summoned the building manager and the police. I awoke to the sound of frantic voices and, moments later, Gary burst in with the paramedics. An ambulance drove me to the UCLA Medical Center.

In the hospital, doctors closed the gash in my lip with nine stitches and advised me to see a dentist about the back molar that had been knocked out of its socket. I learned that my throbbing jaw was dislocated and that the blow to my head had caused permanent deafness in my left ear.

Lying on a gurney in the emergency room, I reached out for Gary's hand. Through swollen lips, I asked, "How's Eeyore, Gary? Is he all right?"

"Eeyore's fine, Millicent. He's just fine. And you're going to be fine too. I promise. Everything is going to be all right."

His lips close to my bruised and aching face, he whispered again softly, "I promise you, Millicent. Everything is going to be all right."

1. "The Little Prince," by Antoine de Saint-Exupéry, page 70.

Chapter 15

The account of my injuries on the bus outraged my neighbors. Dan Schwab, who had led the charge into my apartment after seeing blood smears on my door, called the *Los Angeles Times* to report the incident. I had never met this man, but he was furious at the city's insensitivity to an injured citizen; he was appalled that a blind woman, bleeding from the face, had walked fifteen blocks through the "City of Angels," guided by a limping Seeing Eye dog, and not one of the thousands of pedestrians who passed her on Sunset Boulevard had stopped to offer assistance.

Within hours of my release from the hospital, a reporter from the *Times* called me, asking for an interview. My first response was to say no.

"The whole incident is embarrassing," I said. "Why would I want to make my humiliation public? Tell the entire city how helpless and vulnerable I am?"

I haven't even called to tell my own mother what has happened! I don't want to upset her, I'd thought. I don't want to give her more reasons to worry about me.

The reporter didn't give up easily. She would slant the story to be an indictment against a community insensitive toward its disabled citizens, she said, and she would showcase the courage and intelligence of an injured Seeing Eye dog. Finally, reluctantly, I agreed.

Arriving soon with a photographer, the reporter asked questions and listened while I gave her my account of the chaos on the bus and the long walk through the city streets.

"Do you mind if the photographer takes a picture of you both?" she asked, when I introduced her to Eeyore.

I was mortified at the idea of appearing in a photo with my face battered and stitched, but Eeyore deserved the spotlight, so again, I agreed.

Snapping shut her notebook, the reporter stood up and thanked me. "This might make a small human interest story," she said as she left. "Look for it in the 'Metro' section of the paper."

The next morning, when Gary unfolded his copy of the *Los Angeles Times*, my picture stared up at him from the front page.

"Honey," he shouted as he rushed into my apartment, "you'd better call your mother. You've just made the front page of the *Times*."

It was six in the morning. Mama would be opening her newspaper soon. I had to call and prepare her, reassure her that I was all right. I started toward the phone, but before I reached it, it began ringing. And for the next eight months, it continued to ring nonstop.

The intercom in the lobby buzzed constantly as reporters and news teams came seeking interviews. The three major television networks, as well as smaller local channels and radio stations, asked me to appear on their shows. Terry Drinkwater interviewed me on the *CBS Evening News*. Asked about the trek down Sunset Boulevard with Eeyore, and why no one had offered to help me, I answered, "I may be blind, but the world has become emotionally blind. It is blind to the plight of the disabled."

My very private life as a blind woman had suddenly turned very public. I found myself thrust into the role of a spokesperson for the needs of the disabled.

The schedule was dizzying, but I couldn't say no. Each television appearance, each radio show afforded me an opportunity to point out the difficulties that the disabled individual encounters every day. In answer to the questions of talk-show hosts, I spoke about the extreme vulnerability of the disabled, using my own situation as only one example. Many thousands more could have been cited as well—examples of individuals who had been ignored or overlooked because of their particular impairment.

In response to my story, every day for weeks truckloads of flowers arrived at my front door, sent by well-wishers from as far away as Ireland, England, Australia, and New Zealand. A family from Hawaii, visiting California when the story appeared on the news, took a five-hundred-dollar check to my lawyer, Janet Gullixson. (I donated the money to a charity.)

School children sent get-well letters and cards to both Eeyore and me. The Society for the Prevention of Cruelty to Animals called to say that Eeyore was to be named "Hero Dog of the Year." They planned a ceremony to present him with a plaque and a citation for bravery, along with a gift of one hundred dollars.

From every corner of the city and from several different continents, people offered their assurances that the safety and well-being of one blind woman in California did indeed matter. Thousands may have passed me on Sunset Boulevard one day, deliberately blind to my injuries, but many thousands more were outraged by such behavior, and every day I was overwhelmed by their generous outpouring of concern.

Off-duty policemen from local departments called to volunteer their services as chauffeurs, offering to drive me anywhere I needed to go in the city. A stranger sent me a hundred dollars worth of taxi vouchers. Dozens of people called, asking if I needed a ride to the store, wanting to help me with my shopping. And for Eeyore, doggy treats and toys arrived almost daily.

Because of the barrage of publicity, I discovered that I could not leave my apartment without being recognized. In restaurants, the management often approached me to say that complete strangers had recognized me and had paid for my lunch. Out in public, well-wishers often walked up to me and, pressing flowers into my hands, whispered, "I saw you on television... I'm so very sorry."

Each gesture, each apology, each evidence of caring seemed to be an effort to compensate for the gross negligence of those who had not cared. And each expression of kindness continued to astound me. Why should so many people concern themselves with me? The answer was simple: People, huge numbers of people, wanted to go on record as saying that apathy offends them; that the human community does in fact believe that goodness matters; and that, in spite of the behavior of some, thousands more across the globe do still value human kindness over cruelty.

Eeyore and I were featured in several major publications such as *People*, as well as in tabloids like *The Star*. Women's magazines called and asked for interviews. At Janet's law office, her staff was inundated with calls for me, requesting personal appearances.

Gary and I were amazed at the way the public had taken hold of my story. Hollywood, especially, had taken notice of me because, in the first story that ran in the *Times*, the reporter had written that I was studying acting. The headlines had read, "Unemployed Blind Actress Hurt on Bus!"

Gary and I had laughed when we first read it, thinking how "Hollywood" it sounded. But as the story grew, gaining momentum throughout the country, I became quite embarrassed. I hadn't yet worked as an actress, at least not since college. But I was studying the craft, and that had seemed like a good answer when the reporter asked me, "How do you spend your days, Miss Collinsworth?"

How could I tell her that, like most other blind individuals, I spent many hours alone in my home, listening to the drone of the television, held hostage by my own darkness? After being mugged and robbed of my groceries, I made few excursions out alone. I attended acting classes with Gary and practiced what I learned, but lately, I had felt little inclination to leave home. And job opportunities, through the State Rehabilitative Services, had been dismal.

Only weeks before the incident on the bus, I had met with a caseworker who tried to convince me to go live for six months at the Rehabilitation School for the Blind.

"You'll learn the special skills needed to equip you to reenter the work force," she'd told me. "You'll be in a dorm room with three others, but you will be allowed to keep your guide dog."

The thought of being incarcerated for six months sent a rise of bile up into my throat.

"I have skills for the workplace," I had answered. "I don't need to be locked up for six months."

"Miss Collinsworth, it is obvious to me that you have not yet come to grips with the enormity of your disability." I had heard irritation in the caseworker's voice. "Tell me," she'd said, "just what kind of prospects do you think you have?"

"I have owned my own business in the past," I'd told her. "I've been an executive for an international conglomerate. I've been a teacher and a choreographer. I have a degree in recreational therapy and a background in public relations, promotions, and marketing. I don't feel that there is really anything I can't do," I'd said. "I simply need the opportunity to try."

The caseworker had laughed. "Do you know what our rehabilitation program trains blind people to do?" she'd asked, chuckling without mirth. "The vast majority of you people are retrained to do menial factory work. If you show some promise, we might be able to train you to become a data processor. If not, you can learn to tie brooms."

Anger had burned inside me that day. As Eeyore and I had stood to leave the office, the caseworker had said, "Let me offer you one piece of advice, Miss Collinsworth: Your life as a blind woman will be a lot easier if you can face the world looking a lot less attractive and acting a bit more humble."

Act a bit more humble? Just because I can't see? My blindness has not made me less of a woman! It has changed me, yes, but it has not diminished me. Nothing could dilute the pride of generations of Collinsworths.

Many times after that miserable interview with the caseworker, I thought about a comment made by my roommate, Annie, at the Seeing Eye.

"Have you ever noticed," she'd asked, "how many of our fellow students here at the institute hold masters degrees and Ph.Ds? And yet, the majority of our number are unemployed. Think about it, Millicent," she had said. "The tragedy of the blind in America is that we're all dressed up and have no place to go."

It was true. The day I had spoken with the reporter, I was indeed all dressed up, with a college degree and an impressive resumé, but I had no place to go. And so I spent a few hours every week in acting classes, hoping to find a new outlet for my creative abilities, hoping to discover a future for myself that offered something more than an assembly line. Something more satisfying than tying brooms.

Shortly after the release of the story of the fracas on the bus, Hollywood opened its arms to the "blind unemployed actress." Theatrical agencies called my lawyer and asked to represent me. Ken Kragen, along with several other famous managers and producers, called to interview me, asking if I was interested in auditioning for a part in an upcoming miniseries with Kenny Rogers.

Jay Bernstein, who had discovered Farrah Fawcett and Suzanne Sommers, offered me a part in his television series, *Houston Knights*. The story would be an adaptation of the bus incident, entitled "Moving Violation."

"I want her to guest star as herself," he told my lawyer, Janet. "It will be the season's opening episode."

Without asking if I could act, he wrote me into the script. Overnight, I went from being unemployed to being a member of the Screen Actors Guild.

A publicity genius, Jay Bernstein sent me out on a promotional tour with his two young actors from the series, Michael Pare and Michael Beck. Together we appeared on Gary Collins' *Hour Magazine. Entertainment Tonight,* along with *Good Morning, America* and CNN's *Show Biz Today,* visited the set of *Houston Knights,* and once again my story went out on the airwaves.

The day we were to begin shooting, Mr. Bernstein ordered a white limousine to drive me to the studio. Greeted by a bouquet of flowers, wine, and a basket of fruit in my dressing room—as if I were really a star—I began my first day on the set. As shooting began, executives from CBS and Columbia Pictures, as well as the press, crowded the sound stage. None of the crew, nor the director, nor the other actors had ever worked with a blind actor. I knew they were all curious—some might have been nervous—but each scene ran smoothly.

After a week of filming, when the director declared, "That's a wrap," I was sorry to see it all end. The hours of study, memorizing lines and cues and movements, placement on the sets—all of it had been very exciting. I felt stimulated, challenged. I knew I would never return to the State Rehabilitative Services. I knew I would never make brooms.

As the publicity furor over the bus incident faded, I expected my place in the spotlight to fade as well, but interest continued to run high, particularly among groups that represented the rights of the nation's largest minority, the disabled. I continued to receive invitations to address the unique challenges and the special needs of the disabled community. And people listened.

The months after the bus incident passed quickly, filled with speaking engagements, television appearances, magazine interviews, and multiple doctor's appointments and examinations. The damage to my jaw was more serious than it had first appeared. Excruciating pain and stiffness made eating and speaking difficult. Sometimes my jaw locked and could only be unlocked by emergency medical treatment. I learned that a series of operations would be needed to repair my jaw and eliminate the pain.

Throughout the remainder of the summer and on into the winter of 1987, while under constant medical care, I continued with my acting classes, auditioned for parts, and landed a few jobs along the way. And Gary and I began planning our wedding.

Geneva invited us to be married in her home in Princeton. It would be a simple ceremony; I wanted no crowds and pageantry, no Currier and Ives production this time. But set against the splendor of Geneva and Ernie's home, I knew the wedding would be lovely.

Geneva and Ernie lived in a large, gracious house in an exclusive suburb of Princeton. She had decorated with antiques, rich oriental carpets, original paintings, and valuable art objects. With Gary beside me to describe every detail, I walked through her house, room by room.

This suits her, I thought, as I touched the cool surface of a cherry-wood table. I could hear Geneva and Ernie laughing together in the kitchen, and I thought, how happy she is. Her life as the wife of an eminently successful businessman was very different from that of a Hollywood manicurist; but then, Geneva had never really belonged in the false and glittery world of Hollywood. Her sojourn in California had been a detour, nothing more. She had been terribly out of place in the salon, working among pampered socialites, surrounded by mirrors and artifice. But here, in this lovely home in New Jersey, Geneva's Southern roots had found welcome in Northern soil, and she was thriving.

On a snowy New Year's Eve, 1987, Gary and I were married in Geneva's living room. Amid baskets of poinsettias and flickering candles, Eeyore gave me away. His teeth biting the handle of a small blue basket that held our wedding rings, he led me across the floor to stand next to the immense Christmas tree that dominated the room. Wearing a midnight-blue velvet dress and carrying a branch of dogwood, I took my place at Gary's side and breathed in the familiar scent of his after-shave. When he took my hand and placed it in the crook of his arm, I grasped the warm, rough wool of his navy blue suit and silently vowed never to let go of this remarkable, gentle man. His beautiful voice was resonant when he spoke his vows to me.

All my life I had prided myself on my rigid control, my careful metering of tears, but on the day I married Gary, I cried throughout the ceremony. The enormity of my vows overwhelmed me. I was a woman of forty, and only lately had I come to understand the meaning of love. I understood the promises I was making. This time, they were more than a script for a lavish production.

I could feel Gary's steady gaze on my face. I sensed the intensity of his love for me. It seemed to emanate from him as we stood together, his arm touching my shoulder.

"You would never have been attracted to me if you'd had your eyesight, Millicent," Gary told me once. "You'd never have even known I was in the room."

Tall, slender, ordinary, he described himself. Not powerful-looking, or gorgeous. Just ordinary. Blue eyes, brown hair, and not conventionally handsome, and very, very shy.

"I'm sure I would never have had the courage to approach you if you hadn't been blind. You're not the kind of woman who would want to go out with such an ordinary man."

I remember thinking, There is nothing ordinary about you, Gary Krantz. You are the most extraordinary man I've ever met.

The minister said, "You may kiss the bride," and my life as Gary's wife began with a sweetness that was almost painful.

After a short honeymoon at the Nassau Inn in Princeton and a few days in New York City, we returned to Los Angeles and started our life as marriage partners.

I was obsessive about being a good wife to Gary. I wanted to do everything I could to show him how much I loved him. I didn't want him to ever regret that he had chosen a wife with a disability. I set out to prove that I could do anything any other wife could do. I could even iron his shirts.

I had always insisted on a laundry service in the past, but suddenly, foolishly, I believed this was something I needed to do. For Gary. Never mind that for many years he had taken care of himself quite admirably. I wanted this job, if for no other reason than to prove to myself that I could be a "proper" wife.

"I can do this," I protested, when Gary tried to talk me out of ironing his shirts.

"Sit still," he commanded, as he smeared balm on my burned fingers. "From now on, I'll do the ironing."

"No, you will not," I argued. "I'll do it."

It was our first squabble—a minor one—and Gary gave in good-naturedly. "All right," he agreed, kissing my forehead lightly, "you can iron the shirts."

That was too easy, I thought. And I continued to iron and Gary continued to apply burn ointment to my blisters. And he began crawling out of bed at about four in the morning several days a week.

"Aren't you sleeping well?" I asked, as he left the bed one morning while it was still dark.

"I'm fine," he mumbled. "Go back to sleep."

A few days later, I awoke again just as he was creeping out of the bedroom. Quietly, I followed the sounds of activity and discovered him in the laundry room. The "shsshing" sound of escaping steam told me he was re-ironing the shirts I had ironed the day before.

Silently, I crept back to our room, overwhelmed at the lengths to which he would go to ensure that my dignity was preserved.

I promised to find myself another domestic chore better suited to my abilities. From now on, I would let Gary iron his own shirts.

A long-time bachelor before our marriage, Gary was already

adept at the household chores. He was quick to take over the daily routine, but intuitively he knew I needed to feel a part of this team effort. We divided the chores between us, but Gary usually did double duty. If I dusted the furniture, he came along later and dusted it again, quietly and without criticism, catching the dust I couldn't see. If I washed the dishes, he dried them and then often washed them again, never telling me how many dirty ones he found in the cupboard. I let him load the clothes in the washer and dryer, and he gave me the stack of warm, clean laundry to fold. With every act, Gary helped me feel that I was a valuable, contributing member of the team effort. And together we laughed over my mistakes.

Gary learned quickly that I needed a very regimented lifestyle, as do all victims of brain injury. I needed structure, not spontaneity, and it became his daily task to see that I face as little stress as possible.

In a delightful twist of irony, the actor's life turned out to be perfectly suited to my needs. In an environment where every step is planned, every word chosen and memorized, every action directed, I found little reason for stress. I felt secure onstage, where I could move about without hesitation because I had memorized the location of every piece of furniture and every prop. I felt comfortable in each scene, safe enough to allow myself to venture into the farthest regions of my creativity, safe enough on stage or in front of a camera to act with freedom. There, under the heat of the lights, I could indulge in spontaneity that was too risky for me in any other setting.

I had never been so happy. Not only was my marriage a source of joy, but I was beginning to find good work as an actress. Among the more than 87,000 members of the Screen Actors Guild, I was one of only six blind actors who was actually working. When Gary and I were cast together in a production of *Wait Until Dark*, I was thrilled. The female lead portrays a blind woman, and for the first time ever, a blind actor was cast in the role.

Not long after that production ended, Al Burton, the producer of such hit shows as *Lassie, Different Strokes, Facts Of Life,* and *Charles In Charge,* offered me a role that any disabled actor would have killed for. A pioneer when it came to the rights of the disabled, Al Burton was famous for doing the unheard of in his television series. Defying Hollywood's prejudice toward handicapped actors, he set a precedent by casting disabled actors in dignified and responsible roles. When he cast me in a sighted role as a newspaper reporter opposite Scott Baio in the series *Charles In Charge*, he made television history. The show was filmed before a studio audience. Not until the taping was finished and the cast was taking final bows did the producers introduce me as a blind actress. Eeyore led me out onto the sound stage and applause vibrated the building.

"It's a standing ovation, Millicent," someone shouted over the roar. "You should see it!"

Late in 1988, Linda Bloodworth-Thomason contacted me. The producer of *Designing Women*, *Evening Shade*, and *Hearts Afire*, Linda had already established herself as one of Hollywood's most creative and powerful women. She had earned a reputation for dealing with important and sometimes controversial issues in her programs, and she had in mind a *Designing Women* episode that would address the growing problem of violence toward women. Responding to the fact that one in three American women will be assaulted or raped during her lifetime, Linda had an episode written titled "Stand and Fight." She invited me to be a guest star.

"Do you think you could portray a self-defense instructor?" Linda asked me.

"I can portray anything if I'm given the chance to train," I answered.

It was to be an acting job. That was all. I would learn some moves in order to portray a self-defense instructor in front of the camera. I could never have envisioned that a simple acting job would so completely, and so irreversibly, change my life.

Mozark Productions, Ms. Bloodworth-Thomason's company, sent me to train with a self-defense group called Impact. This organization had developed an innovative, if somewhat controversial, self-defense technique designed especially for women. The instructors were a little uncertain about teaching me. "We've never trained a blind person before," they said. "We're not entirely sure you'll be able to grasp the technique, let alone implement it."

Just watch me, I thought, determined once again to prove that I could do anything a sighted woman could do. The technique would push me to the limits of my physical and mental abilities.

The technique was based on skills used in the martial arts, but the most powerful aspect of the program was its ability to give women a sense of power. Rather than feeling defenseless and vulnerable when attacked, women trained by Impact learned to fight back. They learned to repel their assailants. They learned how not to be victims.

After three private lessons, I was sent to a group class—about twenty women who had gathered in a large basement room of a downtown church.

All ages and races, these women had made the decision to learn to take care of themselves. For six weeks, they would meet and learn strategies, practice moves, participate in drills, and then fight off the heavily padded mock assailants. On this first night together, they sat in a circle and talked about their reasons for taking the Impact course. I listened to some of the women around me say that they wanted to be equipped to protect themselves if ever attacked or raped. Others, sobbing quietly, told of wanting to learn how to keep such atrocities from ever happening to them again.

I listened. The memory of being raped clawed at me, and I felt almost ill as I heard other women give their personal accounts of violence and humiliation. But when it was my turn to speak, I found myself unable to share anything more personal than the account of the already much publicized incident on the bus. I mentioned the need for the disabled to be able to protect themselves, and then I smiled and sat quietly while the rest of the circle shared their private horrors.

I listened stoically, saying nothing. I was there to learn a technique for an acting part. I didn't need to travel the path of abuse once again, pointing out the places where tragedy had occurred. I didn't need to reveal myself so completely.

Week after week, I met with the women and practiced drills. The final drill each week was a mock fight. As one woman stood and fought off an attacker, the rest of the group circled her and cheered her on, shouting encouragement. Standing among the group, I recalled Impact's philosophy: We are therapeutic, but not therapy.

It was true. It was therapeutic to be among so many women who were determined to protect themselves. It was therapeutic to hear the voices of encouragement as small, terrified women became fighting machines, able to down an attacker twice their size. And, for some of the women in the class, it was therapeutic to be able to express the long-suppressed emotions of anger and terror that had gripped them since the day they had been victims of a real episode of violence.

In the first weeks, it was not uncommon for a woman to collapse onto the mats during a simulated mugging or rape.

Sobbing, sometimes hysterical, she was suddenly forgetful of what she had learned, unable to remember how to fight and protect herself. Overwhelmed by terror, she would be paralyzed by the power of her memories. Each time that happened, the circle of women around her began shouting, "Fight for your life! Fight for your life!"

Made strong by the chorus of women's voices, the student would get up and take her stance and fight back.

"You are worth fighting for!" The mantra of Impact echoed off the walls in the building.

Each week, I entered class with mixed emotions. I enjoyed the physical challenge of Impact, but I was miserable during the first half-hour when we had to sit in a circle and talk about ourselves. While I felt great empathy with the experiences of these women, I discovered that I had little patience with the recitation of their troubles. I wanted to get up and begin fighting. I wanted no emotional gyrations.

I quickly became adept at the technique. I practiced the movements in drills with the instructors, and then I stood and fought, repelling attacks by mock assailants dressed in heavily padded clothing and helmets. Yelling, "No," I whirled and spun and kicked and elbowed and jabbed! Finally downing the attacker, I ended the drill by shouting, "911," reinforcing the vital last step which teaches students to go for help immediately.

The *Designing Women* episode, "Stand and Fight," was a resounding success and received the Media Access Award. Not only did it play to a huge national audience, but numerous women's organizations across the country asked to use it as a learning tool. It would make a difference in the lives of thousands of women. It had already made a difference in mine.

I had not been startled to learn that a woman's chances of being attacked were so high; and I was dismayed, but not surprised, to learn that a blind woman is even more likely to be the victim of an assault. Studies show that two out of every three disabled women will be attacked or raped in their lifetime. I had already experienced more than my share of assaults, but I knew it could happen again. If it did, I would be prepared. I would never again be an easy prey.

It wasn't enough for me to have simply learned the technique and played a part. I wanted to learn everything I could about defending myself. After six weeks with Impact, I knew I wanted to go further. Acting would be my primary focus, but I wanted to continue training. I wanted to become an Impact instructor.

Finally, after hundreds of hours of classes, I earned Impact's designation of "Expert" in single assaults, multiple assaults, and assaults with a deadly weapon, becoming the program's first certified, blind/deaf self-defense instructor in the United States.

As an Impact instructor, I traveled and spoke to groups, demonstrating the techniques and conducting seminars on self-defense.

My work with Impact thrust me into the community of adult survivors of domestic violence, incest, rape, and assault. I had to study issues and learn basic counseling techniques as well as physical defense skills. As had happened when I was a student in the classes, I struggled with having to deal with the emotions of the women I taught. It was not easy, but I remained distant from the women in my classes, maintaining emotional boundaries that I allowed no one to cross. The directors of Impact couldn't help but notice.

"Part of the job of an Impact instructor is to provide some nurturing, Millicent," one of the directors said to me. "You're not very good at that, are you?"

Something froze inside me when I had to dig into the emotional issues that were such a big part of Impact's methods. I didn't want to dredge up my own painful past—I felt I had dealt with it and I wanted to move forward, not look backward. I couldn't explain it very well, but my friends at Impact seemed to accept my limitation. As I met with the next group I would take through the six-week program, I learned that I had been assigned a "surrogate nurturer" to work with me.

Now that I didn't have to deal with the emotions of my students, I was more at ease as an instructor. The Impact technique, synchronized and regimented, was as close to dancing as I would ever get again. I reveled in what was like choreography for me and, between acting jobs, I accepted every teaching and demonstrating opportunity I was offered.

My association with Linda Bloodworth-Thomason extended beyond the filming of that one episode for her television series. In the months after the *Designing Women* episode aired, Linda and I grew close, finding we shared a common small-town heritage—she from the Ozarks of Missouri, and I from Searcy, Arkansas.

Since our first meeting on the set of *Designing Women* in 1988, Linda and her husband Harry had included Gary and me in many Mozark Production events. We became a familiar part of their production family, as well as a part of their extended family. Representing Linda at various events was a natural progression for me. When she asked me to take Impact to her hometown, Poplar Bluff, Missouri, in 1990, I was delighted.

A junior high girl had been recently raped and murdered on the outskirts of Poplar Bluff, Linda told us. The entire community was in shock. Responding to the town's horror, Linda offered to provide training in self-defense for its citizens, as many as could be accommodated during our short stay. We would speak to students in local schools, as well as address clubs and community groups. On our first day in Poplar Bluff, we found ourselves in a junior high school auditorium, facing more than five hundred restless students.

The young people had come to the assembly that day to see a "real live television actress." Excited and noisy, they whooped and cheered when Eeyore led me onto the stage. Gary joined me at the podium and together we talked about Impact. After we demonstrated several of the movements that could help them escape an attacker, Gary sat down, leaving me alone in front of the students. As my hands adjusted the microphone, suddenly, for the first time in my life, I felt compelled to talk publicly about Mr. Simpson.

Eeyore sat beside me, his body warm against my legs as I told what it was like to be molested as a child. I spoke about the threats that had kept me silent, about the fear that had paralyzed me.

Silence hung over the gymnasium. The restless students sat still in their seats. Not a sound interrupted me as I spoke. As I ended my story, I said, "If what happened to me as a little girl has happened to you, and you have been keeping that secret, now is the time for you to speak. You may not be able to get anyone to listen or to understand at first—maybe no one will even believe you—but the most important thing is for you to keep talking. Keep telling your story until someone listens to you. No matter how long it takes, keep talking until someone believes you. Keep talking until someone takes you seriously."

The assembly over, the children dismissed, Gary and I left the auditorium and went on to our next scheduled appearance. I had no idea what would result from the account of my experiences, but I could no longer keep silent. I prayed that somehow, someone would be helped by it.

The community response to the two four-day workshops in Poplar Bluff was overwhelming. When I was asked to return for a third time to speak to a women's conference, Linda discussed with me her vision of the Claudia Company.

Established in 1989, Claudia Company was a nonprofit organization Linda named in memory of her mother. Its goals included college scholarships for women, a classics reading program for girls and boys from elementary through high school, and a college preparatory program for girls from junior high through high school. In addition, Claudia Company would aid in the design, funding, and administration of programs to combat domestic violence.

Claudia Company's corporate offices would be built in Linda's hometown, Poplar Bluff, and its programs would benefit southeast Missouri and the entire state of Arkansas. Hillary Clinton, Arkansas' first lady, was named chairman of the national advisory board.

I felt great interest in each of the issues Claudia Company intended to address. And I was moved by Linda's commitment to her home region. It was my home, too. I offered, as a friend, to do whatever I could to help advance the goals of Claudia Company. I had no idea, at the time, just how that offer would affect Gary and me.

We had settled into a comfortable lifestyle in Los Angeles. Our acting careers were progressing steadily. I was often invited to give motivational speeches, and both Gary and I volunteered many hours with Impact. We were busy. We were not looking for additional activities to fill our lives. In fact, we had turned down other offers to work with worthwhile organizations. One of those organizations, Kidpower, just wouldn't take no for an answer.

Kidpower was the brainchild of Irene van der Zande, a child development expert and author I met while teaching for Impact. She had developed a self-defense program for children and nothing I said convinced her that I didn't belong in a classroom full of children.

"I find it difficult to empathize with adult students, Irene," I told her with irritation. "I certainly am not inclined to be warm and fuzzy with kids."

"You'd be a natural, Millicent. You taught for years in Torrance; you know children; you already know Impact. The techniques are similar. How can you say no?" Irene insisted.

It was easy. I had barricaded my heart. I wanted to put as much distance as possible between myself and the memories of

my teaching days. The memories of Zach. I wanted to leave all
the old hurts behind me. The girl who had once thrived in the
classroom, teaching fifteen hundred children each week, was dead.
The woman who had survived her was an emotionally detached
technician. Or so I thought, until I began traveling to Poplar
Bluff.

There, standing in junior high auditoriums, meeting the
children of Poplar Bluff, listening to their Southern twangs and
touching their earnest, sweet faces, I felt the barriers begin to
crumble. With each trip, I welcomed these children deeper into
my soul.

By 1991, Gary and I were traveling to Poplar Bluff regularly,
living two weeks of every month in Los Angeles and two weeks in
Missouri. And, when Linda asked me to accept the position of
Executive Director of Claudia Company, offering me a generous
salary, I said yes.

Traveling to Poplar Bluff, walking down small-town streets,
listening to the gentle rhythms of Southern speech—all these
things sent me back to my childhood in Searcy. The route we had
to travel to get to Poplar Bluff took us within scant miles of the
old brick house on Center Street. The airlines could take us as far
as Little Rock, but from there it was a three-and-a-half-hour drive
up Highway 67, past the outskirts of Searcy and Newport and
through Tuckerman. Each time we passed these familiar towns, a
sense of longing broke loose inside me. I wanted to stop and tour
the places that had been a part of my own personal history. But
something always stopped me from indulging in such a
sentimental journey.

Nothing would be the same, I told myself. Remember the pain
of 'going home,' when you made the trip as a family, believing
everything would be just as it was when you left?

I told myself it was foolish to want to wander through a little
town that I hadn't lived in for nearly thirty-five years.

No one would remember you, I said to myself. It would be a
waste of emotion as well as a waste of time.

Cousins who had been children or teenagers when we left
Arkansas were now middle-aged with children of their own. Except
for Aunt Jo, who was confined to a convalescent home, and Aunt
Mary, who suffered from Alzheimer's, all my aunts and uncles
had died.

The old brick house on Center Street was owned by strangers.
How could I bear to drive by it and know that I was no longer

able to run up the front steps and in through the wide front door?

And what of Five Oaks? Was it still standing? And if, after a hundred and fifty years, the elements had destroyed it, could I endure seeing it crumbling and in ruins?

The pull toward home grew stronger. But each time I told myself our responsibilities at Claudia Company were too pressing. We couldn't afford the time to stop and wander down the streets of small country towns. We had a job to do in Poplar Bluff.

Our involvement had begun as a gesture of friendship. Gary and I had volunteered our time and energy—Gary, using his business skills as the controller, and I working in the area of public relations and promotions. In the beginning, I enjoyed the travel, representing Claudia Company and working with women like Hillary Clinton and Mrs. Sam Walton. But as the months passed, the allure of public relations began to fade.

It surprised me to discover that I no longer enjoyed the life of an executive. The thrill was gone. I no longer enjoyed what I was doing.

I knew the reasons. There were several. First, I often found myself diametrically opposed to the methods Linda wanted to employ to reach her goals. We shared many commonalities, and I loved her—her friendship was very dear to me, and I would always be grateful that she gave me a reason to return to the region of my birth. But we were two very different women, in personality and in style, and at times, we found ourselves in conflict.

I struggled with Linda's philosophy of work, which could be summed up in her oft-quoted sentence, "Around here, we fly by the seat of our pants." It worked for Linda, for her creative genius, which seemed to thrive amid, and in spite of, chaos. But for me— blind and partially deaf, organization and carefully ordered plans were essential.

And lastly, I was discovering that I wanted to be "in the trenches." The job of administration was creating a huge chasm between me and the people who had worked their way into my heart. I wanted to close that gap and draw close to the children, but the responsibilities of executive director bound me to the desk, the telephone, and a calendar full of administrative appointments.

Both Gary and I had fallen deeply in love with the children of Poplar Bluff. After seeing us around town and at their schools over a period of months, they overcame their shyness and stopped us on the street to talk. In restaurants, in the aisles of Wal-Mart, they called to us and came over to visit, petting Eeyore and talking, asking questions in their strongly accented style. Some asked if they could make appointments to talk with us at Claudia Company's offices. Two of them, young girls, came to see me privately, and the stories they told broke my heart.

Thin, frail, and soft-spoken, "Amber" was a russet-haired child with a delightful twang in her speech. She said she was from the hill country, but the story she told indicated she had spent most of her life in hell.

"Miss Collinsworth, please let me talk to you," she said in a halting voice. "I heard you in the assembly that day, when you talked about what happened to you when you were a little girl, and I thought, why, she's talkin' straight to me."

Amber told of her mother raping her with a foreign object. Her mother's boyfriends, too many to count, had sodomized and raped her repeatedly over the years. Her life had been an endless series of episodes of torture and humiliation. She was now embroiled in the legal system, and its abuse was equally appalling. She was twelve years old, and she had already suffered a nervous breakdown. I could only listen and weep as Dr. Sandler's voice echoed in my thoughts, "Not alone... not alone."

Amber and I spent many hours together. I grieved for her and with her. And often, after sitting with her and listening to her talk, I thought of the tenacious little woman back in California who had tried to pull me into her self-defense program for children. I thought a lot about Kidpower.

It might have saved her... She might have been able to escape...

It was too late for Amber. It was also too late for "Keesha."

Keesha was a brilliant young black girl whose height and presence made her seem much older than her fourteen years. I was first attracted by the melodious sound of her voice. Her regal bearing belied the humiliation she had endured as a little girl. Assaulted by a family member, her mind and body had reacted to the pain of the experience by developing alopecia, the loss of hair.

Keesha wrapped a turban about her bald head and carried herself as though she were a queen. Slender and tall, she stood proud, never alluding to her condition or the situation that had caused it, and I felt humble whenever I was in her presence. She had no time for self-pity.

I would always worry about Amber's emotional frailty, but Keesha's indomitable strength amazed me. I never allowed myself to pretend I helped her in any way, but rather, I believed she helped me. I placed her among those I list as my personal heroes.

More and more I thought about Irene's Kidpower. I found myself wondering if perhaps I was ready to go back to the classroom. More and more I realized that the work of an administrator did not satisfy me.

In December 1991, before taking a group of Claudia Company girls from the college preparatory program on their first trip to New York City, Gary and I made the bittersweet decision to leave Claudia Company. I could no longer postpone the series of operations I needed on my jaw. The pain had escalated to excruciating proportions, making it almost impossible for me to eat or to sleep. Speaking was difficult with my jaw locked permanently, but between clenched teeth, I had continued with speaking engagements, trying to honor all the public engagements that filled my calendar. But by the end of the year, I knew I could not put off the surgeries any longer.

Our agents in California, who had chased after us trying to work auditions and acting parts into our hectic, cross-country lifestyle, were elated to learn we were coming to California to stay. Our family, whom we had seen only in small snatches of time between trips and administrative duties, were also elated.

I felt both sad and relieved about our decision. Sad, because working with Linda had been a rich experience; sad, to be saying goodbye to the friends we had made. But I was excited as well, because our tenure with Linda and Claudia Company had helped us decipher what we wanted to do with our lives. In addition to acting, we wanted to volunteer to work with Irene's Kidpower. We would begin training as soon as the doctors declared me fit.

With Kidpower, Gary and I would be able to join the forces on the front lines. We would be able to really have a part in the war against child sexual molestation and abuse. Maybe we could prevent the tragedy of another Amber of Keesha.

In January 1992, we made our last trip to Poplar Bluff, Missouri. After several days of attending to final details at Claudia Company, we drove away, steering our rented car onto the highway toward Little Rock.

Driving across the countryside, Gary described for me the scenery I could not see. I visualized the spindly oak trees made naked by winter's assault. I imagined the tall evergreens, dark against the gray sky. The dogwoods, tucked in among the other forest trees, would be ugly at this time of year, their branches bare, their beauty hidden until spring called the foliage back to life.

The pull of home was strong that day. So strong that even the fear of disappointment could not dispel it. We had only a few short hours until our flight left Little Rock, but Gary and I decided to spend those hours in Tuckerman. We would retrace my parents' footsteps, returning to the place where they had lived as newlyweds. Perhaps touching that small piece of the past would be enough for me.

Recalling Mama's vivid descriptions and the memories I had of a few visits there in my childhood, I was able to direct Gary through Tuckerman. Our quest that day was to find the house Mama and Daddy had lived in, the one with the huge magnolia tree in front, where Mama and her little companion, Charles Love, had raked leaves and shared homemade ice cream. To our delight, the house still stood, dwarfed now by the magnolia tree that had grown to immense size over the past fifty years.

As Gary described every detail of the house, I remembered Mama's stories of her life as a young bride in this town. Her daily outing had been a visit to a little drugstore a few blocks away. Every day she had sat on a stool at the soda fountain and ordered a tuna sandwich and a cherry coke and visited with the pharmacist who doubled as a soda jerk.

"Let's find the drugstore, Gary," I exclaimed, pulling him toward the car. "I'm sure I can figure out how to get there."

Driving slowly through the quiet streets of Tuckerman, we searched for a small drugstore that would have been within walking distance of the house where Mama and Daddy had lived. Turning a corner, Gary said, "That has to be the one."

We walked inside the small drugstore, and Gary said to me, "You aren't going to believe this, Millicent. The soda fountain is still here. It looks like nothing has changed in fifty-five years."

"Do you mind if I take a picture?" Gary asked a woman who stood behind the counter. "This is for my mother-in-law in California," he told her. "She lived in this town over fifty years ago, but she always talked about this drugstore. My wife and I would like to take her a memento."

"What was her name?" the woman asked.

"Collinsworth," Gary answered.

A man's voice called out from the back of the store. "Did you say Collinsworth?" he asked. From the timbre of his voice, I guessed him to be a man of about sixty-five or older.

Turning toward the direction of the sound, I said, "Yes, sir. My mama's name is Collinsworth."

"Did she have red hair?" he asked, drawling his words like a man who had lived all his life in the South.

My face split in a huge smile, I answered, "Yes, Mama has always been known for her beautiful red hair."

"Well, ma'am, your mama was my teacher fifty-three years ago," the man said. "Bruce Higgenbottom is my name, class of '39. Never forgot your mama," he went on. "No one could ever forget that red hair."

No one could ever forget, he'd said.

It had been more than fifty years since Mama had been a teacher in this town, but she had not been forgotten. Long after her departure, her presence lingered here still, in this small town that represented little more than a moment's pause in her long journey.

The urgency to go home, all the way home, to Five Oaks, and to the old brick house on Center Street, overwhelmed me. More than anything, I wanted to walk among the flowers in Mama's gardens. I wanted to whirl on the stairs at sunset and try to catch a rainbow. I wanted to sit on the swing at twilight time and recall the courageous acts of storybook heroes and heroines. I wanted to celebrate the slaying of dragons and the conquering of foes.

For me, a long war had finally ended.

I wanted to go home.

Chapter 16

"We'll make the trip to Searcy in April, Millicent, after you've recovered from this operation," Gary promised as he drove me home from the hospital a couple of days after the first surgery on my jaw. It was February. Two more months to wait. "You'll be feeling pretty good by then," he said, reaching over to touch my cheek. "And Arkansas should be beautiful."

He knew that, since the day we stopped in Tuckerman, I had been able to think of little else but the need to go home. It was an urgent, pounding need.

"Maybe a few dogwoods will still be in bloom," I answered carefully, my face and jaw still numb.

For the next two months, my thoughts were filled with remembered scenes of springtime in Arkansas. I visualized dogwoods, their branches sprinkled with delicate pink and white blossoms; and the magnolias that would be laden with heavy, waxy white flowers. The oak trees would be green and lush now, their thick foliage shading the narrow, small-town streets of Searcy.

I saw the cracked sidewalks that ran along Center Street, where blades of grass and dandelions grew between slabs of uneven concrete. Impatient with the doctor's orders to rest, I mentally toured the old brick house, walking through each room. I strolled the acres of Five Oaks and climbed the stairs of my family's ancestral home, feeling my way through memories stashed and buried long ago.

Finally, as April ended, my journey home began.

Driving a rental car, we headed north, up Arkansas' Highway 67, toward Searcy. Once outside of Little Rock's city limits, Gary began describing the countryside. I sat stiffly in my seat, listening, imagining, seeing once again the dense, green-black forests where tiny splashes of dogwood peeked around the verdant stands of evergreens. I envisioned the acres of farmland as Gary described them, deciding secretly that the spiralling smoke, where the farmers were clear-cutting their land, were smoke signals to welcome home a prodigal daughter.

When we pulled off the highway and turned toward Searcy, I began arguing with Thomas Wolfe. His novel *Look Homeward, Angel* may have convinced an entire generation that one can never go home again, that home must reside in the heart, that a physical place called home would be forever altered by time and circumstance, but he had not convinced me.

It will be just as I left it... Nothing will have changed. Not just a thought, or a hope, it was a plea. If there was a power that controlled the fate of small towns, I was beseeching it now, to prove its prowess, to exhibit an unchanged, unaltered place, preserved as I remembered it; a place where the best of all possible dreams had been born.

Thirty-six years had passed since I had lived here, and more than twenty years since I had last visited. I was returning blind, to be led through the streets by a man who had never been here. We would make our way carefully, guided by my memories and Gary's ability to see the landmarks I would describe, landmarks that had been cast upon the mercy of time and the capricious whims of progress.

"I see a small airport on the left-hand side of the road," Gary said, as Searcy came into his view. "Does that sound familiar?"

"Yes, yes! My cousin Ben used to keep his Cessna there!"

Excited, gripped with trepidation, I said, "Start watching for what seems like an endless line of white fencing. It will be old Dr. Rodgers' farm. He used to breed and train Tennessee Walkers."

"No, no white fence, Millicent. All I see is a Wal-Mart distribution center and a modern-looking brick hospital, asphalt and a parking lot, Hon."

"Oh no... it can't be gone. We used to drive past Dr. Rodgers' farm on the way to Grandmother's. I loved watching his horses prance. I can't believe it's a Wal-Mart now. Oh, Gary, we shouldn't have come. Nothing will be left. Why did we come?"

"Try to remember something else, Sweetheart," Gary answered. "We're turning onto Main Street now, there's got to be something else that remains."

I sat silent, thinking, mourning.

"Help me orient myself, Millicent. Think of another landmark."

"As I remember, there used to be a grain and feed store up the road, on the left. About a hundred yards or so beyond the grain store, on the right, should be a long, red brick building that was the old shoe factory. Look for a street called Woodruff off to the left. And there should be an old ice house."

"I see it," Gary answered. "It's all there. A chain-link fence surrounds the shoe factory. It's in pretty bad shape, looks like it's vacant. The old ice house has been turned into an automotive repair shop."

Inside my head, where only landscapes of the past resided, I struggled to accept this new scene. The neat picture of mowed lawns and tended exteriors was replaced with one of overgrown grass and disheveled, unkempt buildings. Familiar, comfortable handholds of time turned prickly and painful to the touch.

"I see a little park on the left, lots of trees, and what looks like a little brook running through it. Does that sound familiar?"

"It's Spring Park!" I began stammering in my excitement. "Laddie and I... we took our sleds there in the winter! We hunted Easter eggs in the spring... We waded in the brook in the summer!

"Gary, that's where Laddie saved the little boy... His clothes caught fire—not Laddie's—it was a birthday party... I told you about it... When we were little you could look across the park and see Yarnell's Ice Cream!"

"Well, you can relax now, Darling," Gary answered, "I can see a Yarnell Ice Cream sign peeking through the trees."

We turned up Pleasure Street and onto Spring, driving past the First Baptist Church, where Laddie and I had been baptized, and past what had once been the very prestigious Mayfair Hotel. It was now a retirement center.

"We're on the square, Millicent, facing the courthouse."

"Oh, Gary, do you see it? There should be a statue of a Confederate soldier on one corner of the courthouse lawn."

"It's there, Honey."

Gary turned the car into a parking place. With fumbling fingers I fastened Eeyore's harness and we stepped out onto the sidewalk.

"The pigeons haven't stopped anointing him, have they?" I asked, laughing as I took Gary's arm and walked toward the town's beloved symbol.

"Some rituals are sacrosanct, Millicent."

The day was grand. Perfect. Sunshine poured over me. My mind tuned to every sound, every nuance of feeling, I forgot my darkness, so keen were my memories. The only reminder of my blindness was the tug of Eeyore as he pulled me forward, leading me down the sidewalk surrounding the courthouse.

"We're in front of the Vietnam memorial, Millicent," Gary said.

He described the large granite monument that bore the names

of Searcy's sons who had gone to war and never returned. He read aloud the names etched there, and when he came to Jimmy Cunningham's, he placed my hand against the cool marble and let my fingers trace the letters. I remembered a little blond boy wearing baggy shorts, a striped jersey, and a red cowboy hat. I remembered laughter and silly childhood games.

"I wish you could have come home too, Jimmy... "

Gary took my arm and we continued our trek around the courthouse.

"The Rialto theater should be just ahead," I said. "Look across the street, kitty-corner from the courthouse."

"It's there," Gary answered. I walked faster behind Eeyore.

"The building looks like it was just painted," Gary said.

"The marquee... describe the marquee!"

"It's just as you always described it, Honey. It's a sort of art-deco design, strips of colored neon lights, blue, pink, yellow, white... "

"It's just the same? Oh, Gary, how wonderful!"

"The theater is closed though, the doors are padlocked. There's a 'For Lease' sign in the window."

Movie houses built in strip malls on the outskirts of town now offered the first-run movies that used to play in this downtown theater. Its art-deco marquee no longer flashed with the promise of entertainment on a Saturday afternoon.

Change had marched here, as I knew it must.

As Gary described the scene, I listened to the hum of car engines on the downtown streets. And I remembered the sound of giggling when, on long-ago Saturday afternoons, Laddie and I had walked down the street, gripping the hands of our family's maid. I remembered her seating us near the front of the theater and then retreating to the balcony to sit with the other black women who cared for the children of rich white families, and I thought, some changes had come too slowly.

Gary took my arm and, with Eeyore in the lead, we walked toward the sight of the old Robbins-Sanford Mercantile. Gary read aloud the sign over the front door: "Ozark Arms."

"The store window used to have a huge stuffed horse," I said, recalling the feelings of both fear and fascination I had felt when I stood close to it. "Laddie and I liked to come here and look at toys, then we'd go home and make our Christmas list for Santa."

When Gary stepped toward the door, I shook my head. I didn't want to disturb the memory of the toys and glittering gifts that once filled the shelves of the store. I wanted to hold onto the picture of leather harnesses, saddles, and a multitude of other small town goods. I didn't want to replace the scent of tobacco and freshly oiled wood floors with the smell of strangers and other foreign odors. I wanted this memory left intact.

My mother and father had begun their history here. In this store.

"Your daddy was working as an accountant for Robbins-Sanford Mercantile," Mama had told me. "He watched me walk home from high school, past the store and up the street to the duplex across from the old brick house on Center Street. We met later, when I went to work for Robbins-Sanford's too, when I was about eighteen, but he said he'd been watching me for a long time."

I imagined my father seeing my mother, her red hair loose and streaming down her back, her schoolbooks in her arms as she walked across the courthouse square.

"You know, he once said that he watched me play basketball at Searcy High School," Mama had told me just before Gary and I had left for this trip. "He said, 'I had my eye on you even then, Pauline.'"

He was a quiet, placid young accountant irresistibly drawn toward a fiery, tempestuous redhead. It is the stuff of which classics are made, their marriage almost archetypal. A study in extreme symbols, I saw it in circular form, their romance the apex from which they began a slow descent into tragedy. Spiralling ever downward, pulled by the power of my father's disease, the elements of anti-romance entered their story. Flawed and broken, they fought to survive against condemnation. Their fall from bliss cast them into a nightmare, but they did rise at times, if only for a moment, lifted by the power of grace.

I could neither fault them, nor pity them, for theirs is the human story. Which of us can escape our own fall from bliss? And once fallen, what more can we do than to seek grace?

I might have stood musing in front of the Mercantile, staring at memories for hours, had not Gary pulled me back to the present.

"Millicent, I noticed an old Coca-Cola cooler in the window of a drugstore up the street. Would you mind if we walked back up there? I'd like something cold to drink."

"Is it Stott's Drug Store?" I asked.

"That's it," he answered.

My feet slowed, weighted with memories, as we approached

the store where, for decades, my Aunt Jo had worked. My hand was damp on Eeyore's leather harness as I stood in front of the large windows, remembering how, as a little girl, I had thought she was the prettiest lady in Searcy—next to Mama, of course. She too had red hair, like Mama's, and pale ivory skin. Smelling of sweet powder and floral perfume, Aunt Jo had reigned over the cosmetic counter at Stott's, giving beauty advice to three generations of Searcy women with all the authority of a Helen Gurley Brown.

Aunt Jo's red hair had turned white. Now well over eighty, she had long ago abdicated her position behind Stott's cosmetic counter, leaving its rule to a younger woman. With age had come illness, and she now lived in a convalescent home, no longer able to care for herself alone. Thoughts of her, weakened and ill, saddened me.

"I don't think I want to go in, Gary," I said. "You go ahead. Eeyore and I will wait out here."

Gary steered me toward a wooden bench on the sidewalk in front of the store. I heard a bell tinkle as he opened the door to Stott's Drug Store. It seemed like hours before he came out again.

"Millicent, you've got to come in here," he said, his voice sounding incredulous. "You've got to see what I've found."

Grabbing my elbow, he pulled me into the store and led me down an aisle toward the back of the store.

"I was just browsing while I drank my Coke, and I started visiting with this old man who was waiting for the druggist to fill a prescription. We started talking about all these old pictures hanging here," he said, placing my hand on the wall. "They're snapshots of old Searcy, scenes of town activities, pictures of high school athletic teams, that sort of thing."

Moving my hand across the surface of the wall, Gary placed my fingers on a frame that hung about eye level.

"What do you think this is, Millicent?" he asked.

"I haven't any idea," I answered.

The garrulous, country voice of an ancient man came from behind me. "Why, it's yer daddy, girl," he rasped. "That there's a picture of the Searcy High football team of 1924. Yer daddy's standin' right there, in the middle."

Gary took the picture off the wall and put it in my hands. Taking my fingers across the glass in front of the photograph, he said, "There he is, Honey, right under your fingers."

"I wish you could have seen yer daddy play, sweet girlie," the old man said. "That was when boys knew how to play ball. There were times I seen him plow plumb through the opposite team and run the full length of the field to score a touchdown. When Collinsworth ran, it was like watchin' the wind. He was what you'd call a hometown hero back then."

A hometown hero.

Hugging the picture and closing my eyes tightly against the threat of tears, I tried to imagine my father in his football uniform, vigorous and athletic, with all the beauty and vitality one would expect of a gridiron hero. But the picture wouldn't come. Every time I tried to summon it, I saw instead another setting. I saw a quiet street in California. No screaming crowds filled a stadium to witness his heroism; no one captured the event on film. But in my mind, it was the occasion of his greatest courage.

I was eleven years old. It was the year of our severe poverty. Daddy, ill and hardly able to walk without help, had to rest for hours after making the trip downstairs from his bedroom. His breathing labored, his wheezing could be heard in every room of the house. But being a child, I did not consider the extent of his pain.

Laddie was thirteen. He was graduating from eighth grade, and the event would be held at the Charter Oak Elementary School. I ran home from school and declared that the principal had asked all the families that lived close to the school to please walk to the ceremony so there would be ample parking for the families that lived farther away.

"Please, Mama, could we walk tonight? All the other families in the neighborhood are walking," I said. "It's only two blocks."

"I don't know, Mitty," Mama answered. "You know how ill your father is. I don't know if he has the strength to walk that far."

"But he has to, Mama," I begged. "He has to walk so everyone can see him, so we can prove, once and for all, to our neighbors and our friends that they're all wrong, that our daddy is not crazy!"

Laddie and I had endured the taunts and the teasing from playmates and neighbors. If they could just see us with our father, walking to graduation like all the other families, perhaps they would end the torment. Perhaps we could pretend, if only for that one night, that our family was no different than any other.

Weary, sighing, Mama said, "I'll talk to Daddy, but I'm not promising anything."

I followed Mama upstairs and stood outside Daddy's room,

my ear pressed against the door, hearing the creaking of his chair as he rocked back and forth.

"Minor," Mama said softly, "I know how ill you feel, but I have to ask you to take a walk for your children. Mitty is begging for us to walk together, as a family, to Laddie's graduation tonight. It's at the school, just two blocks up the street. Do you think you could do that?"

I waited, holding my breath.

"The children at school tease Mitty and Laddie unmercifully about your illness. They think you are crazy. Minor, Mitty wants them to see that they are wrong."

The creaking of Daddy's chair stopped. I heard him draw a deep, wheezy breath, and then he answered, "I'll walk."

That evening, Mama helped Daddy dress in his finest blue suit and tied his tie in a perfect knot. Laddie wore his white shirt, and I put on the best dress in my hand-me-down wardrobe. Mama took Daddy's arm and, with backs straight and heads held high, they walked out the front door of the old manor house behind a somber Laddie. I led the procession down the street, skipping and twirling with excitement.

I heard the whispers as we passed other families on their way to graduation. Mama nodded to our neighbors, acknowledging their presence on the sidewalk as though she reigned over the concrete and, in her benevolence, she was allowing them to share it with her. Daddy leaned heavily on her arm, and by the time we reached the school, his face was the color of ash. He sat in silence throughout the ceremony, nodding only slightly as Mama and I applauded Laddie's commencement.

Standing there, in Stott's Drugstore, thirty-three years later, clutching the photo of my father in his football uniform, I thought of how proud I was of my father, how proud I was to find him hanging in Searcy's gallery of heroes. But I knew his greatest act of heroism had not been accomplished on the field of athletics. To me, my father's most heroic act would always be the walking of the gauntlet outside the villa at Charter Oak.

As we left Stott's Drugstore, Gary put his arm around me and hugged me. Kissing the top of my head, he asked, "Are you ready to go to Center Street now?"

Nodding, I brushed at tears I could no longer contain.

We drove the few short blocks from the town square toward Center Street, and I sat in silence, bracing myself against the onslaught of overpowering emotions.

Would the old brick house still be standing? Would it be as it had always been?

"There it is." Gary's voice was soft. I felt the car slow and then stop as Gary parked against the curb. "It's exactly as you've always described it, Millicent. It's beautiful."

He began describing every small detail of the house, from the dusty gray-pink color of the bricks to the vibrant colors of the stained-glass panels around the front door; from the New Orleans–style balcony on the second floor to the wide, gracious porch where white columns stood like sentries. The willow oak tree in the front yard towered over the lawn, casting early evening shadows across the walk that was now cracked and broken.

I faced the house as though I could see it, my forehead pressed against the cool glass of the car window, and I listened as Gary's voice described my childhood home. I didn't need my eyes to be able to see the herringbone walkways that led through bulb gardens in the side yard; I could envision the purple blossoms of the lavender and lilac bushes and the crape myrtles that grew along the property line.

"Would you like to get out and walk around a bit?" Gary asked. "Maybe I can do a better job of describing things. We can see if the carriage house is still in back."

"Oh no!" I exclaimed, suddenly terrified of being too close, of touching tender places so long untouched. "The new owners might see us," I said. "Just drive around the corner. You should be able to see from there what they've done with the back of the house."

Gary drove around the corner.

"Are you sure you don't want to get out, Millicent?"

"I'm sure... I don't want to have to explain what I'm doing here. How would I explain my attachment to this old house? Do you think anyone would understand?"

"You're going to get a chance to find out," Gary answered. "The new owners just drove up and they've seen us. A young man is walking toward us."

I groaned. "This is so embarrassing. He'll never understand..."

"Roll down your window, Millicent. He's coming to speak with us."

"May I help you?" His voice was soft and only slightly accented.

"Please forgive us," I blurted. "This was my childhood home," I said. "I haven't seen it in over twenty years. I'm blind now, and my husband was taking a moment to describe it for me. I hope you don't mind. We didn't mean to intrude."

"Why, I know who you are." The young man's soft voice cut through my nervous prattle.

"You do?"

"Of course I do. You're Mitty Collinsworth." I could hear the smile in his voice. "And you have a brother named Laddie, and your family lived here for years."

Mitty. He called me Mitty.

Only my family and a handful of close friends ever called me Mitty. How did this stranger learn my childhood name?

"I'm Jeff Taylor," he introduced himself. "Would you like to come in and see the house?"

Jeff opened the car door and reached in for my hand. Tucking it securely in his arm, he led me up the walk and toward the large golden oak doors that led into the old brick house on Center Street. Gary and Eeyore followed behind as Jeff took me up the wide front steps of my beloved childhood home.

"My father and I are restoring the house, Mitty," Jeff told me. "We've tried to keep it as true to its original style and architecture as possible."

Holding Jeff's arm, I walked through the downstairs rooms.

"Here—this is where I sat and listened while Corinne and Ruby Jean sang to us."

"We've remodeled the kitchen, Mitty," Jeff said. "But the house is much the same as you would remember it."

The library, with its fireplace and rich woodwork, held the memory of the first time, the only time, I climbed into my father's arms. My chest ached as I remembered the roughness of his chin with its late afternoon growth of beard against my cheek.

My hands trailed the banister as we climbed the stairs. I paused on the landing.

"I used to stand here, just so, in the evening, as the sun was setting. The stained-glass window used to flash rainbows when it caught the sun, and I used to spin and try to capture the rainbows... "

"You could spin now, Mitty," Jeff said. "The sun is just setting. There are rainbows on the walls."

With his quiet, gentle manner, Jeff told me I was free to dance on the landing, sing in the kitchen, or sob over poignant memories in the library. I sensed he understood the power of this old house, that he too had come under its spell.

Jeff and his professor father lived here together, when Jeff was not studying architecture abroad. He had meticulously planned every inch of the renovation process, believing that the house deserved to be preserved, and believing in the power of love. Like my mother, Jeff's mother had loved this house. She had died before she could see the final renovation. Both Jeff and his father still appeared to be mourning her death. In her honor, they lived here and continued to oversee its restoration. Perhaps it was a kind of personal restoration as well.

"We've done quite a bit with the upstairs, Mitty," Jeff said as we entered the upstairs hallway. "I believe this would have been your old room."

My hands fluttered in my excitement as I caressed the walls. "This was the room I shared with Laddie... Our beds were against that wall... " Stammering, I moved out of the room and toward a doorway. "And this is the balcony... Daddy ran here... "

I was stunned. It had seemed like such a tall, strong railing when I was a child. Standing next to it now, at my height of five feet eight inches, I felt ill. It reached only inches above my knees. How easily Daddy might have tipped himself over it that night...

I turned away quickly.

The tour upstairs finished, Jeff led us back down to the living room. I turned around, adjusting myself to memories, and gestured toward the side yard.

"Out there would be the bulb garden," I said.

Jeff led us out the door and into the side yard. After a walk through a slightly altered garden area, we went into the back yard where the carriage house no longer stood. The wading pool was also gone, but the herringbone walkway remained and another garden bench had been added.

"We've built another room on the back, Mitty, but it is in the same style as the rest of the house," Jeff said as we returned to the house. He took me by the hand and let me feel the great round columns that stood in the room. "We've tried to do everything possible to retain the spirit of the original house."

"It's really beautiful, Millicent," Gary said. "The woodwork is exceptional. It's so much like the inside of the old manor house it's almost eerie."

"My mother never really let go of this house," I explained to Jeff. "When she bought an old villa set in the orange groves in California, she tried to turn it into a replica of the this house. She never stopped loving this house."

Our tour complete, Jeff and his father served us coffee and ice cream and talked about their success in the effort to have the old brick house listed in the National Register of Historic Places; how their renovations had received attention from architectural firms and publications.

Before Gary and I left that evening, Jeff took my hand and, in his mild, gentle tone, he said, "Come with me, Mitty, I have something to show you." Leading me through the house, past furniture and recently erected walls, he said, "When my family and I first moved in, we discovered something, and we realized how special it was. We decided that this part of the house would never be altered."

Passing through the front door and out onto the porch with its graceful columns, Jeff led me to the edge of the porch. Kneeling, he gently pulled me down beside him.

"Let me have your hand, Mitty," he said. With his hand guiding mine, I traced a rough, scrawled etching in the concrete. When he removed his hand, my fingers traveled on their own, reading the childish scrawling of my name dug into the cement. *M-i-t-t-y*. Next to my inscription, I had written my age, "7 years old." Laddie's name and age were inscribed a few inches from mine. Beneath the words and the numbers were the imprints of two small hands. Laddie's and mine.

My hand shook as I placed it over the tiny handprint of the child I had once been. The child who, with her thick glasses and pigtails, had followed me, tormenting me and accusing me. The child whose desperate promise to her father had haunted me for so many years.

Caressing the cold concrete, I felt the presence of that child. Placing my hand upon hers, I felt a sense of completion, as though I had come full circle. As though the child and the woman had finally become one. The woman could no longer be hurt by the hauntings of a terrified child; and the child could now reside safely within the woman I had become.

It was an unlikely place for an epiphany, I suppose, but that night, as I was kneeling on the warm concrete of a wide porch, breathing in the scent of honeysuckle, I knew something mystical had occurred within me. And as though to commemorate it, the darkness in front of my eyes turned into a golden glow. I could not speak of it, nor could I explain it. I could only savor it.

Moments later, as Gary and I said goodbye to Jeff and his father, the glow faded to be replaced by the darkness, but a sense of contentment settled down upon me. As we drove away, I felt, not sadness and loss for the old brick house on Center Street, as I

had felt for so many years—no, there was no sadness. I felt...
peace. The house was loved, as it had always been loved. And it
had welcomed me. It bore my name, carved upon it, and in a
sense, it would always be mine.

I sensed, without his telling me, that Jeff understood. I knew,
as he said goodbye, that he would live in it carefully, as though a
tenant of sorts, the legal caretaker of one family's cherished
memories.

That night, sleep was impossible. I paced the small hotel room
for hours, going over every moment of the day, returning to
every site we had visited. An empty place inside me had been
filled. I felt sated. I felt strong. I picked up the telephone and
called the family members that still lived in Searcy. Cousins I had
not spoken to in nearly twenty years welcomed me home. They
were the children of the relatives who had watched my father's
suffering and my mother's disgrace. But we were a new generation,
and we would release ourselves from the bondage of the past. We
would make new memories. We would begin again. I promised to
make time to see them before Gary and I had to return to
California.

Finally, hours later, I collapsed on the bed and let myself
muse on our plans for the following day. We were going to
visit Five Oaks.

Please, God, let the house still be standing... Let it be
there still...

Early the next morning, Joe Pennington, our farm manager,
met us at the hotel with his four-wheel-drive truck. Once Eeyore
was secured in the back, we set off on this final adventure: to find
my family's ancestral home, if, after all these years, it was still
standing.

"I haven't been up to where the old house was for about five
years," Joe told us. "The last time I tried to get up there, I had to
turn around and go back. But using the four-wheel-drive, we
should be able to get through. I just don't know what we'll find
when we get there."

Years earlier, an international firm had begun farming the
property for us. The land, willed to Laddie and me, provided
Mama with a lifetime trust, and under Joe's wise supervision, the
fields were worked and harvested regularly. But no one had any
interest in exploring the heavily wooded area, anchored by five
huge oak trees, that sheltered the big white house with green

shutters. For years, no one had ventured close to the decaying old house that had been home to generations of Collinsworths.

"We can drive around the property for a bit, if you like," Joe offered. Perhaps he sensed my hesitation, my fear that we would find only a crumbling hulk, sunk in the depths of forest land, like an abandoned ship, left to the powerful tides of time.

"I can give you a tour of your farmland," Joe went on. "Then we can look for the road up to the house."

"That would be great, Joe."

Had my father's home become a cadaver? Would it be scarred and ravaged, a skeleton, bearing no resemblance to the gracious house that had once been Five Oaks?

I let myself be distracted by Joe's narration about the farmland. He listed the crops planted on our land and their yield, entertaining us with the scientific wonders of modern farming. As dust from the dirt roads billowed in the truck windows, I listened, and coughed, and waited for the moment of unveiling that was coming closer with every mile we traveled.

"We could make a quick stop at the old cemetery first, if you like, Millicent," Joe said.

He's reading my mind, I thought.

"It's not far out of the way," he said.

I answered quickly, "That's a great idea, Joe."

Dogwood Cemetery lay a few hundred yards off the main route, down a narrow road that was little more than a trail. I remembered it well. Generations of ancestors lay buried beneath the neatly mowed lawn, their lives and deaths marked by granite, moss-covered tombstones. Years of being blasted by the elements had sanded the lettering off of many of the headstones, but I could still trace on some of them the names of generations of Collinsworths.

Wandering among the stones, listening to the silence, I thought of the day Uncle Rufus had revealed to me the presence of a Yankee in the family plot. Almost laughing, I trailed my fingers over the rough stone that marked the grave of the young Yankee who had died so far away from home.

Eliza Collinsworth Davis would not have been so gracious, I thought. The story of my ancestor had been one of Uncle Rufus' favorites. He loved to tell how, during the War, Eliza had smuggled contraband, medical supplies, and information to the Confederate Army while it was surrounded by the Union forces outside of Nashville.

"The Yankees all knew what she was doing," Uncle Rufus used to say with great pride. "But they couldn't catch her in the act. The Union soldiers forced her to say the vow of allegiance on nine different occasions. Each time she said the vow, she turned right around and continued her underground activities."

I used to imagine Eliza stuffing bandages and ammunition under her skirts or down her blouse, or hiding secret notes in sacks of flour—anything to foil the Yankees and help the Rebs.

"She could have been shot or hanged if she'd been caught," Uncle Rufus used to say, shaking his head and grinning at the audacity of one woman against so large an enemy.

I didn't know where Eliza was buried, but Uncle Rufus lay in Dogwood Cemetery, not far from the Yankee whose presence he had considered such a shameful thing.

Patting their gravestones, I thought about the games Laddie and I had played as children, he the gallant Rebel and I the doomed Yank. I thought about the Confederate soldier on one corner of the courthouse lawn and the Vietnam memorial on the other. And I wondered at a city's, a culture's, fascination with soldiers. And I thought, perhaps nothing so defines a nation as the wars it chooses to fight.

Perhaps the same can be said of individuals.

My battles had defined me. My victories, as well as my defeats, would continue to determine who I was. And in the end, I would lie here, among my ancestors, my death chiseled in granite, my life carved by grace.

Warm wind whipped my hair in my face and twirled my pant legs against my calves. I shivered and, turning toward the sound of Joe's truck engine, I called out to Gary. His hand reached me and I grabbed it tightly. I was ready now to find Five Oaks.

"The dogwoods are in bloom," Gary told me, as the truck forged out across a meadow, bouncing alongside Dogwood Creek.

"I don't know if we're going to be able to make it," Joe said, after the truck pitched forward into a deep rut. Downshifting into low gear, he gunned the engine and the truck lurched up the last small hill with the gears whining in agony.

I felt the truck stop a moment later and as Gary gasped, Joe said softly, "There it is. I can't believe it, Millicent. The house is still standing."

Dense forest and undergrowth, like a jungle, hugged the terrain, hiding in its center a white, two-story house with green shutters.

"How does it look, Gary? Is it in ruins?"

"It looks great... It's unbelievable, really." Gary opened the truck door and I scrambled out behind him.

"You'd better leave Eeyore in the truck," Joe said. "This area is filled with snakes and ticks. Watch yourselves," he warned, as I hurried Gary, anxious to make my way through the tangled vines and tall grass to embrace the old house that stood beneath the shade of five immense oak trees.

"They're overgrown with vines, Millicent, but all five oaks are still standing. Lightning hasn't destroyed them. They're magnificent," Gary said in a hushed voice.

"Take me to the house," I said, reaching out for whatever hand was nearest. Joe caught my hand and led me forward.

"The porch has fallen away from the rest of the house, Millicent, but everything else is standing," he said, speaking quietly, as though we stood in a sanctuary. He placed my fingers on the fretwork of the porch which lay sprawled across the front lawn. I traced the intricate design that craftsmen had proudly carved more than a hundred and fifty years ago.

"What's really amazing is the shutters, Millicent," Gary said. "They're still bright green, almost as though they were painted yesterday."

Standing near the dilapidated porch, I remembered my grandmother's cinnamon rolls and the scent of freshly baked bread that had mingled with the aroma of hams hanging in the smokehouse out back. Unable to see the present, I saw the past through childish eyes, and I mentally toured Grandmother's kitchen, letting my hands fondle the handle of her butter churn. I roamed the house in my memory, seeing my uncles on the porch, hearing their laughter and smelling the tobacco smoke that swirled from their pipes.

"Millicent," Joe touched my shoulder tentatively as his voice broke in on my thoughts, "I don't think the house is going to last much longer. It's good you got here now, before another winter passes. This time next year, I'm afraid there will be little left of the old place. I'm sorry."

I nodded, too overcome to speak.

"Would you like to take something back with you, something from the house, as a memento?"

Swallowing and drawing a deep breath, I said, "Could we salvage one of the shutters?"

"I'll be glad to try," he answered. And he walked away, leaving me standing there, staring blindly at an old white house that, like a dying invalid, had hung on just long enough for that one distant family member to arrive to say a last goodbye.

Gary called to me from the north side of the house. "The chimney's crumbling, but some of the bricks are intact. Would you like to take a couple of them home? They're handmade, aren't they?"

"Oh, yes, I'd love to take some home!" With a quick wipe at my eyes, I started in the direction of Gary's voice.

"Watch your step, Millicent," he shouted to me. "Wait there. I'll come get you."

Stepping carefully and gripping Gary's arm with one hand, I let my other hand trail along the side of the house, feeling the planks of wood that had been cut and shaped out of trees from the forest that now seemed to hover above us, overgrown and overpowering, obscuring the brightness of the spring day.

We passed the huge oak where a tire swing used to hang, and for a moment I fancied I heard the sound of Laddie's childish laughter as he kicked his legs and swung high up into the branches.

As we neared the back side of the house, Joe called to us. From the direction of his voice, I knew he was several yards away, probably near what used to be Grandmother's garden.

"Millicent, smell the air," he shouted. "Do you know what that scent is?" he asked.

A faint whiff of sweetness filled my nostrils.

"It can't be! Is it... ? Joe, what is it?"

Joe hurried to my side and his hand closed on my elbow. "Come with me," he said, pulling me across the sloping back yard. Dropping to his knees, he began digging in the soft, dark soil. I heard his breath expelled as he gave a hard yank, and then he stood up and thrust something into my hands.

"It's narcissus, Millicent. Clumps of them are blooming back here." He drew a noisy breath. "Can you smell them?"

I buried my face in the tangle of leaves and blossoms, sucking in the sweetness. Never had I imagined such a welcome. Never had I imagined such a homecoming.

Clutching the bouquet of narcissus, I set out in the direction of the massive oak tree that I knew stood nearest the house.

"Millicent, wait," Gary called to me. "Here, take my hand."

Crossing the uneven ground, stepping carefully over thick roots and fallen, rotting branches, Gary led me to the base of the tree my family and Old John had joined hands to encircle so many years ago. It had been little more than a child's game then, and the memory of it was sweet. I envisioned Mama that day, her arm linked in Old John's as they walked together, lost in conversation. Old John's head had been tossed back and his deep laughter had rolled across the wide front lawn. I remembered Mama leading him to this tree and placing his hands upon it. His fingers had traveled over its bark, and smiling, he had nodded his head as if in rhythm to a secret song.

On this day, as I stood with my hands upon the tree, my fingers caressing the thick vines that hung against it like careless tendrils, I too heard music. Like a chorus of voices from the past, it reverberated through the forest, reminding me of all the generations of Collinsworths who had lived and died, leaving behind a legacy of courage and strength.

Leaning against the huge oak, I wrapped my arms around the tree and embraced its stolid strength, accepting from it a kind of benediction.

Blinking away tears, I turned and began walking back toward the old house. In my blindness, I stumbled and reached out to steady myself. My hands grasped a plank that protruded from the fallen porch. My fingers roved across it, and I thought of the many times I had stood on Grandmother's porch, leaning against the railing, my eyes trained in the direction of Dogwood Creek, listening for my father's summons.

Had it ever been otherwise?

Had I ever ceased the waiting, the yearning for my father?

Perhaps I would never be able to stop aching for him, for knowledge of him, for love of him. Through all the years of my life, he had been a dark presence, seldom speaking, always beckoning. I had reached out to him and found him here, beneath the oak trees, his arms full of dogwood branches, his face youthful and filled with peace. Here, I had learned of miracles and second chances. Here, my father had bequeathed me hope.

What better gift could a father give his child?

Standing there, beneath the shadow of five towering oaks that had sheltered my family for more than a hundred years, I whispered, "Thank you, Daddy. Thank you."

Select Bibliography

Books

Bass, Ellen and Davis, Laura. *The Courage to Heal, A Guide for Women Survivors of Child Abuse.* New York: Harper Perennial, a Division of Harper Collins Publisher, Inc., 1992.

De Saint-Exupery, Antoine. *The Little Prince.* 1943. Reprint. Orlando: Harcourt Brace Jovanovich, 1971.

Duke, Patty and Hochman, Gloria. *A Brilliant Madness, Living With Manic-Depressive Illness.* New York: Bantam Books, 1992.

Glanze, Walter D., ed. *Mosby's Medical, Nursing, and Allied Health Dictionary,* 3d ed. [definition of "dementia praecox" (obsolete term for schizophrenia)]. St. Louis: The C.V. Mosby Company, 1990.

Kaplan, Harold I., M.D. and Sadock, Benjamin J., M.D, eds. *Comprehensive Textbook of Psychiatry V.* Vol. 2, 5th ed. [Definition: Shock]. Baltimore: Williams & Wilkins, 1989.

Martindale, Don and Martindale, Edith. *Psychiatry and the Law: The Crusade Against Involuntary Hospitalization.* St. Paul, Minn.: Windflower Publishing Co., 1973.

Szasz, Thomas S., ed. *The Age of Madness, A History of Involuntary Mental Hospitalization.* New York: Jason Aronson, 1973.

Warren, Carol A.B. *Madwives, Schizophrenic Women in the 1950's.* New Brunswick: Rutgers University Press, 1987.

Periodicals

Alderson, Jeremy Weir. "In Search of the Perfect Diet: The Thin Binge." *Harper Bazaar* 124, no. 3355 (July 1991): 73, 111.

Arbetter, Sandra. "Obsessive-Compulsive Disorder: When Enough is Not Enough." *Current Health 2* 15, no. 3 (November 1988): 25–27.

Bailey, Carol A. "Family Structure and Eating Disorders: The Family Environment Scale and Bulimic-Like Symptoms." *Youth & Society* 23, no. 2 (December 1991): 251–272.

Brody, Robert. "Update on Anorexia/Bulimia." *Cosmopolitan* 210, no. 1 (January 1991): 80–90.

Brouwers, Mariette. "Depressive Thought Content Among Female College Students with Bulimia." *Journal of Counseling & Development* 66, no. 9 (May 1988): 425–428.

Dunn, Don. "When Thinness Becomes Illness." *Business Week* [Industrial/Technology Edition], no. 3277 (August 3, 1992): 74–75.

Elkind, David. "Eating Disorders." *Parents* 63, no. 4 (April 1988): 190.

Goode, Erica E. "When Dieting Is All That Counts." *U.S. News & World Report* 104, no. 18 (May 9, 1988): 74–76.

Killen, Joel D.; Taylor, C. Barr; Telch, Michael J.; Saylor, Keith E.; Maron, David J.; and Robinson, Thomas N. "Self-Induced Vomiting and Laxative and Diuretic Use Among Teenagers." *JAMA: The Journal of the American Medical Association* 255, no. 11 (March 21, 1986): 1447–1449.

Loomis, Christine. "Anorexia—Signs and Symptoms." *Parents* 63, no. 9 (September 1988): 9, 26.

Newman, Barclay Moon. "Insulin for Schizophrenia." *Scientific American.* Vol. 158. (May 1938): 278–279.

Pope, Harrison G. Jr., and Hudson, James I. "Is Childhood Sexual Abuse a Risk Factor for Bulimia Nervosa?" *American Journal of Psychiatry* 149, no. 4 (April 1992): 455–463.

Ratcliff, J.D. "Bedside Miracle." [Condensed from "Modern Miracle Men" c39] *Reader's Digest.* Vol. 35. (November 1939): 73–75.

Reed, Susan and Bell, Bonnie, et al. "The Weight-Control Urge That Can Kill." *People Weekly.* 38, no. 5 (August 3, 1992): 64–70.

Ruderman, Audrey J., and Besbeas, Maria. "Psychological Characteristics of Dieters and Bulimics." *University of Chicago. Journal of Abnormal Psychology* 101, no. 3 (August 1992): 383–390.

Science Service. "The New Insulin Insanity Treatment." *Scientific American* Vol. 157. (October 1937): 247.

Stafford, Jane. "Insulin in the Treatment of Mental Disease." *Science* 85, no. 2212 (May 21, 1937): 2212, 8.

———. "Insulin in the Treatment of Schizophrenia." *Science* 85, no. 2217 (June 25, 1937): 10.

Warren, Carol A.B. "Electroconvulsive Therapy: "New" Treatment of the 1980's." *Research in Law, Deviance and Social Control* [A Research Annual] 8 (1986): 41–55.

Newspapers

Associated Press. "Court Upsets City's Ban on Shock Therapy." *Los Angeles Times* (March 2, 1986): sec. Sports, 19.

Dorgan, Michael. "Doctor, Patients Ask S.F. to Ban Electroshock Therapy." *San Jose Mercury News* (November 28, 1990): sec. California News, 4B.

Hager, Philip. "Mental Patients' Rights Groups Put Initiative on Ballot: Fate of Electroshock Therapy in Berkeley in Voters' Hands." *Los Angeles Times* (August 17, 1982): sec. I, 3.

———. "Suit Seeks to Void Ban on Shock Therapy." *Los Angeles Times* (December 15, 1982): sec. I, 18.

Horowitz, Joy. "Shock Treatments: Battle Over Policy/Dr. Sues State Agency." *Los Angeles Times* (January 18, 1980): sec. IV, 1.

Kohn, Alfie. "With Safeguards, this Procedure is the best way to treat Depression, Say Doctors. Shock Therapy Makes Comeback." *Los Angeles Times: Science & Medicine* (March 21, 1988): sec. Metro, 5.

Timnick, Lois. "Electric Shock Therapy for Depression: a Second Look." *Los Angeles Times* (January 18, 1980): sec. I, 3.

Other

Brakel, Samuel J., and Rock, Ronald S., eds. *The Mentally Disabled and the Law.* American Bar Foundation Study. Revised Edition. Chicago: University of Chicago Press, 1971.

California Jury, Income Taxes to Injunctions/Incompetent, Etc., Persons. *Involuntary Treatment of Mentally Disordered Persons.* San Francisco: Bancroft-Whitney Co., 4:72–77, 205–207.

Crown, Robert W., Chairman, Subcommittee on Mental Health Services *Hearings on Procedures of Commitment* [edited transcript of proceedings]. Assembly Interim Committee on Ways and Means. Los Angeles, California. December 20, 1965.

————., Chairman, Subcommittee on Mental Health Services. *The Dilemma of Mental Commitments in California.* Report to the California Legislature [4th reprint, June 30, 1978] Prepared for The Assembly Interim Committee on Ways and Means. Los Angeles, California, 1966.

Deering's Welfare and Institutions Code Annotated of the State of California. Adopted 25 May 1937. Session of the 1987–88 Legislature. ss4500–5999. *Involuntary Treatment.* San Francisco: Bancroft-Whitney Co., 1988. 167, 195–212.

Deering's Welfare and Institutions Code Annotated of the State of California. ss4500–5999. *Detention of Mentally Disordered Persons for Evaluation and Treatment.* San Francisco: Bancroft-Whitney Co. January 1992. Pocket Supplement, Article 1, sec. 5150, 52.

Lindman, Frank T., and McIntyre Jr., Donald M., eds. *The Mentally Disabled and the Law.* American Bar Foundation Report on the Rights of the Mentally Ill. Chicago: University of Chicago Press, 1961.

Short, The Honorable Alan, Chairman, Senate Committee on Business and Professions. *Staffing and Care in State Mental Hospitals* [Transcript of Proceedings]. Special Hearing. Sacramento, California. March 28, 1967.

A MESSAGE FROM THE PUBLISHER

W. R. Spence, M.D.
Publisher

"Do you have another chapter yet?"
Our editors heard this request from our
staff so many times we finally developed
what we called "the Millicent Challenge."
If anyone could read the first eight
paragraphs of this manuscript and not
get hooked, we'd buy them a case of Pepsi.
In all seriousness, this is a marvelously
captivating story, full of metaphors that
strike a chord of empathy in all of us.

The book division of WRS Publishing
focuses on true stories about everyday heroes, like Millicent
Collinsworth, who have accomplished their own impossible
dreams. While it is sometimes easy to turn a profit with stories
of greed, sex, and violence, we are not interested in such books.
We only produce books we can be proud of and that can
change lives for the better. **Call us at 1-800-299-3366 for
suggestions or for a free book catalog.**

WATCH FOR THESE RELATED TITLES:

AFTER LOSS, the journal of a man whose wife,
daughter, and parents-in-law were killed in a car accident, and
who was left with two daughters to raise in the midst of his grief.

RIPPLES OF SUICIDE, culled from the experiences
of Harold Elliott, chaplain for the Arlington, TX, Police
Department, the material in this book gives us a thought-
provoking look at suicide.

A VICTORY FOR HUMANITY, the story of the
Achilles Track Club, founded by a lower-extremity amputee,
Dick Traum, for the disabled worldwide.

I LAFFED TILL I CRIED, the story of Patti Lewis,
her thirty-six years of marriage to Jerry Lewis, and the pain
that lay behind the laughter.

WRS
PUBLISHING

A Division of WRS Group, Inc.
Waco, Texas